The Global Politics of the Environment

Second Edition

D0800984

The Global Politics of the Environment

Second Edition

Lorraine Elliott

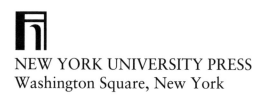

NEW YORK UNIVERSITY PRESS
Washington Square, New York

First published in the U.S.A. in 2004 by
NEW YORK UNIVERSITY PRESS
Washington Square
New York, N.Y. 10003

This book is printed on paper suitable for recycling
and made from fully managed and sustained forest sources.

Library of Congress Cataloging-in-Publication Data
Elliott, Lorraine M.
The global politics of the environment/Lorraine Elliott.—2nd ed.
      p. cm.
   Includes bibliographical references and index.
   ISBN 0–8147–2217–2 (cloth: alk. paper)
   ISBN 0–8147–2218–0 (pbk: alk. paper)
      1. Environmental policy – International cooperation. 2. Environmental degradation.
3. Nature – Effect of human beings on. I. Title
GE170.E47 2004
363.7′0526—dc22   2003066467

Printed in China

For Matthew, Loren, Louise and Benjamin

Contents

Preface to the Second Edition

The first edition of this book was completed just before the Rio+5 conference, the 1997 Special Session of the United Nations General Assembly held to review the implementation of Agenda 21, the programme of action adopted in 1992 at the United Nations Conference on Environment and Development. This second edition has been completed almost twelve months after Rio+10, the World Summit on Sustainable Development in Johannesburg. The years in between have seen the adoption of more multilateral environmental agreements, continued changes in the state of the global environment and, in some respects, a redirection of some of the political debates. This new edition takes account of those changes. It substantially updates and revises the narrative on and analysis of global environmental problems to take account of diplomatic, legal and political events. The distinction made in the first edition between the so-called 'Stockholm' and 'Rio' agendas seems now more difficult to sustain as a distinction between transnational and global environmental problems. Chapters 2 and 3 in this second edition have therefore been structured around an analysis of the global politics of conservation and the global politics of pollution. One of the most important themes of the global politics of the environment is the way in which issues of democratization, ethics and justice have become more crucial to policy debates about environmental governance and to the actual task of meeting the challenges of global environmental change. This edition, therefore, makes these concerns more central. In revising and restructuring the text, I have also included a new chapter on the normative challenges of justice, obligation and rights. Finally, the chapters on the international political economy of the environment have been revised and restructured to take account of a number of important policy debates surrounding the Millennium Development Goals, the Monterrey Consensus on financing for development, and the WTO Doha Declaration.

In thinking further about these events and in preparing this second edition which reflects on those changes, I have incurred a number of institutional, professional and personal debts. I should like to thank the Department of International Relations at the Australian National University for financial support for research and sabbatical leave. Some of the research for this book was undertaken during two visiting fellowships – one at the Asia Research Centre at the London School of Economics, in June and July 2001, and one at Balliol College at the University of Oxford, from January to July 2002. I am grateful to both institutions for providing a welcoming environment and the wonderful opportunity to spend whole days in the library! Thanks are also due to the Department of Politics and International Studies at the University of Warwick, my institutional home during the very final phase of this book.

As I noted in the Acknowledgements for the first edition, many of the debts incurred in this process arise from the willingness of colleagues and friends to debate the themes explored here and to enable me to test my ideas through seminars, conference papers, publications and, increasingly, through email conversations. In particular, I am grateful to Marc Williams, Stuart Harris, Merrilyn Wasson, Bob Wasson, Louis Lebel, John Dore, Diane Stone, Richard Higgott, Amanda Dickins, Rorden Wilkinson, Stephanie Lawson, Adil Najam, Paul Harris, Pauline Kerr, Kathy Morton, James Cotton, John Ravenhill, Stefa Wirga, Bill Tow, Len Seabrooke, my graduate and postgraduate students at the Australian National University and the folk who contribute to discussions (and pleas for help) on the Geped electronic discussion list. A number of people have helped with various research, copy-editing, administrative and computer-related tasks: thanks, therefore, to Mary Louise Hickey, Clare Wilson, James Greenbaum, Amy Chen and Lynne Payne. Nothing happens without the support of family and friends and so thanks are due to my parents, Dave and Allison, and my sisters Barbara, Janet and Heather; to Anna George, Jo Crawford, Heather Devere, Mary Sidney, Tomoko Akami, Jennifer Curtin and to Kathrine and Andrew Crompton to whom I owe more than I can say. Very special and grateful thanks to Graeme Cheeseman for his unfailing affection, support and encouragement, and for taking over my half of the domestic chores when the deadlines got really close!

This book is dedicated, as was the first edition, to my nieces and nephews. They are now in their teens and early adult years. The growing up of this 'next generation' has done nothing to change the obligations associated with intergenerational equity. Indeed, it has intensified them. They still deserve better from us than, I fear, we will be able to leave them.

Lorraine Elliott

List of Acronyms and Abbreviations

ACC	Administrative Committee on Coordination
AGBM	Ad Hoc Working Group on the Berlin Mandate
AIA	Advance informed agreement
AIJ	Activities Implemented Jointly
ANGOC	African NGO Coalition
AOSIS	Alliance of Small Island States
APPEN	Asia–Pacific Peoples' Environment Network
ASEAN	Association of SouthEast Asian Nations
BSE	Bovine spongiform encephalopathy
BSWG	Biosafety Working Group
CBD	Convention on Biological Diversity
CBDR	Common but differentiated responsibilities
CCD	Convention to Combat Desertification [short title]
CCMS	Committee on the Challenges of Modern Society
CCOL	Coordinating Committee on the Ozone Layer
CDM	Clean Development Mechanism
CEB	Chief Executives Board for Coordination
CEG	Criteria Expert Group
CFCs	Chlorofluorocarbons
CH_4	Methane
CIPR	Community intellectual property rights
CITES	Convention on International Trade in Endangered Species
CNPPA	Commission on National Parks and Protected Areas
CO_2	Carbon dioxide
COFO	Committee on Forestry
COICA	Coordinating Body for Indigenous Organizations of the Amazon Basin
COP	Conference of Parties
CPF	Collaborative Partnership on Forests
CRC	Chemical Review Committee
CRIC	Committee for the Review of the Implementation of the Convention [to Combat Desertification]
CSD	Commission on Sustainable Development

CSW	Commission on the Status of Women
CTE	Committee on Trade and Environment
DESA	Department of Economic and Social Affairs
DFNS	Debt-for-nature swaps
DGD	Decision guidance document
DPCSD	Department for Policy Coordination and Sustainable Development
DSD	Division for Sustainable Development
DU	Depleted uranium
DWFN	Distant water fishing nations
EC	European Community
ECE	Economic Commission for Europe
ECESA	Executive Committee on Economic and Social Affairs
ECOSOC	Economic and Social Council
EEZ	Exclusive Economic Zone
EIA	Environmental Impact Assessment
EITs	Economies in transition
EMG	Environmental Management Group
EMIT	[GATT Group on] Environmental Measures in International Trade
ENB	*Earth Negotiations Bulletin*
ENMOD	Environmental Modification Convention [Convention on the Prohibition of Military or any other Hostile Use of Environmental Modification Techniques]
EPA	[US] Environment Protection Agency
ETIS	Elephant Trade Information System
EU	European Union
ExCOP	Extraordinary Conference of Parties
FAO	Food and Agriculture Organization
FCCC	Framework Convention on Climate Change
FDI	Foreign direct investment
FFP	Food, feed or processing
FIELD	Foundation for International Environmental Law and Development
FLS	[Nairobi] Forward Looking Strategies
FoE	Friends of the Earth
FSC	Forest Stewardship Council
G77	Group of 77
GATS	General Agreement on Trade in Services
GATT	General Agreement on Tariffs and Trade
GDP	Gross domestic product
GEF	Global Environment Facility
GEO	*Global Environment Outlook*

GEO	Global Environment Organization
GHG	Greenhouse gas
GMEF	Global Ministerial Environmental Forum
GMO	Genetically modified organism
GNP	Gross national product
HCFCs	Hydrochlorofluorocarbons
HFCs	Hydrofluorocarbons
HIPC	Heavily Indebted Poor Countries
HLAB	High-Level Advisory Board
IACSD	Inter-Agency Committee on Sustainable Development
IAEA	International Atomic Energy Agency
ICC	International Chamber of Commerce
ICCBD	Intergovernmental Committee on the Convention on Biodiversity
ICCP	Intergovernmental Committee for the Cartagena Protocol
ICSU	International Council of Scientific Unions
IET	International Emissions Trading
IFAD	International Fund for Agricultural Development
IFCS	Intergovernmental Forum on Chemical Safety
IFF	Intergovernmental Forum on Forests
IGBP	International Geosphere–Biosphere Programme
IIED	International Institute for Environment and Development
IISD	International Institute for Sustainable Development
ILO	International Labour Organization
ILO 169	International Labour Organization Convention Concerning Indigenous and Tribal Peoples in Independent Countries (1989)
IMF	International Monetary Fund
IMO	International Maritime Organization
INC	Intergovernmental Negotiating Committee
INCD	Intergovernmental Negotiating Committee for the elaboration of an international convention to combat desertification in those countries experiencing serious drought and/or desertification particularly in Africa
IOMC	Inter-Organizational Programme for the Sound Management of Chemicals
IPCC	Intergovernmental Panel on Climate Change
IPE	International political economy
IPF	Intergovernmental Panel on Forests
IPRs	Intellectual property rights
ITTA	International Tropical Timber Agreement

ITTO	International Tropical Timber Organization
ITWAN	International Toxic Waste Action Network
IUCN	International Union for the Conservation of Nature and Natural Resources
IWC	International Whaling Commission
IWGF	Intergovernmental Working Group on Forests
JI	Joint Implementation
JUSCANZ	Japan, United States, Canada, Australia and New Zealand Group
LDC	London Dumping Convention
LMO	Living modified organism
LRTAP	Long-Range Transboundary Air Pollution
MAPW	Medical Association for Prevention of War
MARPOL	International Convention for the Prevention of Pollution from Ships
MDG	Millennium Development Goals
MEA	Multilateral Environmental Agreement
MNC	Multinational Corporation
MOP	Meeting of Parties
N_2O	Nitrous oxide
NAM	Non-Aligned Movement
NASA	National Aeronautics and Space Administration
NATO	North Atlantic Treaty Organisation
NCPCs	National cleaner production centres
NEPAD	New Partnership for Africa's Development
NFAP	National Forestry Action Plan
NFPs	National Forest Programs
NGO	Non-governmental organization
NICs	Newly industrialized countries
NOAA	National Oceanic and Atmospheric Administration
NOx	Nitrogen oxide
NOZE	National Ozone Expedition
O_3	Ozone
OAU	Organisation of African Unity
ODA	Official development assistance
ODS	Ozone-depleting substances
OECD	Organisation for Economic Co-operation and Development
OOTW	Operations other than war
OTA	Office of Technology Assessment
OTP	Ozone Trends Panel
PACD	Plan of Action to Combat Desertification
PCB	Polychlorobiphenyls

PIC	Prior informed consent
PNG	Papua New Guinea
POP	Persistent organic pollutant
ppb	Parts per billion
ppm	Parts per million
PPP	Polluter pays principle
PrepComm	Preparatory Committee
PRIO	Peace Research Institute, Oslo
RECIEL	Review of European Community and International Environmental Law
SAR	Second Assessment Report
SBI	Subsidiary Body on Implementation
SBSTA	Subsidiary Body on Scientific and Technical Advice
SIDS	Small island developing states
SIPRI	Stockholm International Peace Research Institute
SLORC	State Law and Order Restoration Council
SO_2	Sulphur dioxide
SPDC	State Peace and Development Council
SPS	Sanitary and Phytosanitary Measures
STAP	Scientific and Technical Advisory Panel
SWAGSD	[UNEP] Senior Women's Advisory Group on Sustainable Development
TAR	Third Assessment Report
TBT	Technical Barriers to Trade
TFAP	Tropical Forestry Action Plan
TOMA	Tropospheric ozone management area
TRIPs	Trade-Related Aspects of Intellectual Property Rights
UN	United Nations
UNCED	United Nations Conference on Environment and Development
UNCHE	United Nations Conference on the Human Environment
UNCLOS	United Nations Convention on the Law of the Sea
UNCOD	United Nations Conference on Desertification
UNCTAD	United Nations Conference on Trade and Development
UNDP	United Nations Development Programme
UNDPI	United Nations Department of Public Information
UNEP	United Nations Environment Programme
UNESCO	United Nations Educational, Scientific and Cultural Organization
UNFCCC	United Nations Framework Convention on Climate Change
UNFF	United Nations Forum on Forests
UNGA	United Nations General Assembly

UNGASS	United Nations General Assembly Special Session
UNHCHR	[Office of] the United Nations High Commissioner for Human Rights
UNIDO	United Nations Industrial Development Organization
UNIFEM	United Nations Development Fund for Women
USIS	United States Information Service
USSR	Union of Soviet Socialist Republics
UVB	Ultraviolet B radiation
VOC	Volatile organic compound
WAA 21	Women's Action Agenda 21
WBCSD	World Business Council for Sustainable Development
WCED	World Commission on Environment and Development
WCS	World Conservation Strategy
WEDO	Women's Environment and Development Organization
WEO	World Environment Organization
WIPO	World Intellectual Property Organization
WMO	World Meteorological Organization
WRI	World Resources Institute
WRM	World Rainforest Movement
WSSD	World Summit on Sustainable Development
WTO	World Trade Organization
WWF	World Wide Fund for Nature

Introduction

One of the questions asked by many policy-makers, activists and scholars after the 1992 United Nations Conference on Environment and Development (UNCED) was 'Did we save the earth?' Needless to say, the answers varied: some answered yes, some answered no and some answered maybe but it's too soon to tell. The ideas explored in this book, however, canvass more than responses to that specific, albeit important question. The main purpose of this text is to focus attention on a more fundamental question, 'how *should* we save the earth?', and to examine the often competing answers offered in response. In many respects, in fact, it is no longer helpful to talk simply about the global politics of the environment. The agenda of protecting the environment is now inextricably linked with protecting people, with sustainable development, with the disproportionate impacts of a globalized economy, with the relationship between rich and poor, and with the demands of global justice. While the issues discussed in Chapters 2 and 3 take concerns about the environment as their starting point, the analysis there demonstrates that these are also concerns about the nature of economic activity, social exploitation and power and powerlessness.

The reasons why these questions should be asked is increasingly obvious. At the beginning of the twenty-first century, human activity is changing the environment, and not for the better, in a way unlike that of any other era. Extensive and excessive resource use, energy-inefficient lifestyles, industrialization and the pursuit of economic growth are inextricably linked to environmental degradation, within and across state borders. The global economy has expanded 'five-fold in the past half-century, three-fold since 1980 alone' (Rees, 2002, p. 24). World exports have increased to be worth more than $US7 trillion, over 20 per cent of world GDP (World Bank, 2003, p. 25). Since the 1950s, world industrial production has increased fourfold (see Sitarz, 1994, p. 38). Energy consumption grew by an average of about 2 per cent a year between 1972 and 1999, a total of almost 70 per cent over that time (UNEP, 2002a, p. 35). Estimates suggest that the world has consumed something now close to a half of estimated ultimately recoverable oil supplies (MacKenzie, 2000). The annual use of fertilizer declined to about 120 million tonnes in 1993

1

but has since increased again, especially in developing countries (World Energy Council, 2001). By the mid-1990s per capita water supply in developing countries was only one-third of its 1970 levels (UNDP, 1996, p. 26). By 2020, water use is expected to have increased by 40 per cent over demands in 2000 (UNEP, 2002a, p. 150). Atmospheric concentrations of carbon dioxide emissions have increased exponentially since the Industrial Revolution and now stand at something in the vicinity of 370 parts per million (ppm). This number may mean little on its own but scientific consensus confirms that it will contribute to interference with the climate system with a rate of change in average global temperatures faster than at any time in the last 10,000 years and sea level rises about three to six times faster than in the last 100 years (see Houghton *et al.*, 1990, p. xxviii). Much of this activity is unsustainable in the way it depletes resources and affects the environment and the lives and livelihoods of the world's peoples, especially in the developing world.

The environmental impacts of this economic activity have been widespread to the extent that human activities may now have 'exceeded the biosphere's capacity since the mid-1970s' (Sachs, 2002, p. 13). Since the 1950s, almost 2 million hectares (about 23 per cent of all cropland, pasture, forest and woodland) has become degraded (World Bank, 2003, p. 3). Water scarcity is on the increase, with over 80 countries now facing water shortages, 26 of them officially designated as water-scarce. Air pollution and contamination of waterways and coastal areas have become a standard feature of industrialized and developing country ecosystems. The world's forests, both tropical and temperate, are in decline. Every day, as many as 50 of the earth's species become extinct. Environmental degradation increases the poverty of those who are already poor, especially in those parts of the world where livelihoods and lives are closely dependent on ecosystem and resource viability. Desertification and land degradation undermine the agricultural and subsistence practices of peoples in the developing world. Pollution of rivers and streams affects the irrigation of farms in developed and developing countries. It undermines access to clean drinking water and kills fish upon which local peoples rely for food. Deforestation denies sources of food, medicine and the basics of daily life to millions of forest dwellers and indigenous peoples as well as undermining their cultural and spiritual identity. Increasing scarcity of fuelwood and water increases the burden of the lives of developing world women. In both developed and developing countries, hazardous waste dumping and toxic pollution cause severe illness (recall Minimata or Love Canal) and death (recall Bhopal), and the United Nations Environment Programme (UNEP) now suggests also that 'poor environmental quality is directly responsible for some 25 per cent of all *preventable* ill health' (2002a, p. 306; emphasis added).

These issues cannot be separated from inequities in cause and impact and the 'increasing polarization between the haves and the have nots [that] has become a feature of our world' (UNGA, 2001b, p. 3). Inequities between rich and poor countries, unequal trade and international capital transactions, the paucity of international development assistance in the pursuit of basic human needs, and the ever-growing burden of developing country debt are entwined with environmental degradation in complex cause-and-effect relationships. The processes of economic globalization have intensified the exploitation of environmental goods and services while, at the same time, increasing inequity between the rich and the poor, not just between countries but also within them. The World Bank reports that the average income in the richest twenty countries is 37 times that in the poorest twenty, double the ratio in 1960 (2003, p. 3). The United Nations Development Programme (UNDP) puts it even more starkly, reporting that by the late 1990s, the income gap between the world's richest and poorest 20 per cent of people was 74 to 1, compared with 30 to 1 in 1960 (UNDP, 1999, p. 3). Almost half the world's people live on less than US$2 a day and almost a quarter on less than $1 (United Nations Secretary-General, 2000, p. 19). The World Bank reports that 'the assets of the three richest people [in the world are] more than the combined GNP of the 48 least developed countries' (2003, p. 37). The richest 20 per cent of the world's population (most of it in the industrialized world) accounts for 86 per cent of total private consumption expenditure and consumes 58 per cent of the world's energy whereas the world's poorest 20 per cent consume less than 5 per cent of global resources (UNEP, 2002a, p. 35). Yet the local impacts of global environmental decline will be felt first, and disproportionately, in those countries and among those peoples who have contributed less to the causes.

Environmental degradation is now a global issue – ecologically, politically and economically. Global environmental problems, it is argued, require global solutions. This simple aphorism hides a multitude of political and economic difficulties, not the least of which is how we should understand the 'global' as an organizing principle. The difference between local environmental problems and what we understand as a global problem has come to be often simply a matter of degree:

> at the local level, a problem such as deforestation primarily affects slash and burn cultivators and peasants attempting to establish stationary farms. But the same problem, multiplied by thousands of small farms and combined with extensive commercial logging, can exacerbate the global-level issue of accelerated atmospheric warming (Wood *et al.*, 1989, p. 32).

That there are no simple solutions might be a second aphorism. Multilateral cooperation among states has become a necessary (but not sufficient) condition for controlling or preventing the causes of environmental degradation and for finding ways to overcome or at least mitigate both the global environmental consequences of local human activity and the local impacts of global environmental degradation.

Yet while there are now many, many thousands of words on paper – in conventions, protocols, declarations, statements of principle, management programmes, action plans, communiqués – environmental degradation continues to worsen. Thus there is a crisis in capacity, a failure of governance, an apparent lack of political will. In seeking to overcome these problems, the first-order questions for many are those related to the kinds of targets and commitments which should be incorporated into international environmental agreements, how scientific evidence should be translated into policy, how implementation can be ensured, how compliance should be monitored and verified, the nature of liability and accountability, whether to focus on symptoms or causes (or both), whether agreements should attempt to prohibit or control activities and behaviours that are the cause of environmental degradation, and what kinds of institutions should be established to oversee these agreements and to manage global environmental programmes.

For others, including this author, these are second-order questions. The questions to be asked *first* are those which focus attention 'on the underlying structure in which this process is being played out' (Thomas, 1993, p. 2). It is important, as Cox suggests, to appraise the 'very framework for action' (1986, p. 208). In this view, environmental degradation is not simply a 'glitch' (albeit a rather large one) in the otherwise reasonably smooth running of the contemporary political and economic world order. Rather the contemporary political and economic order is quite likely to be part of the problem. At the very least, we should not assume that it is not. This introduces a different set of questions. What prospect, for example, is there for effective environmental governance in a decentralized system of sovereign states? Does the liberal international economic order, with its emphasis on freer international trade, modernization and export-led growth, provide a firm basis for the elaboration of principles and strategies which will overcome global environmental decline, or is the liberal international economic order part of the problem in the first place? Can we achieve environmental security in a militarized world? It is those questions which provide the structure for much of this book.

The purpose here, in examining these questions and the answers to them, is not to persuade readers of a particular point of view. Rather it is to try to make some sense of the different ways in which scholars, commentators and practitioners have sought to understand the global politics of the environment and the means by which we should 'save the earth'. Throughout the book, equal attention is given to the orthodox reformist views which have generally informed the practice of states and many other actors – as well as much academic research and analysis – and to alternative critical perspectives which pose a more radical challenge to the contemporary world order and its guiding principles and values.

Structure of the book

The first three chapters of this text examine how the environmental agenda became a global one. Chapter 1 focuses on significant events in that globalizing process – the 1972 UN Conference on the Human Environment (the Stockholm Conference), the 1992 United Nations Conference on Environment and Development (the Rio Conference) and the 2002 World Summit on Sustainable Development (the Johannesburg Conference). The two subsequent chapters explore the expanding agenda of environmental concerns in two stages, showing how environmental degradation moved from national jurisdictions to become first transboundary and then global and how the politics followed suit. Chapter 2 explores the global politics of the more traditional, 'green' agenda – conservation – beginning with protection of species and biodiversity, then moving to consider living resources and then habitat and ecosystem resources, the latter especially through the lens of the politics of desertification. Chapter 3 focuses on the 'brown' agenda – the global politics of pollution. It begins with the political debates on hazardous wastes and toxic chemicals. It then explores (briefly) the challenges of oceans pollution before turning to a more lengthy exploration of atmospheric pollution including ozone depletion and global warming. While these chapters are primarily descriptive of environmental concerns and the politics of negotiations, they illuminate the political problems, tensions, issues and debates which provide the focus for the rest of the book.

Chapters 4, 5 and 6 explore various aspects of the processes of and debates about environmental governance. Governance is understood here as something more than simply (or even) the formal, material organizations which exist to address environmental concerns. Rather it includes the broader social institutions, rules and practices which provide the framework for decision-making and cooperation. While there is often agreement that we face some kind of crisis in environmental governance, demands for better governance beg at least two important questions. First, why is there a crisis of governance? Second, what are the characteristics of better environmental governance and how, if at all, can this be achieved? The analysis in the first three chapters of the book identifies three major themes in the debates about global environmental governance which need to be further investigated. The first, which is explored in Chapter 4, is that of institutional competence and the nature of institutional reform, revolving especially around the adequacy of the state as actor and agent. The second, which provides the focus for Chapter 5, is that global environmental governance must be democratic and inclusive. The third theme, the subject of Chapter 6, is that global environmental governance requires a normative shift which responds to the inequities in the global politics of the environment and which elaborates a more robust structure of rights and obligations.

Chapters 7 and 8 focus more closely on the international or global political economy of the environment. The relationship between the structures and processes of the world economy – trade, debt, development – and environmental degradation is complex and in dispute. That relationship is further complicated, and the dispute exacerbated, by the competing interests and concerns of rich and poor countries (as well as rich and poor peoples). Chapter 7 considers the tensions between developing and developed countries which have become a central characteristic of the global politics of the environment. Concerns about inequities in cause and impact are revisited in political debates about commitments, obligations, costs and benefits, the contested meaning of sustainable development (the catch-cry of the post-UNCED era) and the best strategies for achieving it. Those strategies are explored further in Chapter 8. They range across resource transfers of various kinds, more effective utilization of trade mechanisms, attempts to address the high level of developing country debt and the application of financial, market-based mechanisms at an international level. It will come as no surprise that the usefulness of any of these strategies, and the manner in which they should be applied, is contested.

Chapter 9 turns to another much used but less well-understood phrase of the post-Rio era, albeit one which travels in tandem with sustainable development, that of environmental security. In particular, it questions the extent to which this concept should be understood primarily as an 'add on' to a traditional security agenda or whether it invokes a rethinking of accepted wisdoms and practices about political orthodoxies. Chapter 10, the concluding chapter, specifically addresses the respective merits of the two broad traditions of analysis – a generally orthodox reformist position on the one hand and a more critical transformative or cosmopolitan perspective on the other – which have shaped the global politics of the environment and which have informed the ideas explored in this book.

Chapter 1

From Stockholm to Rio to Johannesburg

Introduction

The globalization of environmental politics was shaped by two land-mark events – the 1972 United Nations Conference on the Human Environment (the Stockholm Conference) and the 1992 United Nations Conference on Environment and Development (the Rio Conference or the Earth Summit). The Stockholm Conference is frequently described as a watershed in the development of international environmental law, as the beginning of serious international cooperation on the environment and as 'the event where international debate on the environment began' (Tolba, El-Kholy et al., 1992, p. 742). Two decades later, the Rio Conference was hailed as firm evidence that environmental concerns had moved to occupy a central place in the agenda of world politics. It established new benchmarks for global attention to environmental decline and the importance of sustainable development. The plan of action adopted at Rio – Agenda 21 – became the focal point for a con-tinuing review process, through the annual meetings of the Commission on Sustainable Development, the 1997 United Nations General Assembly Special Session (sometimes called Rio+5) and the World Summit on Sustainable Development in Johannesburg in 2002 (Rio+10). This chapter traces these key 'moments' and introduces the institutional and normative themes which are examined in more detail in later chapters.

The decade before the Stockholm Conference witnessed growing sci-entific and public concern about environmental degradation, the slow development of international environmental law and an equally slow democratization of international environmental policy-making. That process, spurred by a growing sense of planetary crisis, continued in the two decades between the Stockholm and Rio conferences. The number and scope of environmental concerns on the international agenda increased, as did the number of multilateral treaties adopted to respond to those concerns. However the optimism which was the hallmark of the Rio Conference was short-lived. By 1997, the multilateral consensus was looking fragile and the political commitment to sustainable development had become caught up in disputes over how to manage the processes and consequences of globalization, a process that was not overcome by the negotiations surrounding the World Summit on Sustainable Development in 2002.

Before Stockholm

Three broad areas of concern characterized the pre-1972 agenda of international environmental issues: wilderness and wildlife conservation, maritime pollution and the spread of nuclear weaponry (see Caldwell, 1991, p. 6). This agenda reflects a progressive 'deterritorialization' – from issues where state jurisdiction over particular kinds of behaviour was usually clear to concerns for the high seas outside the reaches of national jurisdiction and then to issues such as nuclear pollution likely to affect the planet as a whole (although nuclear concerns do not feature prominently in this book). Of these three, conservation concerns have the longest history. As far back as 1872, the Swiss government proposed an international commission to protect migrating birds. In 1900 the European colonial powers signed a convention for the preservation of animals, birds and fish in Africa. The North Pacific Fur Seal Treaty was adopted in 1911 and the *Convention on Nature Protection and Wildlife Conservation in the Western Hemisphere* in 1940. One of the earliest global conservation agreements still in force – the *International Convention for the Regulation of Whaling* – was adopted in 1946 although its membership was initially small and its primary purpose to prevent resource depletion through regulation rather than to conserve whale species per se. Efforts to protect wildlife habitat were reflected in agreements such as the 1971 Ramsar *Convention on the Conservation of Wetlands*. From the mid-1950s, environmental disasters also spurred agreements on the prevention, or at least control, of maritime oil pollution, including the 1954 *International Convention for the Prevention of Pollution of the Sea by Oil* (usually agreed to have been fairly ineffectual) and the 1958 *Convention on the High Seas* (a forerunner to the 1982 *Convention on the Law of the Sea*).

Much of this early multilateral activity was dominated by states and governments. During the 1960s, however, non-governmental environmental and conservation organizations became increasingly activist on transboundary and international environmental issues. Non-governmental organization (NGO) membership grew in the 1960s. In the US, for example, membership of two long-standing organizations concerned primarily with wilderness conservation – the Sierra Club and the National Audubon Society – increased from a few tens of thousands to 140,000 and 200,000 respectively by the early 1970s (Brenton, 1994, p. 19). New NGOs with a more activist focus and a wider agenda of environmental concerns were also established. Greenpeace was founded in 1969, following a campaign against atomic testing at Amchitka. Friends of the Earth was born of a serious difference of opinion in the Sierra Club over tactics and strategy.

Intellectual debate in the years prior to 1972 also set the scene for the Stockholm Conference. The most influential work, much of it written by biological scientists at the forefront of the new science of ecology, challenged conventional views of the impact of human activity on the environment and the impact of a degraded environment on human society. The publication in 1962 of Rachel Carson's book *Silent Spring* was, as many have noted, seminal to these intellectual developments. Carson, a biologist, was concerned specifically about the impact on birdlife of the use of pesticides but her book generated a debate about the whole impact of human activity on the environment. A powerful metaphor for understanding this impact came from Garrett Hardin's 1968 article in the reputable journal *Science*. In an historically inaccurate but much quoted (and misquoted) piece, Hardin likened the unregulated use of the oceans and atmosphere to the pre-Industrial overuse of the English commons. He argued that the outcome of such unregulated use would be a 'tragedy of the commons' because 'freedom in a commons brings ruin to all' (Hardin, 1968, p. 1244). In the absence of individual ownership, he argued, everyone has an incentive to exploit the resource to their own advantage, resulting in resource overuse.

Hardin's concern was not primarily environmental: rather it was for the overall sub optimal effects of unrestricted population growth, for which his solution (drawing an analogy with the enclosure of the commons) was mutual coercion and the 'relinquishing of the freedom to breed' (Hardin, 1968, p. 1248). He returned to this issue in later work arguing, among other things, that food aid to Third World countries should be discontinued to compel those countries to limit their populations (see Hardin, 1974). Population growth was a popular concern at this time. In his seminal work *The Population Bomb*, Paul Ehrlich drew attention to the consequences of rapid population growth but also to inequities embedded in population pressures, noting that the environmental impact of one American (that is someone who lived in the United States of America) was the same as that of two Swedes, three Italians, 13 Brazilians, 35 Indians or 280 Chadians or Haitians (see Brenton, 1994, p. 14). In *The Limits to Growth* – an influential 1972 report for the Club of Rome – Donella Meadows and her colleagues drew on predictions about resource carrying capacity generated by their global-systems computer modelling to argue for a reduction in resource-intensive industrial activity (Meadows *et al.*, 1972).

This sense of impending disaster, of a shrinking planet, of a planet reaching its carrying capacity, was reinforced by the first photos of the earth from space which portrayed a fragile earth, giving rise to the image of 'spaceship earth' and its human passengers. In a 1969 speech, United Nations Secretary-General U Thant suggested that

> members of the United Nations have perhaps ten years left in which to subordinate their ancient quarrels and launch a global partnership to curb the arms race, to improve the human environment, to defuse the population explosion (cited in Brenton, 1994, p. 28).

This doomsday theme was subject to trenchant criticism. John Maddox in *The Doomsday Syndrome* (1972) and Julian Simon and Herman Khan in their collection *The Resourceful Earth* (1984) challenged the limits scenario. They argued that the human capacity to invent and find substitutes, along with market responses to scarce resources, would ensure that the carrying capacity and limits to growth could be overcome. Despite this background of academic and scientific dispute, a growing public awareness of the social consequences of environmental degradation and concerns about resource scarcity and population growth spurred demands for multilateral action.

The United Nations Conference on the Human Environment (UNCHE), 1972

In establishing the UNCHE, the General Assembly at first anticipated a consciousness-raising exercise to provide a 'framework for comprehensive consideration within the United Nations of the problems of the human environment ... to focus the attention of governments and public opinion on the importance and urgency of this question' (Resolution 2398, cited in Rowland, 1973, p. 34). A second resolution (Resolution 2581) ensured that the conference would generate a more vigorous outcome 'as a practical means to encourage and to provide guidelines for action by governments and international organisations' (see Brenton, 1994, p. 36).

The Conference was contentious from the start. The Communist bloc countries withdrew from the preparatory process and the final conference on ideological and political grounds, confident that environmental degradation was a capitalist problem and angry that East Germany was excluded from negotiations. Developing countries were wary that 'Northern' concerns with pollution and nature conservation would take precedence over poverty and underdevelopment. At a meeting in Founex in 1971, developing-country scientists and experts voiced their concerns over issues of responsibility for environmental degradation, appropriate levels of development assistance, funding, technology transfer and population. The Founex Report emphasized the importance of development and made it clear that developing countries would oppose strategies which could slow their industrialization or place environmentally motivated restrictions on aid, investment and trade (see Brenton, 1994, p. 38).

The Stockholm Conference, held from 5 to 16 June 1972, was attended by about 1,200 delegates from 114 countries. Only two heads of government were there – Olaf Palme from the host government and Prime Minister Indira Gandhi of India. There was also a formal NGO conference and an informal People's Forum which together set a precedent for what is now a standard feature of UN thematic diplomacy. Accredited NGOs were able to lobby delegates and present formal statements to the Conference. The Preparatory Committee had anticipated three substantive outcomes: a declaration, an action plan and an organizational framework within the United Nations which would address environmental concerns. Maurice Strong, the Canadian Secretary-General of the Conference, favoured a declaration which would establish the 'rights and obligations of citizens and governments with regards to the preservation and improvement of the human condition' (Strong, 1972a). The Stockholm Declaration, a non-binding declaration of 26 principles, did not meet this test. It was a compromise which accommodated the *shared* interests of states in maintaining the sovereignty principle and the *competing* interests of developed and developing countries. The most quoted principle is principle 21 which asserts a state's sovereign rights over its resources *and* its responsibility for environmental damage beyond its borders but which gives no guidance as to how these two potentially competing purposes might be reconciled. The Declaration balanced a global commitment to protect resources and limit pollution with the needs of economic development. In principles 9 to 12, it emphasized the importance of aid, technology and other assistance for overcoming underdevelopment as a cause of much environmental decline in developing countries. The Declaration is most often characterized as a 'wish list of items that were inconsistent with one another and ... to some extent intellectually incoherent' (Palmer, 1992, p. 266).

The less well-known Stockholm Action Plan detailed 109 recommendations on human settlements, resource management, pollution, development and the social dimensions of environmental degradation. Maurice Strong (1972b) called it a 'blueprint' for a continuing environmental work programme but its relative brevity ensured that it was a catalogue of concerns rather than a strong basis for environmental progress. The third and most important outcome was institutional. Stockholm paved the way for the General Assembly to establish the United Nations Environment Programme (UNEP), ensuring that the UN system would become the major site for international environmental diplomacy and the development of international environmental law (see more in Chapter 4). Political factors nevertheless constrained UNEP from the start. Developed countries were cautious about any institution which would require substantial funding. Developing countries were reluctant to support an institution whose decisions might restrict their own development. Existing UN agencies were intent on jealously guarding their own environment-related activities. Thus UNEP was established as a programme, with a role as coordinator and catalyst, rather than as a specialized agency with a more explicitly operational mandate.

Stockholm was not the 'new liberation movement' Maurice Strong called for in his opening address to the Conference (see Strong, 1972a). While it addressed some of the systemic issues of poverty and underdevelopment, there was little real practical commitment to halting and reversing the causes of environmental degradation. The major achievement of the Stockholm Conference was that it brought governments together to debate environmental issues and provided a basis for the slow development of international environmental law in the years to follow. Its success, then, was primarily political rather than environmental.

Stockholm to Rio

The conference report was submitted to the General Assembly at the end of 1972. The period following Stockholm has been described as a relapse after the 'high point in Western public attention to the environment' (Brenton, 1994, p. 51). Scientific knowledge expanded, the activities and expertise of environmental NGOs increased and there was a greater recognition that environmental problems required not just scientific and technical solutions but attention to the complexity of social, economic and political causes and consequences. However, despite many international environmental conferences and the adoption of a number of international environmental agreements, progress in halting and reversing environmental degradation was incremental and piecemeal. There was a lot of activity but not much real action.

Expert conferences and publications were important in placing scientific advances before policy-makers and the public. In 1977, UNEP convened an Ad Hoc Committee of Experts which formulated a World Plan of Action on the Ozone Layer. The First World Climate Conference was convened in 1979 under the auspices of the World Meteorological Organization (WMO) in Geneva. In 1980, UNEP and the International Union for the Conservation of Nature (IUCN) launched the World Conservation Strategy (WCS) and in 1982 the UN General Assembly adopted a World Charter for Nature focusing on the conservation and use of living natural resources. In 1984 the International Council of Scientific Unions (ICSU) sponsored the International Geosphere–Biosphere Programme (IGBP) to understand the relationship between the earth's systems and to assess the extent of change in those systems caused by human activity. It was followed, in 1987, by the Human Dimensions of Global Change Programme, established by ICSU in collaboration with the International Council of Social Sciences.

In the West at least, public concern about environmental problems was heightened by a series of environmental disasters. The 1976 dioxin leak at Seveso in Italy, the 1978 Amoco Cadiz oil spill and the partial meltdown at the Three Mile Island nuclear power plant in Pennsylvania in 1979 all grabbed headline space in the media. In 1984, the methyl isocyanate gas leak at Bhopal in India, which killed 2,000 and injured 200,000, drew attention to the activities of multinational corporations, especially in developing countries. In 1986, 30 tons of toxic chemicals were washed into the Rhine following a warehouse fire in Switzerland. The 1986 explosion at the Chernobyl nuclear power station in (Soviet) Ukraine reminded people once again of the transboundary consequences of pollution (the radiation spread across 21 countries in Europe) and raised questions about state responsibility, accountability and liability. Such accidents were increasingly perceived not as isolated incidents but as evidence of the dangers of unregulated industrialization and industrial pollution.

In response to scientific analysis and public concern, governments adopted a number of agreements to mitigate or control transboundary environmental degradation. These included a series of agreements on oceans pollution (the 1972 London Dumping Convention and the 1973 International Convention for the Prevention of Pollution from Ships – the MARPOL agreement), on endangered species (the 1973 Convention on International Trade in Endangered Species) and on acid rain (the 1979 Geneva Convention on Long-Range Transboundary Air Pollution). The first major agreement on the degradation of the global atmosphere, the Vienna *Convention for the Protection of the Ozone Layer*, was adopted in 1985. Two years later, before that Convention had come into force, governments established reduction targets in the Montreal *Protocol on Substances that Deplete the Ozone Layer*. In 1989, 116 countries adopted the Basel *Convention on the Control of Transboundary Movements of Hazardous Wastes and their Disposal*.

However the political and economic issues that had been important at the Stockholm Conference did not figure prominently in public debate again until the mid-1980s when, in 1983, General Assembly resolution 38/161 established a special independent commission to 'propose long-term environmental strategies for achieving sustainable development to the year 2000 and beyond' (UNGA, 1983, para. 8(a)). The World Commission on Environment and Development (WCED), known as the Brundtland Commission after its chairperson Gro Harlem Brundtland, the Prime Minister (and former Environment Minister) of Norway, comprised 23 members from 22 countries, each serving in their independent and expert capacities. More than half came from developing countries, ranging from China, India and Brazil to the Ivory Coast, Guyana and Zimbabwe. Those from the 'developed' world came from most but not all of the G7 countries (there was no one from France or the UK) as well as from the then socialist bloc. The Commission appointed a number of expert Special Advisers and three Advisory Panels (on energy, industry and food security). One of the hallmarks of the Commission's work was the public hearings held around the world from March 1985 to February 1987, enabling Commissioners to hear from a wide variety of interested people and organizations. The Commission's report, *Our Common Future* (WCED, 1987), which was finally tabled in 1987, placed the concept of 'sustainable development' firmly into the global environmental lexicon (see Chapter 7).

The late 1980s were marked by a more active public debate and multilateral attention. Mostafa Tolba (at the time Director of UNEP) described 1988, the year following the publication of the Brundtland Report, as the year in which environmental concerns (finally) became a top item on the international agenda (see Soroos, 1991, p. 1). In January 1988, scientists, policy-makers and representatives of intergovernmental and non-governmental organizations met in Toronto for the 'Changing Atmosphere: Implications for Global Security' conference, adopting voluntary targets for reducing greenhouse gas emissions. In the same year, the World Meteorological Organization (WMO) and UNEP established the Intergovernmental Panel on Climate Change (IPCC), involving over 1,000 scientific, legal and policy experts from over 60 countries. The momentum of 1988 carried over into 1989. In March, 24 heads of government met in the Hague at a conference convened by the prime ministers of France, the Netherlands and Norway. They adopted a declaration acknowledging the seriousness of threats to the atmosphere and the inadequacy of the existing machinery of environmental governance. However, neither the United States nor the Soviet Union was invited for fear that they would oppose any declaration or recommendations which seemed to undermine state sovereignty. Environmental concerns were also inscribed on the agenda of the G7 meeting in Paris in July 1989, the first time any serious attention had been given to such concerns in this forum. The seven wealthiest industrialized countries proclaimed that 'decisive action [was] urgently needed to understand and protect the earth's ecological balance' (cited in Fairclough, 1991, p. 96).

Late in 1989 (22 December to be exact), the UN General Assembly (UNGA) adopted a number of resolutions on the global impact of environmental degradation. Resolution 44/207 – Protection of the Global Climate for Present and Future Generations of Mankind [sic] – acknowledged an urgent need to address climate change as an issue of common concern (UNGA, 1989a). A second resolution – 44/224 – declared that deterioration of the environment was 'one of the main global problems facing the world today' (UNGA, 1989b). A third resolution – 44/228 (UNGA, 1989c) – paved the way for what was intended to be the environmental highlight of the 1990s – the United Nations Conference on Environment and Development, known also as the Rio Summit, the Earth Summit, or just UNCED.

United Nations Conference on Environment and Development (UNCED), 1992

Resolution 44/228 expressed concern at the 'continuing deterioration of the state of the environment and the serious degradation of the global life-support systems' (UNGA, 1989c, preamble). It identified a number of major environmental problems – protection of the atmosphere, freshwater and oceans resources, land resources, biological diversity and biotechnology, waste management (including toxic wastes) and issues related to urban settlements, poverty and human health conditions. It recognized the global character of environmental problems and identified unsustainable patterns of production and consumption, particularly in industrialized countries, as the cause of much of that deterioration. It stressed the importance of international cooperation, scientific research and access for developing countries to technology and new and additional financial resources. The Conference was therefore required to elaborate 'strategies and measures to halt and reverse environmental degradation in the context of increased national and international efforts to promote sustainable and environmentally sound development in all countries' (UNGA, 1989c, Part I, para. 3), an objective which was supplemented by a long list of more specific purposes (UNGA, 1989c, Part I, para. 15, sub-paras (a) to (w)).

The Preparatory Committee (PrepComm) was established as a committee of the General Assembly and chaired by Ambassador Tommy Koh of Singapore who had chaired the Law of the Sea negotiations. Maurice Strong, who since Stockholm had been the first Executive Director of UNEP as well as a member of the Brundtland Commission, headed the conference secretariat in Geneva. In Koh and Strong, UNCED benefited from extensive diplomatic experience in the difficulties of reconciling environment and development concerns. All states were requested to take an active part in preparations and to submit national reports to the Secretariat. UNEP and other UN bodies were asked to 'contribute fully' to the preparations. NGOs with consultative status with the UN Economic and Social Council (ECOSOC) were also invited to contribute. The preparatory process was funded through the regular budget of the UN. A voluntary fund was also established to assist developing countries ('in particular the least developed among them' in the words of resolution 44/228) to participate in the PrepComms and Conference.

The PrepComm held an organizational session in New York in March 1990 and four substantive sessions (one in Nairobi, two in Geneva and a final session in New York) to 'prepare draft decisions for the Conference and submit them to the Conference for consideration and adoption' (UNGA, 1989c, Part II, para. 8(c)). Decision-making was by consensus. Cross-sectoral issues, such as financial assistance, technology transfer and the international economic system, were addressed in plenary meetings. Other issues were addressed by three working groups: one on atmosphere, land resources (including deforestation, desertification and drought) and biodiversity/biotechnology; one on oceans, seas, coastal areas, freshwater resources, waste management and trade; and the third (established at the second substantive PrepComm) on legal and institutional issues. These three working groups often broke into smaller groups known in UN-speak as the 'formals' (those meetings at which delegations could make official statements and which were open to NGOs), the 'formal informals' (informal meetings, often open to NGOs, with proceedings translated but not transcribed) and the 'informal informals' (small meetings, often conducted in English and open only to government representatives). It was at these latter meetings that final compromise decisions were often made. Many smaller national delegations, who faced problems in attending simultaneous meetings, found this a burdensome process. Environmental NGOs, who were typically excluded from the informal informals, were concerned at the lack of transparency.

There was little real progress on the substantive agreements until PrepComm III. The bulk of the negotiation did not begin until the fourth and final PrepComm in New York – the five-week 'New York Marathon' – where agreement was finally reached on a declaration of principles and about 85 per cent of the programme of action that would be presented to the Conference. Much of the work was completed during the last days before the final session closed at 5.10 a.m. on 4 April. The draft declaration of principles was only agreed to at 3.30 a.m. that morning and only after Tommy Koh had three days earlier ordered delegates to select a new panel of negotiators and to compile a new working draft (see Halpern, 1992). Fifteen per cent of Agenda 21 went to the Conference bracketed (that is, without consensus).

UNCED convened in Rio de Janeiro in Brazil from 3 to 14 June 1992, following two days of procedural consultations (including the election of the 39 conference Vice-Presidents!). There were 178 national delegations, over 1,400 officially accredited NGOs and a strong media presence although the exact number of journalists may never be known. At the same time but almost 40 kms away at Flamengo Park over 30,000 people attended the parallel NGO conference – the Global Forum. The work of the Conference proceeded in two main bodies – general debate in the Plenary and substantive negotiations in the Main Committee and its subsidiary groups. Each of those chapters on which agreement had not yet been reached in the PrepComms – atmospheric protection, high seas fisheries, biotechnology safety concerns, technology transfer, institutional arrangements, poverty and consumption and financial resources – was dealt with by a contact group. The Main Committee ran out of its allotted time at 6.00 a.m. on Thursday 11 June and disputes on three chapters – forests, finance and atmosphere – still had not been resolved. They were forwarded to the ministerial session on the final two days of the Conference, attended by over 100 heads of government and state.

The conference agreements – the Rio Declaration, Agenda 21 and the Statement of Forest Principles – were formally adopted in those final two days and two separately negotiated conventions – the UN Framework Convention on Climate Change (UNFCCC) and the Convention on Biological Diversity (CBD) – were opened for signature. The UNCED reports were endorsed by the 47th session of the General Assembly at the end of 1992. The Assembly established a standing agenda item on implementation of decisions and recommendations of the UNCED and decided to convene, not later than 1997, a special session for the purposes of an overall review of Agenda 21. It also established the Commission on Sustainable Development, recommended by UNCED, with the mandate to monitor and review the implementation of Agenda 21 (discussed in more detail in Chapter 4).

Maurice Strong had hoped the Conference would move 'environmental issues into the centre of economic policy and decision-making' (Strong, 1991, p. 290) and 'establish the basis for the new dimensions of international cooperation that will be required to ensure "our common future" ' (Strong, 1991, p. 297). The discussion here focuses on the Rio Declaration and Agenda 21. Other outcomes of the Rio Conference, and the extent to which they met Strong's expectations, are discussed in more detail in later chapters.

The Rio Declaration on Environment and Development

The 27 principles of the Rio Declaration were eventually adopted in the same form as they came from the Preparatory Committee. The Declaration's goal is 'a new and equitable global partnership through the creation of new levels of cooperation among States, key sectors of societies and people' (UNCED, 1992a). Principle 1 locates 'human beings' (rather than the planetary ecosystem) at the centre of concerns for sustainable development. The second principle reasserts principle 21 of the Stockholm Declaration, confirming states' sovereign rights over resources as well as recalling their transboundary responsibilities. Several principles give voice to the political and economic concerns of developing countries. The controversial right to development is asserted in principle 3. Principle 5 emphasizes the importance of eradicating poverty, principle 6 gives priority to the special needs of developing countries and principle 7 confirms that developed and developing countries have common but differentiated responsibilities. Principle 8 calls for a reduction in, and the elimination of, unsustainable patterns of production and consumption and the promotion of 'appropriate demographic policies', a rather oblique and finessed response to disagreements over population pressures. Principle 12 calls for a 'supportive and open international economic system' and principle 16 reinforces the polluter-pays principle in encouraging the full internalization of environmental costs. Principle 15 asserts the precautionary principle, demanding that 'lack of full scientific certainty shall not be used as a reason for postponing cost effective measures'.

The Rio Declaration is more inclusive than its Stockholm predecessor. Women, youth and indigenous communities are recognized as important participants in the pursuit of sustainable development. Principle 10 identifies public awareness and access to information as crucial to achieving sustainable development. Principle 23, the subject of some controversy, calls for the environment of people under oppression, domination and occupation to be protected, an injunction that Israel opposed as an intrusion into Middle Eastern politics. It was accepted in the Rio Declaration only on the understanding that the same wording would not be used in Agenda 21. The Declaration also draws attention, in principle 24, to warfare as inherently destructive of sustainable development and notes that 'peace, development and environmental protection are interdependent and indivisible' (principle 25). In a final flourish echoing the UN Charter, states are to solve their environmental disputes peacefully (principle 26) and states and peoples are to cooperate in good faith and a spirit of partnership in fulfilling the principles in the Declaration (principle 27).

Despite this extensive list, the Declaration really only codified existing principles and statements rather than providing guidance and inspiration in the pursuit of a new global ethic of sustainable development. Some criticism was muted, suggesting only that the Declaration was 'less inspiring and coherent than originally proposed' (Parson *et al.*, 1992, p. 12). Others argued that it 'fail[ed] to provide the kind of framework needed to deal with global environmental problems' (Davison and Barns, 1992, p. 6). Ileana Porras, an adviser to the Costa Rican government during UNCED, has argued that the Rio Declaration was driven by development concerns and, as a result, is a 'text of uneasy compromises, delicately balanced interests and dimly discernible contradictions' (Porras, 1993, p. 23). Two themes which characterize the global politics of the environment are evident in these critical views and both are examined in greater depth in later chapters. First, the Declaration and its principles are shaped by and reinforce the imperatives of state sovereignty rather than global stewardship. Second, the Declaration exemplifies the difficulties of reconciling environment and development in the concept and practice of sustainable development.

Agenda 21

Agenda 21 is, like the Rio Declaration, a non-binding agreement. In 40 chapters, grouped together in a preamble and four sections, it sets out a detailed plan of action for implementing the principles of the Declaration and for achieving sustainable development. Each chapter adopts the same format – identification and elaboration of the issue, a description of the proposed programme and a cost estimate. The first section of Agenda 21 groups a number of chapters on social and economic dimensions, including combating poverty, changing consumption patterns, managing demographic dynamics, human health and human settlements. Under the broad heading 'Conservation and Management of Resources for Development', Section 2 contains the chapters on major environmental issues: atmosphere, land resources, deforestation, desertification and drought, sustainable agriculture and rural development, biodiversity, biotechnology, oceans, freshwater resources and various aspects of waste management. Sections 3 and 4 hold the governance chapters. Section 3 (Chapters 23–32) focuses on strengthening the role of what are called the major groups – women, children and youth, indigenous peoples, NGOs, local authorities, trade unions, business and industry, science and technology, and farmers. Section 4 – means of implementation – covers financial resources and mechanisms, technology transfer, institutional arrangements and legal instruments as well as less contentious chapters on science, education and capacity-building.

The preamble includes several diplomatic compromises. It retains references to the 'particular circumstances facing the economies in transition' (the EITs) but all other references to the EITs were removed because of developing country concerns that too extensive a recognition of the former Soviet bloc countries could jeopardize their own development needs. As agreed in negotiations on the Rio Declaration, all references to 'peoples under occupation' were removed from Agenda 21. At PrepComm IV, the Yemeni delegation acting on behalf of the Arab Group bracketed all of Chapter 9 on atmospheric issues in response to what they perceived as an undue emphasis on energy efficiency and a general antipathy to fossil fuels. Differences arose over commitments to renewable energy resources and references to 'environmentally safe and sound energy systems', which some took to embody an anti-nuclear bias. The solution was to include a footnote statement in the preamble that all references in the Agenda to environmentally sound energy sources, systems, supplies and technologies should be read to mean 'environmentally safe and sound' (see UNCED, 1992b). The Saudi delegation, which had wanted the whole of Chapter 9 removed, entered a formal reservation to the chapter because of its references to renewable energy, although the reservation has little practical significance given the non-binding nature of the Agenda. Other difficult issues were postponed entirely. For example, in the absence of any consensus on how to balance sovereign rights with high seas freedoms, the problem of straddling and migratory fish stocks (those which move between territorial waters and high seas) was referred to a separate UN conference.

Careful diplomatic compromises also characterized the debates on financial resources and mechanisms. In Chapter 33, donor governments 'reaffirmed' their commitment to the United Nations official development assistance target of 0.7 per cent of donor country gross national product (GNP). Few countries had met this target and others, such as the United States, had never accepted it. There were no deadlines (despite an attempt to establish 2000 as a target year). There was no agreement on the replenishment of the International Development

Agency of the World Bank, although World Bank President Lewis Preston had proposed an 'Earth increment' in his address to Plenary. There was also no consensus on increased funding for the Global Environment Facility (GEF) established under World Bank, UNEP and UNDP auspices in 1990, although Chapter 33 acknowledged developing country demands for the GEF to be restructured to make it more democratic and transparent. There were also no specific commitments on technology transfer. Chapter 34 simply suggested that it should be 'promoted, facilitated and financed as appropriate' (UNCED, 1992b, para. 34.11). The environmental impact of military establishments proved a sticking point in Chapter 20 on hazardous wastes. The United States claimed national security interests and governments are required only to ensure that militaries conform to national norms on the treatment and disposal of hazardous waste (see Parson *et al.*, 1992, p. 15).

For some, Agenda 21 made a substantial contribution to the pursuit of sustainable development. In his closing address (reproduced in Johnson, 1993, p. 522), Maurice Strong said that although it had been weakened by compromise and negotiation, Agenda 21 was still the most comprehensive programme of action on environmental concerns ever sanctioned by the international community. Haas *et al.* suggest that it 'reflects a far more sophisticated appreciation of the ecological links that must be addressed to achieve sustainable development than did the Stockholm Action Plan' (1992, p. 32). Others are more cautious, concerned that it is largely unfinanced and 'contains no priorities of any kind' (Susskind, 1994, p. 41).

It is not surprising, then, that the Rio Conference as a whole also attracted mixed reviews. For some, UNCED laid a strong foundation for continuing commitment and momentum on environmental issues (Haas *et al.*, 1992, p. 32). Holmberg claimed it to be a 'momentous exercise in awareness-raising at the highest political level' which should be judged not 'by its immediate outcomes but by the processes it set in motion' (1992, p. 4). Others are less persuaded by procedural success, concerned instead whether the conference advanced global environmental protection. Sir Crispin Tickell, a former British ambassador to the United Nations, diplomatically called the Rio Conference an 'interesting mix of some success and *much failure*' (1993a, p. 80; emphasis added). Alberto Szekely, a member of the International Law Commission, argued that the 'appalling poverty of the legal achievements of the Rio Conference provide[d] very little scope for optimism' (1994, p. 66). Governments were criticized for failing to meet either of Rio's twin goals of establishing a firm basis for defining and achieving sustainable development, and halting and reversing global environmental degradation.

There were, Koy Thomson argued, 'no leaps towards a sustainable future' (1992, p. 4). Even Maurice Strong in his closing address pointed out that commitments on funding, technology transfer and elimination of poverty had been insufficient (in Johnson, 1993, pp. 522–3).

Rio to New York

Despite disagreements about its success or failure, UNCED did mobilize a flurry of multilateral activity on global environmental change which seemed to suggest that UN member states were energized by the Rio process, despite its limitations, and were prepared to move quickly to establish and implement further legally binding rules to mitigate environmental degradation. The two UN treaties which were opened for signature at Rio – the UN Convention on Biological Diversity and the UN Framework Convention on Climate Change (discussed further in Chapters 2 and 3 respectively) – were given international legal effect within two years. In the five years following Rio, governments negotiated (among others) a UN convention to combat desertification (see Chapter 2), a UN Agreement on Straddling and Highly Migratory Fish Stocks (see Chapter 2), a protocol on biosafety (see Chapter 2) and a protocol establishing legally binding targets for reducing greenhouse gas emissions (see Chapter 3).

By 1997, however, the Rio spirit had been substantially weakened and the multilateral optimism of 1992 was proving to be severely misplaced. Two events are noteworthy – the United Nations General Assembly Special Session (UNGASS) to review the implementation of Agenda 21 which met at UN headquarters in New York from 23 to 27 June and the third Conference of Parties under the Framework Convention on Climate Change, convened in December. Two reports made public before UNGASS made clear the imperatives for rejecting 'business as usual' practices. The Secretary-General's report, *Global Change and Sustainable Development: Critical Trends*, drew attention to continued dangers associated with patterns of unsustainable development, while still holding out the possibility of positive and effective policy interventions (UNSG, 1997a). UNEP's first *Global Environment Outlook* described several advances in institutional development, the application of sustainable development principles, attention to pollution and resource depletion and increases in non-governmental participation in environmental governance. However its blunt conclusion was that 'from a global perspective the environment has continued to degrade … [and] progress towards a sustainable future is just too slow' (UNEP, 1997a).

United Nations General Assembly Special Session (UNGASS), 1997

The atmosphere at the Special Session (also called Rio+5) has been described as 'acrimonious' (Osborn and Bigg, 1998, p. 12) and 'tense and febrile' (Jordan and Voisey, 1998, p. 95). The outcomes were disappointing. The 1997 meetings of the Intersessional Working Group of the Commission on Sustainable Development (CSD) along with the Commission's fifth annual session were given over to preparation for UNGASS. CSD-5 submitted two key documents to the Special Session, both replete with square brackets. The first, adopted as a Programme for Further Implementation, was watered down in New York. Many of the compromise outcomes on specific points differed little from previous agreements or were 'no more ambitious than the positions officials had already identified as fallbacks' (Osborn and Bigg, 1998, p. 12). The second document, a 26-paragraph political statement, was abandoned after it proved impossible to reach consensus. It was replaced with a six-paragraph statement of commitment inserted as a preamble to the Programme.

The General Assembly President, Malaysian Ambassador Razali, suggested that the fate of the political statement demonstrated that the nations of the world could not agree on how to work together to halt environmental degradation (cited in Rogers, 1997). As one report from within the UN observed, the only real agreement to come from the Special Session was that 'five years after the Rio Earth Summit, the planet's health is generally worse than ever' (UNDPI, 1997). The problems were extensive: continued disagreement over the meaning of sustainable development, let alone how to implement it; a general unwillingness to accept any new commitments especially on funding and technology; confusion over how to respond to the global economic agenda, including the impacts of globalization and the pursuit of trade liberalization. UK Environment Minister, Michael Meacher, was moved to describe the session as a 'chaotic and disconnecting experience' (cited in Jordan and Voisey, 1998, p. 94).

Later in 1997, the parties to the UN Framework Convention on Climate Change met in Kyoto for the third Conference of Parties. Their primary purpose was to finalize negotiations for a legally-binding instrument which would establish formal targets for reducing greenhouse gas emissions. Those negotiations, which had proceeded under the Berlin Mandate adopted in 1995, are described in more detail in Chapter 3. They were characterized by deep divisions over obligations, financial commitments and reduction targets. The Kyoto Protocol establishes individual emissions targets for industrialized countries with an aggregate reduction of only 5.2 per cent as against 1990 levels with a target date of 2012. Three industrialized parties – Australia, Iceland and Norway – were permitted to *increase* their emissions under the Protocol, on the grounds of special circumstance. Governments are expected to have made some progress towards meeting their targets prior to this target date, but there are no formal sanctions if they do not. Indeed, emissions could increase prior to the first budget period. Despite claims that the Protocol was a successful and carefully balanced consensus outcome, the postponement of binding action to a date 15 years from adoption of the agreement confirms again the impression of international negotiation lagging behind the environmental changes and challenges they are intended to meet.

New York to Johannesburg

Perhaps one of the most important events following UNGASS was the publication of the Millennium Report (in 2000) and the adoption of the Millennium Development Goals (MDG). In his report submitted to the Millennium Assembly of the UN General Assembly, the Secretary-General stressed that the challenges of sustaining our future and ensuring freedom from want were as important as freedom from fear in the pursuit of human security and the objectives of the UN Charter. The Development Goals focused on sustainable development, poverty alleviation and improvement in the quality of life of the world's poorest and most disadvantaged. They included halving by 2015 the proportion of people on incomes of less than a dollar a day, those suffering from hunger and those unable to reach or afford safe drinking water. The MDG also called for entry into force of the Kyoto Protocol, intensification of collective efforts on the sustainable management and conservation of forests, full implementation of the conventions on biodiversity and desertification, and a halt to unsustainable exploitation of water resources.

In December 2000 the UN General Assembly adopted Resolution 55/199 to prepare for the ten-year review in 2002 of Agenda 21. This review was to be known as the World Summit on Sustainable Development (WSSD), indicating in theory at least that the environmental agenda was inextricably connected with the development one and that environmental problems could not be resolved without attention to a range of broader concerns associated with poverty, equity and the nature of the global political economy. While the primary purpose was to accelerate implementation of Agenda 21, the resolution suggests a more broadly normative purpose as well. WSSD was intended to *reinvigorate* at the highest political levels the global commitment to sustainable development, international solidarity and the North/South partnership (UNGA, 2001a, para. 17(b)). The Commission on Sustainable Development again acted as the preparatory committee. Multi-stakeholder dialogues and regional roundtables of eminent persons were held in the middle of 2001. Five regional PrepComm meetings were held in the last four months of 2001 to examine issues of concern to each region and identify future priorities, and the CSD convened four global preparatory committee meetings, chaired by Emil Salim, former Environment Minister of Indonesia (see Steiner, 2003, for a brief discussion of the preparatory process).

In December 2001, UN Secretary-General Kofi Annan released a report on the implementation of Agenda 21, drawing on reviews submitted to the Secretariat by the UN task agencies for the various chapters of Agenda 21. The Secretary-General's report was blunt: 'progress towards the goals established at UNCED [had been] slower than anticipated, and in some respects conditions are actually worse than they were 10 years ago' (UNSG, 2001, p. 4). The report identified a gap in implementation, arguing that there was a fragmented approach to sustainable development, that there had been no changes in the 'unsustainable patterns of production and consumption', that there was a 'lack of mutually coherent policies ... in the areas of finance, trade, investment, technology and sustainable development', and that the necessary financial resources had not been forthcoming (UNSG, 2001, pp. 4–5). It also questioned the notion that globalization had been beneficial, observing that 'the world's poorest countries have generally been left behind' (UNSG, 2001, p. 54).

Two further events helped to set the scene for WSSD. At the Fourth Ministerial Meeting of the World Trade Organization (WTO) in Doha in November 2001, governments agreed to launch discussions on the relationship between WTO rules and the trade rules in multilateral environmental agreements (MEAs). Early in 2002, governments met in Monterrey in Mexico for an international conference on Financing for Development and adopted the Monterrey Consensus which recognized that substantial increases in official development assistance (ODA) would be required if sustainable development goals were to be realized (see Chapters 7 and 8).

The World Summit on Sustainable Development was held in Johannesburg from 26 August to 4 September, brought forward from dates earlier agreed upon to avoid coinciding with the anniversary of the September 11 terrorist attacks in Washington DC and New York. It was allegedly the largest gathering of people at a UN (or any) meeting in history. The broadly held view was that the Summit would succeed only if it was accompanied by concrete commitments rather than a reprise of the disputes and arguments which characterized UNGASS. Resolution 55/199 required the CSD, as the Preparatory Committee, to 'propose specific time-bound measures' (UNGA, 2001a, para. 16(d)). Fears that WSSD would be little more than a 'conference to celebrate a conference' (cited in Brack *et al.*, 2001, p. 1) were only partly alleviated. Two documents were adopted. The Political Declaration departs from the usual formality of statements of principle associated with the Stockholm and Rio conferences. It is presented as a 'solemn pledge' of collective responsibility to the peoples of the earth, to the 'children who represent our collective future' (United Nations, 2002b, pp. 1–5).

The Plan of Implementation contains ten chapters and a number of fairly broad commitments. Some repeat the Millennium Development Goals. Others are watered down versions of what governments had adopted in other multilateral fora (see Pallemaerts, 2003). There are a number of more specific commitments on what has become known as the WEHAB agenda – water, energy, health, agriculture and biodiversity. Fisheries are to be restored to maximum sustainable levels by 2015. Biodiversity loss is to be slowed by 2010 (whereas in the Declaration adopted at the sixth Conference of Parties to the Convention on Biological Diversity only a few months before, governments had committed 'to strengthen [their] efforts to put in place measures to *halt* biodiversity loss ... by the year 2010' (UNEP, 2002f, p. 340; emphasis added). Governments agreed to act 'with a sense of urgency' to increase susbtantially the use of renewable energy resources (although there is no *specific* target – suggestions for a 10 per cent increase did not make it to the final agreement). Governments also announced a number of specific funding and project commitments in some key priority areas, including water and sanitation, energy, health, agriculture, biodiversity and ecosystem management and on cross-cutting issues. One of the most significant was the agreement to establish a world solidarity fund to alleviate and eventually eradicate world poverty (United Nations, 2002b, para. 7b). Finally, the Summit generated a number of 'type II' partnership initiatives – private–public agreements involving government, business and civil society and directed to specific Agenda 21 programmes. Over 220 were announced, with a total financial commitment of $US235 million. While generally welcomed, the partnership initiatives were announced without any 'real discussion on the criteria' and with no clarity on 'how the implementation of these initiatives will be monitored' (Perrez, 2003, p. 13).

Conclusions about WSSD varied. Some argue that it is hard to see it as 'anything other than a failure' (Peake, 2002, p. 46). The most enthusiastic (aside from political leaders and UN officials) are willing to suggest that the outcomes were 'satisfactory' (Perrez, 2003, p. 22). However there was certainly disappointment at the 'dearth of concrete plans' (Kaiser, 2002, p. 1785) to further the implementation of Agenda 21. Explanations for the modest outcomes vary – an overloaded agenda and conference fatigue; distractions associated with the US-led 'war on terror'; and a more general lack of leadership and political will. The US had been especially opposed to any detailed timetables or targets and, as a result, there is little practical detail on how the various goals will be reached, which leaves them 'largely at the level of ambiguous, unenforceable promises' (Wapner, 2003, p. 3).

The Plan of Implementation is particularly weak on the issues of rights and justice which, as later chapters demonstrate, are central to sustainable development and environmental protection. While it includes what appear to be progressive normative statements – about enforceable land and water rights, about indigenous knowledge, about good governance for example – each is qualified by a deference to national law. This is not surprising, but it weakens any reinforcement of global norms and provides governments with an effective 'opt-out clause' in terms of their own obligations. The 'hotly disputed paragraph on corporate accountability' (IISD, 2003b, p. 17) has been decried as 'weak and permissive' (Steiner, 2003, p. 36). There was also considerable difficulty over the meaning of 'precaution', its impact on trade and the extent to which it had relevance to issues beyond the environment, such as human health (Pallemaerts, 2003; see Perrez, 2003). The relationship between trade rules and multilateral environmental agreements was also a sticking point, with disputes over whether the text should give the trade regime priority over MEAs.

Conclusion

United Nations Secretary-General Kofi Annan proclaimed that the Johannesburg Summit made 'sustainable development a reality' (UN-DESA, 2002). As the following chapters demonstrate, that may be optimistic. Despite the increasingly congested terrain of international environmental law, many of the issues on the agenda at Johannesburg echoed those which had been unresolved at Stockholm and at Rio 20 years later. Political will has not kept pace with environmental change. The extensive programme of action established under Agenda 21 has done little to diffuse the political differences at the centre of debates over sovereignty, sustainable development, funding, and the tensions between the Organization for Economic Cooperation and Development (OECD) and G77 countries over responsibilities and relative vulnerabilities.

The rhetoric of a global partnership is not matched by any practical ethic of global stewardship or a willingness to pay serious attention to environmental problems grounded in structural inequities and injustice.

This chapter has provided a brief introduction to the expansion of the environmental agenda. The following two chapters trace this in more detail, demonstrating how the problems first of conservation (Chapter 2) and then pollution (Chapter 3) have become both politicized and globalized. This distinction between conservation and pollution problems is itself increasingly arbitrary, especially as pollution undermines the vitality of species and living resources and the viability of the ecosystems and habitat on which they rely. The environmental issues explored in Chapters 2 and 3 are selective but they demonstrate a number of features which characterize the global politics of the environment and which are relevant to the main themes of this book. They point to the difficulties of securing effective environmental protection in a decentralized world of sovereign states when agreements are sparse on enforcement and compliance mechanisms and implementation relies on what Soroos calls 'good faith efforts' (1986, p. 314). They illuminate tensions over how the 'global' is to be defined and in whose interests. They reveal the gap between commitments on paper and the political and financial commitments required to ensure the effective implementation of those agreements. They also show how transboundary environmental problems, and the search for solutions to those problems, are embedded in the global political economy and, in particular, the relationship between the industrialized countries of the North and the poorer countries of the South.

Chapter 2

The Global Politics of Conservation: Species, Resources and Habitat

Introduction

Conservation issues have been fundamental to the globalizing environmental agenda. Traditional concerns with the preservation of nature and wildlife in pristine wilderness areas have shifted to encompass concerns about the conservation of species and biodiversity, the protection of living, renewable and supposedly inexhaustible resources and the protection of habitat and ecosystems, including biologically productive land. Collective action is now necessary for the management and protection of endangered wildlife, species, genetic diversity, habitat and resources. Political tensions arise over more than appropriate management strategies. They have become bound up in disagreements over sustainable use, commodification and intellectual property rights, utility rather than amenity value, the imperative of sovereign ownership of natural resources, conflicting values and cultural traditions, and disputes about what constitutes a local or global problem.

Debates about conservation and protection are no longer simply 'environmental' or 'national' in scope and focus. The conservation and protection issues explored in this chapter are transboundary and global. Biodiversity and species protection – the first conservation issue addressed here – takes on a transboundary dimension in the migratory patterns of birds and animals (and those who hunt them) and the cross-border trade in such species. It is global in that concern about the loss of diversity has come to be shared among a range of international actors. The conservation of living resources tied more specifically to economic exploitation – marine resources and forests in the cases explored here in the second section of this chapter – is also transboundary and global. Neither fish stocks nor the sources of maritime depletion confine themselves to any one national jurisdiction. Often they are confined to no national jurisdiction, ranging over the oceans commons. International cooperation is thus required if those stocks are to be managed sustainably. Deforestation (or, put differently, the conservation and protection of forest resources and habitat) is a 'local' problem with transboundary and planet-wide or global causes and consequences. Deforestation and biodiversity demonstrate tensions over the claiming of sovereign or national 'resources' as the global or common heritage of humankind, as well as revealing the structural connections between 'local' environmental problems and the 'global' political economy. This local–global connection, and the relationship with the pollution problems addressed in Chapter 3, is evident also in debates about water scarcity which are explored briefly here. Desertification, the final issue examined in this chapter, is caught up in the broadest dimensions of the conservation agenda as the viability of terrestrial ecosystems and habitat is compromised or lost through extreme land degradation. As with deforestation and biodiversity loss, there are consequences also for human lives and livelihoods. The global nature of desertification lies in an often reluctant recognition that there is, or should be, a shared and common concern for those peoples and countries (usually developing) which face extensive degradation.

Protecting and conserving biodiversity

Biodiversity is colloquially used as a synonym for the number of species, but it encompasses diversity *of* species, genetic diversity *within* species and the diversity of habitat that supports biological life. Biodiversity is concentrated in the tropical countries of the developing world. Of the 12 'megadiverse' countries, 11 are in the developing world – Brazil, China, Colombia, Ecuador, India, Indonesia, Madagascar, Malaysia, Mexico, Peru and Zaire. Australia is the only developed megadiverse country. Over half of all species live in the 6 per cent of the earth's land surface that is covered by tropical forest (Brenton, 1994, p. 198). One river in Brazil alone contains more fish species than are to be found in the whole of the United States and a small reserve in Costa Rica contains more plant species than the whole of the United Kingdom (WRM, 1990, p. 16).

Loss of diversity within and of species has a number of causes. Individual species may be endangered to the point of extinction through a range of direct and indirect economic pressures including exploitation for commercial gain or for food. The introduction of or invasion by exotic species can threaten indigenous fauna and flora. Species numbers are vulnerable also to the unintended consequences of habitat loss as a result of changes in land use practices, overuse of water resources, drainage of wetlands, pollution of and damage to coral reefs through sedimentation and the direct and indirect impacts of climate change. The changing political economy of agriculture through mono-cropping and Green Revolution technology has resulted in loss of genetic diversity within plant species, often 'at the expense of indigenous practices that helped sustain genetic diversity' (Soto, 1992, p. 694).

One of the most authoritative analyses of species in danger is the IUCN's *Red List of Threatened Species*. The 2002 update lists 11,167 species threatened with extinction (IUCN, 2002). The loss of numbers within individual species has, in some instances, been substantial. Elephant numbers in Africa are estimated to have halved from 1.2 million to just over 500,000 in the 1980s and 1990s (Barbier, 1995, p. 3; WWF, 2003): in some countries up to 90 per cent of the populations have been lost (UNEP, 1994d, p. 1). Tiger numbers in the 14 tiger range countries (that is, those states in which the species is found) are now estimated to be no more than something between 5,000 and 7,000 and several sub-species are now believed to be extinct (UNEP, 2001c). Rhinoceros numbers in Africa were depleted by 97 per cent in the last half of the twentieth century (UNEP, 1994d, p. 1). By the early 1990s, chimpanzee numbers in Western Africa had declined from a peak population of over one million to about one-tenth of that number and the number of wild mountain gorillas was estimated to be no more than 350 (Karno, 1991, p. 990).

Quantitative information on the extent of species loss and on rates of extinction is difficult to determine because we do not know how many species there are in the world. Recent estimates have revised numbers upwards and suggestions stand at anything from 8 million to 30 million (and, indeed, perhaps even much higher). Only about 1.5 million species have been identified and classified. We know much more about vertebrate and plant species than we do about the 'less conspicuous organisms' (Kassas, 2002, p. 44) such as fungi, bacteria, algae and protozoa. In spite of this uncertainty, there is agreement that species extinction is increasing. Walter Reid (1992, p. 1090) argues that the rate of extinction could be higher than at any time in the last 65 million years. Murray (1993, p. 70) has suggested that, at present rates, up to 8 per cent of all species could become extinct by about 2020. Some scientific opinion estimates that perhaps 50 species become extinct each day (see Bragdon, 1992, p. 382). This extinction rate is generally accepted to be much faster than the natural rate – something between 50 to 100 times (Reid, 1997, p. 19), 400 times (WRM, 1990, p. 27) and 1,000 times (Porter and Brown, 1991, p. 15) higher. This loss is irreversible.

The proposition that *all* species, not just humans, should be respected and protected in and of their own right – sometimes referred to as intrinsic value – is an important ethical theme in conservation debates. However much of the contemporary debate about the loss of species and biodiversity has come to focus on utility value, especially with respect to pharmaceutical, medicinal and agricultural purposes. The commercial value of plant- and insect-derived medicines is estimated at $US75 to $US150 billion per annum (UNEP, 2002a, p. 121). Genetic diversity enhances the disease- and pest-resistance of domesticated plant crops whereas genetic uniformity can result in widespread and costly vulnerability to disease. There is also an ecosystem value to biodiversity: we cannot predict how the loss of a species (or many species) might affect the balance of the ecosystem nor how long it might take an ecosystem to recover from this damage. Berlin and Lang note that 'palaeontologists have estimated that it took the environment 20 million years to heal fully after the last great episode of mass species extinction' (1993, p. 37).

Protecting wildlife

The protection of wildlife and the conservation of living resources have invoked two distinct and often competing approaches to non-human species and to individual creatures. Preservationist concerns focus on the inherent or intrinsic value and 'right to life' of non-human species. The extinction or endangering of individual species by humans, with a particular but not exclusive emphasis on terrestrial and marine mammals and some bird species, is understood as a denial of that right to life. This runs counter to the 'resource conservation' ethos, where the primary imperative is to maintain the economic viability of a species especially those which have a food or other commodity value for humans. This approach encourages conservation in the interests of 'human use of the biosphere and of the ecosystems and species that compose it, so that they may yield the greatest sustainable benefit to present generations while maintaining their potential to meet the needs and aspirations of future generations' (World Conservation Strategy, cited in Miller, 1983, p. 250).

International efforts to conserve or protect wildlife have focused primarily on support for *in situ* conservation and protection of species, habitat and ecological processes *within* national jurisdictions. Scientific monitoring and the coordination of resources and expertise has been undertaken by institutions such as the International Union for the Conservation of Nature and Natural Resources (IUCN) and its Commission on National Parks and Protected Areas (CNPPA) and the United Nations Environment Programme (UNEP). Non-governmental organizations, such as the World Wide Fund for Nature (WWF), the

Sierra Club, the Audubon Society and the US-based Nature Conservancy, have been active contributors to global conservation programmes. Regional and international agreements have sought to protect habitats or important ecosystems through the designation of biosphere reserves (under UNESCO's 1970 Man [sic] and the Biosphere programme), national parks or world heritage sites under the 1972 *Convention Concerning the Protection of the World Cultural and Natural Heritage* (the World Heritage Convention) and the IUCN's *World Conservation Strategy* or through protecting specific kinds of habitat such as that pursued under the 1971 *Convention on Wetlands of International Importance especially as Waterfowl Habitat* (the Ramsar Convention). Other agreements have sought to protect individual members of migratory species. The 1979 *Convention on the Conservation of Migratory Species of Wild Animals* (the Bonn Convention), for example, provides protection for endangered migratory species through a listing procedure. Species listed in Appendix I of that agreement are to be given strict protection. Appendix II species are to be the subject of further multilateral agreements. Although the Convention came into effect in 1983 progress has been 'disappointingly slow' (Bowman, 1991, p. 137).

The trade in endangered species has attracted perhaps most international attention with respect to wildlife protection. Live creatures and their products (fur, ivory, organs) are traded predominantly, but not exclusively, from developing to developed countries. The economic value of the illegal trade in wildlife is estimated at approximately $US10 billion a year (Stoett, 2002, p. 195). This trade endangers species not only because individual animals or birds are involved but also (if poaching or smuggling is involved) because the death of infants or mothers or older adults, or disruption to breeding, ensures a greater incidental death rate.

Convention on International Trade in Endangered Species (CITES)

CITES was adopted in March 1973 and came into effect in July 1975. The Convention regulates and, where necessary, prohibits commercial trade in those species (whether alive or dead) and in parts thereof (such as skin, eggs, bone, seeds and bark), including plant species, which are placed in danger through trade. Guidelines adopted in 1994 require that a precautionary approach must inform decisions on whether species are threatened with extinction or are likely to withstand the pressures of international trade.

Categories of protection are established in three appendices to the Convention. Appendix I lists those species which are determined to be vulnerable to or endangered by existing or potential trade. Appendix II lists species which *might* become threatened by large volumes of trade. Appendix II also covers species for whom it is difficult to distinguish between an endangered and non-endangered subspecies so as to prevent a rare or endangered animal being passed off as a more common member of the species (the 'look-alike' provision). Appendix III identifies species which are protected in at least one country which has requested assistance in managing trade. Commercial trade in Appendix I species is prohibited under CITES except that Article VII(4) allows limited trade if they have been bred in captivity. Any non-commercial transaction requires permits from both importing and exporting countries. Any cross-border movement of Appendix II and Appendix III species requires a permit from the exporting country. The Convention does not cover species which might be endangered for reasons other than the pressures of trade. It also excludes scientific samples and specimens collected before the Convention came into effect. Despite this, coverage is extensive. As of May 2003, approximately 5,000 species of animals and 25,000 plants were listed under the CITES appendices.

The Convention has been controversial and its contribution to wildlife conservation and the protection of endangered species a matter of some debate. Two concerns dominate: compliance and the adequacy of trade bans. As with all international law, the provisions of the Convention apply only to signatory parties. Parties have been slow to adopt national implementing legislation. National reporting to CITES has been lax: up to 50 per cent of parties have failed to submit timely reports on implementation and CITES transactions (see Ong, 1998, p. 294). Smuggling, mislabelling and diversion through non-party countries are used to circumvent the Convention. There are no agreed sanctions for non-compliance and penalties remain the province of individual governments. The burden for export permits and controls falls primarily on developing countries whose capacity to manage this system is often limited.

The trade restrictions under CITES are seen by many as 'too little, too late' responses to the problem of species protection on the one hand, and as a possible incentive to illegal trade and increased poaching on the other. Trade bans are also criticized for denying range states income from sustainably managed exploitation which could be used to support conservation programmes. However the main issue which bedevils this debate is whether the '*economic* value of wildlife, as realised through international trade [should be] fostered and encouraged through the CITES process in order to realise the goal of protection and recovery of listed species' (Favre, 1993, p. 883; emphasis added). In other words, can the killing of wildlife under a sustainable-use regime be compatible with the imperatives of protecting that same wildlife? Swanson (1992) and Barbier (1995) argue in favour of such a sustainable-use principle which, they suggest, *is* compatible with the provisions and purpose of CITES. CITES resolutions also now accommodate ranching proposals, which allow for particular species in selected countries to be downlisted for sustainable resource management, and species quotas which set strict limits for the taking of a named species to be distributed among range states. The ranching strategy was adopted, for example, for the Zimbabwean population of the Nile crocodile and a species quota approach has been applied to a number of species including the African leopard and four crocodile species (see Swanson, 1992, p. 61; see also Wilder, 1995, pp. 61–2, 69). These innovations have, however, been subject to problems because of the difficulties of establishing effective control structures within producer states (Swanson, 1992, p. 61).

These debates have come to a head over the protection of the African elephant. In 1989, the relisting of the African elephant from Appendix II to Appendix I established a ban on the trade in ivory. It was controversial and the extent to which it has enhanced or undermined elephant conservation efforts has been seriously questioned. The widely held view is that CITES has failed to halt the overall decline in elephant numbers (although the rate of decline slowed) but differences arise over whether this is because the agreement has been poorly implemented or because the basic approach is flawed. Wilder argues that continued but often illegal trade in ivory has been possible because CITES provisions are circumvented and because the Ivory Export Quota System is ineffective (1995, pp. 63, 66–7). Barbier (1995, p. 9), on the other hand, has suggested that increases in the price of ivory, reflecting scarcity under a trade ban, could have encouraged illegal trade and increased poaching. Other criticisms arise because the ban does not recognize differences between those countries where elephant numbers are severely depleted and those, such as South Africa, where populations are healthy and where selective culling may be required to keep numbers within the range that can be supported by the habitat. In response to lobbying from a key group of elephant range states, elephants in Zimbabwe, Botswana, and Namibia were downlisted to Appendix II status at the tenth Conference of Parties (COP) in June 1997. Severe restrictions were applied to subsequent elephant-related trade, especially in ivory (see Ong, 1998) and income thus derived had to be used for conservation programmes. In 2000, South Africa's elephant population was partially downlisted (see Favre, 2001). In 2002, COP-12 reconfirmed restrictions over one-off ivory sales for Botswana, Namibia and South Africa. In the same year, a report from the Elephant Trade Information System (ETIS) established by CITES in 1997 and managed by the non-governmental organization TRAFFIC, revealed a rise in the illegal ivory trade although the direct connection to CITES was unclear (TRAFFIC, 2002). Nevertheless, concern remains that the apparent 'relaxing' of the ban has encouraged an increase in poaching and illegal trading in countries whose elephants have not been downlisted, such as Kenya or the Democratic Republic of Congo (see Ong, 1998; Favre, 2001, p. 282).

Conserving biodiversity

As noted earlier, concerns about protecting species expanded into a more general concern with biological resources, driven in part by disputes over utility, property rights and economic benefit. The first suggestions for a convention to protect biodiversity date to 1974. A number of non-binding instruments were adopted in the 1970s and 1980s. The Stockholm Action Plan contained six recommendations on the preservation of the world's genetic resources with the Food and Agriculture Organization (FAO) in the lead role. The 1980 World Conservation Strategy (WCS) included the preservation of genetic diversity among its objectives. In 1983, the FAO passed a non-binding Undertaking on Plant Genetic Resources which established that such resources were the 'heritage of mankind [sic]' and should be 'available without restriction' (see Hendrickx *et al.*, 1993, p. 258), although this did not mean they should be free. In 1985 the World Bank established a Task Force on Biodiversity which led to a Biological Diversity Action Plan drafted by UNEP, IUCN, the World Resources Institute and WWF-US and, in turn, to a Global Biodiversity Strategy in 1992. The IUCN began work on a draft convention in November 1987. In November 1998, UNEP took over these deliberations and convened an Ad Hoc Working Group of Experts on Biological Diversity. Formal negotiations for a legal instrument officially began in 1990 with the Ad Hoc Working Group of Legal and Technical Experts, the third session of which was constituted as the Intergovernmental Negotiating Committee. The Committee met another five times and the Convention was adopted at an 'extremely bad-tempered and confused' (Brenton, 1994, p. 203) final session in Nairobi in May 1992.

Tensions during negotiations were driven not so much by questions of appropriate conservation strategies for species and ecosystems as by questions of ownership of and intellectual property rights to genetic material and biotechnology and the distribution of benefits from genetic exploitation. Countries cleaved between the gene-rich South and the (bio)technology-rich North. Genetic resources had traditionally been treated by the North at least as a 'common heritage' or, if not owned by all in common, then owned by no one. In this way, companies in developed countries were able to utilize the species and genetic resources of developing countries as a free resource, a process which Shiva (1990) likens to gene robbery and which is now more commonly referred to as biopiracy. Developing countries argued that genetic resources were not a global heritage but sovereign national resources. They perceived Northern concern for the protection of (mainly) Southern biodiversity and the continued emphasis on biodiversity as a 'global' issue as eco-imperialist and driven by economic concerns rather than environmental ones. They argued also that if Northern companies were to continue to exploit the species and genetic resources of the South, an equitable sharing of benefits would be required to compensate for the problem of unequal exchange and, further, that they should have access to Northern biotechnology to exploit their own genetic resources. The response of developed countries and the biotechnology industry was, in summary, that '[i]t is not the products found in plants that are offered for sale, but derivatives which have been isolated and synthesised at considerable expense ... legal protection is needed to safeguard the large investments required for future work' (Murray, 1993, p. 79). The question of who 'owned' extracted genetic material was thus made a legal one, complicated by political tensions and economic imperatives which contributed to the difficulties in reaching agreement.

The concerns of indigenous peoples who sustain and depend on bio-diversity for foods, medicine and way of life became a key theme in this debate, often at the urging of NGOs rather than governments. Plants in particular hold medicinal and cultural value for indigenous peoples and local communities and the World Health Organization lists over 21,000 plants used in traditional medicines (see Murray, 1993, p. 75). Indigenous peoples' knowledge about traditional medicines, for which little compensation or recognition had been given, has made an important contribution to the pharmaceutical biotechnology industry (discussed further in Chapters 5 and 6).

The Convention on Biological Diversity

The Convention has a fairly lengthy preamble, 42 articles and two annexes, one on identification and monitoring and one on arbitration and conciliation. Article 1 identifies the Convention's purpose as the conservation of biological diversity, the sustainable use of its components, and the fair and equitable sharing of the benefits arising from the utilization of genetic resources. The reasons for doing so: because biological diversity has 'intrinsic ... ecological, genetic, social, economic, scientific, educational, cultural, recreational and aesthetic values' and, rather curiously, because 'the conservation and sustainable use of biological diversity will strengthen friendly relations among States and contribute to peace for humankind' (UNEP, 1992, preamble). Parties are to meet their obligations through the development of national strategies, plans and programmes (article 6), identification and monitoring (article 7), *in situ* (article 8) and *ex situ* (article 9) conservation and impact assessment (article 14).

The preamble identifies the conservation of biodiversity as a common *concern* (not a common heritage!) of humankind. Article 3 reinforces sovereign rights over resources although states are encouraged not to impose any restrictions on access that would 'run counter to the objectives' of the Convention (article 15.2). Access to genetic resources has to be on terms mutually agreed (among states) and has to be based on informed prior consent (again the consent of states). Research is to be shared in a 'fair and equitable way' (article 15.7). Technology for the conservation of biodiversity and the use of genetic resources is to be 'provided and/or facilitated' by developed countries (see article 16). 'Effective' participation in biotechnology research for parties who provide genetic resources (likely to be developing countries) is to be facilitated 'as appropriate' (article 19.1). Intellectual property rights (IPRs) and patents are to be adequately and effectively protected (see articles 16.2 and 16.3). Boyle (1994, pp. 124–5) suggests that this leaves unresolved the question of whether IPRs are intended to benefit the providers or users of genetic resources. It also leaves unresolved the question of whether IPRs are appropriate tools for the protection of indigenous knowledge (an issue explored in Chapter 6). The preamble 'recognizes' the traditional dependence of indigenous and local communities on biological resources and the 'desirability' of equitable sharing in benefits from the use of traditional knowledge, but the Convention includes little in the way of specific provisions to ensure that this dependence is protected and those benefits distributed, leaving it up to individual governments. Boyle (1994, p. 117) notes that Brazil objected to draft wording to the effect that biodiversity was the common concern of 'all peoples' because it might be taken to confer rights on indigenous peoples. The GEF was nominated to operate as the Convention's financial mechanism on an interim basis, provided it was appropriately restructured. Developing countries had favoured a separate Biodiversity Fund with compulsory contributions. Developed countries favoured voluntary contributions, although the Convention provides that developed countries *shall* provide new and additional financial resources (article 20).

Elizabeth Dowdeswell, then Executive Director of UNEP, called the Convention a 'unique opportunity for achieving a new contract between people and nature ... a contract characterised by solidarity, independence and equity' (UNEP, 1994c). It has been praised for its attention to equity concerns (McNeely *et al.*, 1995, p. 33) and described as a 'courageous political document but also a rather clumsy and cumbersome political text' (McGraw, 2002, p. 23). Others are not so sanguine. Boyle finds 'serious flaws' (1994, p. 112), particularly in the priority given to 'human use' rather than preservationist principles (1994, p. 115). The obligations have been called 'soft' (Redgwell, 1992, p. 265), 'vague in the extreme' (Brenton, 1994, p. 204) and a 'pastiche of vague commitments, ambiguous phrases and some awkward compromises' (Raustiala and Victor, 1996, p. 19). Chatterjee and Finger characterize it as 'just one of many typical examples where the concern for exponential destruction has been perverted into a preoccupation with new scientific and (bio-)technological developments to boost economic growth' (1994, p. 42). They argue that it focuses too much on profits, patent rights, access and control and not enough on the main causes of the destruction of biodiversity. It is for these kinds of reasons that Guruswamy calls it 'deeply flawed' (1999, p. 82).

The Convention was opened for signature at UNCED in June 1992 and came into effect on 29 December 1993. By the end of the Rio Conference it had been signed by over 150 countries. The US was not among them, arguing that the provisions went beyond legitimate biodiversity protection goals and that the Convention would unduly restrict the biotechnology industry. In a statement which referred to the Agenda 21 recommendations on biodiversity but made no reference at all to the Convention the US government called for a comprehensive international survey of plants, animals and natural resources under the guidance of a multidisciplinary scientific committee (see USIS, 1992). The Clinton administration signed the Convention in 1993 but at time of writing the US government has not yet ratified it.

In May 1993, UNEP's Governing Council established the Intergovernmental Committee on the Convention on Biodiversity (ICCBD) to prepare for the first Conference of Parties held in the Bahamas (28 November to 9 December 1994). Early COPs focused, perhaps naturally, on the basic machinery for the Convention's implementation although the decision to locate the secretariat in Montreal (under UNEP auspices) was not taken until COP-2. The GEF was finally approved as the funding mechanism at COP-3 in 1996 although many developed countries were adamant that the COP should not be authorized to make decisions on the size or frequency of country contributions to the GEF for its biodiversity programme (see Anon., 1994c, p. 265). Debate continued also on the often contentious need to address biodiversity conservation in the context of forests, agricultural production and fisheries management, on the general difficulties of defining sustainable use of biodiversity resources and on the implementation of an ecosystem approach to species conservation. The latter, which 'integrates ecological, economic and social factors ... to restore and maintain the health of ecological resources together with the communities and economies that they support' (Johnston, 1997, p. 228) was confirmed as a key principle at COP-6 in 2000. The issue of protecting traditional knowledge and ensuring the equitable sharing of benefits, in accordance with article 8(j), was taken up at COP-3 in 1996 and has continued to be a focus of discussion through an open-ended working group.

Parties have manoeuvred to make the Convention a focal point for biodiversity issues and to elaborate the role of the COP *vis-à-vis* other international fora, such as the WTO and the World Intellectual Property Organization (WIPO) on intellectual property issues, and the FAO on plant genetic resources and forest biodiversity. For this reason, and to give some guidance for assigning priority to work programmes and related issues, COP-6 (April 2002) adopted a Strategic Plan, guidelines on access and benefit-sharing and a revised forest work programme. The Plan commits parties to a more effective and coherent implementation of the Convention's objectives, with the broad goal of achieving a significant reduction in the current rate of biodiversity loss by 2010. This will be a difficult goal to achieve. A decade after the Convention's entry into force there is little evidence that the loss of biodiversity or genetic erosion has been slowed. Most parties to the Convention have established national biodiversity strategies or action plans but many are poorly developed and implemented. Where protected areas are established within countries to contribute to the purposes of the Convention, they are often too small and fragmented to provide appropriate habitat conservation and biodiversity protection remains poorly integrated with key economic sectors in fisheries, agriculture and forestry. While 'the scope of data and information needed to support CBD objectives is vast' (Kimball, 1997, p. 242), there are still considerable gaps in knowledge and scientific capacity.

Biosafety and biotechnology

One of the most contentious issues associated with the Convention has been the safety of biotechnology and genetically modified (GM) seeds and food products. Debate continues on whether GM seeds and foods provide significant benefit to developing countries seeking to raise crop yields in the face of population increases, particularly if those modified seed crops are less reliant on fertilizers and pesticides and can be grown in marginal land, or whether the potential human health and environmental consequences are too high or simply not yet well enough known or understood. The United States has taken the lead in the use of GM technology. Estimates suggest that by the late 1990s, approximately 60 per cent of processed foods available in the US were derived from genetically modified organisms (Pollock and Shaffer, 2000, p. 41). Consumer opposition in other parts of the world, however, was heightened by agriculture-related food and health scares, including the spread of bovine spongiform encephalopathy (BSE or mad-cow disease), foot-and-mouth disease, revelations about dioxin-contaminated animal feed, and the 'Starlink' maize controversy in the United States (on the latter, see Burgiel, 2002).

Article 19 of the CBD foreshadowed negotiations for a protocol on the safe management and transfer of living modified organisms (LMOs) resulting from the application of biotechnology. An open-ended ad hoc working group on biosafety (BSWG) was established at the second COP in 1995. Negotiations did not proceed in a legal vacuum. The international framework for the management of biotechnology is rather crowded. Chapter 16 of Agenda 21 established a framework for the environmentally sound management of biotechnology. Other relevant agreements include the Agreement on Sanitary and Phytosanitary Standards, the FAO's draft Code of Conduct on Biotechnology, UNEP's guidelines for safety in biotechnology, the Bonn guidelines on access to plant genetic resources, and (after seven years of difficult negotiations) the FAO's International Treaty on Plant Genetic Resources for Food and Agriculture (adopted in 2001).

The expectation was that the biosafety negotiations would be limited to six sessions and would be finalized late in 1998. A two-day Extraordinary Conference of Parties (ExCOP) which followed the final negotiating session in Cartagena in Colombia in February 1999 was suspended without consensus and, therefore, without a Protocol. A number of informal meetings followed, paving the way for the resumption of ExCOP. The Protocol was finally adopted in Montreal in January 2000 and was opened for signature at the fifth COP for the CBD in Nairobi in May of the same year. Its stated purpose is to ensure the safe transfer, handling and use of living modified organisms that may have adverse effects on the conservation and sustainable use of biological diversity, also taking into account risks to human health.

Given differences over the need for a Protocol let alone its content, some have argued that it is 'perhaps remarkable' that a Protocol was adopted at all (Newell and Mackenzie, 2000, p. 316). Differences between the main negotiating blocs under the BSWG revolved around the scope of any agreement (that is, what categories of living modified organisms would be subject to its provisions), the relationship between the Protocol and existing trade rules, whether socioeconomic impacts should or could be included in risk assessment, and the extent of identification and labelling which should be required (see Newell and Mackenzie, 2000; Burgiel, 2002; Newell, 2003). Much of this set the precautionary principle against demands for strict and demonstrated scientific criteria as the only basis upon which importing countries could reject LMOs or products containing LMOs. The precautionary principle won out. Article 1 states clearly that the Protocol must be pursued in accordance with the precautionary approach elaborated in the Rio Declaration. It is central to the Protocol's procedural provisions which implement an advance informed agreement (AIA) strategy based on risk assessment and risk management. This version of prior informed consent requires exporting parties to notify an importing party in writing of any international transfer (that is, trade) of LMOs covered under the Protocol. Based on a risk assessment, the importing party then has 90 days in the first instance to respond to the notification and, if deemed necessary, 270 days from date of notification to provide a decision in writing on whether the LMOs will be accepted or prohibited, whether further information is required, or whether the deadline for response is to be extended further. Article 10(6) provides that a lack of scientific certainty shall not prevent parties taking decisions to prohibit the transfer of LMOs. Several categories of LMOs are not subject to the AIA procedure – pharmaceuticals for human use, LMOs in transit or destined for contained use, those LMOs declared safe under the Protocol, and what are known as LMO-FFPs (food, feed or processing) which are not intended for deliberate introduction into the environment. However rules on the latter, particularly on their segregation, labelling and notification, are to be adopted within two years of entry into force of the Protocol.

A second, related issue was how the trade restrictions in the Protocol would relate to WTO rules and whether there should be a 'savings clause' which gave priority to the trade regime in the event of a dispute. The compromise wording provides that nothing in the Protocol changes pre-existing rights and obligations under international law but that this should not be taken to mean that the Protocol is subordinate to other agreements. As Cosbey and Burgiel observe, this is a 'conflict postponed, rather than a conflict avoided' (2000, p. 9). Following adoption of the Protocol, the Intergovernmental Committee for the Cartagena Protocol (ICCP) took a number of important steps, including establishing the pilot phase of the Biosafety Clearinghouse to which all AIA decisions must be reported. The Global Environment Facility also financed a multi-million dollar project to build capacity within developing countries for assessing the impacts of LMOs. The fiftieth ratification was received in June 2003, activating the countdown to entry into force in September the same year.

Sustainable living resources: 'forests and fish'

Protecting species has been bound up in the issue of conserving living resources. As with species protection, debates over forest and marine resources (the two issues explored here) have focused on whether sustainable use of living resources should be driven by economic or ecological imperatives and whether management strategies should focus on minimizing the causes or alleviating the symptoms of excessive harvesting.

Ocean wildlife and ocean resources

The oceans, which cover about 70 per cent of this planet we call Earth, are 'in trouble – serious and potentially catastrophic trouble' (Sitarz, 1994, p. 144). Pollution of the oceans (explored in Chapter 3) threatens marine and coastal ecosystems. Marine mammals are, in many cases, severely threatened and the world's major fisheries are being overfished. The problems arise not only from high consumer demand and unregulated fishing but also from subsidization and general over-capitalization of the fishing industry. Threats to marine mammals such as whales and seals come from hunting and disruption to the marine food chain through overfishing. Some species populations have recovered from earlier decimation but others continue to decline. Right whales are now estimated to number about 7,000. Southern hemisphere blue whales are thought to have declined to no more than 400 (see Browne, 2000). Other marine mammals, such as dolphins, may not be threatened in terms of overall numbers but their deaths as bycatch to commercial fishing operations have attracted much public concern. Many endangered marine species are now subject to national laws and conservation agreements. Yet again there are tensions between the ecological imperatives of protecting wildlife and the counter-claims of the economic imperatives of continued exploitation, perhaps no more so evident than in the debates over protection of whales. The UN General Assembly did little to alleviate this tension when it declared 1998 as the International Year of the Ocean 'to raise awareness of the oceans ... as finite-sized *economical* assets' (in Dubner, 1999, p. 627; emphasis added).

The 1946 International Convention for the Regulation of Whaling, which established the International Whaling Commission (IWC), was initially intended as a management regime for a severely depleted resource, although Reader (1993, p. 82) suggests that the Convention had the opposite effect and that more whales were taken *after* the entry into force of the agreement than when whaling was unrestricted. In the 1970s wildlife conservation became the dominant theme at the IWC, mobilized by non-governmental organizations and non-whaling countries.

In 1982, the Commission adopted a moratorium on whaling (except for whales taken for scientific purposes) which came into effect at the end of 1985. The moratorium was upheld in 1993, and in 1994 the IWC established a whaling sanctuary in the waters of the Southern Ocean and Antarctica. Proposals to establish sanctuaries in the South Pacific and South Atlantic have not attracted sufficient support. The Commission has also been grappling with the issue of indigenous whaling and has adopted a number of provisions which allow for limited catches by indigenous communities in specific circumstances.

The moratorium is strongly opposed by whaling countries – Iceland, Norway and Japan – who argue that the whaling industry is of economic importance (and, in some cases, that whale meat is culturally significant) and that sustainable harvesting is possible for some species, such as the minke whale. All three countries have continued to take whales under the scientific purposes provisions and all three have either entered formal objections to the moratorium provisions, proposed to recommence commercial whaling outside the provisions of the IWC or threatened to withdraw from the Convention altogether. Japan and Norway have also tried to use the provisions of CITES to overturn a ban on the trade in whale meat, raising fears of a possible return to industrial-scale whaling (see Browne, 2000). The IWC contains no formal sanctions and has therefore come to rely on publicity from NGOs and general public and international outcry to keep whaling states in line.

Depletion of fish stocks has generated far less public concern than the taking of marine mammals although it is an equally if not more serious problem. The Food and Agricultural Organization has confirmed a worldwide trend in vulnerability of fish stocks and reduction in harvesting yields (see Weber, 1994; Vigneron, 1998). Of the 9000 or so species which are harvested, only about 20 support major commercial fisheries and they are therefore vulnerable to overfishing which has increased with the development of sophisticated detection and catch technology. The loss is more than a commercial one: as well as the flow-on effect for the robustness of the marine food chain and therefore marine ecosystems, fish accounts for about 16 per cent of the world's total protein consumption (Sitarz, 1994, p. 154), a dependence that is even higher in the developing world. As Wilder points out, the 'development of principles for the conservation of international fisheries has been slow' (1995, p. 76). In regional fisheries agreements – of which there are now a number – disputes over appropriate regulatory strategies have included whether equipment and fishing techniques should be controlled; whether access to fishing grounds should be restricted or whether a more appropriate strategy is to limit or regulate catches; whether catch restrictions should address individual species or take into account the ecosystem impacts of species depletion; and whether restrictions should be based on a total allowable catch or a distributed quota system.

Attempts to establish a global, comprehensive agreement on fisheries management have been constrained not so much by differences over wildlife versus resource values as by political differences between distant water fishing nations (DWFN) and coastal states seeking to exercise sovereign rights over coastal waters. The establishment of Exclusive Economic Zones (EEZ) under the provisions of the 1982 UN Convention on the Law of the Sea (UNCLOS) (which finally came into effect in November 1994) extends to 200 nautical miles the maritime zones over which coastal states have national jurisdiction and sovereign rights to resources. UNCLOS included only general provisions on conservation and management of global fisheries. This has further complicated the transboundary aspect of any negotiations on managing the living resources of the seas. Much of the world's commercial fish harvest is taken in coastal waters and EEZs. Only about 5 per cent comes from the high seas. Yet managing fish resources requires international cooperation to regulate fleets which harvest outside their own territorial waters, and to regulate access to highly migratory and straddling stocks which move between territorial waters or across the boundaries between high seas and EEZs.

Debates over high seas and EEZ fishing rights, which were contentious at the UNCLOS negotiations, reemerged at UNCED in 1992. Agenda 21 includes an extensive chapter on oceans and coastal management (Chapter 17) but it proved impossible to get agreement on the management of marine living resources, especially straddling and highly migratory stocks. In a compromise move, the issue was deferred to a later international conference – the UN Conference on Straddling Fish Stocks and Highly Migratory Fish Stocks. In August 1995, after four substantive rounds of 'tense and at times bitter' negotiations (Anon., 1995c, p. 179), parties adopted an agreement which reaffirms the provisions of UNCLOS as the basis for conserving and managing straddling and migratory fish stocks. Formally known as The United Nations Agreement for the Implementation of the Provisions of the United Nations Convention on the Law of the Sea of 10 December 1982 relating to the Conservation and Management of Straddling Fish Stocks and Highly Migratory Fish Stocks, it encourages compatibility between conservation and management measures in EEZs and high seas but gives much of the policy and enforcement role to regional fisheries organizations. However in a significant departure from usual maritime jurisdictional provisions, the Agreement provides for comprehensive 'board and inspect' procedure. It also incorporates both the precautionary principle and the ecosystem approach as the basis for conservation and management measures. The Agreement entered into force in December 2001 (but without the participation of some important distant water fishing nations such as Japan and South Korea).

Forests and deforestation

The protection and management of forests is both a resource and habitat issue and one which is central to disputes over sustainable use, sovereign ownership and ecological viability. Forests are ecologically, economically and culturally important at local and global level. They help to maintain soil quality and manage water flows. They contribute to the regulation of local climate systems. The ecological consequences of deforestation therefore include soil erosion, nutrient loss, siltation of watershed and downstream ecosystems, possible increase in floods and droughts, and changes in local and regional weather patterns. Because tropical forests (approximately 6 per cent of the world's land surface) contain at least 50 per cent and possibly up to 90 per cent of the world's species (WRM, 1990, p. 16), forest loss is also a major factor in loss of biodiversity. In Madagascar alone, for example, at least 1,000 and possibly up to 2,500 endemic plants have been lost because of deforestation (Thomas, 1992, p. 256). Forest destruction contributes to climate change in a 'double assault': deforestation releases stored CO_2 and it removes an important carbon sink. While the pattern and extent of carbon release and sequestering is as yet unclear, forest destruction contributes at least one-sixth of annual global CO_2 emissions and possibly more (see Chapter 3). Forest burning also releases nitrous oxide and the agricultural practices which often supplant forest use are a source of methane emissions.

The extent of present-day forest loss is unclear. No fully accurate baseline information is available and patterns of forest use and forest destruction vary from region to region. Despite an increase in forest lands associated primarily with plantations, UNEP's third *Global Environment Outlook* estimated a net global loss of nearly 100 million hectares between 1990 and 2000 (UNEP, 2002a, p. 91), conservatively estimated at about 1.2 per cent a year (see Laurance, 1999, p. 110). Tropical forests are the most vulnerable. Since the 1970s, approximately 40 per cent of rainforests have disappeared and the rate of deforestation may well be on the increase. Murray (1993, p. 72) notes that in 1980 about 113,000 square kilometres of tropical forest were cleared. By 1990 annual clearance was 169,000 square kilometres. In regions such as Southeast Asia all countries except Singapore and Vietnam suffered a net loss in forest cover in the decade from 1990 to 2000 (Asian Development Bank, 2002, p. 4). While the contemporary concern is with tropical forests, much of the world's deforestation prior to the Second World War took place in temperate regions. The World Rainforest Movement suggests that Western Europe, for example, has lost 70 per cent of its forests since Roman times and argues that fully one-third of 'temperate broadleaved forests have been lost since the dawn of agriculture' (1990, p. 21).

There are a number of causes of deforestation which is rather drily defined as a change in land use from forest to non-forest purposes. The slash-and-burn agriculture traditionally practised by shifting cultivators – up to 10 per cent of the world's population – is designed to minimize threats to the forest by leaving land fallow over periods of time long enough for regeneration. However the numbers of people pursuing this kind of subsistence lifestyle have been increased by what Norman Myers calls the 'shifted cultivator' (1992, p. 444), landless peasants who have been forced from their own lands. The result is further encroachment on forest lands and reduction in fallow times. Caution is required here, however, not to cast as culprits those who are forced into more unsustainable uses of forest land as less land becomes available through land accumulation for large-scale agriculture and mono-cropping. Uneven land tenure contributes even further to this problem – 75 per cent of people in developing countries depend on agriculture for their livelihood, but do not own the land they farm (Thomas, 1992, p. 247), making them vulnerable to land clearance and development programmes.

Large-scale land conversion for agricultural ranching and cash cropping is substantially more destructive of forests except in Africa where small-scale agricultural conversion has accounted for over half of the loss of forest area (see UNEP, 2002a, p. 92). Conversion of this large-scale kind is often related to the production of elite wealth, supported by financial incentives. In Brazil, for example, ranching attracted subsidies and zero tax rates on income, thus making land conversion an attractive financial proposition. The policy was abolished in 1989 but cattle ranching accounted for 38 per cent of all deforestation in Amazonia in the years between 1960 and 1976 (Woodliffe, 1991, p. 61). Forest land is being cleared for mono-cropping to service debt rather than grow food for local consumption. Former forest land in Thailand, for example, is used to grow cassava for EC feedstock and soybeans grown on once-forested land in Amazonia are destined for overseas markets (see Opschoor, 1989, pp. 139–40). Land clearance and forest loss arise also from internal colonization, the two best-known examples of which are the Indonesian Transmigration Scheme, which was funded partly by the World Bank, and the Brazilian Polonoroeste Programme.

Commercial logging – both legal and illegal – is another source of deforestation, responsible for something between 10 per cent (WRM,

1990, p. 51) and 25 per cent (Porter and Brown, 1991, p. 97) of annual forest loss, depending on regional variation. Logging is probably the major cause of primary rainforest destruction in Southeast Asia and Africa. There is little disagreement over the damage caused by most commercial logging. As Thomas observes, 'to date and almost without exception, logging has been undertaken in an environmentally harmful, economically unsustainable and socially destructive fashion' (1992, p. 252). Unsustainable logging results in a loss of future economic resource – in 1998 gross production from the forestry industry was valued at $US160 billion globally (Brack *et al.*, 2002, p. 9). It also undermines the regenerative capacity of the forest, leads to erosion, loss of fauna and forest canopy and contributes to 'collateral' forest damage through the opening up of access roads which facilitates settler movements and further conversion to agricultural land. This has been accompanied by an increase in South–South colonialism where the foreign companies which gain logging concessions in tropical regions come from newly industrialized countries (NICs) such as Malaysia and South Korea. The harvesting of wood for energy in many developing countries is exacerbated by urban preferences for charcoal which is less energy-efficient than 'unadulterated' wood. Nevertheless, in rural communities in developing countries, fuelwood for domestic use, collected primarily by women, is usually taken from open forests and fallow land rather than closed forests (see WRM, 1990, p. 79) and rarely involves the destruction of large stands of trees. Pollution and pollution-related diseases have become an increasing cause of deforestation or 'forest death' (*waldsterben*) in both developed and developing countries. Estimates suggest that about 60 per cent of European forests are seriously or moderately degraded (UNEP, 1999a, p. 39).

These kinds of practices also affect those who live in or rely on the forests. Loss of forest land (and forcible removal and resettlement) is a major factor in the destruction of cultural identity for indigenous forest dwellers. Approximately 50 million indigenous peoples plus another 90 million forest dwellers rely on forests not only for food, fodder, building materials and medicines but also for cultural and spiritual identity (see WRM, 1990, p. 18). Yet as Colchester notes, the 'land rights of forest dwellers have consistently been denied and native leaders [have been] bought off or eliminated' (1994, p. 48). The most well-publicized cases of destruction of indigenous forest habitats have been those of the Penan in Sarawak and the Yanomami Indians in the Brazilian Amazon but the pattern is repeated in a number of other countries.

Prior to UNCED, international action on forests was the realm of two agreements – the International Tropical Timber Agreement (ITTA) and the Tropical Forestry Action Plan (TFAP). The ITTA came into effect in

1985 as a commodity agreement focusing on trade in tropical timber products. The International Tropical Timber Organization (ITTO), which began operational activities in 1987 as a forum for producers and consumers of tropical timber, has two, possibly mutually exclusive, objectives. The first is to promote the expansion and diversification of international trade in tropical timber; the second is to maintain the ecological balance of the timber-producing regions. The Agreement was initially welcomed as a real opportunity to curb the excesses of the timber industry. More recently it has been criticized as little more than a lobbying group for timber interests which promotes trade at the expense of conservation and the 'survival, social and cultural significance [of forests] to the local people' (Native Peoples of Sarawak, 1991). Attempts to restrict imports from countries which do not practise sustainable logging techniques have run into difficulties within the free-trade ITTO. Consumer and producer states have opposed proposals to certify logs as sustainably grown, with Malaysia leading producer resistance. The successor agreement to the original ITTA, adopted in January 1994, was little changed from its predecessor, in spite of some hopes that it would extend coverage to temperate forests and require tropical timber products to come from sustainably managed forests. Target 2000, the Organization's (non-binding) attempt to reconcile its trade and conservation objectives by requiring that all tropical timber entering the international trade should come from sustainably managed forest sources by the year 2000, has had little impact on logging practices. At time of writing, negotiations were under way for a successor to the 1994 Agreement.

The Tropical Forestry Action Plan was established in 1985 by the World Bank, UNEP, the FAO and the World Resources Institute (WRI) under the coordination of the forestry department of the FAO. Its primary focus is the sustainable management of the forestry industry rather than forests per se. It emphasizes financial flows, technical assistance and policy advice to recipient countries for the development of National Forestry Action Plans (NFAPs). For some, the Plan was a mechanism to harmonize development assistance for forestry; for others it was to enhance attempts to address the fundamental causes of deforestation (see Thomas, 1992, p. 261). It is not clear that it fulfilled either expectation. The World Rainforest Movement identified it as 'an attempt to legitimise the commercialisation of the world's tropical forests' (WRM, 1990, pp. 76–8). By 1990, annual funding for TFAP had reached $US1 billion per year, yet only about 9 per cent of that budget had been spent on conservation (see Thomas, 1992, p. 262). In the mid-1990s, the Plan was restructured with more of a country focus, and renamed the National Forestry Action Program. The inadequacies of ITTA and TFAP and the increasing public demand for timber products from well-managed forests, contributed to the founding in 1993 of the Forest Stewardship Council (FSC). The Council brings together forestry stakeholders with the goal of supporting 'environmentally appropriate, socially beneficial and economically viable stewardship of the world's forests' (Schmidt, 1998, p. 24). It is best known for the certification and labelling system to assess forest management which it established and which it monitors through accrediting certification bodies.

Attempts to forge a comprehensive and binding global forests agreement have thus far been unsuccessful. However, the various agreements and initiatives constitute what some have called an 'incipient and contradictory forest regime' (Sears *et al.*, 2001, p. 345). Humphreys also argues that, despite the absence of a legally binding agreement on global forest policy, 'an emerging ... forests regime ... developed in the 1990s' based on a normative understanding that 'forests should be conserved and used in a sustainable manner' (1999, p. 251). In 1990, FAO's Committee on Forestry (COFO) and the FAO Council discussed the possibility of treaty negotiations although many countries were reluctant to see such negotiations proceed under FAO auspices. The 1990 G7 summit in Houston called for a convention on the protection of the world's forests to be negotiated for signature at Rio. There was a 'general air of weariness and pessimism' (Johnson, 1993, p. 108) associated with the forest negotiations during the Rio PrepComms. Preliminary discussions on a convention broke down after objections from tropical timber producer countries. The chief Malaysian negotiator at UNCED took the view that 'forests are clearly a sovereign resource ... we cannot allow forests to be taken up in global forums' (cited in Brenton, 1994, p. 216). Developing countries were concerned that a forests convention would divert attention from developed country commitments on climate change. There was also little agreement on what kinds of forests should be covered in any international agreement – the developing countries argue that it is discriminatory for agreements to refer only to tropical forests – and how questions of responsibility and compensation should be addressed. Producer countries expected compensation if they were asked to forgo short-term gain from forest resources in the interests of a greater global good. As one Brazilian politician has claimed, 'if the Amazon is a world resource, the world will have to pay for it' (cited in Woodliffe, 1991, p. 69).

UNCED *Statement of Forest Principles*

Chapter 11 of Agenda 21, on combating deforestation, is managerial rather than preservationist in its approach. It emphasizes sustainable forest management and effective utilization of the goods and services provided by forests, forest lands and woodlands. In the absence of any agreement on a convention, but unwilling to leave the matter altogether, delegations at UNCED negotiated a weaker statement of principles which even then went to Rio from the PrepComms in a 'state of disarray' (see Johnson, 1993, p. 109). What was finally agreed at Rio was, to give it its full title, a 'Non-legally binding authoritative statement of principles for a global consensus on the management, conservation and sustainable development of all types of forests'.

The Statement is based on the concept of multiple value, acknowledging forests as both ecological and economic resources which should be 'sustainably managed to meet the social, economic, ecological, cultural and spiritual human needs of present and future generations' (UNCED, 1992c, principle 2(b)). On the whole, though, the Statement is little more than a general guideline which responds to political concerns brought to the negotiations by the various parties. It reinforces states' sovereign rights to resources (principles 1(a) and 2(a)). It emphasizes international cooperation and the equitable sharing of the costs of forest conservation and sustainable development; the impact of external indebtedness and poverty on the ability of developing countries to manage their forests; the need for new and additional financial resources; and the transfer of technology on concessional and preferential terms. It reinforces the principle that trade in forest products should be based on non-discriminatory and multilaterally agreed rules. It pays some attention to the importance of full participation in decision-making and implementation of national strategies by indigenous people(s), local communities, forest dwellers and women. It makes no reference to the relationship between deforestation and climate change, or forests and loss of biodiversity. Alberto Szekely, a member of the International Law Commission, argued that the Forest Principles fell 'one hundred per cent short of providing even the most elementary basis for an international regime for the protection of the world's forests' (1994, p. 67). Both the Statement of Principles and Chapter 11 were criticized as 'legitimizing the policies of those actors – the transnationals, the multilateral development banks, UN agencies etc. – that have to date contributed to a large extent to the crisis of the tropical, temperate, and boreal forests' (Greenpeace cited in Chatterjee and Finger, 1994, p. 47).

The Forest Principles and Agenda 21 called for the issue of further international cooperation on forests to be kept under assessment. Since Rio a number of other fora, both intergovernmental and non-governmental, have sprung up to confer on forest issues. Many of the tensions which characterized UNCED negotiations on forests and deforestation have continued to shape debates in these fora, including criteria and indicators, the certification and labelling of timber products, the role of the FAO and the whole issue of a forests convention (Humphreys, 1996a, pp. 244–51). None has yet emerged as any kind of precursor to formal negotiations on a convention although there has been a slow and painful inching towards some kind of consensus.

In 1993 a Working Group on Criteria and Indicators for the Conservation and Sustainable Management of Temperate and Boreal Forests (the Montreal Process for short) was established to develop a 'scientifically rigorous [but non-binding] set of criteria and indicators' to measure forest management at a national level (see IISD, 1996a). It completed this task in 1995. Another forum, the Helsinki Process, had already begun work in 1990 to develop guidelines on the sustainable management of forests in Europe (IISD, 1996b). A jointly sponsored Malaysian/Canadian initiative – the Intergovernmental Working Group on Forests (IWGF) (initially 'Global Forests') – was established to focus on Agenda 21 commitments and the 1995 Commission on Sustainble Development (CSD) review of forests although it provided opportunities only for discussion, not negotiation. The Commission on Sustainable Development then established the Intergovernmental Panel on Forests (IPF) to 'pursue consensus and coordinated proposals for action to support the management, conservation and sustainable development of forests' (Rosendal, 2001, p. 449). The Panel negotiated a number of proposals for sustainable forest management and encouraged governments to establish National Forest Programs (NFPs). In the absence of consensus on financial issues, trade-related issues and whether or not to begin formal negotiations, the IPF report submitted to CSD-5 in 1997 was only able to note the need for enhanced international efforts on global forest policy. The IPF report was forwarded to the UNGASS which paved the way for the Intergovernmental Forum on Forests (IFF). The Forum, which 'greatly resembled its predecessor' (Tarasofsky, 2000, p. 32), held its final meeting in February 2000. There was continued disagreement on the creation of an international forest fund and on whether there should be a recommendation to begin negotiations for a legally binding agreement on forests. Malaysia and Indonesia had now come to favour such a process, along with the EU and Canada. Brazil and India, in company with the United States, opposed it. NGOs also generally opposed a forest convention, concerned that it would detract attention from the bigger question of biodiversity and would likely be driven by trade rather than environmental interests (see Steiner, 2001).

The IFF recommended the creation of a UN Forum on Forests (UNFF) which would report to ECOSOC and which would, within five years, consider the possible parameters of a mandate for developing an international legal framework on forests. The tasks of the UNFF, with the support of a Collaborative Partnership on Forests (CPF), are both dialogue- and policy-focused with an emphasis on transparent and participatory decision-making. In June 2001 the first meeting of the UNFF adopted a multi-year work programme and a plan of action for implementing IPF/IFF proposals. It also recommended three intersessional ad hoc expert groups: one on mechanisms for monitoring and reporting; one on finance and transfers of environmentally sound technologies; and one to focus on the parameters of a mandate for a legal framework. The continued political tension over forest policy was demonstrated when UNFF-2, held in March 2002, was unable to agree terms of reference for these three working groups. These were finally adopted at UNFF-3 in mid-2003 along with a number of other resolutions on voluntary reporting, the UNFF Trust Fund and the importance of strengthening the UNFF Secretariat.

Water resources

The concern with species and biodiversity is with living resources that can be irretrievably lost. The concern with forests is with living resources that are, in theory at least, renewable. A third type of resource now figures prominently on the global agenda – that which cannot be depleted but which is becoming increasingly scarce: water. Less than 1 per cent of all water on earth is available for human consumption. Per capita availability is being undermined by increased demand, by changing precipitation patterns associated with climate change, and by pollution. Over one billion people do not have access to safe drinking water and almost twice that number are without adequate sanitation. Estimates also indicate that three million people die each year, primarily in poorer countries, from diseases related to unsafe water (see IISD, 2003a, p. 2). Increasing amounts of fresh water are being called upon 'to supply agricultural, industrial, domestic and municipal needs' (Rodenburg and Bryant, 1994, p. 181). Land degradation and deforestation affect the rate of run-off and groundwater recharge. Overuse of groundwater results in salt-water pollution of aquifers and, in some cases, land subsidence. Other pollution sources include industrial pollutants, untreated sewage and agricultural chemicals. Irrigated agriculture is a major cause of inefficient water use and the use of polluted water for crops contributes further to environmental degradation as well as disease. Projects to manage water demand, including the construction of large dams, have affected freshwater ecosystems, including important wetland and marsh sites.

Environmental scientists argue that 'water use will need to be reduced by at least 10 per cent to protect the rivers, lakes and wetlands' which are crucial for local livelihoods (International Water Management Institute, 2001). Estimates suggest, however, that water use is expected to increase by as much as 40 per cent by 2020 (see UNEP, 2002a, p. 150). Globally, water availability on a per capita basis declined from 17,000 cubic metres in 1950 to 7,000 in 1997 (UNDP, 1998). The IPCC reports that in the large catchment basins of Niger, Lake Chad and Senegal, 'total available water has decreased by 40 to 60 per cent' (UNEP, 2001b, p. 2).

International attention to water management and water scarcity issues dates at least to the International Decade for Drinking Water Supply and Sanitation (1981–90). In 1999, the UN Secretary-General prepared a comprehensive assessment of the world's freshwater resources and UNESCO now hosts the World Water Assessment Programme and prepares a biennial World Water Development Report. The UN's Millennium Development Goals set the target of halving by 2015 the proportion of people without access to safe drinking water. The WSSD confirmed this commitment and included a similar target for adequate sanitation. Estimates suggest that 'developing and transitional countries will require $180 billion annually in order to produce global water security over the next 25 years' (World Water Council, 2003) but there is little evidence that funding of this kind is being committed by donor countries.

Common interest and global burden-sharing: desertification

Desertification is the reduction in or loss of the biological productivity of land (land degradation), particularly in drylands ecosystems. As a conservation issue, it focuses attention on the ecological and economic importance of habitat and ecosystems. Conventional wisdom is that desertification is on the increase, threatening about 70 per cent of the world's drylands (UNCED, 1992b, para. 12.2). Approximately 23 per cent of 'usable land ... has been affected by degradation to a degree sufficient to reduce its productivity' (UNEP, 2002a, p. 64). Between one-sixth and one-quarter of the world's population, many of whom already live in poverty, are vulnerable to the consequences (Abate and Akhtar, 1994, p. 72; UNEP, 1995b).

Desertification arises from human activities and climatic variations. Changing land-use patterns and ecologically unsustainable agriculture – including overcultivation, overgrazing of stock, planting of inappropriate crops, heavy use of fertilizers and chemicals – contribute to the kind of soil erosion and land degradation that results in desertification.

According to the FAO (cited in UNEP, 2002a, p. 64), deforestation, overgrazing and agricultural mismanagement are the major causes of land degradation. Such practices are often the unintended consequences of development programmes, inequitable land tenure and the enforced unsustainable use of marginal lands rather than the result of conscious and deliberate negligence by local communities. Changes in climate patterns, chronic drought and dessication also contribute to desertification (see Hulme and Kelly, 1993). The ecological impacts that help to define desertification include decline in soil fertility and soil structure, loss of biodiversity, degradation of irrigated cropland and loss of arable land. The socioeconomic consequences include food insecurity and loss of subsistence livelihoods, increased poverty, malnutrition, starvation and forced movements of peoples. There are also extensive economic costs: UNEP (1995a) estimates the direct loss of annual income through desertification at about $US42 billion per year but is reluctant to put an estimate on indirect costs.

The definition of desertification, in both its causes and impacts, as a transboundary or global conservation problem has been contentious. Even if it is not transboundary in the usual sense there are, as Abate and Akhtar suggest, still good reasons for addressing desertification issues in a global regime, not least of which are the 'principles of burden-sharing and a common interest in the global environment' (1994, p. 77). The negotiations on desertification resulted in the first post-UNCED convention mandated by the Rio Conference although international deliberations on this issue date to the 1970s. A general lack of funding and political support, poor integration with other socio-developmental programmes, failure to include local populations and the dominance of political and economic problems over environmental ones limited the success of early attempts to address desertification. Those efforts included UNEP's Plan of Action to Combat Desertification (PACD) adopted after the 1977 UN Conference on Desertification (UNCOD). There were also various attempts in the mid-1980s to manage and halt desertification in Africa, including the establishment in 1984 of a four-year drought and desertification control programme for the mid-Sahel and, in 1985, the Cairo programme for African cooperation on desertification.

The resolution that established UNCED also called for 'high priority' to be given to drought and desertification control and enjoined the Conference to consider *all means necessary* to halt and reverse the process of desertification (UNGA, 1989c, para. 15(g); emphasis added). The G77 countries argued that those means should include a desertification convention. At a regional preparatory meeting for UNCED in November 1991, representatives of African countries adopted the

African Common Position on Environment and Development along with the Abidjan Declaration which called, among other things, for a convention to combat desertification as one of the specific UNCED outcomes (see IISD, 1993). The industrialized countries, particularly the EC and the US, were less persuaded that desertification was an international issue and no negotiations for a convention were set in train prior to UNCED. Chapter 12 of Agenda 21 – the chapter on combating desertification and drought – remained bracketed until the final PrepComm. It identified programme areas for mitigation and response strategies and requested the General Assembly to convene negotiations on a desertification convention (UNCED, 1992b, para. 12.40). At the end of 1992, General Assembly resolution 47/188 established what was formally known as the Intergovernmental Negotiating Committee for the Elaboration of an International Convention to Combat Desertification in those Countries Experiencing Serious Drought and/or Desertification, Particularly in Africa – known (thankfully) as the INCD for short. The Committee held a preliminary organizational session and five substantive negotiating sessions. A special voluntary fund was established to provide assistance for developing countries to participate in the negotiations.

There were a number of difficult issues but the negotiations seem to have been less acrimonious than those on biodiversity or forests although the United States and the EC continued to object to desertification being designated a global problem rather than a regional issue of concern only to affected countries. There were differences over whether the Convention should focus on causes or symptoms, whether natural climatic factors placed limits on strategies and whether drought should be considered on an equal footing with desertification. Debates over commitments focused on the extent to which affected (mainly developing) countries should be required to take action to halt or reverse desertification and the degree of obligation on the part of developed countries to provide assistance to them. Developing countries, while seeking to maintain sovereign rights, were keen that a convention acknowledge the importance of economic growth, social development and the eradication of poverty as relevant strategies for which they required assistance. The Africa Group (representing that part of the world most affected) called not only for new resources but also for debt relief and commitments to the UN official development assistance (ODA) target of 0.7 per cent of GNP. Industrialized countries argued that any financial assistance should be conditional upon a complementarity of commitment. One of the most difficult issues, on which negotiations almost stalled at the first substantive INCD in 1993, was that of the regional instruments as annexes to the Convention. The INCD's initial mandate was to negotiate an annex on Africa, with annexes on Latin America and the Caribbean, and Asia to follow once the Convention had been agreed. Regional groups outside Africa emphasized the importance of extending this mandate to include other regions in the draft Convention and in 1993 the General Assembly adopted a resolution which did just that.

UN Convention to Combat Desertification in those Countries Experiencing Serious Drought and/or Desertification, Particularly in Africa (CCD)

The Convention was finalized in June 1994 and opened for signature in Paris on 14–15 October 1994. Four regional annexes (for Africa, Latin America and the Caribbean, Asia and the Northern Mediterranean) were adopted at the same time. The African annex was the most 'elaborate in form and content' (Anon., 1994b, p. 229) and the INCD adopted a resolution on urgent action for Africa, recommending a range of further measures including the establishment of partnership arrangements between African countries and developed countries (see UNEP, 1994b). The preamble to the Convention suggests that desertification has a 'global dimension' (in that it affects all regions of the world) which requires joint action. In contrast with the precedent set by other negotiations, this Convention is more than a framework agreement. As well as the usual statements of principle and procedural and institutional articles, the Convention contains detailed provisions for action. Much of it is concerned with the development of action programmes at national, subregional and regional levels, scientific and technical cooperation and supporting measures such as capacity-building, education and public awareness.

The rather awkwardly phrased objective of the Convention (article 2) is to

> combat desertification and mitigate the effects of drought in countries experiencing serious drought and/or desertification, particularly in Africa, through effective action at all levels, supported by international cooperation and partnership arrangements, in the framework of an integrated approach which is consistent with Agenda 21, with a view to contributing to the achievement of sustainable development in affected areas (UNEP, 1994d).

Such action should, according to the Convention, be informed by the principles of participation, cooperation and attention to the special needs of affected developing countries. Affected countries are required to enact or strengthen laws, policies and action programmes to combat desertification. Developed countries are obliged to provide support and financial resources and facilitate access to technology, knowledge and know-how. The Convention places particular emphasis on participation (including that of local communities, indigenous peoples and women), decentralization and 'bottom-up' planning. As with other conventions discussed in this chapter, the CCD is a compromise. Nevertheless, this Convention has been received with more optimism (albeit still cautious) than other global agreements: as one commentator notes 'few were totally pleased with the outcome ... most were hopeful that this Convention could have some positive impact' (Anon., 1994b, p. 230).

The INCD continued to function prior to entry into force, meeting twice in 1995 and twice again in 1996 in preparation for the first Conference of the Parties and making progress on procedural matters relating to scientific and technical cooperation. Financial issues, especially those relating to the Global Mechanism (whose purpose is to mobilize and channel financial resources, including the transfer of technology to affected developing-country parties) and its likely host institution, remained contentious (see IISD, 1996c, 1996d). The requisite fiftieth ratification (from Chad) was deposited on 27 September 1996 and the Convention came into effect on 26 December 1996. The first COP was held in Rome late in 1997. The meeting confirmed Bonn as the location for the secretariat and the International Fund for Agricultural Development (IFAD) as the Global Mechanism although the final arrangements were not confirmed until COP-3 in November 1999. COP-1 also adopted decisions which established an ad hoc panel of experts on indicators regarding the Convention's implementation and a work programme to explore the importance of traditional knowledge. COP-4 in December 2000 adopted a fifth annex for Eastern and Central Europe. In October 2001, the fifth Conference of Parties established a Committee for the Review of the Implementation of the Convention (CRIC). Financial resources available to address desertification were strengthened when the Global Environment Facility formally designated land degradation as one of its focal areas for funding.

Conclusion

The conservation issues discussed in this chapter demonstrate the difficulties of negotiating and adopting comprehensive environmental protection agreements. The agreements have all been criticized for their vague language, their limited response to the problems they were intended to address and for their permissive approach to environmental management. Responses have been sectoral, ad hoc, often not well-coordinated and driven by political and economic interests as much as by environmental ones. The 'better than no agreement at all' syndrome has often prevailed: the very fact that an agreement exists has been claimed as some measure of success. Implementation has relied very much on national action and the success of the strategies adopted and compliance with various agreements is at least open to dispute. Opt-out clauses, reservations and cautious language characterize these agreements. Negotiations and implementation problems point to the importance, especially for developing countries, of funding and technology and the difficulties of getting real commitments from developed countries. These trends were reproduced in debates about how best to manage transboundary and global pollution, issues to which the next chapter turns.

Chapter 3

The Global Politics of Pollution

As the scope of environmental concerns expanded in the 1970s and 1980s, greater attention was paid to the transboundary and then global aspects of pollution, as pollutants dispersed across state borders through air and ocean currents, or were physically displaced through trade or dumping. Political action often followed scientific concern and pressure for action from non-governmental environmental organizations. Debates have centred on whether pollution should be regulated or prevented and increasing attention has come to be given to precautionary action, at least in principle. The problems and difficulties in the negotiations echo those demonstrated in Chapter 2: competing interests between polluter and victim states, the imperatives of sovereignty, compromises between substantive agreements and declaratory frameworks, resistance to targets and firm commitments, and permissive compliance and verification procedures. The chapter begins with an examination of the problem of the transboundary dispersal and displacement of hazardous waste and toxic chemicals. It then turns to the management of pollution in the oceans and the atmosphere which provide the second and third case studies in this chapter.

Hazardous waste and toxic chemicals

The transboundary politics of hazardous and toxic substances has focused primarily on the problem of displacement. The environmental and public health problems were brought to public attention through a number of accidents in the 1970s and 1980s (see Chapter 1) and the much publicized journey in 1986 of the *Khian Sea* which spent over two years looking for a site to dump its cargo of toxic incinerator ash. The movement of waste and toxic chemicals between industrialized and developing countries has attracted most attention. The transboundary displacement of hazardous wastes and toxic chemicals increased in the late 1980s as industrialized countries adopted stringent waste disposal regimes and either banned or regulated the use and production of dangerous chemicals. Waste producers sought disposal sites in countries where environmental regulations were more permissive, or where the costs of doing so were lower than in the country of production. Developing countries were also attracted by revenue. The government of Guinea-Bissau, for example, agreed to accept over 15 million tons of toxic waste for payment of $US600 million, an amount four times its annual gross national product and 35 times the value of its annual exports (see Puckett, 1994, p. 53; Godwin, 1993, p. 196). The deal was later cancelled after pressure from other developing countries.

The amount of hazardous waste generated annually is not known, but estimates suggest some 300–500 million tonnes (see Krueger, 1999b, p. 12), around 95 per cent of which is produced by the developed world. It includes non-nuclear industrial waste, pesticide sludge, chemical wastes, uranium mining waste and incinerator ash. The total amounts exported are difficult to determine with accuracy (in part because of persistent non-reporting). UNEP reports that the level of waste which is legally exported to developing countries is low (1999a, p. 29) although estimates suggest that it could be as much as 20 per cent of hazardous waste trade (see Murphy, 1994, p. 30). Since the end of the Cold War, former Central and Eastern European countries have also become major hazardous waste disposal sites. Illegal waste is often transported covertly and highly sophisticated technology is required to determine its contents. Technical facilities in developing countries for the safe disposal of such wastes are often limited. Disposal therefore often means dumping – in used mines, on the surface or in poorly managed landfills where seepage into soils and waterways is not uncommon. The clean-up costs are high. The environmental and human impacts, which include contamination of the food chain, increases in cancers and birth defects and shortened lifespans, can be disastrous for local communities. UNEP Executive Director Klaus Töpfer has called the illegal trade in hazardous waste a 'crime against mankind [sic] and nature' (cited in Krueger, 1999b, p. 53).

Convention on the Control of Transboundary Movements of Hazardous Wastes and their Disposal (the Basel Convention)

Until the late 1980s, the movement of hazardous wastes was managed primarily through national or regional initiatives such as the 1984 Hazardous and Solid Waste Amendments to the US Resource Conservation and Recovery Act and the EC Directive on the Transfrontier Shipment of Hazardous Waste adopted in the same year (see Nanda, 1991, p. 507). OECD recommendations on the transfrontier movement of hazardous wastes, adopted in 1984 and 1986, were a precursor to UNEP's 1987 Cairo Guidelines and Principles for the Environmentally Sound Management of Hazardous Waste. At the time the Cairo Guidelines were adopted the Executive Director of UNEP convened an Ad Hoc Working Group to negotiate an international legal instrument on hazardous wastes. One of the key issues in these negotiations was whether a regime should regulate or prohibit the movement of hazardous wastes. A second related concern was how to incorporate trade restrictions in the convention in a way that did not contravene the principles of the General Agreement on Tariffs and Trade. A third theme in the negotiations, and one which remains central to political tensions in the Convention, was the relationship between industrialized and developing countries.

The Basel Convention was adopted by 116 countries on 22 March 1989, although only 35 countries signed at the time. The Convention calls on countries to minimize the generation and movement of hazardous waste and requires that any such waste should be disposed of as close as possible to its source. Waste is rather broadly defined as substances and objects which are either disposed of, or intended or required to be disposed of (article 2(1)). The Convention classifies wastes according to source (for example, clinical wastes or wastes produced in chemical production processes), constituent parts (including arsenic, cadmium, mercury, asbestos, phenols and organohalogen compounds) and characteristics (explosive, flammable, corrosive or infectious). It excludes radioactive wastes (the responsibility of the International Atomic Energy Agency (IAEA)) and hazardous wastes dumped from ships (covered by the London Dumping Convention which is discussed later in this chapter).

Parties may export waste only if they do not have the facilities to dispose of the waste in an environmentally sound manner (a term which is not defined) and only if they can be certain that it will be disposed of in such a manner in the importing country. If that proves not to be possible, the exporting state is obliged to reimport the waste. Movement of hazardous wastes may not proceed unless and until the exporting state has received, in writing, the prior informed consent (PIC) of the importing state and any transit states. The Convention recognizes the sovereign right of states to prohibit the import of hazardous waste. Trade with non-parties is prohibited unless it is covered by a bilateral or regional agreement. Any movement of waste which does not meet the provisions of the Convention is deemed illegal and parties are required to introduce legislation to prevent and punish such trade. Non-compliance is difficult to track, however, because the Convention does not require notification of all transactions.

The Convention was characterized by some as an 'effective starting point' (Howard, 1990, p. 227) with 'many useful features in protecting human health and the environment' (Sens, cited in Nanda, 1991, p. 508). For others, it had too many loopholes, added nothing new to existing rules and did little more than legitimize the trade in hazardous waste (see Godwin, 1993, p. 203; Nanda, 1991, p. 508). The Convention came into effect on 5 May 1992. Mostafa Tolba, then Executive Director of UNEP, described this three-year delay as an 'unreasonably long period in which to transform strong words and good intentions into real action' (cited in Anon., 1993a, p. 14). At the time, the two largest producers of hazardous waste (the EU and the United States) had not ratified the Convention. The US is still not a party although it attends meetings as an observer.

The Convention is characterized by a 'fundamental disparity between the objectives of developed countries (along with certain multinational industries)' who 'seek to legitimise the continued generation and disposal of hazardous waste' and 'developing countries (along with environmental groups)' whose purpose is to 'reduce and ultimately eliminate the production and dumping of such waste' (Rosencranz and Eldridge, 1992, pp. 318–19). A range of regional agreements outside the Basel framework, many of which ban the import of all forms of hazardous and sometimes nuclear waste, hint at continued developing country dissatisfaction with the Convention (see Krueger, 1999b, p. 83 for a list). Developing countries have sought to strengthen the Convention, often in coalition with NGOs working through the International Toxic Waste Action Network (ITWAN). One of the most contentious 'North–South' issues has been that of a ban on the export of all hazardous wastes from OECD to non-OECD countries. In 1994, parties agreed in effect to a full ban on trade for final disposal (between industrialized and developing countries) and advocated the phasing out of trade for recycling purposes by the end of 1997. The Convention was amended to take account of this decision in 1995 but at time of writing the amendment has still not been ratified by a sufficient number of countries to bring it into force. Supporters of a full ban argue that it will force countries to take steps to manage their own waste within national boundaries and, in the long run, to minimize waste production. Trade for recycling has not been phased out and the not-yet-in-force ban remains contentious. Recycling can provide opportunities for the recapture of valuable raw materials that might otherwise be lost and opponents of the ban argue that it will simply drive the trade underground. However, recycling is also open to abuse in the form of sham and dirty recycling. Waste is often labelled as recyclable when there is in fact no recuperation or reprocessing intended and genuine recycling processes can still release highly polluting contaminants and heavy metals which are dangerous to workers and to the environment.

It is unclear how much the Basel Convention has done to control the movement in hazardous waste – the Secretariat itself acknowledges that 'it is extremely difficult to produce reliable statistics on the generation and cross-border movements of hazardous waste' (UNEP, 2002b, p. 2). Problems continue in the lack of an adequate control and verification system, especially for monitoring or preventing illegal trade. Kummer identifies a 'certain helplessness in the attempts to control illegal traffic' (1998, p. 233). A survey undertaken by the Secretariat in 1997 revealed that in about half of the Parties the enforcement system and legislation on the prevention and punishment of illegal traffic was non-existent or inadequate (see Rummel-Bulska, 1998, p. 430). The problem is compounded by lack of technical expertise in developing countries and limited commitment from industrialized countries to transfer technology for detection and disposal. Funding has been limited and generally inadequate, with persistent problems of non-payment or late payment to the voluntary trust fund and continued under-resourcing of the regional training centres established in the late 1990s. At COP-5, in December 1999, parties adopted a Protocol on Liability and Compensation to overcome a serious weakness in the Convention but differences among the parties remain over financial limits for strict liability. At time of writing the Protocol still fell far short of the required number of ratifications to bring it into effect. COP-6, in December 2002, examined a number of issues relating to implementation and, after lengthy debate, adopted a Strategic Plan and agreed on a compliance mechanism as well as a budget until 2005. In 2001, the Secretariat reported to UNEP on the possibility of 'clustering' activities with the two other major global conventions on hazardous or toxic chemicals explored below.

Convention on the Prior Informed Consent Procedure for Certain Hazardous Chemicals and Pesticides in International Trade (the Rotterdam Convention)

The Prior Informed Consent (PIC) procedure which is codified in the Basel Convention to manage hazardous waste was established by UNEP and the FAO in 1989 as a voluntary mechanism to manage trade in banned or restricted chemicals. In 1996, governments began negotiations under an Intergovernmental Negotiating Committee (INC) to give legally binding weight to this specific application of PIC. A number of lessons had been learned from the implementation of PIC under the

Basel Convention, not least of which is that it requires good information and monitoring to influence practice and that governments require the institutional and technical capacity to assess notifications. The Basel application of PIC had also come under scrutiny for taking little account of economic disparities between developed and developing countries and the extent to which financial inducements (such as the offer of investment in power plants in return for using hazardous waste as a fuel) undermine the 'free choice' component of 'consent' (see Clapp, 1994, p. 508).

The PIC Convention (known as the Rotterdam Convention) was adopted on 11 September 1998. It covers 22 pesticides and five industrial chemicals and codifies the UNEP/FAO process which establishes procedures for collecting and disseminating information about whether individual governments will receive further shipments of designated chemicals. Proposals for additional chemicals will have to be accompanied by decision guidance documents (DGDs). Recommendations to the Parties will be the responsibility of a Chemical Review Committee (CRC). At time of writing, the Convention has 44 of the 50 ratifications required to bring it into effect. In the meantime PIC remains a voluntary commitment for the pesticides and chemicals listed in the agreement. The INC has continued to meet prior to entry into force to prepare for implementation of the Convention. In 1999, it established an interim Chemical Review Committee which has since adopted decision guidance documents for a number of other chemicals for listing in Annex III (chemicals subject to the PIC procedure). The success of the Rotterdam Convention will rely not only on implementation at a national level but on the availability and level of funding for the clearing-house process and assistance to developing countries to develop their infrastructure for controlling toxic substances and for education.

The Convention on Persistent Organic Pollutants (the Stockholm Convention)

The Basel Convention restricts trade but does not regulate or prohibit the production or use of toxic chemicals. Between 1998 and 2001, governments struggled to reach agreement on another convention that seeks to control the production and trade of the broad category of synthetic chemicals known as persistent organic pollutants (for a brief history of the emergence of the POPs issue, see Selin and Eckley, 2003). POPs are a problem of displacement and dispersal. They are both traded and transported by air and ocean currents. They can be passed quickly up the food chain because they bioaccumulate in living tissue and have been linked to a range of physiological and neurological defects and illnesses (for a summary of scientific research on POPs see Baldwin, 1997).

Chapter 19 of Agenda 21 established an Intergovernmental Forum on Chemical Safety (IFCS) and an Inter-Organizational Programme for the Sound Management of Chemicals (IOMC). Both were mandated by UNEP in 1995 to begin what was essentially a pre-negotiation process. The IFCS report, finalized in Manila in 1996, was accepted by UNEP in 1997. Formal negotiations began in 1998 with an initial list of twelve chemicals, the so-called 'dirty dozen' first identified in the Convention on Long-Range Transboundary Air Pollution (LRTAP). This twelve comprised nine pesticides, polychlorobiphenals (PCBs) and the industrial by-products dioxins and furans. Most were already banned in industrialized countries such as the US and Canada.

As with the hazardous waste negotiations, one of the key issues in the POPs negotiations was the allocation of responsibility between developed and developing countries and the provision of technical and financial assistance to developing countries to assist them to implement the agreement. Substances banned in industrialized countries are often exported to developing countries where regulations are often more lax and where pesticides are often used heavily to generate short-term agricultural income in the face of the challenges of poverty, despite the environmental and social consequences. A second key issue was that of timing and standards, including formal mechanisms for adding to the initial list of POPs in the Convention, a task which fell to the Criteria Expert Group (CEG). The negotiations were complicated further by concerns on the part of some developing countries that banning substances such as DDT would hinder their efforts to fight vector-borne diseases such as malaria, especially in the absence of substantial financial support for effective substitutes. Business interests sought a lengthy delay before the introduction of a ban to give them more time to develop alternatives.

The Stockholm Convention on POPs was finally adopted in May 2001. It gives specific recognition to the precautionary principle in its general sense – that precaution underlies the concerns of the Parties and is embedded in the Convention. The Convention is designed to protect human health and the environment by restricting the production and use of, as well as the trade in, chemicals listed in two annexes. Governments are expected to prevent the development of new POPs and to promote strategies for replacing existing ones. The agreement anticipates that additional chemicals will be added to the list and a POPs Review Committee has the responsibility of undertaking assessments and making recommendations to the Conference of Parties. The criteria adopted for this process are similar to those in the LRTAP agreement, based on 'specified criteria, consisting of threshold values of persistence and bioaccumulation, combined with a risk characterisation' (Selin and Eckley, 2003, p. 36). The negotiations and Convention have been called 'laudable but rather timid' (McGinn, 2000, p. 29). Since the Convention was adopted the INC has continued to meet in preparation for entry into force. At time of writing, 41 of the required 50 ratifications have been deposited.

Oceans pollution: protecting the commons

For a long time, pollution of the oceans was paid little attention in international circles. The oceans were deemed to have unlimited capacity as a dumping ground and environmental degradation was not considered a serious problem. Accidents such as the *Torrey Canyon* oil spill in 1967, however, sharpened public concern about ship-based pollution of coastlines and coastal wildlife. Oceans pollution arises through dispersal and displacement. Pollutants are carried by ocean currents across jurisdictional boundaries between high seas and territorial waters and also across states' sea-based territorial boundaries. Between 70 and 80 per cent of marine pollution is from land-based sources which include agricultural run-off (pesticides and fertilizers), sewage, oil and hydrocarbons, synthetic compounds and a range of heavy metals (see Sitarz, 1994, p. 145). Pollution from rivers causes damage to coastal ecosystems and disrupts coastal fisheries and can also extend well into the oceans. Pollution plumes from the Amazon, for example, can extend up to 2,000 kilometres from the mouth of the river (Holdgate, cited in Soroos, 1986, p. 297). In the case of pollution displacement, pollutants are dumped in the oceans or coastal regions through deliberate or accidental discharge from ships. Conservative estimates suggest that about 1.3 million tonnes of oil enter the oceans each year with approximately half of that coming from operational discharges from ships and land-based sources as well as accidental spills from ships (UNEP, 2003b).

Governments turned serious attention to the problem of marine pollution at the 1972 Stockholm Conference which adopted General Principles for Assessment and Control of Marine Pollution. Part XII of the 1983 UN Convention on the Law of the Sea also contains provisions 'for the protection and preservation of the marine environment ... [including] measures to prevent the pollution of the oceans by pollutants carried through the atmosphere' (Ramakrishna, 1990, pp. 431–2). In Chapter 17 of Agenda 21, states were urged to take action to prevent, reduce or control land-based sources of oceans pollution. In general, however, there was a general reluctance to address the 'pressing issues of land-based sources of pollution [and] habitat destruction' in deference to the 'traditional line of national sovereignty over coastal waters' (Weber, 1994, pp. 54, 55). Regional agreements, such as the 1974 Paris Convention on land-based sources of marine pollution in the Atlantic and Arctic, had some legal impact. For the most part, however, states were urged to comply with UNEP's 1985 non-binding Montreal Guidelines for the Protection of the Marine Environment Against Pollution from Land-Based Sources and to promote (where appropriate) regional arrangements in support of UNEP's regional seas programme. Only after UNCED did governments meet, under the auspices of UNEP, to draft a global Programme of Action on the protection of the marine environment from land-based sources of pollution. The Programme was finally adopted in late 1995 as the Washington Declaration. The (non-binding) Programme is intended to provide an information clearing-house and central resource for governments. It was reviewed in 2001 and delegates committed to improve implementation.

International agreements on ship-based sources of marine pollution date to the 1950s. Negotiations have been dominated by the interests of maritime states (those with long-distance shipping capabilities) and the shipping industry. Agreements have, for the most part, adopted a regulatory approach through the use of discharge restrictions and equipment standards. The 1954 International Convention for the Prevention of Pollution of the Sea by Oil established restricted discharge zones, although the provisions were generally ineffective. Amendments to the Convention, which extended the restricted discharge zones and placed equipment requirements on new tankers, effectively reversed a permissive approach by prohibiting discharges except under certain conditions rather than allowing discharge except in prohibited zones (Mitchell, 1993, p. 208).

The two main agreements on the prevention of ship-based sources of marine pollution are the 1972 Convention on the Prevention of Marine Pollution by Dumping of Wastes and Other Matters (the London Dumping Convention (LDC), sometimes just referred to as the London Convention) and MARPOL 73/78, that is, the 1973 International Convention for the Prevention of Pollution from Ships and its 1978 protocol. The London Dumping Convention deals with the dumping of dangerous substances at sea through a list process – a blacklist of prohibited wastes and a graylist of other substances, such as lead, arsenic and copper, for which permits are required and with which special care must be taken. The dumping of highly toxic pollutants and high-level radioactive wastes in the oceans is banned. In 1985, a two-year non-binding moratorium on the dumping of low-level radioactive waste was extended for an unlimited duration against, Lang (1991, p. 157) suggests, the interests of the major dumping countries, France, the United Kingdom and the United States. In 1993, the parties adopted an unconditional ban on dumping of any nuclear wastes in the seas (see Moody-O'Grady, 1995, p. 700). In spite of this progressive tightening of the rules on dumping, the obligations were considerably weakened by caveats which require parties only to take 'practicable steps' to prevent pollution and to take 'effective' measures only in accordance with their 'scientific, technological and economic capabilities' (Lang, 1991, p. 156). In many respects the LDC had come to be viewed as a 'dumpers' club' (Stairs and Taylor, 1992, p. 122), a view reinforced by the 1996 Protocol (which substantially rewrote the 1972 agreement) which excludes from its coverage the disposal or storage of wastes arising from off-shore minerals activity. At time of writing, the Protocol has not yet attracted the required number of ratifications and therefore has no legal force. The problems are compounded by a poor reporting record, with half of the contracting parties regularly failing to lodge reports on their compliance with the Convention (Stokke, 1998, p. 40).

MARPOL was intended to address more general ship-based pollution, to eliminate international pollution of the marine environment and to minimize accidental discharge of pollutants from ships and tankers. It is broader in scope than earlier agreements. It covers a range of maritime vessels including oil platforms as well as a wider range of controlled substances including oil, liquid chemicals, sewage, garbage and harmful packaged substances (see Mitchell, 1993, p. 210). The agreement also imposes tougher equipment standards than had hitherto been the case and expanded verification and inspection procedures. It did not, however, come into effect until 1983, ten years after its adoption (and the 1973 Annex IV, on ship-based sewage pollution, did not come into effect until September 2003). In 1978, however, the Parties negotiated a protocol to the original 1973 agreement which tightened equipment standards and extended the verification regime to allow for unscheduled inspections. Regular amendment processes have expanded the scope of the MARPOL provisions. Amendments in 1992 made double hulls mandatory for new tankers (accelerated by further amendments in 2001); a new 1997 protocol established limits on air pollution from ships at sea; and amendments in 1999 extended guidelines to tankers carrying heavy diesel oil and fuel oil. As with the London Dumping Convention, the extent of compliance may be difficult to determine with accuracy because submission of monitoring reports has been erratic.

Atmospheric pollutants

The atmospheric issues examined here are transboundary and global. The legal regimes which have developed to address these display many of the characteristics of other pollution regimes – differences over the science, disputes between polluter and victim countries (and an unwillingness of the former to shoulder responsibility), substantial time lags in taking action and agreements that are flawed in their ability to address the problem. At the same time, they have given rise to a number of conceptual and practical advances which, if properly implemented, could have an important impact on atmospheric pollution. These include critical loads and freeze-and-roll-back as management strategies as well as the more politically challenging issues of differentiation and contraction and convergence.

Long-Range Transboundary Air Pollution (LRTAP)

Tropospheric (lower-level) air pollution and its impacts are readily visible although the problem of cross-border air pollution did not generate a great deal of public concern until the 1960s and was not inscribed formally on the international agenda until the 1970s. While initially an issue addressed primarily by the industrialized countries, transboundary air pollution has become a growing problem for developing countries. The pollutants of most concern have been sulphur dioxide (SO_2) and nitrogen oxide (NOx) released when coal and gas are burned. The chemical reaction between these oxides and water vapour and sunlight causes the acidification of precipitation (acid rain, a term first coined by Scottish chemist Robert Smith). The irony is that this kind of pollution is the consequence of national laws requiring taller smokestacks (up to 500 feet) to disperse pollutants which would be otherwise be dangerous at lower, local levels. Acid rain damages the built environment as well as lake, river and terrestrial ecosystems. Public health concerns are more likely to arise from the impact of what are now referred to as volatile organic compounds (VOCs). VOCs, along with nitrogen oxides, are precursors of ground-level ozone which, in contrast to its crucial protective role in the stratosphere, 'is just as harmful to forests and agricultural crops' as sulphur emissions (Levy, 1993, p. 94).

The Scandinavian countries were the first to express concern about the detrimental environmental impacts of long-range air pollution, claiming that the acid rain damaging their lakes and fisheries was caused by industrial sulphur emissions from the United Kingdom and Central Europe. An Organisation for Economic Co-operation and Development (OECD) programme inaugurated in 1972 to identify and measure long-range air pollution confirmed in 1977 that pollutants could be dispersed over long distances. By the 1980s the problem was recognized as serious enough to warrant discussion on mitigation efforts. Within Europe, these proceeded under the auspices of the United Nations Economic Commission for Europe (ECE). The major cleavage of interests was between net-importer or victim states, who suffer greater effects of acid deposition than might be expected given their emissions of pollutants, and net-exporter states whose emissions are dispersed and who therefore suffer less than would be commensurate with their level of emissions. Over half of the sulphur deposits in Finland, Norway, Sweden, Austria and Switzerland, for example, come from foreign sources (Schwarzer, 1993, p. 14). The victim states consistently supported stringent regulations, calling for a freeze and then 50 per cent cut on sulphur dioxide and nitrogen oxide emission. Polluter states favoured only minimum commitments.

Convention on Long-Range Transboundary Air Pollution (LRTAP)

In November 1979, 35 countries, including Eastern bloc countries and the United States and Canada, adopted the Convention on Long-Range Transboundary Air Pollution (the Geneva Convention). The Convention recognized airborne pollutants as an environmental problem but did little more than require parties to 'endeavour' to limit and if possible reduce air pollution. The Convention did not come into effect until 1983 and Schwarzer suggests that it had little initial impact on practice within the polluting countries (1993, p. 16). However, by emphasizing exchange of information and research as the basis for further consultation on appropriate strategies, the Convention locked the then Eastern bloc countries into the monitoring and reporting programmes established for Western Europe. It also provided an opportunity for countries to place pressure on laggard states through voluntary commitments to more stringent targets.

Subsequent negotiations on reduction targets resulted in a number of pollutant-specific protocols plus one on cost-sharing. The 1985 Helsinki Protocol on the Reduction of Sulphur Emissions established reduction targets of at least 30 per cent of 1980 levels by 1993 at the latest. Although this built in part on the commitment of the so-called 'Thirty Percent Club' (ten countries which had pledged to reduce their own sulphur emissions by 30 per cent), the choice of 1980 as a baseline and the reduction target of 30 per cent seem to have been arbitrary (Wettestad, 1995, p. 170). Three major polluters, the US, the UK and Poland, which together contributed over 30 per cent of global sulphur dioxide emissions

(Porter and Brown, 1991, p. 74) did not sign the agreement then and have not done so since. The Protocol did not come into force until 1991. A new sulphur protocol – the Oslo Protocol on Further Reductions – was adopted in June 1994 to take account of differing economic and technical capacities for emission reductions. The Oslo Protocol is based on a critical loads formula which factors into emission levels the resilience threshold of the environment (which will vary from location to location) below which no damage to the ecosystem should occur. A different emissions target is therefore calculated for each party. The advantages of a critical loads approach are that it emphasizes equity over equality, but it can also be time-consuming and difficult to agree on those loads.

The 1988 Sofia Protocol committed parties to a freeze on nitrogen oxide emissions at 1987 levels by 1994 (thus allowing for an *increase* in emissions in the interim). While Eastern bloc countries opposed reduction targets primarily because their outdated automobile technology meant there was little likelihood they could meet any targets, twelve European countries declared their intention to *reduce* nitrogen oxide emissions by 30 per cent by 1998. Five countries – Sweden, Switzerland, Austria, the Netherlands and the Federal Republic of Germany (motivated by increasing acid rain damage to its forests) – were prepared to commit to a 30 per cent reduction by 1995. In 1991 the parties adopted a protocol to deal with volatile organic compounds (VOCs). The VOCs protocol establishes varying commitments to freeze VOC emissions or reduce them by 30 per cent by 1999 (but with different baseline years for different countries) either at a national level or within designated tropospheric ozone management areas (TOMAs). Despite attempts to take individual country circumstances into account, these reduction targets are generally considered too low (Schwarzer, 1993, p. 19). In 1998, LRTAP adopted two more protocols, one on heavy metals and one on POPs, neither one in force at time of writing. The heavy metals protocol targets lead, cadmium and mercury and requires parties to reduce emissions below 1990 levels and to cut emissions from industrial sources. The POPs protocol (the Aarhus Protocol) lists 16 POPs with the objective of eliminating their discharge, emission and loss. Some are banned outright and others are severely restricted. The Gothenburg Protocol adopted in 1999 sets emission ceilings for 2010 for four pollutants – sulphur, NOx, VOCs and ammonia – in order to abate acidification, eutrophication and ground-level ozone.

The impact of these agreements has been mixed (and three of the five have not yet come into force). By the mid-1990s, overall sulphur emissions had been reduced by 40 per cent (Soroos, 1998, p. 11). However an increase in nitrogen oxide emissions in the early 1990s meant that 'damage to forests, soils, inshore waters and historical monuments' continued to worsen and critical loads [were] exceeded in almost all parts of Europe (Schwarzer, 1993, p. 21). UNEP reports, however, that 'emissions of most key air pollutants have [now] declined over the whole of Europe since the early 1980s' (2002a, p. 224). On the other hand, sulphur emissions are thought still to be 'too high to avoid serious effects in sensitive ecosystems' (UNEP, 2002a, p. 224). Compliance with reporting requirements has been uneven (Levy, 1993, p. 91) and monitoring of some pollutants in Central and Eastern Europe has been inadequate. Indeed, UNEP's conclusion is that 'many air pollution targets have still not been met' (2002a, p. 235).

The global commons of the atmosphere: ozone depletion

The 1970s and 1980s also saw increased attention to global atmospheric pollutants and their global consequences – ozone depletion and climate change. Ozone (O_3 – three atoms of oxygen) was discovered in 1840. In the stratosphere – that is, the lower atmosphere about 10 to 50 km above the earth's surface – it performs the important function of filtering harmful ultraviolet B radiation (UVB) even though it exists there only in a few parts per million. Stratospheric ozone is, however, vulnerable to destruction in chemical reaction with chlorine and bromine gases. The anthropogenic (that is, human-made) sources of those gases are found in chlorofluorocarbons (CFCs) (which are used as propellants for aerosols, refrigerants, solvents for cleaning electrical components and the manufacture of rigid and flexible foam products); in the organic solvents carbon tetrachloride and methyl chloroform; in methyl bromide (which is used primarily as a fungicide); and in halons which are found primarily in fire extinguishers. The release of chlorine as a by-product of volcanic eruptions and biomass burning is a possible non-anthropogenic contributor to ozone depletion. Because sources are so stable (CFCs can remain in the atmosphere for up to 120 years before breaking down) chlorine and bromine concentrations have increased since pre-Industrial times, reaching a peak in the mid-1990s (European Environment Agency, 1999, p. 103). This has, in turn, accelerated the destruction of ozone and increased the amount of UVB radiation reaching the earth. Increased UVB radiation leads to an increase in skin cancers and cataracts, suppression of human and animal immune systems, increased vulnerability to infectious diseases and reduced productivity in plants and phytoplankton, the latter the basis of the marine food chain (and also a carbon dioxide fixer). A 1 per cent decrease in stratospheric ozone is thought to cause a 2 per cent increase in surface UVB radiation and as much as a 4 to 6 per cent increase in skin cancers (Shea, 1989, p. 82).

Much of this knowledge is relatively new. In the 1960s, debates about damage to stratospheric ozone focused on the possible consequences of supersonic air transport, although the culprits were water vapour and nitrous oxide. In 1974, two US scientists hypothesized that accumulated chlorine gases could lead to depletion of stratospheric ozone (Molina and Rowland, 1974). In 1977 a UNEP-convened meeting of experts drew up a World Plan of Action on the Ozone Layer which emphasized further scientific research. The Coordinating Committee on the Ozone Layer (CCOL) established at that meeting met annually from 1977 to 1985. In 1981, UNEP's Governing Council convened an Ad Hoc Legal and Technical Working Group to draft an ozone protection convention. Negotiations began in 1982 and are generally considered to have been one of the more successful examples of international environmental cooperation.

Convention for the Protection of the Ozone Layer (the Vienna Convention)

The Vienna Convention was adopted by 20 countries plus the EC on 22 March 1985. It is a framework convention of 21 articles, most of which are procedural and administrative. It contains no firm targets or controls, only general obligations emphasizing the importance of cooperation and scientific research. Specific commitments were contentious because the negotiating parties favoured different management strategies. The US, Canada, Finland, Norway and Sweden (collectively known as the Toronto Group) had already banned non-essential aerosol uses of CFCs. The European Community countries argued that a production cap, which they had adopted in 1980, would be easier to monitor. Industry opposition to reductions in either consumption or production was stronger in Europe than in the United States (Benedick, 1991, pp. 30–4).

The Convention's potential lay in its precautionary nature. There was still no scientific certainty on the causes or impacts of ozone depletion and thus the agreement departed from usual reactive practices of international environmental law. Scientific evidence and changing industry attitudes were important in mobilizing negotiations for specific reduction targets. In 1985, a team of British Antarctic Survey scientists reported readings which indicated a 40 per cent reduction in springtime ozone over the Antarctic since 1979. These results were initially treated with some scepticism because none of the atmospheric models had predicted such an outcome. In July 1985, a scientific team sponsored by UNEP and the National Aeronautics and Space Administration (NASA) reported that the ozone layer was already damaged. Two subsequent NASA-sponsored expeditions (National Ozone Expedition (NOZE) I and II) demonstrated the 'undoubted chemical cause in destruction of ozone by atmospheric chlorine' (Rowlands, 1991, p. 106). Ozone depletion was no longer theory. By 1988, there was strong evidence of an increase in ozone depletion over middle latitudes. In March, NASA's Ozone Trends Panel (OTP) reported a total decrease in stratospheric ozone of between 1.7 and 3.0 per cent in latitudes 30 and 60 degrees north since 1969 (see Shea, 1989, p. 81). Almost immediately, chemical giant Du Pont announced that it would phase out its CFC production (about 25 per cent of global output) although three weeks earlier, before the OTP report, the company had argued that the 'scientific evidence does *not* point to the need for dramatic CFC reductions' (see Benedick, 1991, p. 111; emphasis added).

Protocol on Substances that Deplete the Ozone Layer (Montreal Protocol)

On 16 September 1987 (before the Vienna Convention had come into effect) 24 countries plus the EC adopted the Montreal Protocol which adopted a freeze-and-roll-back approach to reduction targets and consumption controls for two groups of ozone-depleting substances. Group I substances – five fully halogenated CFCs – were to be cut to 50 per cent of 1986 levels by 1999. Group II substances, halons, were to be frozen at 1986 levels by the end of 1992. The value of the 1986 baseline meant that there would be no advantage to governments in delaying their accession to the Protocol. The Protocol included a number of other provisions to support these control measures. There were restrictions on trade with non-parties in controlled substances and products containing controlled substances (article 4). Review of the schedules of controlled substances was to be based on scientific evidence. A modified amendment procedure ensured that changes to schedules already agreed would come into effect six months after adoption, thus avoiding lengthy domestic ratification processes.

While the Protocol was hailed as a successful piece of environmental diplomacy and an important step in addressing ozone depletion, it contained exceptions and loopholes which ensured that, at best, it would not stop depletion, but only slow its acceleration. Targets were emission rather than concentration-driven. Not all ozone-depleting substances were covered, and many of the substitutes which were not at that stage covered by the Protocol – such as hydrochlorofluorocarbons

(HCFCs) – were still ozone-depleting as well as greenhouse-enhancing. Non-depleting substitutes, the hydrofluorocarbons (HFCs), had a very high greenhouse potential.

The industrialized countries, 25 per cent of the world's population, contributed almost 90 per cent of ozone consumption and were rightly required to shoulder much of the responsibility for reductions. However, consumption of ozone-depleting substances in developing countries was predicted to increase and neither China nor India, whose participation was essential to the control of future emissions and concentrations, were signatories at that stage. Developing countries argued, first, that ozone depletion was a problem created by, and therefore to be solved by, the industrialized countries and, second, that they were not prepared to forgo the benefits of existing investment in technology, even if it were ozone-depleting, when alternative substances and technologies were so expensive. Developing countries were granted a ten-year compliance grace period, as long as their annual consumption did not exceed 0.3 kilograms per capita (about one-quarter of US per capita consumption). Only a few of the advanced developing countries – Bahrain, Malta, Singapore and the United Arab Emirates – exceeded this level (see Gehring and Oberthür, 1993, p. 9).

Exceptions also accommodated the planned economies of the then Eastern bloc (article 2.6); allowed limited transfer of production for industrial rationalization purposes (article 2.5); and allowed for production increases to meet the import demands of developing countries (articles 2.1 to 2.4; see Benedick, 1991, p. 81). There were no enforcement or verification procedures except for national reporting provisions. The US Office of Technology Assessment (OTA) estimated that if only the original signatories complied with the Protocol's provisions, consumption of CFCs and halons could increase by as much as 20 per cent by 2009 (see Morrisette, 1989, p. 818). The US Environmental Protection Agency calculated that even full global participation in the Protocol could still result in a threefold increase in stratospheric chlorine concentrations by 2075 (Caron, 1991, p. 762).

Since the Montreal Protocol entered into force on 1 January 1989, after being ratified by at least eleven countries representing two-thirds of global consumption of halons and CFCs, the parties have met regularly under the review procedures to revise and ratchet existing schedules, to adopt new schedules and to increase the coverage of controlled substances. The parties have been reluctant to allow exceptions to the controls, especially if technically and economically feasible alternatives are available. Major amendments were adopted at the second Meeting of Parties (MOP) in London in 1990, in Copenhagen in 1992, in Montreal in 1997 and in Beijing in 1999. Phase-out dates on CFCs and carbon tetrachloride were initially set for 2000 and later ratcheted to 1996. Halons were to be phased out by 2000 (later ratcheted to 1994). The original 2005 phase-out date for methyl chloroform, adopted at the London meeting in 1990, was later revised to 1994. Targets for the substitute components HCFCs were more difficult. A complicated schedule was finally adopted in 1994 with a 1996 consumption cap (based on the aggregate of 1989 consumption plus 3.1 per cent of 1989 consumption of CFCs). The phase-out date, however, was set at 2040 although it was later revised to 2020 for developed countries. The Beijing amendments included new controls on HCFCs, banning trade between parties who had not ratified the 1992 Copenhagen amendments. Methyl bromide also proved challenging. An initial freeze on production and consumption (at 1991 levels by 1995) was finally adjusted to a 2010 phase-out at the Vienna meeting but with exceptions for quarantine, pre-shipment and critical agricultural-use applications to take account of the interests of those parties (many of them members of the EC) who used it as a commodity fumigant and pesticide. The Montreal meeting in 1997 agreed to a ban on trade in methyl bromide with non-parties.

As well as the formal commitments, the Montreal process has also been characterized by voluntary declarations on more stringent phase-outs by parties concerned at the slow progress in adopting and revising controls. In 1989, for example, the EC announced a commitment to phase out CFCs by 2000, before this target was formally adopted under the Protocol. In 1995, 22 countries pledged to phase out HCFCs by 2025 when no agreement could be reached under the formal negotiations and 16 countries signed a voluntary declaration to cut methyl bromide consumption by 25 per cent by 2000.

A number of problems, relating to funding and technology transfer and compliance, remain on the agenda. In 1990, the Parties established an interim Multilateral Fund (confirmed in 1992) to provide for financial and technology transfer to assist developing countries meet their obligations. The Fund functions under the day-to-day administration of UNEP, the United Nations Development Programme (UNDP) and the World Bank, with overall guidance provided by a larger than administratively necessary executive committee of seven developed and seven developing countries. The record of replenishment and payment has not been altogether smooth. As an incentive for developing countries to sign on to the Montreal process, the initial commitment of $US160 million was to be increased to $US240 million if and when China and India became parties. At the 1991 meeting in Nairobi, the Fund was increased to $US200 million after China's accession, but there were already problems with non-payment of contributions, especially from France and the new Russian Federation. There was no consensus on replenishment at the 1992 meeting and by the 1993 meeting, only $53 million of the $114 million pledged for that year had been received. Agreement was reached in 1994 for a three-year funding of $US510 million, in 1995 for a $US466 million replenishment for the 1997–99 triennium and in 1999 for $US477.7 million for 2000–02. By 2000, the Fund had disbursed over $1 billion to help phase out production and consumption in developing countries.

The Protocol's impact on emissions and concentrations has been slow. In 1994, the Protocol's Scientific Assessment report concluded that the rate of chlorine loading (but not the level of concentrations) had finally slowed, but that depletion would continue for at least another fifty years, with a slow recovery in ozone loss not anticipated until about 2045 (Anon., 1995a, p. 22). UNEP confirms that 'the global consumption of ODS [ozone-depleting substances] has decreased markedly and the ozone layer is predicted to ... return to a pre-1980 level by the middle of the 21st century' (2002a, p. 213). Those predictions are, however, based on two assumptions: that there will be no new threats to the ozone layer and that there will be full compliance with the Montreal Protocol and its amendments. The ten-year grace period for developing countries ended in 1999. Despite earlier concerns, the 1998 data showed that many developing countries were on track with their commitments to freeze CFC emissions at 1995–97 levels by mid-2000 (with a complete phase-out by 2010). Almost all of the developing country producers had cut production to baseline levels. In 2002, the Multilateral Fund adopted a new Compliance Assistance Programme to work more closely with developing countries through regional offices and the delivery of projects and services.

One of the most challenging problems for the efforts to halt and reverse ozone depletion is now the 'disturbing volume of illegal traffic in controlled substances' (Leubuscher, 1996, p. 186) which is characterized by practices such as fraudulent labelling and diversion to and reimport from third countries. Estimates suggest, for example, that by the middle of the 1990s between 16,000 and 38,000 tonnes of illegal CFCs were being traded annually, possibly as much as 15 per cent of the world CFC trade (UNEP, 2001e, pp. 3, 4), at least some of it involving organized criminal activity. The problem is not that the alternatives are expensive – in most cases they are not – but that equipment has to be adapted or even replaced to use the alternatives, and that *can* be an expensive task. It is generally accepted that parties to the Protocol simply did not anticipate the emergence of a black market and it was not until the 1997 meeting in Montreal that they adopted a licensing system for the import and export of ODS which, it was hoped, would assist governments to combat illegal trade.

The global commons of the atmosphere: climate change

If Benedick was able to refer to the Montreal Protocol as 'the impossible accord' (1991, p. xiii) it was nothing compared with the difficulties of addressing climate change. Scientific uncertainty, economic interests and costs, political tensions and the fundamental question of equity between developed and developing countries all came to bear on an issue which one diplomat has called perhaps 'the most complex public policy issue ever to face governments' (Reinstein, 1993, p. 79).

The greenhouse effect is a natural phenomenon. Atmospheric gases – carbon dioxide (CO_2), methane (CH_4), nitrous oxide (N_2O), tropospheric ozone (and water vapour) – as well as CFCs and their substitutes which do not occur naturally in the atmosphere, absorb infra-red radiation which is reflected from the earth's surface as heat. Without this, average global temperatures would be about 33°C cooler than they are now. The problem arises when the trapping effect is enhanced by increased concentrations of these gases (with the exception of water vapour which is not increased anthropogenically). The sources of greenhouse gas emissions are varied. CO_2 emissions arise primarily from the burning of fossil fuels – about five-sixths of annual CO_2 emissions – and the rest from deforestation (World Bank, 2003, p. 175). Methane, which is a very efficient greenhouse gas, is produced by agricultural processes, particularly rice cultivation and livestock. It is also released during the extraction and transportation of fossil fuels. Nitrous oxides come from biomass burning, fertilizer use, fossil fuel combustion, land clearing and deforestation. Since pre-Industrial times (the mid-1700s), atmospheric concentrations of CO_2 have increased by 31 per cent and are now higher – at approximately 370 parts per million (ppm) – than at any time in the past 420,000 years and possibly the last 20 million years (IPCC, 2001, p. 7). About three-quarters of the increase is from fossil fuel burning, the rest from changes in land use, especially deforestation. The IPCC also reports that concentrations of methane have increased by about 151 per cent in the last 250 years and nitrous oxide concentrations have increased by about 17 per cent in the same period (2001, p. 7).

While there is general agreement on the measurements, there is much less scientific certainty on the likely effects of those increased concentrations. There are a number of problems associated with predicting impacts. First, despite scientific advances, it is still difficult to model the relative contribution of gases. Methane, for example, is 32 times more efficient in trapping heat but it has a much shorter atmospheric lifespan than carbon dioxide. Second, the complex interaction of positive and negative feedbacks and the still only partially understood impact of carbon sinks (those parts of the biosphere such as the oceans and forests which absorb carbon dioxide) have also been difficult to determine. Positive feedbacks, such as the release of methane from thawing tundra, enhance the greenhouse effect. By contrast, negative feedback processes such as reforestation may help retard warming. Third, scientists are also uncertain about the threshold level for concentrations and about whether, when that threshold level is reached, the inherent resilience of the climate system might be overwhelmed.

Scientific research therefore confirms trends rather than proof, emphasizing probable rather than certain outcomes. Nevertheless, there is a high degree of consensus within the climatological community on those likely outcomes, expressed most clearly in the reports of the Intergovernmental Panel on Climate Change (IPCC). The balance of probabilities favours an enhanced global warming: the no-climate-change scenario is considered the least likely. Predicted climate-related impacts include increases in average global temperatures, rises in sea levels and an increase in the frequency and intensity of extreme weather conditions. Climatological history indicates that the planet has always been subject to temperature fluctuations and changes in sea levels: it is the rate and degree of contemporary change that is cause for concern. Global average surface temperature increased by about 0.6°C in the twentieth century (IPCC, 2001, p. 2). The IPCC has predicted that with no action taken to reduce emissions or concentrations (a business-as-usual (BAU) approach), average surface temperatures could increase by as much as 1°C by 2030 and by anything between 1.4 and 5.8°C by 2100 (against a 1990 baseline) (IPCC, 2001, p. 13). Temperature changes are likely to be uneven with changes minimal close to the equator and as much as 8°C near the poles. Between 1970 and 1998 average global surface temperatures increased from 13.8 to 14.35°C (see Worldwatch Institute, 2000, p. 10) and scientific findings suggest that the 1990s was the warmest decade in 1,000 years (IPCC, 2001, p. 2). By the year 2030, average global temperatures could be higher than at any time in the last 120,000 years (see Grubb, 1990, p. 68).

Sea-level rises, as a result of thermal expansion of the oceans and, in the first instance, melting of non-polar glacial ice are conservatively estimated at 0.09 to 0.88 metres by 2100 (against a 1990 baseline; see IPCC, 2001, p. 16). This could be three to six times faster than in the previous 100 years (Houghton *et al.*, 1990, p. xxviii). The National Oceanic and Atmospheric Administration (NOAA) reports that northern hemisphere tropical waters are heating at almost ten times the global rate (NOAA, 2000). The IPCC's Third Assessment Report (TAR) identified a 'widespread retreat' of non-polar mountain glaciers in the twentieth century and increases in global average sea level of up to 0.2 metres

(IPCC, 2001, p. 4). Densely populated coastal areas will be inundated, possibly displacing up to one billion of the world's people. Coastal erosion and salt-water pollution of inland waterways, in conjunction with changes in climate zones, could affect up to one-third of the world's croplands. Shifts in climate and agricultural zones may occur more rapidly than the adaptive capacity of plants or animals, resulting in a loss of biodiversity and agricultural output. Those parts of the world which are already ecologically and economically marginal are likely to be worst hit by the consequences of climate change, and they are the peoples and countries which have, for the most part, contributed little or nothing to the problem. Countries such as Bangladesh, Egypt, Gambia, Indonesia, Mozambique, Pakistan, Senegal, Surinam and Thailand are high-risk countries because of their coastal concentrations. People living in the islands of the Southwest Pacific have already reported severe coastline erosion with islands standing below sea level at high tide. Low-lying island states such as Tuvalu, Tonga, Kiribati, the Marshall Islands and the Maldives might become uninhabitable and, at worst, simply cease to exist. Insurers, working with UNEP's Financial Services Initiative, have estimated that the annual cost of global warming could be over $US300 billion (UNEP, 2001a, p. 1; see also Glasby, 2002).

Climate policy

General climate issues were addressed at a series of scientific conferences in the 1970s and early 1980s, including the First World Climate Conference convened by WMO in 1979, the 1972 Stockholm Conference on the Human Environment (see recommendation 70 of the Action Plan), the UN World Food Conference in 1974, the UN Water Conference in 1976 and the UN Desertification Conference in 1977. However, it was not until the rather ponderously titled International Conference on Assessment of the Role of CO_2 and other GHGs [greenhouse gases] in Climate Variation and Associated Impact, held in Villach, Austria in 1985, that scientific concern began to translate into demands for international political action. The Villach meeting recommended that UNEP, WMO and ICSU 'initiate, if deemed necessary, consideration of a global convention' (cited in Bodansky, 1994, p. 48). The Villach Conference was followed by workshops in Bellagio, Italy in 1985 and 1987. The 1988 Toronto Conference on the Changing Atmosphere recommended a 20 per cent reduction in CO_2 emissions by 2005 (the so-called Toronto target), and called for an international convention and action plan.

The most important contribution to scientific consensus, and to the process of negotiating an international agreement on climate change, has been the work of the Intergovernmental Panel on Climate Change

(IPCC). This expert body was established in 1988 by the WMO and UNEP (see Shackley, 1997 for a description of the Panel's structure and working practices). The IPCC released its first major assessment in August 1990, drawing attention to the environmental and socioeconomic impacts of climate change and the disproportionate impacts on regions already under stress (see Tegart *et al.*, 1990). It suggested that developing countries would need assistance to adapt to changes and limit their emissions and cautioned that 'global warming and impacts must not widen the gap between developed and developing countries' (IPCC, 1990, p. 32) but offered no detailed action guide for policy.

In December 1988, the General Assembly requested the WMO and UNEP, through the IPCC, to begin to think about the possible elements of a convention on climate change (UNGA, 1988, Resolution 43/53). As these formal negotiations drew closer, governments became increasingly cautious about their commitments. At a ministerial conference in Noordwijk in the Netherlands in 1989, delegates debated a Dutch proposal that industrialized countries should stabilize their CO_2 emissions by the year 2000. Neither the US nor Japan would agree to such a commitment, and the Declaration articulated only the general aim of limiting or reducing emissions (see Bodansky, 1994, p. 55). At the Second World Climate Conference in November 1990, some governments were prepared to support a final statement which would commit industrialized countries to stabilizing CO_2 emissions at 1990 levels by 2000. US opposition again resulted in vague language on targets and national strategies (see Reinstein, 1993, p. 83). In December, under resolution 45/212, the UN General Assembly formally established negotiations for a climate change convention, removing this task from UNEP and the IPCC. The Intergovernmental Negotiating Committee for a Framework Convention on Climate Change (INC/FCCC) was given 18 months to produce a convention in time for signature at the Rio Conference in June 1992. The INC met five times. The first two sessions dealt mainly with procedural matters. The fifth and final meeting began in February 1992 in New York and resumed again at the end of April with a large number of brackets remaining in the draft text.

Negotiations were driven as much by political and economic interests as by environmental imperatives. The head of the INC Secretariat, Michael Zammit Cutajar, described them as a 'process of two steps forward and one step back' (United Nations INC/FCCC, 1991, p. 2). The first area of dispute was *how* to stabilize and reduce emissions and concentrations. This is more than a scientific and technical exercise. It is a highly political and politicized one. Strategies for addressing the greenhouse effect have been contentious because they 'reach into the heart of countries' political and economic structures' (Paterson and Grubb, 1992, p. 294). The IPCC has estimated that to stabilize *concentrations* at 1990 levels, emissions would need to be reduced by over 60 per cent for CO_2, 15–20 per cent for methane and 70–80 per cent for nitrous oxide (Houghton *et al.*, 1990, p. xxiii) and 70–75 per cent for CFC-11, 75–85 per cent for CFC-12 and 40–50 per cent for HCFC-22 (Houghton *et al.*, 1990, p. xviii). Even then, stabilizing at 1990 levels would only reduce the estimated 0.3 °C increase in global temperature per decade to 0.23 °C because of the long-term impact of concentrations (Pearce, cited in Hanisch, 1992, p. 64). Carbon dioxide emissions can be reduced through energy efficiency, use of alternative renewable energy sources, changing the mix of fossil fuels to avoid the more dirty, high emitting sources, imposing penalties or financial mechanisms such as carbon taxes or tradeable permits, slowing deforestation or putting efforts into reafforestation. Yet the industrialized countries (and traditional energy industries) have been generally reluctant to adopt these strategies.

The second major area of dispute was over responsibility to act. Countries vary not only in their contributions to greenhouse emissions, but also in the ease with which they can reduce emissions, in their capacity to pay for response policies and in their degree of resilience or vulnerability to impacts. The allocation of responsibility and obligation on a country-by-country basis is controversial. It depends on which gases are counted and whether they are counted on a total output basis, a per capita basis, a per GNP basis, or on the basis of current levels, historical contributions or projected future emissions (see Rowlands, 1997 for a comparison of reduction targets based on different forms of allocation; see also Pan, 2003). Developed industrialized countries cannot escape the major burden of responsibility. The OECD countries, approximately one-quarter of the world's population, contribute about three-quarters of global radiative forcing. The US contributes about 25 per cent of global CO_2 emissions and the EU contributes about 14 per cent. Per capita CO_2 emissions in rich countries average 12.4 tonnes per annum. In developing countries, the figure is 1.0 tonnes (UNDP, 2003, p. 10) and (in 1999) only 0.2 tonnes in the least developed countries (UNDP, 2003, p. 124). Greenhouse emissions from the developing countries are, however, increasing. Some industrialized countries – the US chief among them – argue that any reductions in their own emissions will be futile if developing countries do not also commit to reduce CO_2 and methane. Developing countries respond that this smacks of environmental colonialism and is an attempt by developed countries to shift the blame, to avoid their own responsibilities and to restrain the economic growth of developing countries (see Agarwal and Narain, 1991;

McCully, 1991a). It also ignores or downplays the differences between luxury emissions (from unrestricted energy use, for example) and survival or subsistence emissions (see Shue, 1993).

A third area of contention arises over how best to factor scientific uncertainty into any agreement. The United States in particular has cautioned against commitments beyond those supported by current scientific research, arguing for 'no regrets' policies which will incur minimal cost if the predictions turn out to be inaccurate. Many developing countries interpret this as a strategy by which developed countries could extricate themselves from meeting obligations based on their historical and current contributions as well as the rather selfish actions of countries which are better placed, economically and technologically, to deal with the impacts of climate change.

Within the INC, governments coalesced into a series of interest-based coalitions. Although there was a 'North–South' dimension to the negotiations, political cleavages went beyond this simple bifurcation. Negotiating coalitions included the 37-member Alliance of Small Island States (AOSIS) formed at the Second World Climate Conference, the oil-producing and -exporting countries, the newly industrialized countries (NICs) who were dependent on energy-intensive patterns of production, the economies in transition (EITs) of the former Soviet bloc and the OECD countries. Some suggest that the United States stood apart from its industrialized counterparts in a bloc on its own (see Pulvenis, 1994, p. 85 and Sands, 1992, p. 271). Nor was there always agreement within these blocs. There was, for example, general agreement among the OECD countries (with the exception of the US) on the need for targets, but there was disagreement on what those targets should be (see Reinstein, 1993, p. 89). The EC, Japan and the US were cautious about any agreement which would affect the trade balance between them or 'endanger their competitive ability' (Hanisch, 1992, p. 72). The oil-producing countries and the US favoured only a framework convention (the Vienna model). Other developed countries and AOSIS wanted a convention with specific commitments and implementation measures, although there were also serious fears among developing countries that the convention would limit their development opportunities by placing restrictions on energy use and agricultural practice (see Agarwal and Narain, 1991).

UN Framework Convention on Climate Change

The UN Framework Convention on Climate Change (UNFCCC) was finalized at 6.10 p.m. on Saturday, 9 May 1992 (after days on which delegates often met until 3.00 or 4.00 in the morning). It is not a long document: a preamble, 26 articles and two annexes. Its principles (article 3) include precaution, equity (both inter- and intragenerational), cooperation and sustainability. The Convention's objective is to stabilize atmospheric greenhouse gas concentrations at levels that will prevent human activities from interfering dangerously with the global climate system, within 'a time frame sufficient to allow ecosystems to adapt naturally to climate change, to ensure that food production is not threatened and to enable economic development to proceed in a sustainable manner' (United Nations INC/FCCC, 1992, article 2). This is to be achieved through limiting emissions, enhancing sinks and protecting reservoirs. However, the Convention contains no authoritative targets or deadlines, in large part because of opposition from the US and oil-exporting countries. Article 4.2(a), which Sands calls possibly 'the most impenetrable treaty language ever drafted' (1992, p. 273), refers only to the value of returning emissions to 'earlier levels' by 2000. Developed countries, including those undergoing transition to a market economy, are encouraged, individually or jointly, to bring their emissions of gases not controlled by the Montreal Protocol to 1990 levels (article 4.2(b)). This voluntary target is less stringent than the 1988 Toronto target and nowhere near the 60 per cent reduction which the IPCC suggested would be necessary to stabilize concentrations.

Equity between developed and developing countries is mediated through the principle of 'common but differentiated responsibilities and respective capabilities' (article 3.1). Developed countries are required to take the lead in mitigating climate change and to report on the strategies they adopt. The Convention recognizes their general obligations for the transfer of financial resources and technology to assist the developing countries to meet their general commitments and to prepare for and adapt to the adverse effects of climate change. The Convention also recognizes a range of other vulnerabilities (including those of countries with low-lying, coastal, arid and semi-arid areas) and special circumstances, especially those of countries which are highly dependent on either the production or consumption of fossil fuels.

Much of the Convention is given over to institutional and procedural mechanisms, establishing the Conference of Parties (COP), a Secretariat and two subsidiary bodies – on Scientific and Technical Advice (SBSTA) and on Implementation (SBI) – to assist, provide advice to and report to the COP (articles 9 and 10). Article 11 establishes a financial mechanism for the Convention and article 21 entrusts the Global Environment Facility with the responsibility of operating the mechanism 'on an interim basis'. Also here, buried in article 21, is the terse but significant injunction that 'the Global Environment Facility *should* be appropriately restructured and its membership made universal' (United Nations INC/FCCC,

1992, article 21; emphasis added), an issue addressed in more detail in Chapter 4.

The Convention has been called 'pathbreaking' (Chadwick, 1994, p. xiii) and a 'powerful force for change in North–South relations' (Mintzer and Leonard, 1994b, p. 21). Sands suggested that it 'mark[ed] an important new phase in the development of international environmental law' (1992, p. 271). Ted Hanisch (a member of the Norwegian delegation to the INC) argued that the Convention was successful because it established a first step in building a regime for climate change even though it would not stop the trend of increasing global emissions and concentrations (1992, p. 67). Yet it is precisely those flaws which have led to much harsher assessments which suggest that the Convention is internally contradictory and unsatisfactory. Greenpeace lobbyists Jeremy Leggett and Paul Hohnen (1992, p. 76) have argued that the Convention fails to establish targets which would enable its own stated objectives to be met. Farhana Yamin (n.d., p. 5), writing for the Foundation for International Environmental Law and Development (FIELD), a non-governmental organization which worked closely with the AOSIS during the negotiations, observed that the continuation of emissions is inconsistent with the Convention's objectives and obligations and noted the absence of any reference to energy efficiency, even though Chapter 9 of Agenda 21 clearly identified this as an important strategy.

The Convention was opened for signature at UNCED on 4 June where it was signed by 154 countries and the EC. The necessary fiftieth ratification was deposited on 21 December 1993, and the Convention entered into force on 21 March 1994. The INC met a further six times after the Convention was opened for signature to prepare for implementation. The first Conference of Parties was held in Berlin in March 1995. As well as a number of procedural issues, the Berlin meeting focused on the adequacy of commitments after the year 2000 given that most of the OECD countries were not on track to meet even their vague commitments under the FCCC (Rowlands, 1995b, p. 153). In a replay of earlier disagreements, AOSIS and the EU favoured stringent targets but were opposed by other developed countries. AOSIS submitted a draft protocol which would have required developed countries to reduce their CO_2 emissions to 20 per cent below 1990 levels by 2005. Japan, the US, Canada, Australia and New Zealand (the JUSCANZ group) were especially reluctant to accept further obligations and focused instead on the importance of developing countries committing to reductions within a comprehensive approach which would include sources, sinks and reservoirs. China and the Group of 77 (G77) continued to emphasize developed country responsibility and the oil-exporting countries remained opposed to any action at all. In the face of no consensus, the COP adopted the so-called 'Berlin Mandate' which set in train a process to elaborate a protocol or other legal instrument on further commitments. This became the responsibility of an Ad Hoc Working Group on the Berlin Mandate (the AGBM) which was authorized to have a draft prepared for adoption at COP-3 in 1997.

COP-1 also addressed the practice of Joint Implementation (JI) which allows 'one country [to] fulfil its obligations by helping to reduce greenhouse gas emissions, enhance carbon sinks or preserve reservoirs in another country' (Rowlands, 1995b, p. 148). Concerns focused on whether developed countries would endeavour to meet their obligations by funding cheaper options in developing countries rather than taking action 'at home'. This, it was thought, enabled developed countries to determine reduction strategies for developing countries and reduce options for the latter when the time came for them to commit to formal, legal reduction targets. In the end, a pilot phase (to be known as AIJ or Activities Implemented Jointly) was adopted on the basis of voluntary participation with no credits for emissions reductions.

Berlin to Kyoto

In an interim report released at the end of 1994, the IPCC noted that, even with a stabilization of current emissions, concentrations of CO_2 would continue to increase for at least two centuries (see Oberthür and Ott, 1995, p. 145). The IPCC Second Assessment Report (SAR) of December 1995 confirmed this likely increase in atmospheric GHG concentrations and interference with the climate system (IPCC, 1995, para. 1.7). It reinforced, with some modifications, its 1990 projections. It also confirmed the reality of climate change, advising that the increase in global mean surface temperature of between 0.3 and 0.6°C since the late nineteenth century was 'unlikely to be entirely natural in origin' and that the 'balance of evidence ... suggests a discernible human influence on global climate' (IPCC, 1995, para. 2.4). At the second Conference of Parties (COP-2) in Geneva in July 1996, the oil-exporting countries, with the support of Russia, nevertheless argued that there were still too many uncertainties to use the SAR as the basis for recommending urgent action. In the absence of a consensus, and in the face of opposition from a small number of 'laggard' states, the meeting was only able to 'note' rather than adopt its own (non-binding) Ministerial Declaration – the Geneva Declaration – which endorsed the IPCC conclusions and called for legally binding objectives and significant reductions in GHG emissions (Oberthür, 1996, p. 200). In a major shift, however, the US government committed to the need for legally binding targets, although this seems to have been linked to its preference for the introduction of a system of tradeable permits. The negotiations attracted extensive non-state activity from environmentalists and from industry. The Global Climate Coalition, for example, was prominent in lobbying for the interests of the major oil companies sometimes in opposition to the insurance industry, the latter increasingly concerned at the level of risk exposure likely to accompany the impacts of climate change.

The AGBM tabled its draft protocol at the third Conference of Parties at Kyoto in December 1997. Negotiations were heated and fractious. One of the most contentious issues was whether targets should be based on a percentage reduction (favoured by the EU and AOSIS) or upon differentiation – the setting of targets to take account of different capabilities – a strategy favoured by the US, Australia and New Zealand among others. The EU had committed to an ambitious, overall goal of a 15 per cent reduction in emissions by 2010 which gave it the 'moral upper hand' (Andresen and Agrawala, 2002, p. 47) and placed significant pressure on other parties, such as the US and Japan. Other differences arose over the degree of freedom parties should have over policies and measures; whether emissions should be counted on a gross or net basis (the latter including a calculation for sinks such as reafforestation); whether reductions in land clearance would be taken into account (advocated in particular by the Australian government; see Elliott 2002a); the extent to which the parties listed in Annex I to the Convention (developed countries and those undergoing transition to a market economy) could meet their targets by taking action outside their own borders (the question of supplementarity); and whether developing countries should also be required to commit to formal reduction targets.

When the Protocol was finally adopted after a 36-hour non-stop final session on 11 December, the parties listed in Annex B to the Protocol (with only a few exceptions, the same as the parties listed in Annex I to the FCCC) had agreed to reduce overall emissions of six greenhouse gases to at least 5 per cent below 1990 levels by 2008–12. Individual targets vary. Russia and Ukraine have a zero reduction although they already emit considerably less than their 1990 levels. Three industrialized countries are permitted to increase their emissions: Norway (1 per cent); Australia (8 per cent) and Iceland (10 per cent). The agreement covers a comprehensive basket of six gases and includes an array of options for reductions in emissions. These include energy efficiency, sequestering (that is, establishing or enhancing sinks) and 'bubble' arrangements which would allow countries (such as members of the EU) to meet their obligations jointly. The inclusion of the 'do-nothing' sinks associated with land-use change and agricultural soils was controversial not least of all because they 'apply to activities that already occur' and because of the lack of any agreed method of accounting (see Begg, 2002, p. 332).

The Protocol also provides incentives for developed and developing countries to reduce greenhouse emissions and compliance costs through the so-called flexibility mechanisms (the 'flex mechs'). The International Emissions Trading (IET) scheme allows Annex I parties to achieve reductions by trading emissions permits with other Annex I parties. The Clean Development Mechanism (CDM), which developed from a Brazilian proposal for a clean development fund, allows developed countries to gain credit for part of their reduction targets by investing in abatement activities in non-Annex I countries as long as those reductions are additional to what might otherwise have been achieved. The CDM is also intended to contribute to the flow of financial and technological resources to developing countries (see Werksman, 1998 and Haites and Yamin, 2000 for details). Finally, under Joint Implementation (JI) Annex I parties can receive credit by investing in abatement activities overseas, but only in other Annex I countries and, again, only if this results in *extra* reductions in emissions.

The Kyoto Protocol has been described as a 'remarkable achievement' (Grubb, 1998, p. 140), a 'major step forward' (Ott, 1998, p. 17) and 'truly historic' (Burke, 1997, p. 16). Salt has suggested that on entry into force it will be 'one of the most powerful and far-reaching pieces of international law ever drafted' (1998, p. 160). But it was also 'a very long way from what [is] ... needed to ... avoid further climate change' (Burke, 1997, p. 16). The past Chair of the IPCC, Bert Bolin, suggested that the Protocol 'did not achieve much with regard to limiting the buildup of greenhouse gases in the atmosphere' (1998, p. 331). Not surprisingly, the Protocol left a very large number of matters 'ill-defined or undecided' (Lanchbery, 1998, p. 16). These included the question of developing country commitments and the manner in which the various mechanisms would actually be put into practice. The Protocol was criticized for doing little to address the real equity concern that developed countries, and people within them, continue to emit GHG at a much higher per capita rate than do poorer countries. The Global Commons Institute has proposed a 'contraction and convergence' strategy which aims to make both burden-sharing and emissions levels more equal and equitable (see Lisowski, 2002, pp. 165–6; Global Commons Institute, 2003). In fact, many developing countries have adopted energy efficiency policies and other initiatives which will help to reduce their greenhouse emissions (see Dunn, 1998). There were other equity issues as well. Indigenous peoples organizations expressed concern that the 'inclusion of carbon sinks in the CDM will constitute a dangerous tool for the expropriation of [their] lands and territories and culminate in a new form of colonialism' (Indigenous Peoples and Local Communities Caucus on Climate Change, 2001, p. 7). Emissions trading was controversial, in part because it facilitates 'hot air' trading. Because of the collapse of their economies, Russia and the Ukraine are already below their 1990 emissions. The Kyoto targets effectively permit them to 'sell' the difference between this and their 1990 baseline (see Lisowski, 2002, p. 164).

Kyoto to Marrakesh

To come into effect, the Protocol required 55 ratifications including Annex B countries who account for 55 per cent of 1990 carbon dioxide emissions. In effect, this meant that without US participation (36 per cent of industrialized country 1990 emissions) entry into force would be difficult. The Kyoto Protocol ran into trouble almost immediately. The issue of voluntary commitments for developing countries generated heated debate at COP-4 in 1998 and was finally struck from the agenda. At COP-4, parties adopted the Buenos Aires Plan of Action which established a timetable for negotiating the 'modalities' to give practical form to the various broad strategies incorporated in the Protocol. As Bodansky observes, the Kyoto mechanisms require 'a complex institutional apparatus' (2002, p. 2) and few countries were willing to ratify the Protocol without clarity on what that apparatus and rules would look like.

Under the Buenos Aires Plan, rules on the Kyoto mechanisms were scheduled to be adopted at COP-6 in The Hague in November 2000. Despite the best efforts of the President of COP-6, Jan Pronk, the meeting collapsed because of fundamental disagreements between the EU and a loose coalition known as the Umbrella Group (the US, Japan, Canada, Australia, Norway and New Zealand and, later, Russia and Ukraine) over a range of issues, including sinks, compliance, finance, supplementarity and credits (see Begg, 2002 and Egenhofer and Cornillie, 2001 for summaries). Behind-the-scene attempts to reach a deal between the US and the European Union were unsuccessful. In good diplomatic fashion, the meeting was suspended rather than declared closed as a failure. An informal follow-up meeting was held in Ottawa but a later summit in Oslo to bring together EU and Umbrella Group members was cancelled. In March 2001, the US administration announced that it would no longer support the Kyoto Protocol on the grounds that it was 'fatally flawed in fundamental ways' (cited in Lisowski, 2002, p. 162), not least of which because it did not include formal targets for developing countries. The US announcement raised serious concerns that the Protocol would not attract the required ratifications. EU environment ministers reaffirmed their pledge to unilateral action to meet their targets even if the Protocol did not come into effect.

Following further high-level informal consultations in New York in April 2001, COP-6 resumed in Bonn in July 2001 and adopted a package of decisions – the Bonn Agreements – which included text on supplementarity, technology transfer and finance, including the establishment of three new funds for developing countries (see Ott, 2001 for a summary). However, the meeting deferred other important decisions on mechanisms, land-use change and compliance to the seventh Conference of Parties which met very soon thereafter (November 2001) in Marrakesh in a mood of 'exhaustion and impatience' (Boyd and Schipper, 2002, p. 184). The Marrakesh Accords require a significant element of domestic action from parties in meeting their commitments rather than a specific cap on the use of the flexibility mechanisms. Sinks are permitted as CDM projects, but only those relating to afforestation and reforestation. The Accords also established the ground rules for a two-track process of verifying emission reductions under JI projects as well as for evaluation and validation of CDM projects under the oversight of an Executive Board. Projects established as early as 2000 can be eligible for CDM verification. In 2002 the Executive Board announced that companies and other organizations could begin to apply for accreditation as operational entities under the Mechanism although the technical requirements for CDM projects were deferred until COP-9 in 2003. The starting date for IET and JI was set for 2008. There was also agreement that compliance rules would be based on emissions penalties and eligibility to use the flexibility mechanisms but final negotiations on the compliance regime were deferred until the first Meeting of Parties after entry into force.

The IPCC's Third Assessment Report (TAR), released in 2001, confirmed its earlier view that 'warming over the past 100 years is... unlikely to be...entirely natural in origin' (2001, p. 10) and predicted that 'human influences will continue to change atmospheric composition through the 21st century' (IPCC, 2001, p. 12). In February 2002, the US President, George W. Bush, announced a domestic programme for greenhouse reductions, based on voluntary targets (breaking a campaign pledge to impose mandatory reductions for power plants). While criticized for its inadeqacy, some suggest that this policy, tied to the Kyoto reporting dates, appears to leave open the option of the US rejoining the Kyoto process at some stage (see Babiker *et al.*, 2002, pp. 203–4). Japan finally ratified the Protocol in June 2002. At WSSD, Canada and Russia announced that they would do likewise. These three ratifications will mean that the 55 per cent threshhold commitment will be met (although at time of writing the Russian Federation has still to deposit an instrument of ratification) and the Protocol and its various mechanisms for emissions trading and forms of joint implementation will come into legal force.

This changes the political context of the Protocol and it is notable that business interests in the US and in countries such as Australia, which has also refused to ratify, are now split on the value of the agreement and are concerned that they will miss out on opportunities under the CDM and emissions-trading arrangements. Some argue that US rejection of the Protocol may have saved the political process by rallying other countries in support of the results of many years of difficult negotiations (see Claussen, 2001, p. 3). At the same time, the political negotiations since Kyoto have weakened the environmental integrity of the Protocol. Indeed, reports from the UNFCCC reveal that, while emissions from industrialized countries declined overall during the 1990s, they have since risen again and could *increase* to about 17 per cent over the 1990 level by 2010 (UNFCCC, 2003).

Conclusion

The agreements covered in this chapter have been greeted with both optimism and pessimism. In the former case, success is measured in part by the processes of negotiation and the adoption of an agreement, especially those which seem to give voice to the principles of sustainable development and precaution. In the latter, the fact that agreements have relied as much on declaratory principles as they have on specific targets or agreements, with little in the way of effective provisions for implementation, verification and compliance, suggests that they will do little to mitigate the environmental problems they purport to address.

The description of the negotiations and agreements in Chapter 2 and in this chapter have focused primarily on difficulties specific to each of these environmental concerns. Clearly, however, there are patterns of dispute which they share in common. It is those patterns and the questions to which they give rise that are examined more closely in the following chapters of this book – questions of governance and participation, questions about the international political economy, the pursuit of sustainable development and tensions between developed and developing countries, and questions on the fundamental understanding and purpose of environmental security. It will come as no surprise that the answers to those questions and, indeed, the very framing of the questions in the first place, are contested.

Chapter 4

Global Environmental Governance: The State and Institutional Design

Introduction

The globalization of environmental problems described in the first three chapters of this book demands international agreements that can respond to incomplete but changing scientific information and that establish environmental standards and compliance mechanisms by which those standards can be verified and, if necessary, enforced. Environmental governance needs to be cooperative and collective because unilateral action by states is ultimately ineffective in the face of transboundary and global problems and inefficient in the face of shared or common problems. Environmental agreements and the procedures by which they are negotiated also need to account for the interests of a range of stakeholders including environmental non-governmental organizations, grassroots movements, indigenous peoples, industry, financial institutions, scientific bodies and intergovernmental organizations as well as states and governments.

Since the early 1970s, the terrain of environmental governance has become congested with formal and informal institutional structures dedicated to environmental negotiation, standard-setting and the management of transboundary and global environmental change. This includes the various issue-specific secretariats, working groups, conferences of parties and scientific and technical assessment panels identified in Chapters 2 and 3. It also includes regional organizations and associations such as the European Union (EU) or the Association of Southeast Asian Nations (ASEAN) which have inscribed environmental concerns on their agenda. Environmental issues have also been taken up by organizations which represent states defined broadly (sometimes very broadly) by their economic status, such as the OECD, the G7/G8 and the G77.

Despite this institutional attention and despite the declarations, resolutions, conventions and protocols that have been adopted in the years since Stockholm, the overall state of the environment continues to deteriorate (see UNEP, 1997a, 1999a, 2002a). As earlier chapters have suggested, environmental treaties and international environmental institutions have often been less effective than the environmental tasks at hand require. They either lack formal competence, because states are reluctant to give it to them, or they lack real powers, usually for the same reason. Existing institutions are often poorly funded with little political clout. Nor is there much beyond a rhetorical commitment to important cross-sectoral issues of financial and technology transfer, debt relief, unequal trading relationships or poverty alleviation, all of which are crucial to sustainable development. In general, the 'unprecedentedly high degree of international cooperation and mutual understanding' (Fairclough, 1991, p. 83) that is required has not been forthcoming.

This image of a crisis in governance has become central to the global politics of the environment. While there is little dispute that better governance is required, a precise definition of what this means or what it requires is elusive. Analyses of why there is a crisis in governance and what should be done to respond to it fall, admittedly a little untidily, into two broad categories. In liberal-institutionalist terms, governance is embedded in the 'laws and policies that regulate behaviour as well as the institutions that facilitate the adoption and implementation of them' (Soroos, 1994b, p. 301). Better governance is generally perceived as a more effective and efficient form of multilateral management. However, as the Introduction to this book pointed out, governance is something more than institutional structures and processes. It includes the norms, principles and political practices which inform decision-making and influence social and economic behaviour. A more critical approach understands governance as a political practice which simultaneously reflects, constitutes and masks global relations of power and powerlessness. Scholars working within such a tradition question the usefulness of existing institutions and the values that underpin them which are interpreted as representing the interests of states, not peoples, and as reinforcing the practices and beliefs of a neo-liberal economy based on market freedoms. They seek a sometimes radical transformation in the structures, practices and norms of international politics to emphasize social justice, equity and obligations which transcend borders.

In a reformist tradition, international institutions are assumed 'necessarily [to] follow the principle of state sovereignty' (Levy *et al.*, 1992, p. 13). There are, however, doubts as to the extent of cooperation and collective action that can be achieved, through diplomacy, international law and the development of international institutions, in a system of governance in which the sovereignty of states remains a fundamental organizing principle. Hurrell and Kingsbury, for example, question whether 'a fragmented and often highly conflictual political system made up of over 170 sovereign states and numerous other actors [can] achieve the high (and historically unprecedented) levels of cooperation and policy coordination needed to manage environmental problems on a global scale' (1992b, p. 1). Given this, one solution has been to seek ways to make the institutions of the state system more effective and to modify rather than overturn sovereignty. International cooperation is to be achieved 'not by a denial of sovereignty but by new and effective means of enabling nations to exercise ... sovereignty collectively where they can no longer exercise it effectively alone' (Strong, 1973, p. x). Effective institutions are expected to 'nudge countries further along [the] continuum of commitment and compliance', 'promote concern among governments [and] enhance the contractual environment by providing negotiating forums' (Levy *et al.*, 1992, p. 14). In this generally reformist tradition, stronger environmental governance, a kind of collective sovereignty, can best be achieved and indeed perhaps can only be achieved within the institutions of or under the auspices of the United Nations. The United Nations is argued to be uniquely positioned to help governments in the pursuit of environmental security because of its extensive experience, its multidisciplinary capabilities and its (almost) global membership.

As earlier chapters have shown, a considerable amount of environmental activity has proceeded under UN authority since the 1972 Stockholm Conference. Indeed, while institutions outside the United Nations contribute to research and debate on environmental issues and to the body of both soft law (that is, non-legally binding declarations and resolutions) and hard law on international environmental concerns, it is now difficult to think of an environmental issue with global relevance (with the exception perhaps of the Antarctic) which is not in some way managed primarily within the United Nations system. In light of claims about a crisis in global environmental governance and given that many proposals for institutional reform or new institutional structures 'take as their starting point existing weaknesses in the way the UN addresses global environmental problems' (Newell, 2002, p. 660), it is useful to examine how the United Nations *has* responded to the imperatives of global environmental governance.

The United Nations

The management of environment and sustainable development issues is dispersed throughout the United Nations organization and the UN system. Environmental issues are regularly on the agenda of the General

Assembly (GA) and its Second Committee and are given some purpose through GA resolutions. The various commissions of the Economic and Social Council (ECOSOC) have taken up environmental concerns which touch upon their areas of interest. The Commission on the Status of Women, for example, has addressed environmental and development issues as they impact on the world's women. The specialized agencies address environmental issues in accordance with their own mandates. The Food and Agriculture Organization (FAO) focuses on agriculture, forestry and marine resource issues and has been the task manager for the Tropical Forestry Action Plan. The World Meteorological Organization (WMO) has mobilized debate on atmospheric and climate issues, convened the World Climate Conferences and has been a lead agency in the Intergovernmental Panel on Climate Change. The International Maritime Organization (IMO) continues to address marine pollution. The United Nations Development Programme has a mandate which encompasses the environmental impact of development activities and the relationship between poverty, maldevelopment or underdevelopment and environmental degradation. Indeed, the UNDP is an important actor within the UN system in terms of the cross-sectoral complexities of environmental insecurity. Environmental governance also extends to those institutions, such as the World Bank, which are not directly responsible to the UN organization but which are nevertheless considered part of the broad UN 'family'. Within the UN system, three bodies have mandates which are specifically directed towards environmental issues. They are the United Nations Environment Programme, the Commission on Sustainable Development and the Global Environment Facility.

The United Nations Environment Programme (UNEP)

UNEP was a product of the Stockholm Conference. It was established in 1973, in accordance with General Assembly resolution 2997 of December 1972. UNEP was a political compromise. As noted in Chapter 1, developed countries were reluctant to agree to a new institution that would require further funding commitments from them. Developing countries, concerned that the Stockholm environmental agenda was being defined by the industrialized countries, were reluctant to agree to any new body which they thought could place constraints on their development. UN agencies which were already undertaking a range of environment-related tasks were generally suspicious of a new specialized agency that might challenge or undermine their responsibilities. UNEP was therefore established as a programme within the UN system, not as a specialized agency. A secretariat is charged with the day-to-day running of the programme under the guidance of an Executive Director, but overall policy responsibility lies with a 58-member Governing Council which reports to ECOSOC and through it to the General Assembly. UNEP is headquartered in Nairobi, a concession to developing countries. Administrative expenses for the Council and Secretariat come from the UN general budget, but all programme activities are funded from a Voluntary Fund established for that purpose.

UNEP has no executive powers. Its mandate is to monitor, coordinate and catalyse and its main areas of activity derive from the functional components of the Stockholm Plan: global environmental assessment, environmental management activities and supporting measures. Despite its lack of executive powers, UNEP has had some success in overcoming, or at least working around, its rather vague mandate. Imber describes it as a 'modest but energetic catalyst' (1999, p. 331). UNEP has forged partnerships with other intergovernmental and non-governmental organizations, working in partnership with, for example, the WMO to sponsor the World Climate Conferences, the 1987 Bellagio and Villach workshops on climate change, the 1988 Toronto Conference and to convene the IPCC. UNEP and the IUCN took the lead in the development of the 1980 World Conservation Strategy. As previous chapters have shown, it has coordinated international negotiations on ozone depletion, biodiversity and desertification, species and habitat protection, and various aspects of the international chemicals and waste regime, and has taken a lead role in regional seas protection. Through its successful Earthwatch programme, which now has a UN-wide focus, UNEP collects, assesses and monitors information about the environment. UNEP provides secretariat support for a number of multilateral environmental agreements and is now responsible for producing the *Global Environment Outlook* reports.

As Gray points out, UNEP's achievements have been 'substantial, even remarkable, considering the inherent limitations in its mandate and powers, the jealously guarded state sovereignty ... and the sheer complexity and enormity of the problems at hand' (1990, p. 297). However UNEP faces a number of challenges. It has suffered from geographical isolation within the UN system and from a lack of political support from governments. Member states have also been 'singularly parsimonious in their contributions' to UNEP (Hurrell and Kingsbury, 1992b, p. 31). UNEP's total financial resources in its first two decades totalled less than $US1 billion and its annual budget is less than that of most other UN agencies and some of the larger NGOs (see French, 1995, p. 29; WRI, 2003, p. 153). In 1992, for example, the year in which governments committed themselves to the global partnership of Agenda 21, only 75 out of 179 UN member states made contributions to the voluntary Environment Fund, an amount which that year totalled only $62 million and led to suggestions that core programme activities would have to be cut to something in the vicinity of $120 million for the 1994–95 budget (see Anon., 1993b, p. 119). In 2000, governments' contributions to the Environment Fund totalled only $US41 million and UNEP was able to afford its core programme work (estimated at $US50 million) only because it had a carry-over from the previous budget (UNEP, 2001d). Its professional staff is small (about 300 to 400) compared even with its counterparts in national governments (see Biermann, 2002, p. 298). Finally, UNEP now 'faces challenges from a diverse array of other international organisations involved in environmental management' which often have 'better funding...clearer and stronger mandates, and greater support' (Downie and Levy, 2000, pp. 358, 359).

The Commission on Sustainable Development

The Commission on Sustainable Development (CSD) was the product of contentious debates at UNCED about the Conference's institutional recommendations. Some delegations favoured strengthening UNEP. Others wanted a new UN organization which would provide a specifically post-Rio focus. Chapter 38 of Agenda 21, on international institutional arrangements, sought to clarify UNEP's mandate and suggested, *inter alia*, that UNEP should be better provided with financial resources. It also recommended the establishment of a new UN body – CSD – in a 'spirit of reform and revitalisation' (UNCED, 1992b, para. 38. 1). CSD's terms of reference, its composition, guidelines for participation of NGOs and relationships with other UN bodies were set out in General Assembly resolution 47/191. The Commission is comprised of 53 member governments, elected by ECOSOC on the basis of regional representation. As with UNEP, it reports to ECOSOC and through it to the General Assembly. CSD has two broad areas of responsibility. The first is to monitor and examine progress of the UNCED agenda, especially the implementation of Agenda 21 and any problems arising therefrom. This task is to be undertaken primarily through consideration and analysis of information provided by governments in national reports. As part of this responsibility, CSD is expected to review progress on financial resource and technology transfer commitments, on commitments to the UN target of 0.7 per cent ODA/GNP and on the adequacy of funding mechanisms. The Commission has no powers of enforcement if it finds that progress has been slow or non-existent. The Commission's second area of responsibility is the integration of environment and development concerns within the UN system and among governments.

The Commission meets in annual substantive sessions. At its first substantive session in 1993, the Commission adopted a thematic programme of work, focusing on the sectoral and cross-sectoral issues in Agenda 21. Early in 1994, the Commission convened two ad hoc open-ended working groups, one on financial flows and mechanisms and the other on technology transfer and cooperation. In 1995, it established the Intergovernmental Panel on Forests, later replaced by the Intergovernmental Forum on Forests (see Chapter 2). In 1996 CSD-4 (having completed the first programme cycle) took up a number of newer issues including progress on the Programme of Action for the Sustainable Development of Small Island States. The fifth annual meeting was essentially a preparation for the UN Special Session (UNGASS). As well as discussing a draft programme of work for CSD for 1998–2002, and conducting dialogue sessions with all the major groups, delegates worked on preparing the draft final documents for the Special Session. The 1998–2002 Work Programme confirmed at UNGASS identified sectoral, cross-sectoral, economic sector and major group themes with poverty and consumption and production as overarching themes for each year's deliberation. Following WSSD in 2002, the Commission has moved to two-year 'implementation cycles' with review and policy sessions in alternate years. CSD-11 in 2003 adopted seven such cycles, effectively establishing a work programme through to 2017. Poverty eradication, production and consumption, and protection of the natural resource base remain the overarching themes for each of these cycles, the first of which focuses more specifically on water, sanitation and human settlements.

Under-Secretary-General for Policy Coordination and Sustainable Development, Nitin Desai, argued early on that the success of the Commission would depend on the 'political weight given to it by governments' (in Anon., 1995b, pp. 163–4). There is little evidence that governments have been prepared to give the Commission that necessary weight. Charnovitz reports a 'consensus that on the whole the CSD adds little value to the debate on sustainable development' (2002, p. 18). CSD has not been able to move easily from rhetoric and speech-making to dialogue and action. Despite much activity (which has included many intersessional meetings and ad hoc working groups) and despite apparent support from governments in the Johannesburg Declaration and Plan of Implementation, substantive progress has still to be made on states' commitments to the cross-sectoral concerns of financial and technology resources, poverty alleviation or changes in patterns of production and consumption. From the beginning, CSD was weakened by compromise, consigned 'to the dungeon' as Imber puts it (1999, p. 330). Despite the apparent urgency generated at UNCED, the Commission's first session in 1993 (CSD-1) was poorly resourced with 'only a handful of staff...some...borrowed from other departments' and 'difficulty on some days to secure enough rooms for the meetings' (Khor, 1994, p. 103). CSD sessions have been characterized by political disputes and a general reluctance to 'focus on concrete initiatives and proposals aimed at implementing the promises of Rio' (Blumenfeld, 1994, p. 4). There has been, 'even among the seasoned delegates...evidence of increasing cynicism' (*Earth Negotiations Bulletin*, cited in Hyvarinen and Brack, 2000, p. 25). According to Esty, some have even suggested that CSD seems 'designed to waste time and money' (2001, p. 75). The Chair of CSD-4, Henrique Cavalcanti from Brazil, suggested in a frank admission to an NGO meeting that 'he was not sure the CSD would be around after 1997' (in Doran, 1996, p. 100). Clearly that was premature but, as Chasek observes, 'unless...individual governments have the political will to move the dialogue forward, the CSD will not be in any position to prioritize issues or set the international sustainable development agenda' (2000a, p. 390).

The Global Environment Facility

The GEF sits rather awkwardly within the UN system. It was established by the World Bank, the UNDP and UNEP, at a meeting in Paris in November 1990, as a pilot programme to finance projects and training programmes 'for innovations that protect the global environment – through investment, technical assistance...and, to some extent, research' (El-Ashry, 1993, p. 91). Each of the managing agencies plays a specific role in the functioning of the GEF. The UNDP focuses on technical assistance, institutional capacity and project preparation (as well as administering the NGO-linked small-grant programme and the country dialogue workshops). UNEP provides secretariat support for the expert group – the Scientific and Technical Advisory Panel (STAP) – convened to elaborate eligibility criteria and priorities for selecting GEF projects. The STAP also reviews project proposals and coordinates research and data collection. The World Bank administers the Facility, is the repository for the Trust Fund that is the GEF's core fund, and also implements investment projects.

GEF's terms of reference restrict it to funding projects which are of global rather than local environmental significance and which are therefore assumed to benefit the world at large. Its six priorities are the protection of biodiversity, climate change, degradation in international waters, ozone depletion, land degradation and persistent organic pollutants (the latter two added to the GEF portfolio in October 2002). It is the designated financial mechanism under the biodiversity, climate change and POPs conventions. The various Memoranda of Understanding between the GEF and the Conferences of Parties established under those environmental conventions for which it is the interim financial mechanism have been contentious at times. Developed countries in particular have been reluctant to accept any agreement which might seem to abrogate to the Facility *their* decision-making authority on funding. Developing countries accepted the GEF as a funding mechanism reluctantly and only on the grounds that it be restructured to make its processes more transparent and to give them equal representation in decision-making (see UNCED, 1992b, para. 33.16(a)(iii)). That was a slow process. Developing countries, UN agencies and NGOs favoured a governance mechanism that was transparent, accountable and universal whereas OECD countries and the World Bank wanted a tighter, more executive-based structure (see Streck, 2001, p. 4; Sjöberg, 1999). Early discussions broke down at a meeting in Cartagena in 1993 and agreement on the restructured GEF was not reached until March 1994. What is sometimes know as GEF-II has a 34-member council – 16 members from developing countries, 14 from OECD countries and two from economies in transition – which meets every six months. In theory the Council has a double-majority voting system which requires a majority of participating countries plus 60 per cent donor support. This was adopted to meet G77 demands of democracy and transparency (or at least to prevent the donor countries dominating). In practice decisions are taken by consensus. The GEF Assembly meets every three years during which time countries agree on the level of 'replenishment' of the GEF Trust Fund.

While there have been a number of criticisms of the GEF, the most enduring have related to concerns about the lack of transparency and representation and the role of the World Bank (issues which are explored in more detail in Chapter 8). According to Tickell and Hildyard (1992, p. 82), early discussions about the GEF were held only among Northern countries (primarily the G7) with a select group of Southern governments being included only after the World Bank had been selected as the lead agency. Werksman (1993, p. 82) points out that developed countries dominated decision-making in the pilot phase of the GEF, when membership was restricted to those countries which could contribute $US4 million to the Facility's Trust Fund. As noted above, the restructuring of the GEF prior to 1994 was intended to overcome the charges of a lack of transparency and democratic process. As well as the shift in an internal balance of power to provide a greater voice for developing countries, the GEF has also worked to expand its 'engagement with developed and developing country NGOs' to the extent that some suggest it is now 'one of the most transparent international organisations' (WRI, 2003, pp. 152–3; see also Young, 2002, p. 10).

Institutional reform

The United Nations has increasingly come to be perceived as ineffective in providing a lead in environmental governance. For many, the reasons are to be found in the structure of the organization. The UN is viewed as unwieldy, unresponsive and underfunded, characterized by demarcation and duplication of responsibilities. Maurice Williams argues that 'the organisation has become too complex ... proliferation has produced too many bodies ... with overlapping agenda and fragmentation of efforts. As a result, authority and responsibility have become blurred and coordination almost an end in itself' (1992, p. 24). Environmental governance has also been seen as hostage to intra-UN politics and claims to issue-sovereignty among UN bodies. The President of the UNEP Governing Council has defined the problem thus: 'the proliferation of institutional arrangements, meetings and agenda is weakening policy coherence and synergy and increasing the negative impact of limited resources' (cited in Charnovitz, 2002, p. 17).

Two themes have been central to debates about reform of the United Nations. The first is the need for an authoritative environmental body with the 'capacity to control and deploy ... resources' if it is to meet the environmental objectives member states set for it (Commission on Global Governance, 1995, p. 4). The second is that the growing institutional and policy complexity brings with it demands for effective coordination. The UN has generally failed on the first – or perhaps it is more accurate to say that member states have failed – and it has struggled with the second.

There has been no scarcity of suggestions about how to reform, strengthen and better coordinate the institutions of the UN to improve its contribution to environmental governance. Some have sought to strengthen General Assembly competence over environmental issues by reconstituting one of its committees as an 'environmental committee' or by creating a new committee. Yet the committee system mirrors General Assembly state-centric politics and neither the committees nor the Assembly have executive authority. Suggestions have also been made for a standing commission on the environment and development or an international environmental ombuds-office (Schrijver, 1989) which could receive petitions from individuals and NGOs and possibly even have the authority to establish multilateral inspection teams for environmental fact-finding and monitoring. There have been suggestions that the

Trusteeship Council, now well past the end of its useful life, be revamped as an Environmental Trusteeship Council. This suggestion seems to have been first made by the President of the World Federation of United Nations Associations (see Palmer, 1992, p. 279) but was also taken up by UNCED Secretary-General Maurice Strong (see Imber, 1994, p. 106) and by United Nations Secretary-General Kofi Annan (UNSG, 1997c, para. 85). Whether it would be accepted as such by developing countries, given its neo-colonial history, and whether this would be possible under its existing mandate, is another matter. Other proposals have called for environmental threats to be incorporated into the mandate of the Security Council, or for the Security Council to convene special sessions on environmental insecurities, in much the same way that it holds special sessions on disarmament, or for an Environmental Security Council to be established. Some proposals have anticipated a new body of some kind. The World Commission on Environment and Development recommended strengthening UNEP and called for better and more effective inter-agency coordination (WCED, 1987, pp. 316–23). It anticipated a new Board of Sustainable Development with powerful supervisory and coordination functions (WCED, 1987, pp. 318–19). The Hague Declaration of 1989 recommended a new international authority with decision-making powers and the right to act without consensus to overcome the inadequacies of existing institutions. In the same year, the New Zealand government proposed the establishment of a UN-based Environmental Protection Council (see Palmer, 1992, p. 279).

The UN Conference on Environment and Development was convened in 1992 with calls for some kind of institutional renewal. Conference objectives included the 'review and [examination] of the role of the United Nations system in dealing with the environment and possible ways of improving it' (UNGA, 1989c, Part I, para. 15(q)) and a whole chapter in Agenda 21 (Chapter 38) was devoted to institutional issues. Five years later, the Secretary-General's 1997 Program for Reform included the objective of strengthening the UN's capacity in its sustainable development and environmental dimensions. In 1998, as part of that reform process, the Secretary-General appointed a Task Force on Environment and Human Settlements, chaired by UNEP Executive Director Klaus Töpfer. The report, which was submitted to the General Assembly in 1999, reflected the view that 'the institutional fragmentation and loss of policy coherence ... had resulted in a loss of effectiveness in the work of the UN in the area of environment and human settlements' (Töpfer, 1998, p. 1). The institutional problems in the UN were characterized as 'basic and pervasive' (United Nations Task Force, 1999, para. 20). The Task Force made a number of recommendations which called for a results-oriented approach to effective inter-agency coordination and the strengthening of UNEP as the lead environmental agency within the UN.

Charnovitz points out that governments, in response to their concern 'about the fragmentation of environmental institutions ... [then] created *three* new ones to deal with the problem' (2002, p. 18; emphasis in original). General Assembly resolution 53/242 established a Global Ministerial Environmental Forum (GMEF) tied to UNEP (see UNGA, 1999). The same resolution approved the Secretary-General's proposal for an Environmental Management Group (EMG) to enhance inter-agency coordination in the field of environment and human settlements. UNEP's Governing Council, in Decision 21/21 of 2001, also established an Open-ended Intergovernmental Group of Ministers or their Representatives to examine options for strengthening international environmental governance. The World Summit on Sustainable Development in 2002 was also expected, in much the same way as UNCED and UNGASS, to 'address ways of strengthening the institutional framework for sustainable development' (UNGA, 2000, para. 15(e)). France and Germany led an unsuccessful push for a world environment organization. The Johannesburg Plan of Implementation made a number of general statements about the institutional framework and the importance of good governance and a vibrant and effective UN system. It called for stronger collaboration within the UN system (United Nations, 2002b, para. 140(b)) and encouraged the General Assembly to consider the 'important but complex' issue of universal membership of the UNEP Council (United Nations, 2002b, para. 140(d)). Under the Plan, governments also targeted CSD as the 'forum for consideration of issues related to the integration' of various dimensions of sustainable development and argued that the Commission should be 'strengthened' (United Nations, 2002b, para. 145) although it gave little guidance as to how this might happen.

Suggestions for a new institution have coalesced around the need for some kind of World or Global Environment Organization (WEO/GEO). The motivation has been not only to overcome the problems of fragmentation and duplication but also to provide a counterweight to the power of the WTO and what is seen to be the increasing dominance of trade principles over environmental concerns. Such a body would, as German Chancellor Kohl has put it, provide a 'clearly audible voice at the United Nations' for global environmental protection and sustainable development (cited in Simonis, 2002, p. 30). A variety of models have been proposed for such an organization, ranging from a hierarchical and centralized body with considerable powers to a more loose form of clustering of MEAs and their secretariat (for a summary of the history and the main proposals see Charnovitz, 2002; Lodefalk and Whalley, 2002; Simonis, 2002). There are considerable differences over the role of such a body with respect to rule-making, standard-setting and enforcement; its relationship with existing MEAs; whether it should be part of the UN or independent of it; whether it would advantage or disadvantage the interests of developing countries; and the scope of the problems any such body should address. Opposition to such a body rests on concerns about the rigidities of centralization as opposed to consolidation (although few proposals anticipate a hierarchical body) and the consequences of what some have interpreted as a focus on environment to the exclusion of development, a separation that former Executive Director of the Convention on Biodiversity, Calestous Juma, has called 'impracticable and tactless' (2000, p. 9).

Strengthening UNEP

It is generally accepted that the most realistic proposals are those which anticipate a WEO or GEO that either 'adds new flanks to UNEP' or actually incorporates UNEP (see Charnovitz, 2002, p. 20). Proposals for reform have included strengthening UNEP through providing it with more resources, reforming its mandate to give it more political authority, or reforming the role of the Executive Director, perhaps as a Special Commissioner for the Global Environment (on the latter, see PRIO, 1989, p. 22). There has been a repetitive monotony to the political rhetoric that has accompanied calls to enhance UNEP. Agenda 21 sought to clarify an 'enhanced and strengthened' role for UNEP (UNCED, 1992b, para. 31.21) and recommended that UNEP would require access to 'greater expertise and provision of adequate financial resources' (1992b, para. 38.23). At the same time, however, the decision to establish the Commission on Sustainable Development 'undermined UNEP's prestige and confused its mission' (French, 1995, p. 32). The requirement that CSD facilitate the integration of environment and development concerns within the UN seemed to relieve UNEP of its own coordinating role but left it open to be coordinated by the Commission.

By the mid-1990s there was a strong feeling that UNEP was facing an institutional crisis, that it was increasingly undemocratic and directionless despite its achievements to date (see Sandbrook, 1999; Downie and Levy, 2000). The 19th session of the UNEP Governing Council, held early in 1997, adopted the Nairobi Declaration in which Council members called for a 'strong, effective and revitalized' UNEP, declared that UNEP should be the 'leading global environmental authority' and stated that they would work to improve the Programme's governing structure. They called for 'adequate, stable and predictable financial resources'

(UNEP, 1997b). Less than six months later, at the 1997 General Assembly Special Session, the governments of Germany, Brazil, South Africa and Singapore submitted a joint declaration calling for UNEP to be 'reformed and strengthened ... [as] the world's environmental conscience' and for the 'establishment of a global environmental umbrella organisation of the UN' (Joint Declaration, 1997). As Charnovitz observes, the declaration 'did not meet with enthusiasm' (2002, p. 8). The only consensus that could be reached was (echoing Agenda 21) to call again for an enhanced role and adequate funding for a revitalized UNEP. Kofi Annan's 1997 reform agenda averred, yet again, that high priority had to be given to UNEP to ensure the 'status, strength and access to resources it requires to function effectively as the environmental agency of the world community' (UNSG, 1997c, para. 176). At UNEP's 20th Governing Council in February 1999, governments promised, as they had done so many times before, to provide 'adequate, stable and predictable financial resources' (UNEP, 1999b, para. 1). General Assembly resolution 53/242, which established the Global Ministerial Environmental Forum (GMEF), requested the Secretary-General to strengthen UNEP by ensuring that it had adequate support and predictable financial resources. At its first meeting in Malmö, Sweden in 2000, the GMEF stressed the importance of a 'greatly strengthened institutional structure for international environmental governance' and called for UNEP's role to be 'strengthened and its financial base broadened and made more predictable' (Global Ministerial Environment Forum, 2000, para. 24). As noted above, the WSSD Plan of Implementation did little more than to offer a general endorsement of these earlier commitments to strengthen UNEP and improve coordination with the UN system.

Better coordination?

Despite or perhaps because of this almost constant focus on reform and reorganization, responsibility for environmental protection and sustainable development remains dispersed throughout the UN system. Sandbrook describes it as 'Byzantine' (1999, p. 173). Further, the administrative structures for environmental protection and sustainable development are geographically scattered. UNEP resides in Nairobi, the CSD Secretariat is based in New York. The Global Environment Facility is headquartered in Washington, DC. The secretariat for the various global conventions are also scattered: Montreal for the Biodiversity Convention; Bonn for the Climate Change and Desertification conventions; Geneva for CITES and the Basel Convention. As conventions become more cross-referenced and entwined, and as policy becomes more complicated, there is (as UNEP has acknowledged) a 'compelling rationale for ... rationalising, streamlining and consolidating the present system' (cited in Biermann, 2002, p. 300).

Coordination on environmental issues has become increasingly confused since Rio, comprehensible only to the most assiduous observer or the most experienced UN insider. Konrad von Moltke has argued that the United Nations is 'famously resistant to coordination' (2001, p. 24). It seems rather less allergic to coordinating bodies. Coordination among various UN bodies and agencies was initially the responsibility of the Environment Coordination Board established following the Stockholm Conference in 1972. It was wound up in 1977 and its responsibilities taken over by the Administrative Committee on Coordination (ACC). Chapter 38 of Agenda 21 identified the need for 'a coordination mechanism under the direct leadership of the Secretary-General' (UNCED, 1992b, para. 38.16), recommending that the task be given to the ACC but also suggesting that there should be a high-level advisory body to provide expert advice on sustainable development issues (UNCED, 1992b, para. 38.18). Within a few months of UNCED a flurry of reform gave rise to the Department for Policy Coordination and Sustainable Development (DPCSD), the High-Level Advisory Board on Sustainable Development (HLAB) and the Inter-Agency Committee on Sustainable Development (IACSD). DPCSD included the Division for Sustainable Development (DSD) which in turn was to act as the Secretariat for the CSD. The IACSD was mandated to 'identify major policy issues and ensure effective system-wide cooperation and coordination' (see Flanders, 1997, p. 392). The implementation of its functions, however, was turned over to a series of Task Managers involving almost *every* other organization or programme within the UN.

Following more reform in mid-1997, the Division for Sustainable Development (DSD) became part of the new Department of Economic and Social Affairs (DESA) which was itself formed from the merger of DPCSD with two other secretariat departments to achieve further streamlining and efficiencies. Expectations within the UN were that the DSD would 'enhance the capacity of the Secretariat to support action at all levels to implement Agenda 21 and to ensure greater coherence in the Secretariat's work in the area of sustainable development in general' (UNGA, 1997, para. 19), which would suggest (even with a generous interpretation) that earlier reforms had not worked. Both DSD and UNEP participate in the Executive Committee on Economic and Social Affairs (ECESA), one of four new executive committees established in 1997 to 'sharpen ... the organization by reducing duplication of effort and facilitating greater complementarity and coherence' (UN-DESA, 1999). In 1999, as noted above, the General Assembly approved the establishment of an Environmental Management Group, chaired by the Executive Director of UNEP, to improve inter-agency and inter-MEA coordination. In October 2000, the United Nations System Chief Executives Board for Coordination (CEB – the old Administrative Committee on Coordination) established a High-Level Committee on Programmes to ensure coordination in programme areas including sustainable development. A year later, new administrative arrangements saw the abolition of the Inter-Agency Committee on Sustainable Development (established after UNCED), replaced by an Inter-Agency Meeting on Sustainable Development as part of a process to pursue coordination through more informal and flexible mechanisms. As Mark Imber has noted elsewhere, the UN's 'way of streamlining itself can move grown men [sic] to tears' (1994, p. 116).

The limits to reform: a critical position

If UNCED and its successor negotiations did not respond adequately to 'growing pressure for a more effective system of world governance' (Davison and Barns, 1992, p. 10), the question is why. Where do the problems lie? Is it because of 'shortcomings in institutions, political will and resources' (Thacher, 1991, p. 435) or is there a more fundamental problem? One line of critique focuses on the institutional character of the United Nations itself. Critics identify a cultural resistance to change within the United Nations which means that this is an organization which simply cannot manage a mandate for change. The UN is argued to be an inward-looking, cumbersome body, echoing a distant past of 50 years ago, encumbered with employees whose tenure nearly matches the age of the UN, dominated by appointment on the basis of politics, not merit, at a time when brilliance is needed (see Kildow, 1992; also Imber, 1999 for more on staffing and appointment issues in the UN). In this view, then, the reason that the UN has not been able to respond to growing pressure for change in a more effective way is that it cannot do so and that expectations otherwise are misplaced and unwarranted.

Institutional culture, however, is only part of the problem for critical scholars. Reformist arguments which focus on institutional design suggest that it is possible to manage environmental problems without addressing the underlying political and economic structures in which environmental degradation is embedded. For others, this is inadequate as a response to the crisis of environmental governance. One fundamental cause of institutional failure and the crisis in environmental governance is argued to lie in an incongruence between problems which arise from the interconnected and interdependent nature of the global ecosystem and solutions which are sought in the framework of a geopolitical system based on the state. As the World Commission on Environment and Development observed, 'the Earth is one but the world is not' (1987, p. 27) – and that is part of the problem.

Sovereignty and the inadequate state

Global environmental problems increasingly call into question the adequacy and authority of the state, the reality and utility of sovereignty as a fundamental international norm, and the nature of international governance which the state and sovereignty engender. It is not simply that the unilateral state cannot meet the challenges of global environmental change through self-help when the causes of that change lie outside its borders. It is that the state itself – its autonomy, capacity and legitimacy – is being eroded, or at least challenged, by the very nature of environmental problems which do not respect territorial borders. Brenton argues that the 'emergence of the [environmental] agenda is plainly a symptom of the diminishing authority of the nation-state' (1994, p. 7). Doubts about the ability of the state to fulfil the social contract to provide security for its citizens by 'defending' them against, in this case, externally sourced environmental threats create ambivalence about its normative appeal as the basis for political community. The state is, at best, an ambivalent defender of environmental security (Boulding, 1991). Gwyn Prins goes even further: we live, he suggests, in the era of the incapable state, an era characterized by the 'waning ability of state power to engage with the environmental security agenda' (1990, p. 722).

This focus on the state is inextricably linked with the principle of national sovereignty and its relevance in a world now beset by the competing trends of globalization and fragmentation which blur the distinction between domestic jurisdiction and the realm of international relations. As a report on environmental security published by UNEP and the Peace Research Institute in Oslo (PRIO) put it, 'the notion of sovereignty is difficult (if not impossible) to maintain within an ecological frame of reference' (PRIO, 1989, p. 18). Yet the principle of national sovereignty remains central to global environmental governance and, more specifically, to the institutional structures of the UN. Principle 21 of the 1972 Stockholm Declaration provides that:

> States have, in accordance with the Charter of the United Nations and the principles of international law, the sovereign right to exploit their own resources pursuant to their own environmental policies, and the responsibility to ensure that activities within their jurisdiction

or control do not cause damage to the environment of other States or of areas beyond the limits of national jurisdiction.

This was revamped as principle 2 of the Rio Declaration with the inclusion of sovereignty over developmental as well as environmental policy. The Rio agreements reinforced the 'rhetoric of responsible states' (Davison and Barns, 1992, p. 10) and sustained rather than challenged the primacy of national (environmental) sovereignty. The wording of principle 2 appears in some form in almost all of the global MEAs. This dominance of sovereignty concerns has been reinforced rather than challenged by continued tensions between the developed and developing countries. In the absence of any firm commitments from the developed countries on financial and technology transfer, or assistance to address causes and impact, the developing countries have reasserted sovereignty to protect their right to development. The sovereignty imperative also explains why states are generally reluctant to abrogate authority to international environmental institutions on issues such as standard setting, monitoring or enforcement. Institutional frameworks are rarely authoritative and remain under the control of governments. The United Nations is intergovernmental and therefore, as Australia's former Foreign Minister Gareth Evans noted, 'at the end of the day ... [it can] do no more than ... its member states allow it to do or give it the resources to do' (1994, p. 1). Charnovitz points out that 'if governments *wanted* to make UNEP stronger now, they could do so' (2002, p. 15; emphasis added) which raises important quesetions about whether a world environment organization would fare any better.

Sovereignty concerns ensure that questions of sanctions, verification procedures, compliance mechanisms or dispute settlement mechanisms remain politically contentious in environmental negotiations. As sovereign actors, states cannot be bound without their consent in international law. Thus environmental negotiation proceeds on the basis of consensus among parties (although this does not prevent them from then refusing to sign or ratify, as happened with the Biodiversity Convention and the Kyoto Protocol). As Chapters 2 and 3 have demonstrated, it often also results in lowest common denominator agreements shaped as much if not more by political and economic compromises as by environmental concerns. Inordinate amounts of time are often given over to procedural matters, such as the setting of the agenda, the focus and composition of working groups, the election of officers, the nature of seating arrangements, to ensure that no one country or group of countries feels disadvantaged in the subsequent substantive negotiation. The consequence of the sovereignty-driven consensus imperative is that negotiations are often lengthy but final agreements are often cobbled together hurriedly in the final hours of the final days. The agreements adopted might meet the test of success measured in terms of agreement about words on paper but their success as environmental instruments is open to question.

The role of the state is not, however, fixed in the global politics of the environment, particularly in light of the contested and uncertain relationship between globalization and the sovereign state. While the state as interested self-maximizer or agent of elite economic interests is perceived as 'enemy' of the environment, the state is also the vehicle by which those corporate interests can be challenged. The role of the state in the face of the environmental challenges of globalization can thus be strengthened because it has the resources to enforce implementation of environmental agreements even as those international environmental agreements themselves are seen to constrain sovereign choice and actions.

In the face of the ambiguity of the state, better governance requires also that the concept and practice of state sovereignty be reconceptualized (rather than simply made more cooperative) and that the practice of global governance be decentralized and democratized. Without this, institutional reform can only ever be a partial and incomplete response to the environmental crisis. Reconceptualizing sovereignty as the basis for environmental governance is a difficult task. Reeves puts it well: this should not be about giving something up, but about creating something that we lack (cited in Mische, 1989, p. 402). The state should be displaced (not, note, *re*placed) as the '*sole* legitimate source of public policy' (Levy *et al.*, 1992, p. 36; emphasis added). Sovereignty would thus become a multilayered, multifaceted concept and practice incorporating concern for planetary sovereignty and the sovereignty of peoples. French understands this as a 'sovereignty derived and legitimised not through abstract juridical principle but constituted with reference to a new normative framework ... to accomplish ... objectives deemed to be for the public good' (2002, p. 141).

In practice, this requires a greater democratizing of environmental governance to incorporate not only more participants (or 'stakeholders') but also to pay greater attention to and respond more effectively to local voices and local concerns rather than seeing the state as the sole arbiter of competing interests in the determination of public policy. The rationale for this is that the global, as it is presently constructed, does not represent universal human interests, but rather 'a particular local and parochial interest which has been globalized through the scope of its reach' (Shiva, 1993, p. 150). That 'parochial interest' reflects the concerns of the most powerful industrialized countries and the world's elites. Collective sovereignty and institutional reform are perceived as a form of 'globalisation from above' designed to prop up existing power structures and elite interests rather than a genuine attempt at transformation. What is required, then, is that environmental governance is humane governance, based on a bottom-up democratization that emphasizes the participatory, dialogic and consent-based ethic of a cosmopolitan democracy (see, for example, Archibugi, 2001). These processes of participation, democratization and the revitalization of civil society as a key component of global environmental governance provide the focus for the next chapter.

Chapter 5

Global Environmental Governance: Democratization and Local Voices

Debates about participation in and democratization of global environmental governance have involved two themes. The first, which is primarily institutional, emphasizes international pluralism and the inclusion of new, non-state players in the processes of negotiation and governance. Agenda 21 devotes several chapters to what are there defined as the 'major groups' or the 'independent sector', identifying for such actors and sectors of the community an important role in the pursuit of sustainable development. This participation of non-state actors is deemed to be important to environmental governance for reasons based on democratic efficiency. Multilateral decision-making and the implementation of environmental agreements is argued to be more effective if all stakeholders are represented and if other actors besides states are recognized as having legitimate interests and a legitimate role to play. In a speech in 1987, Gro Harlem Brundtland argued that a political system that secures effective participation in decision-making is a major prerequisite for sustainable development (cited in Starke, 1990, p. 64). This kind of pluralist analysis of participatory sustainable development tends to focus on the roles that non-governmental actors play and the strategies they adopt as they seek to influence governments and intergovernmental organizations in the making and implementation of international environmental policy.

The second theme emphasizes the significance of global civil society as a site of political action rather than investigating stakeholders as institutional phenomena whose importance is understood mainly in terms of their relationship with a state-centric system of environmental governance. There has been much unrest among NGOs and grass-roots movements that pluralist forms of democratization have done little to ensure that environmental outcomes are democratic or equitable. The poor, indigenous peoples and women, especially in developing countries, continue to be disproportionately affected by the impact of environmental

113

degradation while contributing little, globally, to their causes. Democratization is therefore about opening a political space for marginalized voices and those for whom environmental degradation is symptomatic of a broader structural oppression and silencing. Shiva argues that 'the roots of the ecological crisis at the institutional level lie in the alienation of the rights of local communities to actively participate in environmental decisions' (1993, p. 155). Analyses of this kind have tended to emphasize the dynamic nature of global civil society as 'an alternative organising principle for world politics, based on new constitutive rules and institutional forms' (Conca and Lipschutz, 1993, p. 9). Global civil society, in this view, is something more than an aggregate of non-governmental organizations and community groups. It contributes to 'a renewal of international solidarities' (Chartier and Deléage, 1998, p. 29). It represents the politics of resistance, contestation and transformation, a response to statism and the inadequacies of a geopolitical order which has proved of limited success in addressing global environmental degradation, and which has also marginalized local concerns and the voices of the disadvantaged. Indeed, the latter (marginalization) is offered as an explanation for the former (that is, limited success). Participation and democratization are therefore seen as fundamental to the 'effective control of change by those most directly affected' (Hontelez, 1988, p. 762), a process Tinker identifies as a 'return to the sovereignty of the people' (1993, p. 15).

In exploring these two themes, this chapter begins with an examination of two important 'stakeholder' groups – the scientific community and the corporate community. It then turns to focus on what is broadly understood as global civil society, articulated primarily through the networks of non-governmental organizations and grass-roots movements. As discussed here, this label encompasses a diversity of organizations, ideologies and strategies. The chapter finishes with an exploration of the politics of exclusion or powerlessness that a more radical or more inclusively cosmopolitan approach to the democratization of global environmental governance seeks to expose and overcome. The discussion here focuses on women and indigenous peoples.

Science and environmental governance

The scientific community (in as much as it is possible to speak of a 'community' which covers such a range of scientific endeavour) has become increasingly important to environmental governance through policy advocacy and through contribution to knowledge about the causes and consequences of environmental change. As transnational policy actors, scientists and the scientific knowledge that is their product have also become politicized and caught up in ethical debates about the production and exploitation of that knowledge.

As Chapters 2 and 3 demonstrated, scientists have helped to mobilize public debate and force governments to act on environmental problems. Scientists within government agencies, within intergovernmental organizations (such as the WMO, IMO, UNEP and others) and within nongovernmental scientific organizations (the International Council of Scientific Unions (ICSU) has perhaps the highest profile) have played an important role in the development of international agreements and in the dissemination of information and knowledge about environmental problems. In doing so, they have become part of the political process, contributing to and becoming involved in decision-making and standard-setting. The Brundtland Report summarized this role thus: 'identifying risks … assessing environmental impact and designing and implementing measures to deal with them' (WCED, 1987, p. 326). Most environmental regimes have scientific committees or various expert subsidiary bodies whose purpose is to provide scientific advice. It is now standard practice for scientific organizations to be granted observer status at conferences of parties and other negotiating or consultative fora.

Scientific inquiry is an important factor in determining the level of commitment by governments and encouraging compliance with multilateral environmental agreements. It informs the objectives and targets incorporated in environmental agreements and the reassessment of those targets is expected to proceed on the basis of best available scientific information. The influence of scientific assessment relies on 'scientific credibility, political legitimacy and policy salience' (Selin and Eckley, 2003, p. 19). In fact, Lidskog and Sundqvist go so far as to suggest that 'science has no strength in *itself*' and is given strength only by 'different institutions and actors' (2002, p. 77; emphasis added). Yet science is also 'environmentalism's favourite battleground' (Jasanoff, 1997, p. 582). The processes by which scientific knowledge is legitimized and given authority privileges that knowledge and those who hold it. Knowledge which does not fit within the scientific paradigm – such as indigenous knowledge – is therefore often marginalized and discounted. A more critical approach to the sociology of knowledge is wary of the 'superiority complex' which constructs environmental problems as 'strictly scientific and technical' and devalues the social and political dimensions of environmental degradation (see Gudynas, 1993, p. 172; Breyman, 1993).

Haas has identified the importance of scientists as epistemic communities – 'transnational networks of knowledge-based communities that are both politically empowered through their claims to exercise authoritative knowledge and motivated by shared causal and principled beliefs' (1990, p. 349). This is not always a disinterested participation. As Stairs and Taylor note, 'scientists are a lobby group in their own right' (1992, p. 122), sometimes pursuing their own advantage or particular interests which may be related to funding or disputes within the scientific community as well as the imperative of seeking action on environmental problems. In other words, scientists are often political actors as well as policy actors. Science has also become politicized in the way that the results of scientific research, which are often subject to uncertainties and differences within the scientific community, have been appropriated by policy-makers in the pursuit of political and economic interests. As Rosenau points out, 'perhaps no issue area on the global agenda relies more heavily on scientific proof as the means through which persuasion and influence is exercised' (1993, p. 81). Chapter 3 showed how, with respect to climate change, policy-makers argued against environmental targets based on a lack of scientific certainty. Yet as Litfin demonstrates, with respect to ozone depletion, 'even within a relatively *narrow* range of scientific uncertainty, nations can easily interpret the available knowledge according to their perceived interests' (1993, p. 100; emphasis added). Susskind and Ozawa (1992, p. 160) argue that this can undermine the integrity of scientific analysis. The value of scientific inquiry is also caught up in political tensions between developed and developing countries. Much of the scientific research that is undertaken in support of or in contribution to environmental governance is conducted by 'the nationals of developed countries' which leads 'developing countries ... on occasion ... to be suspicious of assertions of scientific authorities that also happen to serve developed-country interests' (Richardson, 1992, p. 177).

Corporate environmentalism

Corporate interests and actors have become a key aspect of the global politics of the environment, a phenomenon Falkner refers to as 'private environmental governance' (2003, p. 72). Corporate activity has been and continues to be a major direct and indirect cause of environmental decline through industrial pollution, exploitation of resources and environmental services, investment strategies, and the environmental impact of international trade. In the context of the global politics of the environment, considerable attention has focused on multinational corporations (MNCs). MNCs have an influential role in the world economy through their control of global wealth and their ability to influence poor and not-so-poor governments with respect to environmental standards.

In the mid-1990s, the top 500 controlled 70 per cent of world trade and 80 per cent of foreign investment (Chatterjee and Finger, 1994, p. 106) and the top 200 controlled 28 per cent of world GDP (Korten, 1997, p. 231). They often have annual sales income which totals more than the GDP of many countries, not all of them developing ones (see UNDP, 1999, p. 32).

MNCs have made a significant contribution to resource depletion and global pollution. For example, they are 'the largest users of raw materials globally' and, in the mid-1990s, the top 500 MNCs 'generate[d] more than half the greenhouse gas emissions produced annually' (Miller, 1995, p. 19). Twenty of them controlled almost 90 per cent of global pesticide sales (see Chatterjee and Finger, 1994, p. 106) and, globally, they have extensive control over land under cultivation for export crops. MNCs, and industry interests generally, therefore have a major stake in the kinds of rules that are adopted nationally and internationally to control pollution and resource depletion. Corporate actors have adopted network and coalition strategies and have established a prominent presence at international environmental negotiations as well as supporting research and funding think-tanks (see, for example, Beder, 2001). They have influenced the kinds of standards set (or, in some cases, not set) in MEAs, at times relying on political allies in government who are prepared to oppose tight regulations. Industry groups can also influence the scientific research agenda and government policies through alliances with 'research institutes, agricultural colleges, regulatory agencies, government ministries and aid agencies' (Miller, 1995, p. 36). A number of detailed policy studies provide examples of how corporate and MNC interests have organized through industry-based coalitions to influence environmental decision-making and standard-setting. Examples include the US-based Alliance for Responsible CFC Policy which opposed control of ozone-depleting substances (Parson, 1993); industry groups in the LRTAP meetings (Levy, 1993); oil companies and shipping opposing regulatory mechanisms to control maritime oil pollution (Mitchell, 1993); the fossil fuel industry in the climate change negotiations (Hildyard, 1993; Hamilton, 1998; Levy and Egan, 2003); and the biotechnology industry in the biodiversity negotiations (Hildyard, 1993; Miller, 1995). Nevertheless, corporate interests do not always present as a coherent bloc and Falkner cautions against understating the degree of variation within the corporate community and among business actors (2003, p. 74). The climate change negotiations, for example, have seen the insurance and environmental technology industry ranged against the fossil fuel industry and, as the Kyoto Protocol looks set to become a reality, splits within the latter as well.

MNCs have generally resisted formal public scrutiny of their environmental activities. Certainly there was little discussion on corporate pollution at UNCED (Chatterjee and Finger, 1994, p. 106). Draft recommendations on the regulation of MNCs produced by the United Nations Centre on Transnational Corporations included 'proposals for greater accountability, a 10-year goal for harmonising of company-level environmental accounting and reporting procedures, and environmental pricing' (Grubb *et al.*, 1993, p. 38). The G77, with the support of some Northern countries such as Sweden, was keen for these recommendations to go to the early PrepComms. However, they were effectively dropped at PrepComm IV (see Thomas, 1993, p. 19). Grubb and colleagues suggest that many governments were 'reluctant to engage such powerful [business] interests' (1993, pp. 38–9). Agenda 21 generally cast business and industry as a part of the solution rather than as a major source of the problem of environmental degradation and unsustainable development. Chapter 30 ('Strengthening the role of business and industry') praised the corporate sector's voluntary initiatives and self-regulation, and emphasized the importance of economic interests and free-market mechanisms as the best framework within which business and industry could make the most effective contribution to sustainable development. Businesses were encouraged to adopt 'enlightened' practices such as cleaner production and responsible entrepreneurship.

Corporate actors were made even more a part of the solution through the Global Compact, announced by the UN Secretary-General in 1999 at the World Economic Forum in Davos and launched officially on 26 July 2000. The Compact, under the auspices of the ILO, UNEP and the UN High Commissioner for Human Rights, 'seeks to engage corporations in the promotion of equitable labour standards, respect for human rights and the protection of the environment' in order to 'weave universal values into the fabric of global markets and corporate practices' (UNSG, 2000, p. 37). The WSSD Plan of Implementation calls upon the international community to 'promote corporate responsibility and accountability' (United Nations, 2002b, para. 140(f)) but the emphasis on voluntary regulation remains. Hughes and Wilkinson have described the commitments to the Compact as 'a marketing opportunity for large-scale business rather than a brake on the pursuit of profit maximisation for its own sake' (2001, p. 157) and Bruno and Karliner provide examples of the 'Global Compact violators' (2002, pp. 37–8).

In response to public concern and, at times, outrage over corporate activity, as well as demands for green or ethical investment opportunities, business and industry have sought to improve their environmental credentials and their image of good corporate citizenship. The World Business Council for Sustainable Development (WBCSD) argues that there is a 'strong and compelling business case … for pursuing a mission of sustainable development' and that case rests on the 'financial bottom line' (2002, pp. 226, 227). One of the major expressions of international 'green corporatism' has been the Business Charter for Sustainable Development which was launched by the International Chamber of Commerce in 1991 and which has now been adopted by over 1,100 firms worldwide, many of them large MNCs. Nevertheless, this is a voluntary code rather than an industry standard and the ICC does not act as a monitoring or enforcing agency for the Charter. The OECD's *Guidelines for Multinational Enterprises* are similarly non-binding and directed to governments in the first instance although they do involve National Contact Points that are responsible for 'encouraging observance' (OECD, 2003, p. 2).

This 'greening of the corporate boardroom' (Tolba, El-Kholy *et al.*, 1992, pp. 682–3) has a number of themes. In policy terms, corporate actors claim that self-regulation and voluntary codes of conduct are more effective and efficient than government-imposed regulations or command-and-control regimes, issues which are explored in more detail in Chapter 8. In terms of day-to-day practice, green corporatism calls for responsible care, recycling, cleaner production, waste minimization and the introduction of environmental audits. The WBCSD also acknowledges the 'triple bottom line' which encourages corporate social responsibility and attention to social and environmental as well as financial measures of business success (2002, pp. 229–31). However, this move to a more public corporate environmentalism (Karliner, 1997) or what Najam calls the 'charm of the pinstripes' (1999, p. 65) is not without its critics. NGOs in particular have sought to advance 'the corporate responsibility agenda' (see Fabig and Boele, 1999) by calling for a convention on corporate accountability. In drawing attention to serious violations of the Global Compact among its adherents, they have also raised concerns about undue corporate influence on the United Nations (a process now termed 'bluewash' – see Bruno, 2002, p. 6). The 'type II' partnerships adopted at WSSD have also come in for similar criticism, for 'privatizing' international cooperation and for privileging corporate actors without establishing adequate monitoring procedures (see Oilwatch, 2002).

Global civil society

One of the characteristics of post-Stockholm global environmental politics has been the growth of non-governmental environmental organizations and grass-roots movements, a phenomenon often referred to as the growth or perhaps revitalization of civil society at a global level. Civil society is understood variously as evidence of the commitment of states and institutions to a more pluralist form of environmental governance, as an 'expression of the globalization of democratic sentiments' (Litfin, 1997, p. 192) and as evidence of a 'new dialectical surge of countervailing forces' (Cox, cited in Falk, 1995, p. 22). The International Peoples' Tribunal calls it 'people-to-people globalization' (1997, p. 127).

While environmental NGOs are often identified as a comparatively new feature of the political scene, there is a long history of private organization around conservation and environment issues. In Europe and in European settler societies, environmental NGOs developed around local conservation and nature preservation concerns in the latter part of the nineteenth century and the early twentieth century. These were mainly middle-class organizations concerned to preserve nature and natural wilderness against the consequences of the Industrial Revolution and for the enjoyment of city dwellers. This conservationist ethic dominated well into the middle of the twentieth century. In the 1960s and 1970s, however, the number and scope of environmental NGOs expanded as the environmental agenda grew to include pollution, nuclear concerns, resource depletion and waste management. New NGOs were formed with an emphasis on political activism and economic and social change. Friends of the Earth (FoE) was founded in the US in 1969 as a result of a split within the Sierra Club (see Burke, 1982). Greenpeace was founded in 1971 out of opposition to nuclear testing at Amchitka.

In developing countries, non-governmental environmental organizations established prior to decolonization were primarily conservationist groups concerned for the protection of birds and animals. In post-colonial times, however, non-governmental organizations in developing countries have rarely been focused on just the environment or conservation. Rather they have been more broadly based grass-roots organizations, concerned about underdevelopment, poverty alleviation and human rights as well as local problems of environmental decline. In responding to local concerns, these 'second generation' NGOs (Chatterjee and Finger, 1994, p. 74) emphasized self-reliance and bottom-up development as a challenge to the modernization doctrine of the major donor countries and lending institutions. Grass-roots involvement has continued to be a defining theme of environmental activism in the developing countries in concert with a focus on the integral relationship between poor development practices and destruction of both the ecosystem and people's livelihoods and lifestyles. In the 1980s, many 'third generation' NGOs also adopted a broader canvass, concerned that participatory development would be insufficient in managing local environmental issues without a simultaneous challenge to global environment and development frameworks.

The label 'civil society' masks considerable heterogeneity within the global environment movement. NGOs and grass-roots organizations are diverse in scope, size, activity, philosophy and institutionalization. They range from small and sometimes ad hoc groups mobilized around the environmental concerns of local communities to large well-resourced organizations operating, as McCormick puts it (1989, p. x), out of designer offices. Most environmental NGOs fall broadly into the categories of local, grass-roots groups or national organizations. Some have formal membership whereas others are more loosely organized. Some, such as the range of environmental think-tanks or research institutes, have a more corporate structure. Only a few are truly international: Greenpeace International, Friends of the Earth International and the World Wide Fund for Nature fall into this category. The budgets and expenditures of some are substantial. Greenpeace International's 1996 budget, for example, was US$25.9 million (Bergesen and Parmann, 1996, p. 263) and in 1995 the US-based Sierra Club's total budget was US$42 million. Environmental civil society has become transnational and global through the kinds of issues with which groups and organizations are concerned and also through the patterns of cross-border activity and exchange in which they engage. The expansion of the environment movement from national to transnational was accompanied by the establishment of peak or coalition NGOs such as (a small selection) the African NGO Coalition (ANGOC), the Asia–Pacific Peoples' Environment Network (APPEN) or the Pesticides Action Network.

The role played by environmental NGOs and grass-roots groups, the objectives they pursue and the tasks they undertake cover a broad spectrum of activities. This includes agenda-setting and political mobilization; lobbying and international law-making; scientific research, analysis and data collection; monitoring compliance with national and international environmental legislation; environmental project management; and direct action. NGOs have had an important role in political mobilization, helping to define the environmental agenda and pushing governments into multilateral negotiation on environmental challenges as well as 'mobilising public opinion and support for sustainable development' (Williams, 1992, p. 26). At the same time, NGOs 'may usefully open up the debate ... by questioning prevailing expert opinion' (Jasanoff, 1997, p. 581). NGOs and grass-roots organizations have also become important in providing services that governments are often unable or unwilling to and contributing to environmental development assistance, through managing environmental repair, management and training projects in both industrialized and developing countries. This activity increasingly takes place in partnership arrangements across state borders as well as within. The increased participation of civil society in multilateral or international environmental decision-making is usually taken as an important measure of the democratization of global environmental governance. Civil society groups and NGOs help to bring transparency and accountability to multilateral environmental agreements and the state-based diplomatic and institutional structures associated with them. Tinker perceives it as a 'check and balance on unbridled state sovereignty' (1993, p. 14).

In this sense, NGOs are not simply the objects of democratization. They are its subjects – they help to create it. This coordinated rather than ad hoc involvement generally dates to the 1972 Stockholm Conference and was entrenched through various environmental negoti-ations in the 1980s. At UNCED, conference Secretary-General Maurice Strong was determined, in the face of some opposition, to broaden the formal participation of NGOs beyond those who were already accred-ited with ECOSOC. The practice adopted at UNCED – that official accreditation would be given to those NGOs who could demonstrate to the Secretariat that their interests and activities were directly relevant to the agenda – has since become accepted practice at multilateral environ-mental negotiations and consultations. Observer or accredited status usually gives NGOs various opportunities to participate in preparatory and conference proceedings and to attempt to influence the agenda and draft agreements. This can include the right to table documents, speak at plenary and other sessions, and participate in working and expert groups. Governments will sometimes include NGO representatives on their official delegations. However this 'insider' activity is politically constrained in the way that its form and extent are sanctioned by states and NGOs are rarely able to participate in the small, informal groups in which key compromises are often worked out and final decisions made.

At multilateral negotiations, NGOs and other civil society groups will also lobby delegates directly and seek to exercise indirect pressure through their use of the media, through what have come to be known as 'side-events', and through the wide dissemination (often using the Internet) of reports on conference proceedings. They also convene events that run parallel with but are independent of the official summit. At UNCED, for example, some 30,000 people from NGOs, community groups, indige-nous peoples' organizations and women's groups among others partici-pated in the Global Forum. A similar gathering at WSSD – the Global Civil Society Forum – involved about 45,000 people. Reports also sug-gest that civil society participation in the actual meeting halls was greater at Johannesburg than it had been at Rio (IISD, 2003c). NGO advice and expertise have often proved valuable to countries which have small delegations and limited resources upon which to draw. In some cases, the boundaries between state and non-state actors become increasingly blurred. For example, the Foundation for International

Environmental Law and Development (FIELD) has worked closely with governments in the Alliance of Small Island States (AOSIS) providing legal advice on negotiations and preparing draft texts.

The extent of NGO or civil society influence on the policy-making agenda is nevertheless a matter of dispute. The counter-factual seems intuitively persuasive – that without the activity and, increasingly, the expertise of environmental NGOs and other civil society groups, there may well have been fewer and weaker multilateral environmental agreements. Indeed, studies suggest that NGOs and civil society groups have influenced decision-making and state practice on particular environmental issues (see, for example, Stairs and Taylor (1992) on oceans protection and Ringius (1997) on ocean dumping; Elliott (1994) on the Antarctic; Benedick (1991) on the ozone negotiations; Tolbert (1991) on the climate change negotiations; Corell (1999) on the Desertification Convention; and Corell and Betsill (2001) on desertification and climate change). Views are mixed, however, on the impact of NGOs at the broad-based summit meetings such as UNCED in 1992 and WSSD in 2002. Reporting activities such as the NGO publication *Earth Negotiations Bulletin* were important in both raising public awareness and bringing transparency to the proceedings. NGO impact on the actual content of the Rio agreements is argued, by NGOs themselves, to have been less extensive. For example, Mark Valentine from the US Citizen's Network suggests that NGOs 'barely scratched the surface of the official documents' (cited in Chatterjee and Finger, 1994, p. 96) and Larry Williams from the Sierra Club admitted that 'we had almost no impact' (cited in Simms, 1993, p. 99).

On the other hand, there is little doubt that the (enforced) willingness of the institutions of economic governance, such as the World Bank, the World Trade Organization and even the International Monetary Fund, to pay greater public and practical attention to environment and sustainable development concerns is in large measure a result of the pressures of civil society groups over a period of time. That pressure has been imposed through lobbying activities, research and publication, legal action and sometimes through open confrontation and protest. Direct protest action continues to be an important tactic for NGOs to mobilize public awareness and to put pressure on governments or industry. Sometimes it is a tactic of choice and sometimes it is because other avenues of influence are closed. Environmental issues and some grassroots groups have also become part of the anti-globalization movement which arose in particular from the protests in Seattle in 1989 against the World Trade Organization (see Kaldor, 2000). This movement has itself (somewhat ironically perhaps) become 'globalized' in its opposition to the institutions which are the agents of the so-called 'Washington consensus' on the benefits of a neo-liberal world economy based on free trade, foreign investment and export-led comparative advantage.

The logic of pluralist analysis focuses on the ways in which NGOs 'exercise authoritative knowledge' (Haas, 1990, p. 349) and on their ability, or otherwise, to influence the patterns of state or inter-state decision-making and behaviour. What is missing from this is civil society as a transformative political community and a 'system that increasingly engages in a transnational politics characterised by a surprising degree of autonomy from the state (Lipschutz, 1993, p. 8). Environmental civil society is understood in this more critical perspective as resistance activism rather than some form of professionalized non-state activity. NGO activity becomes part of a process of 'constructive vigilance concerning human values and unmet needs' (Williams, 1992, p. 26) and a 'link between the local and international levels of politics' (Chartier and Deléage, 1998, p. 26). NGOs are therefore seen not as a stakeholder group in the global environmental politics of the environment but as part of the move towards a 'decentred globalism' (Gerlach, 1991, p. 122). This emphasizes democratization as the empowerment of marginalized voices, justice and equity in environmental outcomes, and the rehabilitation of the local to counter the centralizing tendencies of a reformist, institutionalist approach to global governance. These values have often informed the policies advocated by civil society groups and have shaped political practice within many (but not all) of those organizations and movements. This is not to overlook, of course, the fact that many non-governmental organizations are strongly committed to the modernist project, seeking to influence policies based on managerial and technocratic solutions, emphasizing the importance of objective science and understanding nature in the service of human species.

Local and direct action also encourages a different way of thinking about what is 'global' in civil society. Shiva argues that 'the real ecological space of global ecology is to be found in the integration of all locals' (1993, p. 155). Community and grass-roots organizations, for example, may focus on local concerns such as water pollution, waste management or other forms of environmental repair and sustainable development, but they often draw on the experience of similar groups working on similar problems in other countries. Even in the absence of specific processes of exchange and sharing, the 'hundreds of decentralised and locally autonomous initiatives' (Shiva, 1989, p. 218) can constitute a process that has a global dimension in that it occurs everywhere.

As active participants in global environmental governance, whether as pressure groups, 'insider' organizations or local/global activists, NGOs are characterized as 'the cutting edge of the common interest' (Barnes, 1984, p. 175). However, participation brings with it its own complexities for NGOs. On the one hand, participatory multilateralism can enhance the opportunities for NGOs to articulate change. On the other, it legitimizes statist and centralized forms of governance. The democratic efficiency justification for a pluralist form of participation reveals little about the power relationships which set the boundaries for who may participate and on what (and whose) terms. Chatterjee and Finger, for example, are concerned that 'over the years parts of the [environment] movement have become bureaucratized and part of the establishment themselves' (1994, p. 65). Participatory rights at multilateral negotiations have become 'meaningful primarily for well-organized, well-financed and well-informed NGOs' (Anon., 1991, p. 1589) and often more for Northern-based NGOs than for those in the developing countries. Tensions between NGOs from developed and developing countries, over agenda and strategies, are not entirely uncommon.

These ambiguities of democratization have been forcefully played out over the gender politics of environmental degradation and the environmental politics of indigeneity. For both women and indigenous peoples, the disproportionate impact of the causes and consequences of environmental degradation on their daily lives and, in the case of indigenous peoples, their cultural and physical survival, is symptomatic of the biases of a more extensive structural inequality.

The gender politics of environmental degradation

Three propositions provide the framework for discussion here. The first is that women are disproportionately disadvantaged by environmental degradation. The second, borrowing from Jacobson (1992), is that this gender bias is a roadblock to sustainable development and the third is that women's participation is essential to the pursuit of sustainable development.

Bearing the burden

Women, especially but not exclusively in the developing world, 'bear the ecological costs of progress and development' (Shiva, 1989, p. 7). Burdensome daily tasks associated with gathering and growing food, collecting water and energy resources are made even more difficult as a result of environmental degradation. Where the key components of the ecosystem – energy, land and water – are degraded it is women's lives that are more likely to be adversely and directly affected, even when women are incorporated into the formal economy. So, for example, 'the expansion of cash-cropping and production for export has not been accompanied by the trickle down of benefits to the poor, especially poor women, while at the same time it has led to water pollution, soil erosion, destruction of firewood resources and loss of genetic diversity of plant and animal stocks' (Momsen, 1991, pp. 93–4). Women have to work harder as food producers to compensate for soil erosion and loss of soil fertility. They have to walk further to collect water and increasingly scarce fuelwood supplies. Where fuelwood is scarce, they have to purchase energy or use less efficient alternatives such as dried dung (which then diminishes soil enrichment). This is complicated further because women are disproportionately found amongst the world's poor (up to 70 per cent of those who live in absolute poverty by some accounts – see Bretherton, 2003, p. 103) and it is the poor who are hardest hit by environmental degradation and who have fewer resources to deal with either causes or impacts. Even in the industrialized world, women's lives are more closely tied to household energy, food and water choices and to managing the impacts of environmental damage, such as illness resulting from water or air pollution.

Women's voices

The disproportionate impact of environmental degradation on women suggests that their participation in decision-making is essential, not only to benefit women but to incorporate vital experience and knowledge in the pursuit of sustainable development. As Maurice Strong has suggested, there is a 'pressing need to continue to centralize women's issues and to ensure the incorporation of their collective perspectives, experiences and contribution to sustainable development' (cited in UNIFEM, 1993, p. 3). The difference and diversity in women's voices and experiences cannot be overestimated or ignored. Yet women also '*share* [their] "otherness", [their] exclusion from decision-making at *all* levels' (WEDO, 1992, p. 7; emphasis added). For some, the role that women have to play in sustainable development arises not just because of their daily experiences but as a result of their very woman-ness, their reproductive and nurturing roles which bring them closer to nature than men. This essentialist argument suggests that women's insights will be different and, indeed, superior to those of men. Others resist this kind of biological determinism, seeing in it the source of much of women's oppression and arguing rather that it is women's *experiences* of environmental degradation and ecosystem management that have given them a particular knowledge and expertise that are crucial to the pursuit of sustainable development.

Policy attention to the gendered nature of environmental degradation and environmental governance is a product of the late 1980s. Neither the impact of environmental degradation on women nor their role in environmental governance were part of the Stockholm debate and, indeed, the Stockholm agreements not only ignore women but are also highly gendered in their language. The Nairobi Forward Looking Strategies (FLS), adopted at the 1985 Conference to Review the UN Decade for Women, observed that 'environmental degradation is ... a contributing factor to deplorable conditions endured by many women' (see UNICEF/UNFPA, 1991, p. 3). In 1986, UNEP established a committee of senior women advisers on sustainable development (SWAGSD). The 1987 Brundtland Report, however, devoted almost no time to women or gender concerns at all. Between 1989 and 1991, UNEP convened four regional assemblies on women and the environment in response to the Nairobi FLS and in 1991 convened the Global Assembly on Women and the Environment (the Partners in Life conference).

Gender issues were also given little attention in the early PrepComms for UNCED and the issue was only taken up after intense lobbying from women and after Filomina Chioma Steady, from Sierra Leone, was appointed a special adviser on women in environment and development to the Conference Secretary-General. Principle 20 of the Rio Declaration and Chapter 24 of Agenda 21 acknowledge that governance should be inclusive of women (the democratization argument) and that the participation of women in environmental governance and the pursuit of sustainable development is vital (the efficiency argument). Principle 20 states that 'women have a vital role to play in environmental management and development. Their full participation is therefore essential to achieve sustainable development' (UNCED, 1992a). In Chapter 24, rather awkwardly titled 'Global action for women towards sustainable development', governments are called on to recognize women's roles and to facilitate their participation in economic and political decision-making for the benefit of women *and* the effective pursuit of sustainable development. Societal change figures prominently: eliminating violence against women, improving women's access to property rights, reducing their heavy workload, ensuring equal employment opportunities and eliminating negative stereotypes and prejudices against women. The executive director of the United Nations Development Fund for Women (UNIFEM) called Agenda 21 a 'tribute to the solidarity of a global women's caucus which has played a strong role in helping to define a document which promises a world of better opportunities for women' (UNIFEM, 1993, p. 2). This may well overestimate the promise of Agenda 21. The primary purpose of the Rio Declaration and Chapter 24 was better environmental policy-making and practice on sustainable development, not alleviating the burden on women. In the Johannesburg Declaration in 2002 governments committed themselves to 'women's empowerment, emancipation and gender equality' (United Nations, 2002b, p. 4) but this commitment has little strength in the absence of any real achievements since Rio in 1992 or since the Beijing Fourth World Conference on Women in 1995.

Important questions arise about whether participation of the kind anticipated in Agenda 21 and reinforced at WSSD is an adequate response to women's disproportionate environmental burden. While full participation is clearly required on equity grounds, it does not necessarily ensure that the disproportionate impact of environmental degradation on women will be overcome. Indeed, incorporation and participation in a structure that has systematically marginalized women may be counter-productive if the underlying gender inequities and power relationships within those structures are not acknowledged and addressed at the same time. For women, then, the 'full participation' recommended by principle 20 has to be more than a simple counting exercise. Nor is it simply that 'women's issues' should be given full attention in decision-making. Both are necessary but not sufficient conditions in the pursuit of sustainable development and the democratization of environmental governance. Women challenge not only their lack of participation in decision-making, and the lack of attention given to their concerns, but also the structures and values which have resulted in 'unacceptable ecological and human costs ... [including] massive environmental degradation' and which have 'reinforced old inequities and generated new inequities' (Asian and Pacific NGO Working Group, 1993, p. 1). Thus gender equity, rather than simply women's concerns, becomes an integral component of sustainable development.

In stark contrast to a rather limited presence in the formal institutional structures of environmental governance, women have been especially active and effective participants in non-governmental organizations and in grass-roots movements. The best-known movements mobilized by women are probably the GreenBelt Movement in Kenya, begun by the National Council of Women in 1977, and the Chipko Movement which began in Northern India as a grass-roots opposition to logging and forest destruction. But there are many other examples of women working together to protect and repair the environment: establishing projects on water quality and health in the Aral Sea region; pursuing environmental justice after the poisoning of the Essequibo River in Guyana; exposing arsenic poisoning of groundwater in Bangladesh; combating soil erosion in Ghana; addressing pollution control on Lake Maruit in Egypt; supporting organic farming practices in Barcelona; encouraging sea-turtle conservation in Brazil; fostering alternative methods of waste collection in Peru; and campaigning against hazardous waste production in the US (see WEDO, 1992, 1998).

Women have also worked internationally through global NGOs, such as the Women's Environment and Development Organization (WEDO), to 'forge links among activists all over the globe' (WEDO, 1992, p. 4), to share experiences and to provide a platform for influencing global environmental policy. That the UNCED agreements address gender concerns in any way, for example, was a result of the lobbying effort which coalesced around the Women's Action Agenda 21 (WAA 21) produced by the 1991 World Women's Congress for a Healthy Planet. A new version – the Women's Action Agenda for a Healthy and Peaceful Planet 2015 (known as WAA 2015) – was released prior to WSSD following extensive consultation among women's groups (see Corral, 2002). It identifies five priority areas – peace, globalization for sustainability, access and control of resources, environmental security and health, and governance for sustainable development. These declarations and plans of action that come from regional and global consultations among women call for development to be people-centred and for the rights and needs of all people (including women, the poor and indigenous communities) to be at the 'core of all policies and programmes' with all people 'empowered and centralised in the processes of planning and decision-making' (Asian and Pacific NGO Working Group, 1993, p. 2). They demand policy initiatives – such as restrictions on resource extraction, land entitlement for women, non-discriminatory credit policies – which address the causes of environmental degradation and the causes of inequity in order to develop and promote sustainable livelihoods for women.

In this context, it is important that women are seen not simply as victims of environmental degradation but as 'voices of liberation and transformation' (Shiva, 1989, p. 47), as 'innovators, activists, conservationists, natural resource managers and agents of change at all levels of society' (Asian and Pacific Women's Resource Collection Network, 1992, p. 6). This grass-roots activism is therefore not simply a response to marginalization from formal structures of governance. It is an act of agency by which women seek to reclaim their rights as subjects in environmental governance rather than as objects of environmental management programmes. It contributes to a global movement of women working for environmental protection and alternative environmental and political practices which emphasize equity, justice, emancipation and bottom-up forms of governance. Nevertheless, there are constraints upon the ways in which women mobilize transnationally and on the success of their campaigns (see Bretherton, 2003). Some arise from divisions within the women's movement itself. Others arise from resource constraints and the challenges involved in maintaining grass-roots links at the same time as mobilizing within what are often male-dominated and masculinist structures and ideologies which privilege certain types of knowledge and practices (such as western scientific paradigms) over others.

Humanity's hope? Indigenous peoples and the environment

Indigenous Survival International defines indigenous peoples (who number more than 300 million people in over 70 countries) as 'distinct cultural communities with unique land and other rights based on original and historical use and occupancy. These are peoples whose cultures, economies and identities are inextricably tied to their traditional lands and resources' (cited in Yap, 1989–90, p. 92). This close relationship between indigenous communities and the land and related ecosystems (rivers, streams, coastal regions) has resulted in traditional practices which are, for the most part, environmentally sound. It has also resulted in indigenous peoples being labelled either as environmental victims or environmental saviours. They have become defined as objects to be acted upon, to be empowered from above or from outside, or as a source of knowledge which can be appropriated and incorporated into the global discourse as and when needed. This is, in effect, an environmental politics of exclusion.

Environmental degradation affects indigenous peoples and communities directly through the damage inflicted upon traditional lands and resources and indirectly through the economic activities associated with modernization and development which are the cause of such degradation. The result is that traditional lifestyles and the cultural strength and viability of indigenous peoples are threatened. As the Brundtland Report noted, the 'forces of economic development disrupt...traditional lifestyles ... some are threatened with virtual extinction by insensitive development over which they have no control' (WCED, 1987, p. 12). For example, the Carajas Dam project in Brazil inundated 216,000 hectares of forest and displaced 13,000 people (Colchester, 1988, p. 450). Military flight testing in Canadian Northern Labrador has affected caribou herds on which the local Innu peoples rely (Samson *et al.*, 1999, p. 33). Traditional Huaorani fishing grounds in Ecuador have been contaminated by oil exploration (see Shutkin, 1991, pp. 493–500). Deforestation in Palawan in the Philippines is 'obliterating the indigenous peoples who belong to the Tagbanuwa and Batak tribes' (Kennedy Cuomo, 1993, pp. 231–2). In Sarawak, dam projects and extensive logging activity have damaged the environment and indigenous rights to traditional lands are being ignored (see Osman, 2000). Measles and whooping cough transmitted by forestry workers have brought death to the Yanomami in Venezuela and Brazil (see Burger, 1990, p. 88; Shutkin, 1991, pp. 496–7; Wiggins, 1993, p. 350).

Resource extraction (logging or mining) and energy development (such as dam construction) result in 'soil erosion, rapid surface run-off, pollution of streams, decline in fish stocks and a further impoverishment of the local diet' (Colchester, 1990, p. 168). The loss of forests, biodiversity and soil fertility compromises indigenous farming. Food, shelter and traditional medicines are lost and an important source of spiritual and cultural identity is denied to indigenous forest dwellers. Global environmental problems such as climate change and ozone depletion also affect indigenous agriculture. The salt-water pollution of inland waterways can threaten traditional hunting and fishing grounds. Development infrastructure, such as road construction, brings non-indigenous workers into indigenous lands, accompanied often by disease and violence towards local and indigenous peoples. In conditions of poverty, indigenous communities have themselves acquiesced in environmentally destructive practices, such as the dumping of toxic wastes or mining activities on their lands, although commentators are usually careful to characterize this as an exception rather than a rule (see Wiggins, 1993, p. 349).

Indigenous peoples and indigenous communities are vulnerable also to the exploitation of their ecological and biological knowledge. As Fourmile observes, 'many of the areas of highest biological diversity on the planet are inhabited by indigenous peoples' (2001, p. 216). Indigenous knowledge includes knowledge about the medicinal benefits of plant and animal species as well as forms of ecosystem and 'natural resource management [which] can enhance biodiversity' (Dutfield, 2000, p. 276). The 'search among organisms ... for biochemically active molecules that may be developed for the treatment of disease' (Clapp and Crook, 2002, p. 80) – bioprospecting – can be done in such a way that it draws on indigenous knowledge. This ethno-botanical model is sometimes accompanied by compensation for those who provide knowledge about the therapeutic and other benefits of plant species in particular. However, when the exploitation of knowledge goes unrewarded or when biological materials are collected from indigenous lands without permission, bioprospecting becomes biopiracy – the 'appropriation of biological resources and knowledge ... for the purposes of asserting exclusive rights over these resources' (Anuradha, 2001, p. 27). This is equivalent, Shiva suggests, to an enclosure of the commons (2000, p. 144).

State policies, by commission or omission, can further undermine indigenous communities and their ability to manage the impacts of environmental change. Government refusal to acknowledge rights to traditional lands leaves indigenous peoples with little authority over their own lands. Many governments not only oppose indigenous self-determination but pursue policies designed to assimilate and de-indigenize traditional communities, such as internal migration which can 'cause environmental havoc on an unprecedented scale' (Colchester, 1988, p. 463). Internal migrants are often allocated indigenous land, further contributing to indigenous dispossession as well as to unsustainable land management. Indigenous lifestyles are frequently cast as backward or pre-modern, as obstacles to economic development and therefore dispensable. As a candidate in the 1990 Peruvian presidential elections argued, modernization is thought to be 'possible [only] with the sacrifice of the Indian [indigenous] cultures' (Llosa, cited in Wiggins, 1993, p. 347). Even when governments have moved to recognize indigenous lands in some form, this is often offset by national laws which determine, for example, that all subsurface mineral resources belong to the state as is the case for the Huaorani in Ecuador (see Lu, 2001). It is not just governments that have overlooked indigenous peoples or their interests. The Coordinating Body of Indigenous Organizations of the Amazon Basin (COICA), which represents over one million indigenous peoples in the Amazon region, made clear in an open letter their concern at the way in which they have been left 'out of the political process', reminding environmental organizations that 'we never delegated any power of representation to the environmentalist community' (COICA, n.d., p. 304).

This politics of exclusion is evident even in policies intended to enhance economic autonomy and self-reliance and protect the ecosystems within which indigenous communities survive. Conservation and environmental programmes, such as the designation of biosphere reserves, can dispossess indigenous communities in areas of traditional settlement. The Shakilla, for example, were driven from the Lake Rukana Park in Kenya, and the Ik were expelled from the Kidepo National Park in Uganda (Clad, 1988, p. 330; see also Fearnside, 2003 on Brazil). Community-based management strategies – for forestry and coastal ecosystems, for example – are intended to involve indigenous and other local communities in decision-making but are often compromised by state practices and, sometimes, by local cultural/political structures that restrict who can participate in decision-making and management practice (see, for example, Argawal, 2001; Johnson and Forsyth, 2002). The strategies for harvesting and marketing rainforest products to reverse deforestation and provide an economic resource for indigenous peoples that underpin the 'fair trade' movement (on the 'trade not aid' principle) have attracted similar criticism. Corry (1993) argues that harvesting has done little to empower indigenous peoples or to protect the forests. Fair trade can still undermine indigenous autonomy through a reliance on foreign intermediaries, vulnerability to price fluctuations and the exigencies of Western consumer demand (see also Leclair, 2003).

From the late 1980s, the institutional structures of environmental governance began to address the challenge of indigenous exclusion. In its 1987 report, the Brundtland Commission argued that indigenous peoples should have 'a decisive voice in formulating policies about resource development in their areas' (WCED, 1987, p. 12), calling for 'the recognition and protection of their traditional rights to land and the other resources that sustain their way of life' (WCED, 1987, p. 115). The 1989 Convention Concerning Indigenous and Tribal Peoples in Independent Countries adopted by the International Labour Organization (and known as ILO 169) is based 'broadly on the principle of self-determination' (Richardson, 2001, p. 5) and 'supports community ownership and local control of lands and resources' (Posey, 2002, p. 9). Since 1990, the IUCN has required that its policy documents recognize the role of indigenous peoples in environmental management. World Bank directive 4.20, adopted in 1991, is intended to 'ensure that indigenous peoples do not suffer adverse effects during the development process, particularly from Bank-financed projects, and that they receive culturally compatible social and economic benefits' (cited in Richardson, 2001, p. 6).

One of the most important but still unfinished processes has been the Draft Declaration on the Rights of Indigenous Peoples coordinated by the UN Working Group on Indigenous Populations which first met in 1982. The Draft Declaration was accepted by the UN Sub-Commission on Prevention of Discrimination and Protection of Minorities in 1994 before then being submitted to the Commission on Human Rights in 1995. The Declaration recognizes the special relationship between indigenous peoples and their environment and contains provisions which recognize indigenous land rights, cultural rights and intellectual property rights as well as the connections between these categories of rights. At time of writing, the Draft Declaration has still not been submitted to the General Assembly.

The UNCED agreements also took some steps in addressing the problems of exclusion. The Rio Declaration recognizes that 'indigenous people and their communities... have a vital role in environmental management and development because of their knowledge and traditional practices' and calls on states to 'recognise and duly support their identity, culture and interests and enable their effective participation in the achievement of sustainable development' (UNCED, 1992a, principle 22). Chapter 26 of Agenda 21, entitled 'Recognising and strengthening the role of indigenous people and their communities', emphasizes the importance of indigenous knowledge and the 'cultural, social, economic and physical well-being of indigenous people' (UNCED, 1992b, para. 26.1). It requires that indigenous people[s] be informed, consulted and allowed to participate (UNCED, 1992b, para. 26.5(b)). But it goes no further than highly veiled references to the ways in which indigenous peoples have been marginalized politically, culturally and ecologically. The WSSD in 2002 simply reaffirmed the UNCED commitments although it also linked these specifically with the challenges of eradicating poverty (see United Nations, 2002b, para. 7(e)). A range of other agreements – such as the Forest Principles and the Convention on Biological Diversity – require governments to promote opportunities for indigenous participation, support the identity, culture and rights of indigenous peoples and to acknowledge, support and compensate indigenous knowledge and capacity.

There are substantial political silences in these agreements. There is little overt recognition of the fundamental features of indigenous empowerment – land rights and political autonomy. In fact, the plural noun – peoples – was apparently struck from every page of Agenda 21 after lobbying by the Canadian and Brazilian delegations (see Chatterjee and Finger, 1994, p. 58) who were concerned that such references would imply nations with a right to self-determination. Japan and the EU took a similar stance at WSSD. Historically, indigenous knowledge has been discounted as unscientific and uncivilized or it has been appropriated by Western science and commercial interests without compensation. Agreements such as the Forest Principles and the Biodiversity Convention incorporate provisions for the equitable sharing of benefits arising from the utilization of indigenous knowledge. They do not, however, specifically recognize the intellectual property rights of indigenous peoples or their ownership of this knowledge (issues addressed further in Chapter 6).

There are dangers also that the rationale for including indigenous peoples and communities in the processes of environmental governance is driven as much by anticipated benefits for industrial society as it is by concerns for the rights of indigenous peoples. The historical emphasis on sustainable lifestyles has fostered the perception that indigenous peoples can be called upon as saviours of humankind, as 'guardians of the extensive and fragile ecosystems that are vital to the wellbeing of the planet' (Strong, 1990, p. 6). The Brundtland Report suggested that indigenous lifestyles 'can offer modern societies many lessons on the management of resources in complex … ecosystems' (WCED, 1987, p. 12) because 'these communities are the repositories of vast accumulations of traditional knowledge and experience that links humanity with its ancient origins. Their disappearance is a loss for the larger society' (WCED, 1987, pp. 114–15). The World Bank makes a similar case, arguing that 'it is in *our* interests and those of the planet to open a permanent space for these peoples and their values' (Davis, 1993, p. xi; emphasis added). The themes of them and us, of inside and outside, are clear. Indigenous voices often resist what they see as an 'enforced primitivism' (Clad, 1988, p. 325) which underpins these expectations. Armstrong Wiggins, a Miskito Indian from Nicaragua, argues that 'it would be a mistake to take too romantic a view', pointing out that 'like all other humans, [indigenous peoples] survive by killing and consuming plants and animals … like other peoples they have utilised and developed their territories' (Wiggins, 1993, pp. 348, 325). In this context, it is also a mistake to see indigenous peoples as anti-development rather than opposed to culturally and ecologically inappropriate forms of development which are imposed upon them.

Indigenous peoples are neither the passive victims of environmental degradation nor passive recipients of economic or political empowerment from elite policy-makers. The growing activism of indigenous peoples within and across political borders has been described as a 'renewed political assertiveness by (and on behalf of) indigenous peoples' (Clad, 1988, p. 321). As Kayapó Indian leader Paulinko Paiakan has argued, 'no one of us is strong enough to win alone [but] together we can be strong enough to win' (cited in Kennedy Cuomo, 1993, p. 233). Indigenous peoples organizations' demands for access and benefit-sharing occur in the context of broader collective rights. For indigenous peoples, the solution to environmental degradation and the impact it has on their lives lies not simply in better environmental management. Rather, it cannot be separated from land rights and human rights, the fight for self-determination, opposition to internal colonization and resistance to cultural and physical extinction as the most appropriate way in which to ensure the sustainable development of indigenous lands and communities. As COICA proclaims, 'the most effective defense of the Amazonian biosphere is the recognition and defense of the territories of the region's Indigenous Peoples' (appended to Davis, 1993).

There is a local and global dimension to indigenous activism which seeks to reclaim authority over an environmental, developmental and human rights agenda. Examples of local activism include resistance to logging (the Penan in Sarawak) or, like the Kayapó in Brazil, to dam construction, or Innu opposition to military activity and hydropower schemes on their land. Indigenous activism is, however, not simply oppositional or directed towards state actors. Indigenous communities have also developed local conservation programmes, such as the forest park and botanical reserve established by the Keina Indians in Panama, the Inuit Arctic Conservation Programme or the forestry management project established by the Quichua-speaking Indian federation in eastern Ecuador. Perreault suggests (drawing on the experience of indigenous peoples in the Ecuadorian Amazon) that as well as helping to consolidate local indigenous communities, indigenous peoples networks are multiscalar, connecting 'local … peoples to regional and national indigenous organisations, state actors, multi-lateral funding agencies' as well as engaging with advocacy networks (2003, p. 83). Globally, indigenous peoples have moved to 'articulate their concerns in many "counter"-declarations, statements and charters of their own' (Fourmile, 2001, p. 218). At a global level, coalitions of indigenous peoples organizations – such as the Coordinating Body of Indigenous Organizations of the Amazon Basin (COICA) – work to support local efforts, lobby and liaise with governments and intergovernmental organizations and present their cases to human rights bodies. Indigenous peoples organizations have established a political presence at conferences of parties and other meetings as lobby groups and as organizations accredited to or associated more closely with the conventions.

Conclusion

A more participatory and inclusive form of environmental governance is not only more democratic but is seen as essential to the pursuit of a more equitable and just ecological world order. This process seeks to connect the global with the local, a form of globalization from below. Yet, as this chapter has shown, the constituency of the 'local' is not homogeneous. Nor are the ways in which non-governmental organizations and social movements conceive of and pursue strategies of democratization and participation. Bretherton points out that 'the exercise of agency is [also] contingent upon access to knowledge and other resources' (2003, pp. 103–4). Political and institutional structures, as well as social and economic ones, also influence those strategies. As the discussion here has shown, those structures cannot be separated from issues of equity, justice and rights, concerns which are addressed in more detail in the following chapter.

Chapter 6

Normative Challenges: Justice, Obligations and Rights

The third dimension of environmental governance explored here is the normative framework. A framework of norms and principles provides ethical as well as legal and practical guidance (should they choose to follow it) for actors involved directly or indirectly in making, implementing and enforcing decisions about how best to respond to the globalized challenges of environmental change. As earlier chapters have shown, the global politics of the environment has become characterized by fundamental inequities and injustices. At the same time, there is some confusion about the range of rights and responsibilities which attend upon states and other actors in dealing with environmental challenges in a way which takes account of and seeks to overcome those inequities.

This normative dimension has come to be 'preoccupied with the fairness, sustainability and democratic quality' of these global arrangements (Falk, 2001, p. 221). Some aspects of this concern with norms and principles are examined in other chapters. The focus here, building on the discussion of institutionalization, democratization and marginalization in the previous two chapters, is twofold – first, the demands for a framework of norms that recognizes and responds to inequities in the global politics of the environment and, second, the nature of rights, duties and obligations that might attend upon such a framework. The interest here is not just in what those norms and principles might be (or should be), but also in the extent to which they have been given form in international environmental law. The years since the Stockholm Conference in 1972 have seen a process of normative development which is expressed in multilateral environmental agreements, in various forms of 'soft law' (that is, not legally binding upon states), in other kinds of declarations, and in the public processes, procedures, debates and disputes around the global politics of the environment.

Environmental inequity and transnational harm

The nature of inequity and injustice in the global politics of the environment is perhaps best captured in two related ideas, displacement and transnational harm. These ideas enable us to understand environmental degradation as an ethical problem as well as an ecological one. Drawing on John Dryzek's work, Paul Wapner argues that displacement is 'about shifting the experience of environmental harm' (1997, p. 217). This 'shifting' occurs across space – that is, the physical transportation or the unintended dispersal from one part of the world to another of the by-products and environmental consequences of economic activity. It also occurs across time, by which future generations will suffer the environmental effects of today's lifestyles. Displacement also applies to the outputs and inputs of economic activity. The outputs are perhaps the most obvious, involving the various forms of waste, pollution and environmental damage that are the result of production and consumption and which are frequently felt somewhere other than the location in which the source activity occurred. The 'input' dimension of displacement refers to the exploitation of the renewable and non-renewable (or non-replenishable) resources and environmental services upon which production and consumption are based. As earlier chapters have demonstrated, present-day economic activity – which includes every-day subsistence and lifestyle activities as well as corporate behaviour – exploits resources unsustainably across space and across time.

Another way of understanding this problem is through the conceptualization of ecological footprints and shadow ecologies. The footprint is a conservative measure of 'how much productive land and water an individual, city, country or humanity requires to produce all resources it consumes and to absorb all the wastes it generates' (Wackernagel *et al.*, 2002, p. 12). Globally, humanity is outstripping biospheric capacity. There is, however, an equity dimension to this as well, in that some countries are running at an ecological deficit – that is, their ecological footprint is both greater than the biological capacity of that country and greater than the per capita global average, based on present economic activity and the level of economic activity that is required to ensure that natural capital is replenished. Sachs argues that the OECD countries 'surpass (in terms of ecology and equity) the admissible average size of [their ecological] footprint by a magnitude of about 75 to 85 per cent' (2002, p. 14). Thus their economies cast an ecological shadow over poorer countries from whom the centres of production and consumption derive their raw materials (see MacNeill *et al.*, 1991).

The ethical challenge arises because this displacement is implicated in transnational harm. Andrew Linklater defines transnational harm in a broad sense relating to 'distress, suffering, apprehension, anxiety or fear' as well as the 'damaging [of] vital interests' (2002, p. 327). 'Damage done to the environment,' Postiglione argues, 'is damage done to humanity' (2001, p. 212). Linklater makes it clear that not all harm is intentional and deliberate. Rather, and this applies especially in the case of environmental displacement, it includes harm through unintended consequences and negligence or 'the failure to take reasonable precautions to prevent the risk of harm to others' (Linklater, 2002, p. 330). Environmental displacement and the transnational harm that it causes are unjust. In other words, it is unfair and inequitable that some are harmed by activities not of their own making and over which they have little or no control. As David Held describes it, 'the quality of the lives of others is shaped and determined in near or far-off lands without their participation, agreement or consent' (1997, p. 244). It is also unfair and inequitable that those who contribute less to the problem end up suffering more and those who contribute more suffer less. The extent to which these harm inequities are unintended or the result of negligence rather than deliberate intent sometimes involves a fine interpretive line. In 1991, Lawrence Summers (then Chief Economist for the World Bank, later US Treasury Secretary) argued that 'the economic logic behind dumping a load of toxic waste in the lowest wage country is impeccable... underpopulated countries in Africa are vastly under-polluted' (cited in Puckett, 1994, p. 53).

As other chapters in this book indicate, two important forms of environmental inequity arise through displacement and harm. The first involves the disproportionate consumption of resources and production of waste. In effect, the rich consume more resources and produce more waste than the poor. In 1998, the richest 20 per cent of the world's population (mainly in industrialized countries) accounted for 86 per cent of total private consumption and consumed 58 per cent of the world's energy (UNDP, 1998, p. 2). Per capita carbon dioxide emissions in the OECD countries average 12.4 tonnes; in the lowest-income countries the average is 1.0 tonnes per capita (UNDP, 2003, p. 10). This disproportionate consumption of resources has a historical as well as a contemporary dimension. The second measure of inequity, which is related to the first, involves the disproportionate impact of environmental change. Those who are most immediately affected by global environmental decline are those who have contributed least to the problem and who are now ecologically as well as economically and politically marginalized (including the poor, women and indigenous peoples). Shiva puts it bluntly: 'the natural resources of the poor are systematically taken over by the rich and the pollution of the rich is systematically dumped on the poor' (2000, p. 136). The poor and disadvantaged are the least able to buy their way out of the consequences of pollution, environmental degradation and resource scarcity. These, then, are ethical problems as much as they are ecological or technological ones.

The principles of justice and equity that should apply to environmental issues are bound up in a number of practical questions relating to burden-sharing and the allocation of costs and benefits, 'justifiable entitlement' (Pan, 2003, p. 1), the nature of fault and complicity and how to account for historical practices in contemporary rights and obligations (see Rowlands, 1997). As earlier chapters have indicated, there would seem to be a growing commitment to the proposition that humankind is bound together as an ecological community of fate which establishes the basis for moral obligation (see Held, 1998 on the concept of a community of fate). The biophysical complexities of the planetary ecosystem help to define it as a global commons and a public good, extending the bounds of those with whom we are connected, to whom we owe obligations and against whom we might claim rights. These obligations are expected to transcend the 'morally parochial world of the sovereign state' (Linklater, 1998, p. 26). The World Commission on Environment and Development identified the importance of 'social justice within and amongst nations' (1987, p. 47) and argued that we have a 'moral obligation to other living beings and future generations' (1987, p. 37). The Rio Declaration called for a 'new and equitable global partnership' (UNCED, 1992a). The whole concept of sustainable development articulated in the Brundtland Report and subsequent agreements and declarations invokes intra- and intergenerational obligations, requiring (as Chapter 7 explores further) that to be sustainable development has to account for the needs of both present and future generations.

Solutions to addressing these inequities and injustices appear in a variety of forms. The following two chapters focus on the political economy of the environment and examine the kinds of strategies which have been pursued under the rubric of sustainable development. The focus in this chapter is on a more explicitly normative or ethical response. The two themes explored here are those of obligations and rights, concepts which are central to understanding ethical concerns in global politics. The purpose is not to provide a detailed exploration of the nature of international ethics or moral philosophy. Rather, it is to examine how ideas about obligations and rights have been developed within the global politics of the environment. An important starting point is international environmental law because, as Falk suggests, 'normative ideas about the environment combine notions of ethics with those of law' (2001, p. 228).

International environmental law

UNCED was expected to promote the 'further development of international environmental law', including the 'feasibility of elaborating general rights and obligations of States' (UNGA, 1989c, Part 1, para. 15(d)). Thus the General Assembly accepted that states were the subjects and agents of international law. Chapter 39 of Agenda 21, which addressed international legal instruments and mechanisms, focused primarily on effective participation by states in international law-making, implementation mechanisms, dispute resolution and general standard-setting. There was little substantive attention to the nature or content of legal principles, except for a long paragraph which sought to ensure that standards should not be trade-distorting. UNCED therefore reinforced the status quo with respect to the holders of rights and duties in international environmental law. WSSD in 2002 was not expected to renegotiate the UNCED agreements or the principles embedded therein. Nevertheless, Pallemaerts suggests that the reaffirmation of the Rio principles was a stalemate with respect to the further development of international environmental or sustainable development law (2003, p. 7).

From a reformist perspective, the problems associated with the 'further development of international environmental law' are primarily procedural and institutional ones. Birnie argues that 'ample techniques derived from traditional sources of international law are available for development of regulations to protect the environment' (1992, p. 82). It is the existing *processes* of making international law that are argued to be 'slow, cumbersome, expensive, uncoordinated and uncertain' (Palmer, 1992, p. 259). The emphasis, then, is on improving regulatory techniques and the way in which international law is made. There is, however, a growing body of work which questions whether 'th[is] existing international legal order [is] fundamentally and inherently inimical to environmental protection, requiring wholesale rejection and re-invention' (Sands, 1993, p. xviii). The problem is identified as one which requires something more fundamental than just regulatory and procedural change. The 'further development of international law' requires a new legal ethic which incorporates not only new understandings about obligations and rights but which also ascribes those obligations and rights to other actors besides states as legitimate subjects and agents of international law.

The rights and obligations of states

As earlier chapters have demonstrated, sovereign *rights* for states over resources and environmental policy have been central to the development of international environmental law. Yet the discussion here also indicates that a normative framework for state *obligations* is essential for better environmental governance. A reformist tradition has paid attention to elaborating and reformulating a legal doctrine of state responsibility and liability. Principle 21 of the Stockholm Declaration and principle 2 of the Rio Declaration – those oft-quoted principles that reinforce sovereignty over resources – also require that states should not cause damage to the environment of other states or to areas beyond national jurisdiction. In effect, this requires them to minimize transnational harm. In theory, this principle of transboundary responsibility establishes an obligation with respect to displacement, requiring states to take action to ensure that the outputs at least of economic activity do not cause damage to the environment, and therefore (by implication) the lives, of peoples and places elsewhere. An obligation not to cause damage to the environment could also address the input problem. In other words, the exploitation of resources and environmental services for economic purposes should not result in a drawing down of the ecological capital of other states or areas beyond national jurisdiction (that is, resources should not be over-exploited), nor should there be irreversible or even severe environmental consequences of such exploitation.

While this would seem to establish the basis for a principle of state responsibility and, therefore, liability for transnational harm, especially as it builds on earlier legal arbitrations, it has proved more difficult to put this obligation into practice. It is open to question whether there is much more than fragmentary evidence that such principles have become customary international law. That would require evidence of general state practice and that, as earlier chapters have demonstrated, is not yet the case. States have paid less attention to their obligations than to their rights. Multilateral environmental agreements continue to affirm the physical rights of states to their resources and the authority rights of states over how those resources can be used and exploited.

Along with responsibility and liability comes the issue of whether states have an obligation to inform and consult other states (and their citizens) with respect to detrimental environmental impact of their activities. This arises from the demand that people should be able to determine freely the conditions of their own lives and that a fair and just global politics of the environment must be based on consent. Principles 18 and 19 of the Rio Declaration called upon states to notify other states of any 'natural disasters or other emergencies that are likely to produce sudden harmful effects', to 'provide prior and timely notification ... to potentially affected States on activities that may have a significant adverse transboundary environmental effect' and to 'consult with those States at an early stage and in good faith' (UNCED, 1992a). A further challenge associated with an ethic of responsibility is that of liability and the nature of legal remedies which might be available in the case of transboundary or potentially global environmental degradation. In other words, what are the remedies for transnational and disproportionate environmental harm? The issues of liability and compensation have been scrutinized by the International Law Commission, by a group of legal experts convened by the World Commission on Environment and Development, and by a UNEP group of experts (the Montevideo Programme). UNCED itself did not really come to grips with these issues, suggesting only (in Chapter 39 of Agenda 21) that future action could include an 'examination of the feasibility of elaborating general rights and obligations of States' (UNCED, 1992b, para. 39.5) which simply repeated the wording of resolution 44/228. The Conference, Peter Sand argues, 'brought no basic changes in the mechanisms of international law-making or dispute resolution' (1993, p. 388). International environmental law and the negotiation of multilateral environmental agreements has, however, provided a focus for the elaboration of new principles such as the polluter pays principle (PPP) and the precautionary principle. Both would seem to extend the obligations of states and to set boundaries to the exercise of both physical and authority rights in a way which seeks to limit transnational harm.

The polluter pays principle (PPP)

The polluter pays principle, which is also discussed in Chapter 8, is not, as often thought, primarily a principle about liability or compensation. Rather it was developed as an economic principle under the auspices of the OECD and was designed to prevent public subsidization of environmental repair or preventive action. In other words, all costs should be borne by the polluter, so that polluters should not otherwise have an unfair commercial or competitive advantage. Principle 16 of the Rio Declaration may give some further effect to the customary intent of the polluter pays principle although it is rather vague in its wording and injunction. It says, in full, that '[n]ational authorities should endeavour to promote the internalisation of environmental costs and the use of economic instruments, taking into account the approach that the polluter should, in principle, bear the cost of pollution, with due regard to the public interest and without distorting international trade and investment' (UNCED, 1992a).

Despite its genesis as an economic principle, the polluter pays principle does have potentially important consequences for addressing the ethical challenges of transnational harm. This is because transnational environmental harm and the injustice often associated with it arise because environmental costs are *not* internalized. Rather, as the discussion earlier in this chapter indicated, they are geographically and temporally displaced. The environmental externalities associated with economic activity are often borne by those who have neither caused nor benefited from that activity (this includes future generations). In general, however, PPP does not seem to have translated well to the global and ethical circumstances of environmental change. In fact, as other chapters show, the proposition that the polluter should pay by bearing the costs of action to prevent global or transboundary pollution has potentially been undermined by mechanisms such as those adopted in the Kyoto Protocol on climate change. Polluters, such as the industrialized countries, are able to 'buy' their way out of taking action at home by paying for emission reduction strategies elsewhere, often in developing countries. This may involve a financial transaction – a payment – but it is not the same as 'bearing the costs'.

The precautionary principle

The precautionary principle is, in effect, a principle designed to manage or prevent harm. It has evolved in international law from domestic application in what was then West Germany. The principle has been incorporated into multilateral environmental agreements such as the Framework Convention on Climate Change, the Biosafety Protocol and the Stockholm POPs Convention. Principle 15 of the Rio Declaration states that 'the precautionary *approach* shall be widely applied by States according to their capabilities' (UNCED, 1992a; emphasis added). Debates over precaution were contentious at WSSD particularly between the EU, which ascribes to it the status of a hard-law principle, and the US and Australia, which prefer to see it only as an 'approach' and are certainly reluctant to see it expanded to other policy areas such as human, plant and animal health (see Pallemaerts, 2003, p. 8; Perrez, 2003). Developing countries were also concerned that it could be used to restrict exports of goods that might have negative environmental (or other) impacts.

The idea that precaution should be a guiding principle in addressing concerns about environmental degradation would seem not only logical but an important contribution to a normative framework that accounts for transnational harm and ethical considerations. The usual presentation of the precautionary principle is that governments should not use the excuse of scientific uncertainty about environmental problems or the environmental consequences of particular activities to avoid taking action. However, the exact content of the precautionary principle and what it means in practice is open to debate. Non-governmental organizations, for example, have generally taken it to mean that the burden of proof is reversed – that is, until and unless it can be determined that an action (for example, the dumping of wastes at sea) does not cause environmental damage, then that action should be prevented or restricted. One of the difficulties attached to these debates is whether the precautionary principle is to be invoked only as a response to scientific uncertainty or whether the principle has more general applicability, requiring that any action be precautionary in content – that is, a cautious action which prevents further environmental damage. The application of the precautionary principle is complicated further because many environmental agreements also incorporate what might be called an 'acceptability' principle, suggesting that some impact on the environment is acceptable but that any actions which are intended or might be expected to cause long-term, severe or irreversible damage are not.

Expanding the normative framework: a rights-based approach

The elaboration of more specific rights and obligations for states within the confines of sovereignty and the development of regulatory techniques are, for some, insufficient to strengthen international environmental law and its contribution to international governance. Falk argues that the 'essence of a humane approach [to environmental governance] is the assurance that all peoples have their individual and collective rights realized' or, at least, that 'such rights are being actively affirmed as policy goals to be seriously pursued' (2001, p. 222). The articulation of rights which can be claimed by individuals (and, more controversially, by collectivities) identifies specific obligations for states but it also encourages people to 'take more responsibility for the conditions of each other's lives' (Thompson, 2001, p. 141).

This requires that new concepts such as the common heritage of humankind, intergenerational equity, prior informed consent and environmental rights must be incorporated into international law, both as principles and as specific provisions designed to give effect to those principles. These principles challenge traditional state-centric jurisdictions and widen the scope of those to whom obligations are owed in international law. They seek to incorporate into law an ethic of justice which suggests that rights claims should take a prior place in articulating the normative framework and ethical principles which inform the global politics of the environment.

The common heritage of humankind

The common heritage of humankind principle amplifies the view that common spaces – areas beyond national jurisdiction such as the high seas, the atmosphere, outer space, Antarctica – should be regulated for the benefit of the international community as a whole rather than being subject to the 'first come first served' law of open spaces. The elaboration of the principle in the United Nations Convention on the Law of the Sea was intended primarily to address issues regarding the management of resource exploitation rather than stewardship of the environment. However the concept has also reinforced the colloquial image of an ecological community of fate in which the health of the environment is shared. The legal and customary content of the common heritage concept is unclear. It has been partially accepted with respect to the high seas, through the UN Convention on the Law of the Sea which has now come into effect, but it has certainly been challenged with respect to the Antarctic, and probably not tested at all with respect to outer space. Efforts have been made to articulate the common heritage principle with respect to the atmosphere and the climate system although the Climate Change Convention acknowledges only that change in the Earth's climate (and its adverse effects) are a common *concern* of humankind. Attempts to apply this principle to biodiversity and tropical forests – areas (or 'resources') which are clearly under national jurisdiction – have been contentious especially if the implication appears to be that such areas must be managed either by an international body, or by a state or group of states acting as trustees or stewards for the benefit of the international community.

Intergenerational equity

The idea of a common heritage implies that future generations have a right to inherit a planetary environment in at least as good a condition as previous generations have enjoyed. It therefore weighs against displacement and environmental harm over time. Janna Thompson suggests that people and their environmental responsibilities constitute an 'intergenerational continuum' (2001, p. 136). Thus present generations have an obligation to ensure that they do not damage the planetary ecosystem in such a way that the environmental rights of future generations are denied. There are legal arguments about what the content might be of a right held by generations as yet unborn. There are also related arguments in philosophical ethics which suggest that the individuals in future generations to whom these rights are supposedly owed in the absence of action will be different from those who do exist if action is taken (see Page, 1999, p. 57).

Despite this, the idea of some degree of intergenerational responsibility would seem to be accepted in general and wording of this nature is often incorporated in environmental agreements. The Stockholm Declaration suggested in principle 1 that we have a solemn responsibility to protect and improve the environment for present and future generations. The concept of sustainable development elaborated by the Brundtland Commission (on which more in Chapter 7) embodies some element of intergenerational equity – that is, it relies on meeting the needs of the present generation without compromising the needs of future generations (see WCED, 1987, p. 8). The difficulty is how to give effect to this and how an obligation to future generations can be tested and operationalized. For example, to what extent is there a 'space' dimension to this 'time' ethic? Does the principle that future generations be left no worse off than present ones require that environmental services and resource stocks should not be depleted in individual countries, or is the principle met adequately if the total global stock of, say, forests is maintained even if it declines in some countries and increases in others? Does the principle allow for some kind of compensatory model, such that depletion of one resource can be compensated for if a commensurable resource is provided (see, for example, Page, 1999)?

Human rights and the environment

The issues of 'rights' includes not only intergenerational equity but also intragenerational equity (an issue addressed also in Chapters 7 and 8) as well as the question of whether there is such a thing as a human right to 'environment'. There is a substantial body of international law which provides the basis for *some* claim regarding a human right to a clean environment or for establishing that a clean environment is essential if other human rights are to be met (for a detailed listing, see Wagner *et al.*, 2003). Some of these move in the direction of a substantive right whereas others focus on procedural rights (particularly related to information and decision-making). However there is as yet no treaty-based right to a clean environment (or an environment of a certain quality) or to sustainable development.

Some of these pronouncements are embedded in human rights law. The UN Commission on Human Rights asserted, in a resolution adopted in 1990, a link between preservation of the environment and the promotion of human rights. In 1989, what was then the UN Sub-Commission on Prevention of Discrimination and Protection of Minorities (and is now the Sub-Commission on the Promotion and Protection of Human Rights) appointed a special rapporteur (Fatma Zohra Ksentini; now Fatma Zohra Ouhachi Vesely) to examine the connections between human rights and the environment. Her 1994 final report included a draft declaration of 27 principles which states, in principle 2, that 'all persons have the right to a secure, healthy and ecologically sound environment' (United Nations Economic and Social Council, 1994). Part II of the declaration provides more detail on the substantive content of this right and part III establishes procedural rights in connection with the right to a clean environment.

The UN Commission on Human Rights considered the report at subsequent meetings and called for comments from governments and NGOs. In 1997, the Commission deferred consideration until its 1998 meeting, but invited the UN Secretary-General to bring the Commission's work on human rights and the environment to the attention of UNGASS and to prepare a special report on these matters. That report was a summary of deliberations at UNGASS and comments offered by the FAO (as the only agency within the UN system which had responded to the Secretary-General's invitation to comment) rather than a clear normative declaration of a human right to the environment. Indeed, the Secretary-General reported that the FAO thought Ksentini's special report 'too academic in nature and lacking pragmatic policy recommendations that could be implemented at field level' (UNSG, 1998b, para. 5). Despite suggestions at the Commission that Ms Ksentini's new mandate as special rapporteur on human rights and toxic waste be converted to a permanent environment and human rights mandate, her 'toxics' mandate was simply extended until April 2004.

The Millennium Development Goals adopted by the General Assembly in 2000 have provided some further impetus for specific attempts to link environmental concerns with human rights. In response, in part, to the requirement in the Development Goals that the number of people without access to safe water should be halved by 2015, in 2003 the UN Committee on Economic, Cultural and Social Rights issued a General Comment (the procedure for interpreting the Covenant on these rights) that access to water is a human right. In April of the same year, the UN Commission on Human Rights adopted a further resolution on 'human rights and the environment as part of sustainable development' which confirmed that 'protection of the environment and sustainable development... contribute to human well-being and potentially to the enjoyment of human rights' and that 'respect for human rights and fundamental freedoms are essential for achieving sustainable development' (United Nations High Commission on Human Rights, 2003). The Commission's decision, however, fell short of proclaiming a specific human right to a clean environment. The Commission requested the UN Secretary-General to submit a report on 'the consideration being given to the *possible* relationship between the environment and human rights' (UNHCHR, 2003, para. 11; emphasis added).

Other international legal agreements also give implicit or explicit recognition to environmental rights. The UN Convention on the Rights of the Child, for example, refers to the importance of educating children with 'respect for the natural environment (see Simpson and Jackson, 1997, p. 270; Shelton, 1991, pp. 103–4). The United Nations Economic Commission for Europe's Aarhus Convention adopted in June 1998 – formally known as the Convention on Access to Information, Public Participation in Decision-making and Access to Justice in Environmental Matters – links the rights in its title to the protection of the 'right of every person of present and future generations to live in an environment adequate to his or her health and well-being' (United Nations Economic Commission for Europe, 1998, article 1). A number of other (admittedly non-binding) regional agreements – such as the African Charter on Human and Peoples' Rights and the Cairo Declaration on Human Rights in Islam – refer to the right to live in a clean environment (see International Peoples' Tribunal, 1997, p. 121). Statements about environmental values, sometimes accompanied by expressions of rights and obligations, have also been incorporated in a number of national constitutions (see the appendix to Wagner *et al.*, 2003) and cases have also been brought to tribunals such as the European Court of Justice which help to establish case law on environmental rights.

Other commentaries on human rights and the environment are located in environmental agreements and declarations. The 1972 Stockholm Declaration declared that people have a 'fundamental right to freedom, equality and adequate conditions of life, in an environment of a quality that permits a life of dignity and well-being' (principle 1), implying that the exercise of other human rights requires basic environmental health (see Shelton, 1991, p. 112). The 1982 World Charter for Nature hinted indirectly at environmental rights when it required, in principle 23, that people should have the right to participate in decision-making about the environment and should also have 'access to means of redress when their environment has suffered damage or degradation' (UNGA, 1982). In 1984 the OECD suggested that 'fundamental human rights should include a right to a "decent" environment' (Bosselmann, 2001, p. 121). The 1989 Hague Declaration recognizes, in paragraph 5, that environmental degradation affects the 'right to live in dignity in a viable global environment'. The Rio Declaration echoed this in principle 1, which states that 'human beings ... are entitled to a healthy and productive life with nature' (UNCED, 1992a). The WSSD Plan of Implementation, adopted in Johannesburg in 2002, suggests that states should 'acknowledge the consideration being given to the *possible* relationship between environment and human rights' (United Nations, 2002b, para. 152; emphasis added). At the same time, the Plan does draw attention to the general right 'of everyone to a standard of living adequate for their health and well-being' (United Nations, 2002b, para. 96). However Pallemaerts suggests that a more rights-oriented statement to the effect that human rights and other fundamental freedoms are '"essential for the full achievement of sustainable development" proved too controversial to be included in the final consensus version of the Johannesburg Declaration' (2003, p. 3).

Earthjustice (formerly the Sierra Club Legal Defense Fund) argues that the 'right to a clean and healthy environment ... has become a prevailing international legal norm' (Wagner *et al.*, 2003, p. 1). However, despite the fairly extensive body of soft law described above which defends the relationship between human rights and environmental protection, there are grounds for suggesting that rights to a clean environment tend to be aspirational and rather vague. At best, they may only provide what Schwartz (cited in Bosselmann, 2001, p. 122) calls a 'surrogate protection' against environmental harm. This surrogate approach is evident in the suggestion that 'most of the acts causing environmental degradation would also violate and interfere with universal human rights, such as the right to life and security of person, the right to health and the right to livelihood' (International Peoples' Tribunal, 1997, p. 121). While Sands identifies the potential difficulties in bringing together environmental concerns and human rights, in that 'a distinction may be drawn between environmental rights, which are collective, and human rights, which under the current regime are characterized as individual' he also accepts that it is 'not farfetched to consider the right to a healthy environment as a human right' (1989, p. 416).

It is not always clear from the debates on the existence or elaboration of a human right to a clean and healthy environment whether such a principle is intended to contribute to environmental protection goals, or whether protection of the environment is effectively subsumed to the imperatives of protecting a variety of other human rights. In this context, Wapner suggests that 'environmental degradation is not simply about how people treat nature but ... how they treat *each other*' (1997, pp. 213–14; emphasis added). He goes on to argue that a proper emphasis on 'just treatment of all human beings enables ... [us] to take seriously the injurious ramifications of environmental displacement' (1997, p. 227). Bosselmann criticizes this anthropocentric approach to environmental rights, by which it appears that 'the environment is only protected as a consequence of protecting human well-being' (2001, p. 125).

In general, the natural world is assumed to have no moral standing. Preserving the aesthetic value of the environment or the integrity of species as a contingent goal, in this view, runs counter to an ecological version of rights. The idea of a more ecological concept of rights *for nature* has been most extensively explored in environmental ethics and environmental philosophy, focusing on the idea that nature and non-human species have intrinsic value (see Eckersley, 1992 for a discussion). For Low and Gleeson, for example, justice needs to incorporate 'the relationship between humans and the rest of the natural world' as well as the 'distribution of environmental quality among people' (1999, p. 177).

A related issue focuses on whether existing human rights law can be deployed to protect the environment or whether this requires 'the vigorous reinterpretation of existing rights to encompass environmental objectives' (Obiora, 1999, p. 469). The American Association for the Advancement of Science suggests that it is both, arguing that 'human rights cannot be fully understood or realised without taking account of their environmental dimensions [and] the health ... of the environment cannot be fully realized in the absence of human rights' (2002). This approach underpinned the Ksentini Report and the 1994 draft declaration on human rights and the environment. A further dimension to the debate on the environment and human rights reminds us that environmental activists are sometimes the victims of specific human rights abuses, including denial of access to due legal process, imprisonment, torture and even death. Two prominent examples of environmental activists who have lost their lives are Chico Mendez fighting on behalf of rubber tappers and for sustainable forest management in Brazil and Ken Saro-Wiwa, a campaigner for rights for the Ogoni peoples (including environmental and resource rights), who was hanged by the Nigerian government.

Intellectual property rights

A rights-based approach to the ethical challenges of global environmental governance has also been adopted as a political mechanism and legal tool to underpin specific claims for access, benefit-sharing and recognition. One of the strongest examples of the way in which general rights have been translated in this way is the application of intellectual property rights (IPR) law to traditional and indigenous knowledge. IPRs were initially envisaged as a way to encourage innovation by 'creating an incentive for inventors to disclose the details of their inventions in exchange for a limited monopoly on exploitations' (AEFJN, 2002, p. 1; for a summary of the key IPR treaties see Ganguli, 1998). They have increasingly come to be seen as a tool to protect corporate monopoly rights at the expense of public rights and human rights. The expectations of IPR law with respect to indigenous and traditional knowledge have been that it would help to define indigenous peoples as 'rights holders – not mere stakeholders' (International Indigenous Forum on Biodiversity, 2001, p. 2), that it would enable them to counter biopiracy, particularly when that involves patenting inventions which are based on traditional ecological knowledge, and that it could provide a mechanism for indigenous peoples to seek and negotiate benefit-sharing and compensation for the use of their knowledge.

As demonstrated in Chapter 5 and as Dutfield confirms, 'traditional knowledge systems, particularly that relating to biological resources, are increasingly accepted as an important source of useful information in the achievement of sustainable development' (2000, p. 277). Traditional or indigenous knowledge is 'far more than a simple compilation of facts. It is ... holistic, inherently dynamic, constantly evolving' (Fourmile, 2001, p. 220). In other words, it is not the physical biogenetic material alone that is crucial to this debate, but also the knowledge about that material. Estimates suggest that between '25 000 and 75 000 plant species are used for traditional medicines ... but only 1% is known by scientists and accepted for commercial purposes' (Aguilar, 2001, p. 241). Prakash reports that indigenous knowledge can increase the efficiency of screening plants for medicinal properties by more than 400 per cent (2000, p. 1). Yet indigenous peoples and their interests have frequently been excluded from negotiations on environmental issues that have direct and indirect consequences for them and the exploitation of their knowledge. In particular, there has been little or no compensation for the exploitation of such knowledge for use in areas such as medicine, pharmaceuticals, agrochemicals and other 'industrial' applications.

The Convention on Biological Diversity (CBD) does recognize traditional knowledge and the importance of benefit-sharing – article 8(j) of the Convention is the most important here. Dutfield (2000, pp. 279–80) suggests that the Convention implies a moral obligation on governments to safeguard indigenous entitlements with respect to knowledge, even if that knowledge falls outside the IPR system. Negotiations on the implementation of the CBD provisions on access and benefit-sharing have enabled indigenous peoples to 'sit at the table' (Fourmile, 2001, p. 227). Even then, benefit-sharing is politically contentious to the extent that it is unlikely to be able to address the *historical* injustices associated with past exploitation of indigenous peoples and their knowledge and resources. However, while the CBD 'has emerged as the primary instrument permitting indigenous groups to express their interests and demands for the protection of their knowledge' (Meyer, 2001, p. 37), it is *not* the primary international agreement which configures IPR law as it might apply to biological materials, including genetic materials, or to indigenous or traditional knowledge. That distinction belongs to the WTO TRIPS (Trade-Related Aspects of Intellectual Property Rights) agreement. The TRIPS agreement was adopted in 1994 as part of the Marrakesh Agreement which brought to a conclusion the Uruguay Round of multilateral trade negotiations under the GATT and which established the World Trade Organization. It covers a number of areas of intellectual property – the most important ones in terms of indigenous intellectual property are patents and the protection of new varieties of plants. TRIPS defines intellectual property rights as monopoly rights for individuals or legal persons (such as corporations) over inventions that are demonstrably new, involve innovation and are capable of industrial application. It says nothing about traditional knowledge.

While IPR law has provided a potential tool for indigenous peoples in their fight for recognition and equity, some have expressed concern that 'even if existing IPR protection and compensation mechanisms were fully applied to traditional knowledge and biogenetic resources, this would not be an appropriate mechanism to strengthen and empower indigenous peoples' (Posey and Dutfield, 1996, p. 1). IPR law is argued to 'contain an in-built bias' that protects companies and fails to recognize 'traditional knowledge as protectable subject matter' (Dutfield, 2000, p. 274). The problem for traditional knowledge, including indigenous knowledge, is that the ownership systems are usually collective ones (although this does not mean that indigenous knowledge necessarily constitutes a public commons; see Dutfield, 2000). Traditional or indigenous knowledge is also developed and transmitted over time and therefore falls outside the bounds of intellectual property as it is understood in the TRIPS agreement. It is difficult if not impossible to identify an 'inventor', more so when similar forms of knowledge exist in different places. Indigenous or traditional knowledge is rarely found in the written form which some countries, such as the United States, require as evidence that the 'invention' for which a patent is sought (by, say, a pharmaceutical company) is, in fact, *not* new (the term used is 'prior art'). The Council of Scientific and Industrial Research in India, for example, had to rely on an 'ancient treatise on home remedies' to challenge (successfully) a US patent on the healing properties of turmeric powder (see Ganguli, 1998, pp. 178–9; Anuradha, 2001).

Further concerns arise in situations where indigenous peoples and local communities might be prevented by IPR rules from using plants which have subsequently been patented. This is particularly important for many farmers who store seeds from one year's harvest to plant the following year. Prakash argues that this concern is misplaced because only 'new plant varieties will be eligible for protection' and that the right of farmers to retain seed is protected under 'farmers' privilege' (2000, p. 4). Indeed, Prakash is concerned that the focus on patents has overlooked other means by which indigenous intellectual property can be protected, including geographical indicators and plant breeders' rights. TRIPS also allows for what are known as *sui generis* (unique or specially generated) systems of rights especially for plant protection, potentially enhancing the provisions of the CBD and ILO 169 (see Posey, 2002, p. 9; Fourmile, 2001, pp. 232–3; see Bhat 1996 for a counter-argument). One option, for example, is the concept of community intellectual property rights (CIPR) to protect 'innovations and intellectual knowledge of local communities in relation to varieties of plants' (Aguilar, 2001, pp. 252–3). Governments have also, in some cases, adopted IPR legislation which acknowledges indigenous rights. The Organisation of African Unity, for example, has developed a model bill as a means of harmonizing legislation in African countries to recognize indigenous ownership of 'new compounds made from natural products' (Ganguli, 1998, p.178). It seems doubtful, however, that any IPR regime which was more sympathetic to indigenous rights would have any retrospective force (that is, over traditional knowledge already lost or appropriated).

Prior informed consent

Henry Shue argues that the responsibility 'not to introduce damaging or dangerous conditions into other people's lives ... without their fully informed consent, is ordinarily taken ... to be universal' (1981, p. 588). People, he continues, 'are entitled to decide for themselves whether they wish to accept additional risks' (1981, p. 593). This is the no-harm principle which is fundamental to liberal thought. It also reflects the much older principle *quod omnes tangit ab omnibus comprobetur* – what touches all should be agreed to by all (see Low and Gleeson, 1999, p. 189). The right of prior informed consent (PIC) has been codified in the Basel and Rotterdam conventions on, respectively, the trade in hazardous waste and hazardous chemicals and pesticides (see Chapter 3). The right, in this case, is generally taken as the rights of *governments* to approve or deny import of the designated materials and requires full disclosure of information from the exporting party. Even so, as Chapter 3 indicated, there are political, economic and technological constraints on government agencies when it comes to the concept of consent. Krueger, for example, doubts 'the ability of the PIC procedure to improve decision-making ... by developing countries' (1999a, p. 129).

The PIC provisions incorporated in the Convention on Biological Diversity require first that collection of biological samples must have the consent of the government of the 'source' country. They also encourage, although they do not require, that consent be sought from local and indigenous communities for the use of their knowledge and resources. A similar position is expressed in the 1989 ILO *Convention Concerning Indigenous and Tribal Peoples in Independent Countries* (ILO 169) and the UN *Draft Declaration on the Rights of Indigenous Peoples*. This issue of 'whose consent' is central to how the PIC principle is given effect in international law and as a more general normative principle. In particular, there are concerns that it is important that consent operates 'at the level of the local community' (Anuradha, 2001, p. 33), for two reasons. The first has to do with the input component of transnational harm – in many cases it is the knowledge and resources of local communities that are being accessed, exploited or expropriated. The second reason arises from the output dimension of transnational harm. Local communities and peoples should have the right to determine, based on accurate knowledge of the environmental and other consequences, whether or not to accept waste of whatever kind which arises from economic activity elsewhere. PIC assumes that the appropriate authority in the importing state will act in the interests of local communities. Yet as Puckett argues, PIC can 'undermine local democracy and institute a system of decision-making that is wide open to abuse' (1994, p. 54). In response, the International Indigenous Forum on Biodiversity has elaborated a more extensive meaning of prior informed consent, which demands (among other things) that consent is determined 'in accordance with customary laws, rights and practices', is 'free from external manipulation, interference or coercion' and is based on 'full disclosure of the intent and scope of the activity' (2001, p. 3).

Conclusion

The issue of ethics and justice in the global politics of the environment is embedded primarily in the relationships between people, or at least other kinds of agents such as states and corporations. As demonstrated here, there has been a normative elaboration of rights claims, primarily in soft law, that seem to encourage a corresponding set of obligations towards people rather than states, and to those who are most disadvantaged of their rights. On the other hand, hard-law articulation of rights (for states and for corporate actors) can been seen more as proprietory than protective and less able, in practice, to address the problems of (in)equity, let alone concerns about protecting the environment. Certainly, in the examples explored above, establishing claims against those rights can prove to be difficult (as in intellectual property rights, for example).

The process of making ethics, justice and rights central to debates about the global politics of the environment supports demands for humane forms of governance (see, for example, Falk, 1995, 2001). What states (and other actors) have agreed upon rhetorically also has to be acted upon behaviourally (Falk, 2001, p. 230). Or, as Shue points out, 'there is a meaningful distinction... between not inflicting harm and protecting against harm' (1981, p. 600). Some aspects of this have been explored in earlier chapters, particularly Chapters 4 and 5 which examined the institutional and participatory themes in more detail. The challenges of ethics and justice and the need for public policy strategies which seek to respond to these concerns are also deeply embedded in the international (or global) political economy of the environment and in the way the global polity has pursued sustainable development. The next two chapters turn to consider these issues in more detail.

Chapter 7

The International Political Economy of the Environment

In spite of assertions of a 'common future' (the title of the report of the World Commission on Environment and Development) and the claims in Agenda 21 about a 'global partnership for sustainable development', the international political economy of the environment is shaped by differences over how that common future is to be defined, what principles should inform it and what strategies should be adopted to achieve it. Those issues have been touched upon in earlier chapters but they are given greater attention here and in Chapter 8. This chapter begins with an analysis of sustainable development, a concept which has become a defining motif of contemporary environmental politics or what some prefer to think of as a 'privileged narrative' (Bourke and Meppem, cited in Hobson, 2002, p. 97). The concept is often deployed as if its meaning is undisputed. Yet, as this chapter demonstrates, nothing could be further from the truth. Disputes over sustainable development and the 'common agenda' are almost always couched, at some point, in terms of a divide between the industrialized and richer countries of the North and the developing, usually poorer countries of the South. Tensions arise not only over what principles should inform and manage the relationship between rich and poor countries but over how those principles should be put into practice. Those tensions and principles are explored in the second part of this chapter.

Sustainable development

Sustainable development is one of the most pervasive but also contested ideas in global environmental discourse. The first site of contestation is definitional. That is, how is sustainable development to be defined and operationalized? What is to be sustained? What kind of development is envisaged? The second area of dispute is ideational. That is, what normative assumptions are embedded in the idea of sustainable development? Is sustainable development locked into a development discourse

and ideology of growth or is it informed by an ecological ethic? While
the use of the term pre-dates the World Commission on Environment
and Development (see Pearce and Warford, 1993; Hecht, 1999), it was
that Commission's report – *Our Common Future* – which established
the phrase firmly in the lexicon of environmental politics (see Chapter 1
for more on the background to and procedures of the Commission).

Sustainable development and the Brundtland Report

The Declaration issued by the Commission at its final meeting in Tokyo
in February 1987 argued that it was possible to build a future that was
'prosperous, just and secure' (WCED, 1987, p. 363) but that this
required all countries to adopt sustainable development as the overriding goal of national policy and international cooperation. Sustainable
development, the Commission argued, is in the 'common interest'
because 'ecological interactions do not respect the boundaries of individual ownership and political jurisdiction' (WCED, 1987, p. 46). The
Commission emphasized the importance of multilateralism, the imperatives of addressing social concerns and the need for institutional reform.
It urged new norms of behaviour and changes in attitudes, social values
and aspirations as necessary (but perhaps not sufficient) conditions for
achieving sustainable development. For the Commission, sustainable
development required

> a political system that secures effective citizen participation ... an eco-
> nomic system that is able to generate surpluses and technical know-
> ledge on a self-reliant and sustained basis, a social system that
> provides for solutions for the tensions arising from disharmonious
> development, a production system that respects the obligation to pre-
> serve the ecological base for development, a technological system that
> can search continuously for new solutions, an international system
> that fosters sustainable patterns of trade and finance and an adminis-
> trative system that is flexible and has the capacity for self-correction
> (WCED, 1987, p. 65).

The Brundtland Report defined sustainable development as 'development that meets the needs of the present without compromising the ability of future generations to meet their own needs' (WCED, 1987, p. 43).
Two principles underpin this. The first is that sustainable development
must emphasize needs (although those needs are not defined) and must
give special priority to the essential needs of the poor. The second is that
sustainable development must take account of the limits that technology
and social organization impose on the ability of the environment to

meet those present and future needs. For the Commission, those limits were not necessarily limits to growth, but limitations on resource use in pursuit of that growth. Sustainable development was also ecologically crucial because, the Commission observed, many of us live beyond the world's ecological means. The overall integrity of the ecosystem is therefore important and, at a minimum, development must not endanger the natural systems that support life on Earth (1987, pp. 44, 46).

The Report argued that resource capacity could be conserved and enhanced through scientific assessment to ensure better productivity without ecological damage, through energy efficiency, through anticipating the impacts of industrialization on the biosphere and through encouraging the use of low-waste technologies (WCED, 1987, pp. 59–60). To do this, technology, which is the 'key link between humans and nature' (WCED, 1987, p. 60), has to be reoriented, technological capacity in developing countries has to be enhanced, and greater attention has to be paid to environmental factors in the development and use of technology. Technology is thus a source of risk *and* a means to manage those risks (WCED, 1987, p. 365). However, while advances in knowledge and technology could, the Report suggested, enhance the carrying capacity of the resource base, they could not extend it indefinitely. For the Commission, it was important that steps be taken long before those limits were reached. Renewable resources must be used within the limits of regeneration and natural growth, taking into account the 'system-wide effects of exploitation' (WCED, 1987, p. 45). Land should not be degraded beyond 'reasonable recovery' (1987, p. 46). The use of non-renewable resources should take into account a variety of factors, including the criticality of the resource and the availability of technology for minimizing depletion and for providing substitutes. At very least, a resource should not run out until substitutes are available (WCED, 1987, p. 46). Plant and animal species should be conserved and adverse impacts on the quality of air, water and other natural elements should be minimized (WCED, 1987, p. 46).

For the Brundtland Commission, economic growth (or achieving 'full growth potential' or 'high levels of productive activity' (WCED, 1987, p. 44)) was an essential requirement if development was to be made sustainable. This was because it was the means to overcoming poverty which the Commission identified as a major cause (if not *the* major cause) of environmental degradation and a barrier to sustainable development. The Commission recommended an annual growth rate of about 3 per cent per capita (or, taking population increases into account, something in the vicinity of 5 to 6 per cent per annum in the developing world). In the Commission's view, however, growth had to be less material- and energy-intensive (1987, p. 52), that is, it had to be sustainable. It should take into account the full environmental costs of economic activity (1987, p. 52) and should not increase vulnerability to crises (WCED, 1987, p. 53). Indeed, for the Commission, a measure of progress might be the *abandonment* of a development project for long-term social and ecological good (1987, p. 54).

According to the Commission, there were other incentives as well for developing countries to pursue 'sustainable growth'. The market for their primary commodities would, the Commission anticipated, shrink as industrialized countries pursued their own growth in a more sustainable way (that is, less energy- and material-intensive and more material- and energy-efficient (WCED, 1987, p. 51)). Growth in developing countries would therefore help to compensate for this loss of external markets by increasing domestic demand for products, goods and services, especially if that growth also took account of equity and basic human needs. However growth strategies in developing countries would be less than sustainable, the Commission predicted, unless they were also accompanied by a reorientation of international economic relations. Trade, capital and technology flows had to be more equitable and take greater account of environmental imperatives. Market access, technology transfer and international finance had to be improved in order to help developing countries to diversify economic and trade bases and to build self-reliance (WCED, 1987, p. 365). This emphasis on growth or increase in economic welfare for developing countries is inspired also by what is known as the environmental Kuznets curve which 'predicts that as societies become richer, the pollution per unit of production will decrease' (Gupta, 2002, pp. 362–3). In effect, according to this model, environmental degradation will decrease because money becomes available for developing countries to spend on environmental mitigation and because the immediate material needs of societies have been or are being met.

The Commission also confirmed social justice and equity within and between generations as a central requirement of sustainable development which had to recognize the impact on 'disadvantaged groups' (WCED, 1987, p. 53) as well as on vulnerable ecosystems. Otherwise growth (or development) would not be sustainable. The Report acknowledged that 'our inability to promote the common interest in sustainable development is often a product of the relative neglect of economic and social justice within and amongst nations' (WCED, 1987, p. 47) noting that the poor and marginalized were disproportionately disadvantaged by environmental degradation, yet often lacked both the political and economic means to address these concerns. Growth had to meet essential human needs for employment, food (or, more importantly, nourishment), energy, housing, water supply, sanitation and health care (WCED, 1987, pp. 54–5). It also had to be balanced by a sustainable level of population, that is, 'population size ... stabilised at a level consistent with the productive capacity of the ecosystem' (1987, p. 56). While the Commission recognized that the question of population could not be separated from patterns of consumption, much of the focus was on reducing fertility rates in the developing world, acknowledging the social dimension of this as well as the importance of education of women, health care and expansion of the livelihood base of the poor (WCED, 1987, p. 56).

The WCED report established the baseline for subsequent discussions on and debates over the pursuit of sustainable development. These discussions and debates were central to the UN Conference on Environment and Development. UNCED's purpose was to manage the links between environment and development and create, in the words of Agenda 21, a 'global partnership for sustainable development' (UNCED, 1992b). Sustainable development is not defined in the Rio agreements – its content is assumed – but those agreements echo the basic themes of the Brundtland Report. Principle 1 of the Rio Declaration places human beings at the centre of concerns for sustainable development. Principle 4 provides that 'in order to achieve sustainable development, environmental protection shall constitute an integral part of the development process and cannot be considered in isolation from it' and notes also that 'eradicating poverty is an indispensable requirement for sustainable development' (UNCED, 1992a). Agenda 21 infers that, for the most part, it is developing countries which lack sustainable development. Chapter 2 of Agenda 21, the first substantive chapter, is headed 'International cooperation to accelerate sustainable development in developing countries and related domestic policies'. It calls for development to be reactivated and accelerated, suggesting that this requires a supportive international economic environment based on trade liberalization, adequate financial resources for developing countries, macroeconomic policies conducive to environment and development and recognition of the problems associated with international debt. Chapter 3, on combating poverty, echoes the Brundtland Report in suggesting that an anti-poverty strategy is one of the basic conditions for ensuring sustainable development. It is not until Chapter 4 that economic activity in industrialized countries – specifically patterns of consumption and production – becomes the focus of attention.

These themes were evident in the UNGASS and WSSD processes and documents as well as in the parallel but increasingly interconnected processes associated with the Millennium Summit and the adoption of the Millennium Development Goals, and with the Monterrey Consensus on financing for development. Text adopted for the 1997 Special Session describes 'sustained economic growth as essential' to integrating the economic, social and environmental components of sustainable development (see Osborn and Bigg, 1998, p. 30). In its very title, the World Summit on Sustainable Development reinforced the centrality of this concept. While these processes reflect a more apparently normative concern for sustainable *human* development of the kind favoured by the United Nations Development Programme, there is little interrogation of the underlying value of economic growth.

Critiques and challenges

While sustainable development may seem to have been generally accepted into the lexicon of global environmental politics, there continues to be much criticism of its content and practice. The grounds for concern include the haziness of the concept, the continued emphasis on growth strategies, the assumptions about poverty as a cause of unsustainable development, and the way in which sustainable development seems simply to reinforce the development status quo.

Despite the efforts of the Brundtland Commission and the rather tortuous and technocratic content of Agenda 21, sustainable development has been criticized as an idea which is not well-articulated in practice. Esty argues that it has become 'a buzzword largely devoid of content' and a failure as an organizing principle (2001, p. 74). Sustainable development often seems little more than a circular argument. For example, the Business Charter for Sustainable Development (initially promulgated in 1991) argues that 'economic growth provides the conditions in which protection of the environment can best be achieved, and environmental protection, in balance with other human goals, is necessary to achieve growth that is sustainable' (International Chamber of Commerce, n.d.). Thus Finger suggests that what he calls the 'sustainable development slogan' has come simply to mean that 'ecological sustainability is good for economic development and economic development is good for ecological sustainability' (1993, pp. 42–3). All this does, he contends, is to promote fuzzy thinking. For others, the concept (to say little of the practice) is simply too all-encompassing to be of use. As Wapner observes, 'if you think about sustainable development long enough, you begin to see how it includes the challenges of the entire world' (2003, p. 9).

One of the major points of difference is the emphasis on and benefits of economic growth (albeit *sustainable* economic growth). Indeed, the goal is sometimes quite explicitly identified as 'sustainable *economic* development' (see El-Ashry, 1993, p. 87; emphasis added). This is about the 'right' kind of development or, as the World Bank put it at the time of UNCED, 'development that lasts' (cited in Sachs, 1993b, p. 10). The World Bank now presents this as a 'comprehensive development framework' for poverty reduction which adopts a long-term holistic vision (World Bank, 2001b). As noted above, the Brundtland Report called for 'more rapid economic growth in both industrial and developing countries' (WCED, 1987, p. 89) as an antidote to poverty. This view remains central to the sustainable development discourse. The World Bank observes, for example, that 'accelerated growth in productivity and income can eliminate poverty and enhance prosperity in developing countries' as long as 'critical ecosystems are improved and the social fabric that underpins development is strengthened' (2003, p. 183). Poverty reduction is expected to increase 'people's ability to invest in environmentally sustainable activities' and decrease their 'propensity to engage in environmentally destructive patterns of behaviour' (El-Ashry, 1993, p. 84; see also Jones, 2002). More obviously self-interested reasons are also offered for the world's richer countries to support poverty alleviation, because 'in the global village, someone else's poverty very soon becomes one's own problem: lack of markets for one's products, illegal immigration, pollution, contagious disease, insecurity, fanaticism, terrorism' (UNGA, 2001b, p. 13).

The focus on poverty, rather than its underlying causes, makes it easier to hold poor people responsible for environmental degradation. This, critics suggest, is too simplistic a view of the relationship between poverty and environmental degradation and one which ignores the fact that 'poverty is structurally determined' (Redclift, 1984, p. 59) and 'socially transmitted' (Redclift and Sage, 1998, p. 500). Poverty, Sachs argues, 'derives from a deficit of power rather than a lack of money' (2002, p. 15). Daly argues that 'poverty cannot be ended by overall economic growth' because the 'costs of growth now approximate or exceed its benefits' and because it overlooks 'social equity' (2002, p. 47). As Lipschutz notes, 'the maximising of economic growth does not ensure that the benefits will be equitably distributed' (1991, p. 192). Further, this emphasis on poverty makes it easier to identify unsustainable development as a problem primarily for developing countries. Yet there is no doubt that in per capita and often in absolute terms, rich countries use more resources and produce more waste than do poor ones, an issue addressed in more detail later in this chapter. At the Stockholm Conference in 1972, the head of the Kenyan delegation made a distinction between the 'environmental problems of poverty' and environmental problems resulting from the 'excesses of affluence' (cited in Ntambirweki, 1991, pp. 907–8). A focus on poverty is often accompanied by a focus on global population or, more particularly, population levels in the developing world even though fertility rates are declining in many developing countries. The most extreme suggestions call for a massive reduction in global population over the next century based on rigorous social engineering associated with one-child families (see Glasby, 2002). Yet as this chapter and others indicate, the challenge of unsustainable development is not simply one of 'too many people' but the practices of unsustainable and inequitable production and consumption (addressed below).

The test of what counts as sustainable or unsustainable development is also argued to be applied differently and inequitably in different parts of the world. While the figures are somewhat dated, Michael Redclift's inquiry regarding differences in energy use per unit of production remain relevant. If, as he observed in 1987, the US uses 370 times as much energy per capita as does Sri Lanka, do we assume that the US cannot achieve *sustainability* given its economic structure, or does it imply that Sri Lanka cannot achieve *development* given its economic structure (Redclift, 1987, p. 17)? Where environmental degradation occurs in the wake of development, the critical argument goes, this is perceived not as a flaw in the development process, but as a failure of the financial, human, technological and organizational capacity of the relevant country, for which the solution is another strategy of development – thus the efficacy of development remains impervious to any counter-evidence. At best, then, for those who are wary of the way in which sustainable development has been elaborated, the idea provides only alternatives within development rather than alternatives to development (Sachs, 1993b, p. 11). Protection of the environment, or ecological sustainability, is not ignored, but becomes a means to an end, rather than the end in itself.

The complexities of the relationship between economic growth, poverty alleviation and sustainable development are amplified by the problems of defining or measuring growth in the first place. Growth, whether sustainable or not, continues to be measured primarily in terms of GNP. American economist Hazel Henderson has argued that trying to measure an economy on indicators such as GNP is like trying to fly a jumbo jet with only one gauge on the instrument panel (in Peet, 1992, p. 209). While GNP measures income flows, it provides no information on how that income is generated or distributed. It makes no distinction between different kinds of production, between, for example, that which is spent on arms expenditure, high levels of dirty industrialization or clean-up after environmental disaster, and that which is spent on education and health. GNP measures only certain kinds of formal, 'productive' economic activity and provides no accurate measure of inequity, injustice or wealth distribution, all of which are relevant to the issue of environmental sustainability.

GNP also overlooks 'external costs' such as environmental degradation or resource depletion. The results of timber felling, for example, are usually treated as a net contribution to capital growth, even when it might lead to long-term deforestation and loss of resources (Pearce, cited in Redclift, 1987, p. 16). Thus the economic benefits of forestry are measured, but not the possible long-term costs of either regeneration or non-regeneration. Internalizing the costs of environmental degradation illuminates the consequences for economic development. For example, conservative estimates for India suggest that environmental degradation in that country costs 4.5 per cent of GDP (UNEP, 2002a, p. 309). The World Bank estimates that pollution-related health costs could be as high as 15 to 18 per cent of urban income and up to 7 per cent of GDP in countries such as the Philippines (cited in Bengwayan, 2000). Environmental decline costs countries in Southeast Asia an average of 3 to 8 per cent of their gross domestic product per year (see Barkenbus, 2001, p. 2). The annual costs of air pollution for Bangkok and Jakarta, two of the region's mega-cities, are estimated at $US5 billion (Asian Development Bank, 2002, p. 11). The costs to ASEAN countries of a doubling of atmospheric CO_2 is estimated to be between 2.1 and 8.6 per cent of GDP, much higher than the world estimate of 1.4 to 1.9 per cent (ASEAN Secretariat, 2002, p. 40).

In response to these concerns, measures of the quality as well as quantity of 'growth' are changing. The World Bank's annual *World Development Report* now uses a number of indicators such as average annual rates of inflation and adult literacy to determine the development status of individual countries. There have been attempts to incorporate the level of environmental degradation and the stock and depletion of natural resources into national income accounts – the concept of green GNP (see Repetto, 1992; Hamilton and Dixon, 2003). This takes account of the 'user costs of exploiting natural resources ... [and] the social costs of pollution emissions' (Hamilton and Dixon, 2003, p. 77). However, this approach remains a broad measure and, as with a more standard GNP measurement, gives little indication of the degree of poverty or wealth disparity within countries.

Sustainable development has also been characterized as 'a radical departure from the conventional objectives of economic policy' because it incorporates welfare, distributive justice and an element of 'futurity' (Jacobs, 1990, p. 3). Koenig argues that it is a 'paradigm shift' which 'changed our concept of development forever in adopting a model that goes far beyond conventional economic theory' (1995, p. 2; see also Bradbury, 1997). Not everyone accepts sustainable development in such radical or subversive terms. Braidotti and her colleagues argue that sustainable development in the Brundtland Report contained no fundamental threat to the status quo which is why, they suggest, it has been accepted by 'mainstream economic, development and political institutions'

(1994, p. 133). Rees takes this argument further, suggesting that as the term has 'been embraced by the political mainstream, ... it has been stripped of its original concern with ensuring future ecological stability' (1990, p. 18). In this view, the Rio and WSSD approach to sustainable development represents the 'culmination of a process of rehabilitation of the ideology of economic growth' (Pallemaerts, 2003, p. 9).

The failure of sustainable development to challenge the modernization paradigm is viewed as inherently problematic because it reinforces a form of development which relies on capital injection, transfer of technology and the cultural transformation of old or traditional ways that are considered to be obstacles to development, a process that Sachs refers to as the 'unfettered hegemony of Western productivism' (1993b, p. 4). What has not occurred, in this critical view, is any sufficient analysis of the political and economic reasons *behind* resource depletion or the environmental and social failure of development or modernization models. Critics take the view that rather than providing a solution to poverty and environmental degradation, development has resulted in *greater* inequities because it has entrenched an exploitative relationship between the industrialized countries and the developing world, and because it has engendered a misplaced belief in the 'linearity of progress' (Braidotti *et al.*, 1994, p. 131).

Beyond sustainable development?

For many critics, the continued emphasis on growth precludes any debate about the need for an intelligent restraint of growth. William Rees argues that the pursuit of sustainable development should 'force a reconsideration of the entire material growth ethic, the central pillar of industrial society' (1990, p. 21), what Sanders calls the 'gospel of export-led growth' (1990, p. 396). The discourse of sustainable development and the logic of practices such as sustainable consumption which are part of the implementation strategies are criticized to the extent that they remain embedded in an 'efficiency-focused rationalisation discourse' (Hobson, 2002, p. 95). Herman Daly (once an economist with the World Bank) has distinguished between sustainable development, which he argued is about quality, and sustainable growth, which is about quantity (see Peet, 1992, p. 208; Daly, 2002). For critics of the Bruntlandt/UNCED version of sustainable development, there has been a failure to distinguish the two. If the distinction has been made, either the emphasis on growth and quantity has overridden the emphasis on quality, or the proposition that growth supports development which then supports more growth is accepted without any serious questioning as to whether this is indeed so. What is required, in this critical perspective, is a reclaiming of a quality- rather than quantity-driven concept. Some scholars prefer the term 'eco-development' although (just as with sustainable development) the phrase has been used in a variety of ways ranging from a planning concept which emphasizes local and regional input (advocated by UNEP) to an 'ethically committed, integrated approach' (Redclift, 1987, p. 34). A more integrated approach of this latter kind explicitly incorporates social and cultural processes, and is shaped by those processes and basic human needs, rather than assuming that those needs will automatically be fulfilled by something called sustainable development (see also Hobson, 2002).

Some prefer to think of sustainable development as a 'moral concept, not one derived from market behaviour' (Jacobs, 1990, p. 9) which starts from a concern with equity, justice and a reclaiming of the local. Sustainable development (as an idea and as a practice) is therefore required to mean more than 'economic growth without ecological disaster' (cited in Asian and Pacific Women's Resource Collection Network, 1992, p. 10) and a way of developing 'a gentler, more balanced and stable relationship with the natural world' (Rees, 1990, p. 18). It should be possible, some argue, to pursue a 'development without growth' model (or at least, development with slow growth) which makes available to a society 'the means of production and levels of income that can make local and regional markets largely self-sustaining' (Lipschutz, 1991, p. 193). It is interesting that the corporate community has also adopted the language of human needs and qualitative growth in the concept of eco-efficiency. The World Business Council for Sustainable Development defines this approach to sustainable development as one which involves 'the delivery of ... goods and services that satisfy human needs and bring quality of life, while progressively reducing ecological impacts and resource intensity ... it helps wealthier countries to grow more qualitatively ... [and] developing countries to grow quantitatively while saving resources' (WBCSD, 2002, pp. 228–9). These debates about production and poverty, income and equity, and exploitation of resources and environmental services have become a central feature of political debates within the global politics of the environment between developed and developing countries.

North and South: managing the 'common agenda'

The terms 'developed' and 'developing' are commonly used in environmental agreements to distinguish the rich (usually industrialized) countries from the poor(er) ones. The former includes the OECD countries and sometimes the transitional economies of the former Soviet bloc. The latter group of countries – the developing world – is defined, in effect, by its exclusion from the former. Other phrases are used: First and Third Worlds; the North and the South. These are loaded terms, not least because (with the possible exception of those based on some kind of loose geographic determination) they suggest a value hierarchy. Nevertheless, they are widely used within the literature, even by 'Third World' scholars and are therefore used here, cognizant of Ann Hawkins's observation that 'we all await new ways to speak (and think) of differing countries' (1993, p. 222). It is not entirely inaccurate to understand the 'Third World' in terms of 'political powerlessness, economic poverty and social marginalisation' (Thomas, 1999, p. 226). However, as earlier chapters have suggested, it can be misleading to conflate the 'North' and 'South' into two implacably opposed but internally cohesive blocs and it would also be incorrect to suggest that the relationship between the two is one simply of confrontation, with no recognition of shared environmental interests. Differences within each group on specifics are, however, often overshadowed by a strong degree of cohesion and agreement among, but not often between, developed and developing countries on fundamental contextual and strategic issues, such as the causes of global environmental degradation, relative vulnerabilities and the relative capacities of rich and poor countries to manage the impact of that degradation.

As earlier chapters have demonstrated, the industrialized countries of the North have been and continue to be a major source of the degradation of the commons through the disproportionate use of their own resources and those of developing countries, and the disproportionate production of waste. Developing countries will suffer from this in ways that are out of proportion to their contribution to the problems of global environmental change. The UNDP notes, for example, that the land area of Bangladesh, a country which contributes about 0.3 per cent of global greenhouse emissions, could shrink by as much as 17 per cent with a one metre rise in sea-levels (1996, p. 26). UNEP (2002d) reports that a rise of a metre could flood large areas of the Nile delta and up to 70 per cent of the Seychelles islands. The costs are also likely to be higher for developing countries. The IPCC estimates that the impacts of climate change could cost developing countries between 2 and 9 per cent of their GNP, compared with only 1 to 2 per cent for developed countries (cited in Dunn, 1998, p. 22).

The rationale for developed countries to provide various forms of assistance to developing countries has both an ethical (other-regarding) and practical (self-regarding) basis. The ethical dimensions of this argument have been explored, in part, in Chapter 6. The practical (or perhaps instrumental) aspects of the environmental relationship between developed and developing countries arise from mutual vulnerabilities. Ecological and economic interdependencies mean that unless developing countries are able to address both proximate causes and impacts of environmental degradation, developed countries will also be increasingly environmentally and economically vulnerable to global environmental degradation. Pursuit of economic development is also slowly changing the relativities between developed and developing countries with respect to resource use and waste production. On this basis, industrialized countries argue that without some kind of mitigating action in the South, their own attempts to halt and reverse environmental degradation will of themselves be insufficient to manage global change. They argue that these actions must be embedded in legally binding international commitments. Developing countries have taken substantial steps to manage domestic environmental problems in the context of global environmental change and sustainable development. They argue, however, that if they are to continue to make their development path a sustainable one, these responsibilities should be formulated as legally binding commitments *only* when the North has taken a lead and *only* with financial and technological assistance. From the perspective of many developing countries, solutions to the global environmental crisis also cannot and should not be considered independently of a reform of the international trading system, substantial improvements in international development assistance and a rescheduling (at minimum) of external debt, issues which are explored in more depth in Chapter 8.

The degree of mutual vulnerabilities suggests that developing countries (or at least those which are the most populous) should have a degree of political leverage in environmental negotiations. China and India, for example, initially refused to participate in the ozone depletion negotiations because they felt that the Montreal Protocol did not and would not address the concerns of the developing countries, especially regarding questions of financial and technological assistance. In response, donor countries committed to increase the size of the fund established under the Montreal Protocol if India and China participated, which they have since done, although the fund remains small. Simonis suggests that developing countries have achieved a number of 'bargaining successes in international environmental policy' (2001, p. 106) in the general recognition of differential responsibilities, the importance of compensation for incremental costs and more democratic decision-making processes. These successes tend, however, to be expressed in MEAs in a general hortatory manner and, as Chapter 8 shows, have not often translated into successful material outcomes. The degree of bargaining leverage is minimized because, while the relative contributions of developing countries to global environmental degradation is likely to increase in the future, they are also the countries which will be most affected. 'Holding out' on negotiations could therefore be counterproductive. Unity among developing countries can also be difficult to achieve. Within the developing world some will be affected to a greater degree and more immediately than others. That immediate impact (for example, the consequences of sea-level rises for low-lying island states) often translates into less rather than more political leverage, especially if such countries have little to offer by way of bargaining chips. Von Moltke suggests that the collapse of the Soviet Union also 'robbed developing countries of an important source of political leverage ... in playing East against West' (2002, p. 343). In fact, the new economies in transition of the former Soviet bloc have now become competitors with the traditional G77 developing countries for development assistance and, in particular, for private capital investment.

The ability for developing countries to bargain and exert leverage in environmental negotiations is also a factor of their ability to participate in those negotiations and of the kinds of expertise upon which a country can call. Put simply, intergovernmental conferences are expensive and have become more so with the proliferation of formal conferences, preparatory meetings, ad hoc working groups, intersessional meetings and a range of regional and other fora into which governments are keen to inject their views and to protect their interests. As Biermann observes, 'developing countries lack the resources to attend all these meetings with a sufficient number of well-qualified diplomats and experts' (2002, p. 300). Developing countries, especially the smaller, poorer ones, often have a limited range of technical, scientific, legal and economic expertise upon which to call, expertise that is therefore likely to be quite thinly stretched. It is now standard practice for voluntary funds to be established with each new global environmental negotiating process to assist developing country participation, although the sums contributed are rarely large. In a report prepared in advance of UNGASS, the UN Secretary-General expressed concern that the level of contribution to these voluntary funds was 'insufficient for the task' (1997d, para. 8). The voluntary fund established for the participation of representatives of small island developing states (SIDS) in the 1994 UN Global Conference on Sustainable Development in SIDS provides one example. The secretariat sought $US950,000 but, by mid-September 1993, only $US154,783 had been received from developed countries (Anon., 1994a, p. 6).

Whose common future?

The Brundtland Report made great play, in its title, of the common future shared by developed and developing countries. Yet developing countries argue that the global environmental agenda has come to be defined by the environmental interests of the affluent North rather than the developmental interests of the South. Concern is expressed about the way in which the 'resources' of the developing world, such as tropical forests or species and biodiversity, are now determined to be the 'common heritage of humankind' amid expectations that the developing countries are now supposed to manage them for the good of all. From a developing country perspective, 'efforts to extend the concept of the global commons to nationally-based resources' are seen as a threat to developing country sovereignty and to their rights 'to benefit economically from indigenous resources' (Soto, 1992, p. 694). Vandana Shiva sums it up this way: the North's slogan at UNCED and other global negotiation fora seems to be 'what's yours is mine. What's mine is mine' (1993, p. 152).

This is argued to be inequitable on two counts (as earlier discussions have shown): first, because in the past, developing world resources were exploited by and for the benefit of Northern countries and, second, because when it comes to issues such as desertification, the causes and consequences of which may also have global implications, the Northern countries resist attempts to have these defined as 'global' concerns. The Stockholm Declaration paid some attention to these issues, driven in part by concerns raised by developing countries at the meeting in Founex convened immediately prior to the UNCHE (see Chapter 1). The Declaration confirmed that most of the environmental problems in developing countries are caused by underdevelopment and, therefore, that the needs of developing countries included access to aid, technology and other assistance (principles 9 to 12). It also acknowledged, in principle 23, that the standards set by industrialized countries might not be appropriate for developing countries.

Differences between the developed and developing countries on the meaning of the 'common agenda' were in evidence from the beginning of the UNCED process and continued through UNGASS and WSSD. That UNCED was devoted to environment and development, not as separate issues but as concerns that were inextricably tied, was an attempt to reconcile the major concerns of both developing and developed countries. The Rio agreements reflect that compromise. The Rio Declaration reaffirms the often controversial right to development (principle 3). It emphasizes the importance of eradicating poverty (principle 5) and requires that the 'special needs' of developing countries be given priority (principle 6). Many of the chapters of Agenda 21 reflect, in their generalities if not in their specificity, developing country concerns. Thus there are chapters on the importance of eradicating poverty, on changing consumption patterns (with an emphasis on the North), on financial resources and mechanisms and technology transfer (although, as explored further in Chapter 8 of this book, these issues were highly contentious).

These general principles have been reasserted in a number of other environmental agreements, many of which have been discussed in Chapters 2 and 3 of this book. The Montreal Protocol, for example, acknowledges that 'special provision is required to meet the needs of developing countries' for substances that might be ozone-depleting. Article 5 established a ten-year grace period for developing countries to comply with restrictions as long as certain requirements were met (see Chapter 3). The Forest Principles also state that developing country access to technology for forest management and conservation should be 'promoted, facilitated and financed, as appropriate' (UNCED, 1992c, article 11) although the provision is so vague as to be potentially meaningless. Both the Biodiversity Convention and the Desertification Convention contain provisions emphasizing the importance of technology and financial resource transfer between developed and developing countries. The Framework Convention on Climate Change emphasizes the right of a country to determine its own development priorities and acknowledges that 'the specific needs and special circumstances' of developing countries 'should be given full consideration' (UN INC/FCCC, 1992, article 3.2). It emphasizes equitable burden-sharing and calls for developed country parties to mobilize financial resources and to provide 'new and additional' financial assistance to assist vulnerable developing countries to meet their obligations and to prepare for and adapt to adverse effects of climate change. Attempts to manage the 'climate bargain' between developed and developing countries were one feature of the flexibility mechanisms in the Kyoto Protocol although, as Chapter 3 has shown, the issue of commitments by developing countries has been at the core of climate disputes.

Two specific 'geographical' clusters within the bloc of developing countries have been singled out for particular attention on the grounds of their exceptional vulnerability – Africa, and small island developing states. Both have their 'own' chapters in the Johannesburg Plan of Implementation. UNEP's comprehensive *Africa Environment Outlook*, released in 2002, chronicled environmental degradation including air and water pollution, land degradation, drought and wildlife loss among other problems against a background of endemic poverty, ill health and disease (see UNEP, 2002d). Land degradation and drought in Africa were one of the key factors behind the Desertification Convention which refers to the continent specifically in its title. Indeed, as Chapter 2 indicated, the original intention was that the Convention would include an annex only on Africa in the first instance (with other regional annexes to be negotiated at a later time). The Plan for Further Implementation adopted at UNGASS in 1997 drew attention to the fact that many of the environment and sustainable development problems affecting developing countries were particularly difficult in Africa. The Johannesburg report observed that sustainable development had remained elusive for most countries in Africa (United Nations, 2002b, para. 62) and called for action in a wide range of areas, calling for more attention to providing various kinds of support to countries in Africa. Little of this was new, however. Rather, it repeated the more general demands of Agenda 21 and the Millennium Development Goals. The only substantially new theme was a rather open commitment to support the New Partnership for Africa's Development (NEPAD) initiative established by leaders of the African states themselves in 2001.

Concerns for small island states arose in tandem with, although initially separate from, the political demands of the Alliance of Small Island States at the climate change negotiations (see Griffith, 1995). The designator is slightly misleading in that the SIDS list of 42 countries (states and territories) includes low-lying coastal countries which have economic and environmental vulnerabilities similar to those of developing island states. Chapter 17 of Agenda 21 (the oceans and coasts chapter) included a programme area specifically focused on small island states on the general grounds of ecological and economic vulnerability and, more specifically, because 'the ocean and coastal environment is of strategic importance and constitutes a valuable development resource' (UNCED, 1992b, para. 17.123). While the concern for SIDS has been driven by the vulnerabilities associated with climate change and other natural disasters (or disasters of nature), other relevant factors include the assault on their natural resource base and a limited adaptive capacity (Matthew and Gaulin, 2001, p. 49) as well as remoteness, excessive dependence on international trade and costly infrastructure (UN Division for Sustainable Development, 2003). The UN Conference on the Sustainable Development of Small Island Developing States (SIDS) was convened in April 1994 in Barbados with a plan of action that contained 14 priority areas focusing on environment and resource issues as well as institutional and administrative challenges which required action by SIDS themselves and by the international community (see UNGA, 1994). The Plan of Action was reviewed and reinforced by a special session of the General Assembly in 1999 which also identified a number of sectoral and cross-sectoral areas which required further attention. These included climate change and freshwater resources in the former category and financial, technological and capacity support for the latter (see United Nations, 1999).

Common but differentiated responsibilities

The concept of 'common but differentiated responsibilities' (CBDR) is an attempt to meet Northern concerns that all countries have obligations and Southern concerns that those obligations are not the same. The concept is meant to convey both solidarity and a particular kind of burden-sharing that takes account of inequities in global resource use and in contribution to environmental degradation. It also draws attention to the technological and financial resources that industrialized countries command. At a minimum, the principle of common responsibilities requires all states to participate 'actively in the formation and implementation of international law' for sustainable development and environmental protection (Matsui, 2002, p. 153). Beyond that, a number of issues remain difficult to resolve when it comes to putting the principle into practice.

While developed countries accept that they have been more resource-intensive in the past, they point out, first, that developing country contribution to the problem at a global level will increase in the future and, second, that energy use in developing countries is very inefficient. They note, for example, that the OECD share of global CO_2 emissions has decreased by 11 per cent since 1973 (UNEP, 2002a, p. xxiii) and that non-OECD countries use '3.8 times as much energy per dollar of GDP' (World Bank, 2002, p. 177). As noted earlier, industrialized developed countries argue that any action that they take will have little effect without action from Southern countries given their future contribution to degradation of the commons. They also suggest that developing countries cannot be free-riders with respect to the mitigation of global environmental problems. On issues such as desertification, deforestation and loss of biodiversity, many developed countries argue that developing countries must take responsibility for proximate degradation and must therefore be prepared to make commitments, especially if they also expect financial and technological assistance. The report of the High-level Panel on Financing for Development (the Zedillo Report), appointed by the UN Secretary-General, made it clear that the 'primary responsibility for achieving growth and equitable development lies with the developing countries themselves' (UNGA, 2001b, p. 3).

Developing countries, on the other hand, want attention paid to the systemic causes of environmental degradation in the functioning of the global economy, the nature of development assistance, inequitable trade and debt, issues addressed further in the next chapter. They argue that because Northern development and consumerism has been and continues to be one of the primary causes of the global environmental crisis, it is incumbent on Northern countries to take the lead in making commitments to reverse environmental degradation. Northern demands for comparable action to be taken in the South are interpreted as one more example of neo-imperialist practices which may place further constraints on economic growth in the South and further exacerbate inequities between rich and poor countries.

Most multilateral environmental agreements, whether legally binding or not, contain some expression of CBDR. The Rio Declaration restates the idea of 'common but differentiated responsibilities' (UNCED, 1992a, principle 7). The UNFCCC refers to the 'common but differentiated responsibilities and respective capabilities' of developed and developing countries (UN INC/FCCC, 1992, article 3.1). It notes, in the preamble, that the largest share of historical and current global emissions comes from the developed countries, but notes also that developing countries' share will increase as they pursue social and development needs. Developed countries are required to take the lead in addressing greenhouse gas emissions and climate change. As Chapter 3 has shown, however, this question of lead action versus relative commitments remains a contentious one on the Kyoto Protocol agenda. The Desertification Convention, on the other hand, is quite specific in its requirements for complementary commitments. Parties affected by desertification (primarily developing countries) are expected to enact or to strengthen laws, policies and action programmes to manage the causes of land degradation and desertification. Developed countries are required to provide support and financial resources and facilitate access to technology. CBDR was controversial at WSSD. Industrialized countries continued to insist that the principle should apply only to global environmental threats and should not invoke specific or detailed legally binding obligations. Segger *et al.* suggest that CBDR 'emerged strengthened, broadened and invigorated by the WSSD' (2003, p. 58), especially because the Plan of Implementation provides the basis for applying the principle beyond the confines of environmental protection to include challenges such as poverty eradication. Pallemaerts (2003) suggests, on the other hand, that the outcome was really more of a continuing compromise between developed and developing countries.

Sustainable production and consumption

The expectation that developed countries will provide technological and financial assistance to developing countries (addressed in more detail in the next chapter) is matched by an expectation that they will also address the domestic challenges of production and consumption. As this chapter and others have demonstrated, richer countries (and richer peoples) consume and produce more on a per capita basis, and often on an absolute basis, than do poorer countries and peoples, outstripping their ecological footprint. Global estimates suggest that 'current levels of consumption and production are 25% higher than the earth's ecological capacity' with the 'richest 15% of the world's population accounting for 56% of the world's total consumption, whilst the poorest 40% account for only 11%' (European Commission, 2002, p. 1). Chapter 4 of Agenda 21 observed that 'the major cause of the continued deterioration of the global environment is the unsustainable pattern of consumption and production, *particularly in industrialized countries*' (UNCED, 1992b, para. 4.3; emphasis added). The Rio Declaration exhorted states to reduce and eliminate unsustainable patterns of production and consumption. Agenda 21 reminded industrialized countries that 'measures to be undertaken at the international level for the protection and enhancement of the environment must take fully into account the current imbalances in the global patterns of consumption and production' (UNCED, 1992b, para. 4.4).

The focus on economic activity in industrialized countries was reinforced by the Malmö Declaration proclaimed at the first Global Ministerial Environmental Forum in 1999 which identified 'unsustainable production and consumption patterns' as one of the root causes of global environmental degradation, along with pervasive poverty, inequities in the distribution of wealth, and the debt burden (GMEF, 2000). The UN Secretary-General's report on the implementation of Agenda 21, prepared for WSSD, was even more blunt, arguing that 'sustainable development cannot be achieved without fundamental changes in the way industrial societies produce and consume' (UNSG, 2001, para. 82). The WSSD Plan of Implementation, on the other hand, refers only to 'the way societies produce and consume' (United Nations, 2002b, para. 14). The Commission on Sustainable Development has made unsustainable consumption and production central to its work plan with an emphasis on deploying market-based instruments and pricing signals to encourage new patterns of behaviour in both producers and consumers (see Chapter 8). As part of this process, in 1999 the General Assembly endorsed sustainable consumption guidelines but a UNEP survey in 2002 revealed that their application was progressing only slowly (UNEP, 2002c). The various reports prepared for WSSD confirmed that little had changed and that, in fact, 'more natural resources are being consumed and more pollution is being generated' (UNSG, 2001, para. 83).

As the discussion here has demonstrated, there are different interpretations of the practical implications of common but differentiated responsibilities. For developing countries, this is a principle which requires the North to take a lead in a variety of ways, including that of consumption and production. For developed countries, the principle acknowledges different contributions to environmental degradation but does not (or should not) absolve developing countries of commitments as well. In whatever way these principles – common but differentiated responsibilities and sustainable development – are understood and defined, they have to be put into practice. The question of strategies is the focus of the next chapter. Not surprisingly, given the themes of this book so far, the nature of those strategies and the means of implementing them have been contentious.

Chapter 8

Strategies for Sustainable Development

Three categories of strategies designed to give effect to sustainable development and to the idea of common but differentiated responsibilities are discussed in this chapter: transfer mechanisms; reform of the structures of and processes within the globalized political economy; and the application of economic instruments to environmental protection. These are, however, not simply technical or regulatory exercises. As the discussion here shows, they involve political and social issues which relate to competing interests, the distribution of costs and benefits, and implementation.

Enhancing the flow of resources to developing countries

As earlier chapters have demonstrated, developing countries demand that the responsibilities of developed countries should include financial and technology transfer or, in the words of the Brundtland Report, 'enhancing the flow of resources to developing countries' (WCED, 1987, p. 76). These issues have been central to multilateral environmental negotiations since the Stockholm Conference in 1972. The points of contention arise not simply over the degree of assistance that should be provided to developing countries, but in what form it should be provided, on whose terms and what institutional structures are most appropriate to manage it.

Developing countries have generally argued that without financial and technological assistance they are unable easily (if at all) to meet the costs of mitigating environmental problems. The political disputes over financial assistance have centred on competing demands for additionality and conditionality. For developing countries, financial resources should be *additional* to those already given through existing bilateral and multilateral development programmes. The reasons? First, development assistance funds are already low ('woefully inadequate', Kofi

Annan has called it; see Annan, 2002, p. 7) – approximately $US53 billion in 2000. In 2000, aid flows were 10 per cent below 1990 levels and totalled only 0.22 per cent of donor GNP (Rajamani, 2003, p. 27). Very few donor countries have ever reached (or even come close to) the UN target of a commitment of 0.7 per cent of GNP for official development assistance (ODA). In fact the net flow of financial resources from the developing to developed countries is increasing. According to Smith (cited in Rees, 2002, p. 29), in the 1960s the ratio was three to one (that is, for every one dollar that went to the developing countries, three went from South to North through debt servicing and other financial flows). By 1998, it was seven to one. Second, substantial additional funds will be required to address the sources and impacts of environmental degradation and to meet the challenges of sustainable development. The UNCED Secretariat calculated, for example, that the cost to developing countries of implementing Agenda 21 would be in the vicinity of $US600 billion per annum, of which $US125 billion would have to come from donor countries. The cost of implementing the more recent Millennium Development Goals has been estimated at 'only' $US50 billion per year in funds additional to existing ODA.

There was no firm commitment at UNCED to funds anywhere near the amount calculated by the Secretariat. Developed countries reaffirmed the 0.7 per cent of GNP as the ODA target but accepted no deadlines and made few new commitments. Pledges from heads of state or government were estimated to add up to approximately $US2 billion (Chatterjee and Finger, 1994, p. 139) but little of that eventuated. In the Monterrey Consensus adopted at the International Conference on Financing for Development in March 2002, participating governments characterized official development assistance as a 'complement to other sources of funding' (United Nations, 2002a, para. 39). They did recognize that substantial increases would be required (United Nations, 2002a, para. 41) and urged developed countries 'that have not done so to make concrete efforts' towards the 0.7 per cent of GNP target (United Nations, 2002a, para. 42). Just prior to the meeting in Monterrey, the EU committed to a target of 0.39 per cent by 2006. While the WSSD noted that the use of ODA needed to be made more efficient and effective, the Plan of Implementation did little more than reiterate earlier commitments although governments did agree to establish and make voluntary contributions to a world solidarity fund to eradicate poverty.

In general, donor countries are nervous about additionality because, without guarantees on how funds will be spent, there is no certainty of *mutual* benefit. They argue that financial assistance should therefore be conditional, tied to particular programmes to ensure that the money is appropriately targeted at global concerns and for global benefits rather than being used only to overcome local environment and development problems. It is not surprising that recipient countries are reluctant to accept such conditions, seeing them as undermining sovereignty and reminiscent of International Monetary Fund (IMF) structural adjustment programmes. In 1989, the Conference of the Non-Aligned Movement (NAM) noted 'with concern a growing tendency towards... increased conditionalities on the part of some developed countries in dealing with environmental issues' (cited in Porter and Brown, 1991, p. 127) and this has not altered much since.

The second component of a transfer of resources focuses on technology. Technology is required by developing countries to mitigate the causes of environmental degradation, to adapt to and manage the impacts of that degradation, to improve monitoring and measuring and to support cleaner production. Technology transfer involves not only specific technologies but also the transfer of scientific and technical expertise and know-how, usually captured in the concept of capacity-building. Developed countries increasingly prefer to define this as technology cooperation rather than transfer. The main point of contention between the sources of technology (usually the developed countries) and those who do not have it (usually the developing countries) is whether technology should be transferred at concessional or commercial rates – that is, should it be a kind of development assistance or should it be a commercial transaction. The 'concessional rates' argument is that developing countries simply cannot afford the technology. Given that its use is of benefit to all and in light of past exploitations and contributions to global environmental insecurities, technology transfer becomes a form of redistributive justice. The 'commercial rates' argument (favoured by the US in particular) is, first, that technology is held not by governments but by private companies which should be fully compensated for their investment and, second, that technology transfer could enable developing countries to 'leapfrog', thus providing them with commercial competitive advantage.

There are also differences over whether environmental agreements should include legal obligations for developed countries to facilitate access to technology and financial resources. India attempted, for example, to have language included in Montreal Protocol amendments that would make developing country commitments to phase out CFCs subject to the private transfer of technology. In the end developing countries had to settle for language which simply noted that their ability to meet obligations would depend on such transfers but did not make that transfer obligatory nor make any developing country commitment conditional upon such transfer. While Agenda 21 included a chapter on 'transfer of environmentally-sound technology, cooperation and capacity building' (Chapter 34) it invokes no firm commitments. Rather, access to technology is to be promoted, facilitated and financed as appropriate (UNCED, 1992b, para. 34.14(b)), with an emphasis on technology cooperation and capacity-building rather than outright transfer. This emphasis also underpins principle 9 of the Rio Declaration and remains the preferred approach for developed countries in the UNGASS and Johannesburg agreements where the transfer of technology is incorporated into more general statements about the implementation of specific programme activities.

The World Bank and the Global Environment Facility

There have been a number of suggestions for mechanisms to manage the financial aspects of environmental development assistance. A World Atmosphere Fund was proposed at the 1988 Toronto Conference on the Changing Atmosphere, to be financed by a levy on fossil fuel consumption in industrialized countries. At the fourth UNCED PrepComm, the G77 and China proposed a new Green Fund to administer the funding of the Rio agreements. Papua New Guinea and the AOSIS countries have called for a global climate insurance fund which would help with disaster relief in developing countries (see McCully, 1991b, p. 245). As noted above, at WSSD governments committed themselves to a (voluntary) solidarity fund for poverty alleviation. In debates about how financial and other transfers for environmental purposes should be managed, developing countries have generally sought to have any MEA-related financial mechanism under the control of the parties to that convention. The richer donor countries, on the other hand, have generally advocated the use of existing institutions, a role that has fallen on the World Bank in general and the Global Environment Facility in particular. The World Bank is important because the scale of its programmes – a lending portfolio of $US144 billion in 2000 (Mucklow, 2000, p. 100) – means that 'it has a considerable environmental and social impact in recipient countries' (Hyvarinen and Brack, 2000, p. 35).

The Bank appointed its first environmental adviser in 1970 and established an Office of Environmental Affairs in 1973 but the number of full-time environmental advisers remained small until the mid-1980s. In 1987, under pressure from NGO campaigns which documented and publicized the poor environmental record of Bank lending projects, Bank President Barber Conable established a central Environment Department and four regional environment divisions. In October 1992, a new Vice-President for Environmentally Sustainable Development was appointed to the Bank – the post is now defined as Environmentally and

Socially Sustainable Development and by 1993 there were approximately 100 staff working on environmental issues in the Environment Department and in five environmental divisions linked to regional operations. Since October 1989, environmental assessments have been mandatory for all Bank projects but they remain the responsibility of the government of the borrowing country. Changes under James Wolfensohn, appointed President of the Bank in 1995, have sought to mainstream environment and sustainable development objectives and to make the Bank's processes more participatory and open to civil society with requirements for in-country consultation with NGOs and affected groups. The process of developing a new Environmental Strategy was set in train in 1999 with three interrelated objectives – to improve people's quality of life; to improve the prospects for and the quality of growth; and to protect the quality of the regional and global environmental commons. The Strategy adopted in 2001 emphasized the importance of mainstreaming environmental concerns and promised to 'accelerate progress toward integrating environment and development' (World Bank, 2001a, p. 3).

At the time, Robert Watson (then Director of the Environment Department) suggested that the emphasis was 'turning from preventing harm to incorporating environmental and social values into the everyday operations of the major sectors in which the Bank operates' (1999, p. 5). NGOs (and some of the Bank's own former employees) have remained sceptical about the Bank's attempts to 'green' itself and, in particular, its commitment to sustainable development lending. There is no doubt that projects funded by the World Bank have resulted in environmental degradation and in the dislocation of large numbers of people. The environmental consequences arise not only from direct degradation such as deforestation, threats to rare and endangered wildlife and pollution. They also arise through the social, economic and health impacts on local communities and through the displacement of peoples (itself a real problem of social marginalization) who are often then forced to utilize the marginal lands to which they are moved in an unsustainable manner. A very small selection of projects which fall into this category would include the Carajás iron ore project in Brazil, the Singrauli coal mine and coal-fired electricity generation project in India, the Narmada Valley dams (the Sardar Sarovar and Narmada Sagar) also in India, as well as Bank-funded transmigration programmes in Brazil (the Polonoereste) and Indonesia. Infrastructure support such as road or dam construction also contributes to the negative environmental impact of projects. Studies of extractive industry projects in Africa that have been funded by the World Bank have concluded that the 'general performance of the Bank with regards to environmental sustainability … is not encouraging' (Pegg, 2003, p. 25).

Environmental improvement projects with a specifically local focus have also been proved inadequate. As one example, local NGOs documented a range of problems arising from the use of pesticides in the Integrated Swamps Development project in Indonesia which violated the Bank's policy on pest management (see WRI, 2003, p. 73).

The Bank's record in adhering to its own internal rules for approving projects and for meeting poverty alleviation and environmental protection goals remains under scrutiny. In 1992, the independent Morse Report, commissioned by the World Bank, found that 'Bank management had abused and neglected stated Bank policies on environment and resettlement, and that this attitude pervaded the Bank's hierarchy of decision-making and project implementation' (Werksman, 1993, pp. 73–4). Almost a decade later, an internal report in 2000 acknowledged that the Bank's 1991 forest strategy had failed to protect either forests or the poor and that its lending strategy was flawed (see Reuters, 2000). In 2000 the Bank's Inspection Panel identified problems in the proposal to provide funding (later rejected by the Chinese government) for a controversial poverty reduction plan in Qinghai in Western China. The Panel raised concerns about the adequacy of the Bank's environmental and social assessments and whether its directives on indigenous peoples had been followed. Indeed, the Bank's own (independent) Operations Evaluation Department concluded in a comprehensive assessment of the Bank's environmental performance that (among other things) more needed to be done in improving environmental safeguard policies and their implementation (see World Bank, 2001a, p. 11).

In light of these various criticisms and revelations, the Bank's central role in the Global Environment Facility ensured that the GEF was and has remained subject to scrutiny. The establishment of the Global Environment Facility in 1991 (see Chapter 4) was characterized as a 'willingness on the part of the world's wealthier states to safeguard the inheritance of future generations by helping developing countries to mitigate their growing contribution to global environmental degradation' (El-Ashry, 1993, p. 93). It is unlikely that the Facility has met this expectation. As noted in Chapter 4, its purpose is to meet the incremental costs of meeting global environmental concerns through investment and technical assistance. For some, the GEF provided an opportunity for the World Bank to ' "greenwash" its operations' (Streck, 2001, p. 75). Certainly the majority of projects funded in the first period of the GEF were tied to existing World Bank projects. In its first ten years, the GEF funded some 700 projects in 150 countries. Despite having dispersed more than $US4 billion from its own project funds (along with as much as $US8 billion in additional financing), 'GEF's official evaluators cannot advertise any serious impact on the rate of causes of global environmental change' (Zoe Young, 2002, p. 4). While the Facility's own review process suggests that its projects have produced 'significant results aimed at improving global environmental problems', it also admits that it is difficult to determine whether there has been a 'measurable impact on most of the global threats it seeks to address' (WRI, 2003, p. 153).

Solutions or flawed strategies?

While there would seem to be good ethical, practical and political reasons for the flow of resources to developing countries to be increased, the short- and long-term environmental and developmental value of these strategies is worthy of further examination. There are, for example, grounds for concern that substantial flows of new and additional financial resources to developing countries may actually increase global inequities and exacerbate rather than solve global environment and development problems. Even at concessional rates and with a grace period, loans still have to be repaid with interest. There is, then, a likelihood that the income required to service new debt will continue to rely on environmentally unsustainable production. Lewis demonstrates also that 'environmental aid does not target [those] most in need of abating local pollution' (2003, p. 144). The decline in ODA has been accompanied by an emphasis among donor countries on the importance of foreign direct investment (FDI) as 'vital complements to national and international development efforts [which] contribute to sustained economic growth over the long term' including, of course, sustainable development and environmental protection (United Nations, 2002a, para. 20). Martens and Paul suggest that private investment is a 'deceptive hope' (1998). By the late 1990s only 37 per cent of FDI went to developing countries and that not to the poorest among them (UNDP, 1999, p. 31), in part because of a preference for investment in manufacturing and service sectors. In fact, 75 per cent of FDI went to just ten middle-income countries (World Bank, 2002, p. 5). The onus, however, is placed on developing countries to establish the appropriate domestic environment to attract investment. Even when foreign investment is drawn to natural resources and primary commodities – the 'comparative advantage' of many poorer developing countries – past practice demonstrates that those industries are often a primary cause of environmental degradation.

Arguments about Northern advantage, Southern dependency, inadequate past practice and potential future exacerbation of environmental degradation are also made about technology transfer. Transferring technology will, in this view, simply entrench reliance on Northern technology and is, therefore, another form of neo-colonialism. For example, the non-ozone-depleting substances and production processes which are transferred (as appropriate) under the Montreal Protocol are owned by Northern chemical companies. The transfer of technology is often tied to development assistance which produces a 'great dependence on expatriate expertise' which, as the World Bank itself has observed, displaces local experts (Martens, 2002, p. 27). A belief in technology as a solution to unsustainable development and environmental damage is claimed to be counter-intuitive when technology has been the cause of much environmental degradation as well as 'disastrous social [and] cultural damage' (Chatterjee and Finger, 1994, p. 59). Past experience confirms that the technology transferred is not always appropriate to local needs or concerns and has sometimes been less than successful in assisting local communities towards what is often a reclaiming of self-sufficiency and meeting basic human needs. Green Revolution technology, for example, was designed to increase agricultural efficiency and yield. Yet it resulted in environmental degradation through extensive fertilizer and water use, and land aggregation (and thus increased poverty for those engaged in subsistence agriculture). It introduced seed types which had to be purchased anew each year, replacing so-called 'inefficient'-yield seeds which could be harvested, stored and replanted, thus minimizing costs for poor rural dwellers. A survey of the specific modality of national cleaner production centres (NCPCs) established by the United Nations Industrial Development Organization (UNIDO) indicates that 'donors have not learned to provide assistance that is unencumbered by their interests' (Muchie, 2000, p. 213).

As noted earlier, commitments (even vague ones) to financial and technological assistance are increasingly couched in language that demands 'structural adjustment' in developing countries. While many developing countries themselves face problems of internal inequities and poor governance structures, this emphasis on domestic enabling environments allows Northern countries to defer the issue of their own unsustainability. It conveys a message that environmental problems and unsustainable practices are to be found primarily in the South and that they can be overcome if only enough money and technology are given. This focus on the transfer of money and machinery can obscure the urgent need for radical changes in First World consumption patterns (discussed in Chapter 7) and also in the structures of a globalized economy.

The global economy and structural reform

Practical (even if highly politicized) strategies such as transfer of financial and technological resources, supported by capacity-building, are seen by many in the developing world to be of little use unless they are addressed in the context of global economic governance which is seen to disadvantage the world's poorer countries and peoples. For many Northern countries, on the other hand, demands for financial assistance, debt rescheduling and trade reform are reminiscent of 1960s and 1970s demands for a new international economic order, part of a larger political agenda that, in their view, has little to do with environmental or sustainable development concerns. Nevertheless, the relationships between debt, trade and environmental degradation have featured prominently not only in the UNCED and Johannesburg processes but also in the institutions of economic governance such as the World Trade Organization and what some call the 'post-Washington consensus' (see Stiglitz, 1998) proclaimed in documents such as the Doha Declaration and the Monterrey Consensus.

Debt and the environment

The Brundtland Report identified Third World debt as a factor in environmental damage and a constraint on sustainable development in developing countries. Despite the Heavily Indebted Poor Countries (HIPC) initiative adopted in 1996 by the World Bank and the IMF to bring global debt burdens to sustainable levels, particularly for the poorest countries, developing country external debt remains high – approximately $US300 billion (Pettifor and Simms, 2002, p. 31). Debt-servicing ensures that the flow of financial resources from the South to the North remains in favour of the latter. Growing debts among the poorer countries of the world have impelled a further selling off of natural resources. In the 1980s, as Sanders notes, developing countries highly dependent on a primary resource base, were 'caught between rising debt and falling commodity prices' (1990, p. 398). As a result, they turned to increased primary production for export (to pay debt and to maintain national income), strategies which resulted in overlogging, overgrazing and, in turn, ecosystem exhaustion. Debt-servicing is not only a drain on a country's economy but much of the burden of debt-servicing falls on the poor.

The Brundtland Commission called for 'urgent action ... [to] alleviate debt burdens' (WCED, 1987, p. 18) but did not specify how this should be done. The UNCED process paid some but not a great deal of attention to the debt issue. Chapter 2 of Agenda 21 does note that the 'development process will not gather momentum if ... the developing countries are weighted down by external indebtedness' (UNCED, 1992b, para. 2.2) and that a supportive international economic climate would include 'dealing with international debt' (UNCED, 1992b, para. 2.3(c)). It encouraged further debt renegotiation, but also commended the actions of low-income countries who continued to service their debt burdens at great cost (thus 'safeguard[ing] their creditworthiness'). For many, debt rescheduling is a short-term answer and the 'growth-oriented solutions' to the debt burden which featured in Agenda 21 simply reinforce the problem. In this view, 'turning the debt crisis around will require more than rescheduling payments or issuing new loans' (Postel and Flavin, 1991, p. 176). Rather it will require, first, a writing off of both public and private debt, a strategy that is however most unlikely to be adopted by commercial or multilateral lending institutions. The lead proponent of a massive forgiveness of global debt has been the NGO Jubilee 2000 which has called for poor-country debt to be written off unconditionally. Indeed, UN Secretary-General Kofi Annan has called Jubilee 2000 (now known, post-Millennium, as Jubilee Plus) as an 'inspiration to us all' (cited in Easterly, 2002, p. 1678). The Millennium Declaration provided some support in calling for the bilateral debt of the poorest countries to be written off. Turning the debt crisis around also requires, second, a more fundamental rethinking about the concept of 'debt' and what is owed to whom. Debates about global debt increasingly refer not just to monetary debt (usually in the context of that owed by developing countries) but also to the *ecological* debt that rich countries owe to developing countries from whom resource and environmental services have been extracted over time. Two debt-related strategies are described very briefly here – debt-for-nature swaps and the HIPC initiative.

Debt-for-nature swaps (DFNS)

One innovative proposal, which attracted a flurry of attention in the late 1980s and early 1990s, was the swapping of a component of a country's debt for conservation or environmental programmes. A debt-for-nature swap (DFNS) involves the purchase of part of a country's debt (usually a very small part) at a discount price by a non-governmental organization (usually) or a government (occasionally). The NGO or third country becomes the creditor although sometimes the debt is then donated to an affiliated NGO in the debtor country. To repay the debt, the debtor government undertakes conservation or environmental programmes in the debtor country to the value of the debt or, at least, for more than the 'purchase price'. Between 1987 and early 1992, 19 DFNS were executed, involving ten debtor countries (including Poland) and, as purchasers, nine organizations, one official aid agency and two governments (see table in Mahony, 1992, p. 98).

At first glance, the strategy seems to be a win–win situation. A debtor country has part of its debt relieved and environmental protection is funded when it might otherwise not have been. The debt is effectively repaid in local currency which relieves foreign exchange pressures on the debtor country. Creditor NGOs acquire local funds to a value greater than its outlay in purchasing the debt and debtor-country NGOs gain access to conservation funds and to further programme experience. Nevertheless, DFNS have not been universally praised and there are a number of problems. Decisions on the use of resources, lands or funds, taken by creditor NGOs or countries, can be seen as an infringement of sovereignty and driven more by Northern interests. Environmental organizations involved in swaps have been criticized for disregarding local communities (often indigenous communities) in making decisions about the environmental component of the swap. COICA has made the point on South American DFNS, for example, that the debt involved was not Indian debt while the 'nature' involved was Indian land that the Indians had not agreed to trade for anything (cited in Wiggins, 1993, p. 350). Because the amounts involved are small, DFNS do little to relieve the debt burden of developing countries, although the *primary* purpose of the swap is environmental protection. Instead they legitimize debt and divert attention from debt relief and the structural problems which lead to debt. The extent of environmental protection is also disputed. Von Moltke and DeLong suggest that 'the resulting conservation programs have had a major impact on environmental protection' (1990, p. 10). Mahony queries this, noting, for example, that 'parks in ... beneficiary countries are being invaded by loggers, miners or the landless' (1992, pp. 97, 100–3). She points out that there is no guarantee that the debtor country will honour its financial agreement with the foreign or local NGO (especially if long-term bonds are involved) or that it can simply cut funding to other environmental programmes or to other programmes, such as welfare programmes, which will affect poor communities. The injection of local currency can also have a potential inflationary effect or, in an inflationary economy, the value of the swaps can diminish quickly (see Patterson, 1990, p. 10). Indeed, Mahony (1992, pp. 99–100) argues that the only ones who can be sure of benefiting, in the long run, are the creditor banks who get something for a debt that otherwise might never have been repaid.

Heavily Indebted Poor Countries (HIPCs)

The HIPC initiative was endorsed in 1996 by the World Bank and the International Monetary Fund as a method to enable very poor countries and those who were heavily indebted to bring their debt burdens to 'sustainable' levels if they could demonstrate that they were committed to macroeconomic reforms. Of 41 HIPCs identified by the World Bank,

33 are in Africa. The logic for this form of debt-restructuring was that at high levels (usually measured by debt-to-export ratio), unsustainable debt (debt overhang) disrupts any chance that poor countries have of economic growth and sustainable development (including, of course, the more specific challenges of environmental protection). Thus, with debt relief and structural reform 'governments will have additional resources available to strengthen their social programs, especially in primary education and primary health' (van Trotsenburg and MacArthur, 1999, p. 1). The demands for demonstrated policy reform were driven by two concerns. The first was that 'countries ruining their economies through irresponsible policies should not be rewarded by debt relief' (Michaelowa, 2003, p. 462). The Zedillo Report (on financing for sustainable development) made it clear that 'the principle that debt obligations should be repaid is central to the functioning of credit markets' and that debt relief programmes should be considered an 'exception for extraordinary circumstances' (UNGA, 2001b, p. 21). Second, responsible fiscal and other policies are important for attracting foreign investment and 'reducing national vulnerabilities' (United Nations, 2002a, para. 47).

In 1999 the initial requirement that debt relief would be available only after six years of such policy adjustment was substantially reduced to one year, provided that governments developed poverty reduction programmes based on wide-ranging participatory processes. At the same time, and to accommodate this change, the IMF structural adjustment programmes associated with the HIPC initiative (known as the Enhanced Structural Adjustment Facility) were renamed the Poverty Reduction and Growth Facility. The criteria for eligibility were also adjusted, from a debt-to-export ratio of 200 to 250 per cent down to a ratio of 150 per cent. The expectation was that this would increase the extent of total debt relief from about $12.5 billion under the original scheme to about $30 billion.

There are a number of concerns about the procedures of and the extent of 'relief' achieved under the initiative. Sharma and Kumar (2002) argue that the amount of relief is minimal – no more than 1 per cent of total Third World debt – and in many cases token. As with DFNS, critics argue that the primary purpose is not to assist developing countries but to ensure only that their debt is made more 'manageable' so that they can continue to service levels of debt that remain high. Martens and Paul (1998) suggest that the 'restrictive definition' for eligibility 'is determined by the interests of the creditors, not by the real needs of the debtor countries and their people'. The initiative also takes no account of what the debt-forgiveness NGO, Jubilee 2000, called odious debt – present-day debt which is supposed to repay funds that were lent by governments and development banks to military dictators and other illegitimate regimes (such as the apartheid regime in South Africa) and which have never benefited the people or the countries that are now supposed to repay the debt.

Trade and the environment

Principle 12 of the Rio Declaration required states to 'cooperate to promote a supportive and open international economic system' and demanded that 'trade policy measures for environmental purposes should not constitute a means of arbitrary or unjustifiable discrimination or a disguised restriction on international trade' (UNCED, 1992a). The principle goes on to proclaim that 'unilateral actions to deal with environmental challenges outside the jurisdiction of the importing country should be avoided', an injunction, in effect, against extraterritoriality (that is, the effective imposition of one country's domestic environmental standards on another). Agenda 21 accepts that international trading relationships between rich and poor countries are inequitable and that this has contributed directly and indirectly to environmental degradation and to underdevelopment. It also accepts without question that trade liberalization and environmental protection are compatible goals. Chapter 2 (entitled 'International cooperation to accelerate sustainable development in developing countries and related domestic policies') suggests that the 'development process will not gather momentum ... if barriers restrict access to markets and if commodity prices and the terms of trade of developing countries remain depressed' (UNCED, 1992b, para. 2.2). Thus trade liberalization (para. 2.3(a)) and 'making trade and environment mutually supportive' (para. 2.3(b)) are necessary.

Trade rules under the WTO now encompass a range of agreements, including the General Agreement on Tariffs and Trade (GATT), the Trade-Related Aspects of Intellectual Property Rights Agreement (TRIPS), the General Agreement on Trade in Services (GATS), the Technical Barriers to Trade (TBT) Agreement (as it applies to labelling) and the Agreement on the Application of Sanitary and Phytosanitary Measures (the SPS Agreement). The debates over the relationship between this body of trade law and environmental policy have centred on a number of questions. Can environmental protection issues be accommodated within the logic of trade liberalization? Can trade liberalization contribute to overcoming environmental degradation or is it likely to contribute to further environmental degradation? Is it possible, in trade liberalization discourse, to distinguish between environmental protection and environmental protectionism? Are trade restrictions 'a legitimate way to retaliate for inadequate environmental standards' (Schoenbaum, 1992, p. 702)? These are important questions because 'trade rules and agreements are a major determinant of how natural resources are used, what pressures are placed on the environment and who benefits from the huge money flows ... that cross borders with the exchange of goods' (Postel and Flavin, 1991, p. 180). At a normative level, answers to these questions rest in part on different views about 'protection' – a 'pejorative term' for the trade community and an 'exemplary one in the environmental community' (Berlin and Lang, 1993, p. 35). At an institutional and legal level, they involve the application and interpretation of trade rules under the World Trade Organization and the relationship between these rules and the trade-related rules adopted in environmental agreements. As well as the more general disputes over the theory of free trade, played out in academic journals as well as policy negotiations, and the issue of whether trade rules should take precedence over environmental concerns, other unresolved issues include 'eco-labelling, process and production methods, approaches to risk management [and] environmental standards' (Thomas, 2000, p. 14).

In conventional trade logic, trade liberalization is good for the environment; non-liberalized trade (that is, protectionism) is bad for the environment; and environmental protection can be bad for free trade because it can mask protectionism. The report of the International Conference on Financing for Development (the Monterrey Consensus) identifies 'international trade as an engine for development' (United Nations, 2002a, para. 4). However the terms of trade have 'moved against the developing [countries] in the last twenty years' (Leclair, 2003, p. 66). Freeing international trade, therefore, is expected to increase economic welfare (wealth) for developing countries and to help reverse this trend. Even a 50 per cent cut in tariffs (primarily in industrialized countries) is expected to bring a gain to developing countries of between $US90 and $US155 billion (see UNGA, 2001b, p. 40). The impact of this increase in wealth is argued to be twofold – less incentive to use resources unsustainably to generate income and higher levels of expenditure on the environment. Resources will be used more efficiently because freer trade encourages the removal of subsidies and other non-tariff barriers which distort trade and environmental costs and act as disincentives to the development of alternative technologies. In other words, freer trade will result in a progressive internalizing of externalities (that is, ensuring that the full environmental costs of traded goods, including production, transportation and disposal, will be taken into account). It will also foster common standards which are argued to be 'a powerful force in support of higher environmental standards worldwide' (Lallas *et al.*, 1992, p. 317). Continued protectionism (non-free trade), on the other hand, is decried because it can raise barriers against manufactured exports from developing countries, thus limiting their opportunities to diversify from commodity-based exports which rely on the unsustainable use of non-renewable resources (WCED, 1987, p. 79). Finally, environmental protection measures are perceived to have potential trade-distorting consequences, either because (as with domestic subsidies) they provide a country or industry with a subsidized competitive advantage or (as with import restrictions related to domestic legislation) they might be used as barriers to trade, a concern that has particular resonance with developing countries.

This approach, however, leaves the logic of trade liberalization untouched. It explores how environmental concerns can be added on to the trade agenda, but does not question whether trade liberalization is appropriate as an environmental protection strategy or whether it might exacerbate environmental decline. From a critical perspective, freer trade may well cause further environmental degradation. This is because it may encourage economic activity which takes no account of external environmental costs (see Neumayer, 2000, pp. 139–41), especially because WTO rules apply to the products traded, not the conditions under which they are produced. This critical position also takes issue with economic welfare claims, arguing that many developing countries engage in trade not to improve economic welfare but to service debt – 'desperation production' (Arden-Clarke, 1992, p. 123) – and that even if further income were generated there is no guarantee that it would be used for environmental protection. Gaines argues that 'the promise that the wealth-generating benefits of market-driven international economic systems can help alleviate grinding poverty comes with the danger that those same unconstrained market forces will perpetuate and even exacerbate economic inequities and environmental harm' (2002, p. 260). As Postel and Flavin have noted, 'much depends ... on who gains from the added export revenue – peasant farmers or wealthy landowners' (1991, p. 180). This equity dimension has encouraged much more attention to the practice of fair trade or alternative trade by which goods produced in developing countries are sold at prices greater than are set by the market, in order to include a social costing associated with a fair standard of living and return for labour (see, for example, Leclair, 2003). Yet the Zedillo Report was able to make the bold claim that 'there is ... little reason to regard trade as inherently biased one way or the other' when it comes to making growth equitable and sustainable (UNGA, 2001b, p. 39).

Many environmentalists are concerned also that trade liberalization might encourage developing countries to perceive a comparative advantage in pollution-intensive industries – the 'pollution haven theory' – and that free(r) trade will simply enable some countries (usually the developed ones) to maintain the integrity of their own environments by using the raw materials (especially non-renewables) of other countries. While high environmental standards in an importing country could be construed as a non-tariff barrier to protect domestic markets, low pollution regulations in developing countries could be understood as a kind of subsidy. Shrybman (1990, p. 31) suggests that while advocates of trade liberalization have defined subsidized pollution control measures as non-tariff barriers, they have not perceived a lack of regulation (in effect the competitive advantage of being able to produce unsustainably) as a subsidy. Yet the standardization or harmonization of environmental standards expected through the freeing up of trade could draw countries into least-common-denominator standards of environmental protection and thereby undermine conservation efforts. This is the so-called 'race to the bottom' (see Muradian and Martinez-Alier, 2001, pp. 285–6). Critics point out also that trade rules under the GATT/WTO have not prevented trade in goods that have potentially severe environmental consequences, such as hazardous waste, and that trade in goods such as tropical timber has contributed to further consumer demand and therefore further unsustainable resource use. The restrictions on extraterritoriality are also perceived to impose a 'major barrier to the use of life cycle assessment as a tool to control global environmental impacts' (Thompson, 1992, p. 765).

Those of a more critical persuasion argue that making environment and trade mutually supportive means adjusting the GATT/WTO rules and ensuring, as Weiss exhorts, that trade becomes a means to an end, where that end is 'environmentally sustainable economic development' (1992, p. 728). She argues that '[m]easures needed to protect the environment [such as trade restrictions] cannot be forsworn simply because they may adversely affect trading relationships' (1992, p. 728). In this view, then, it should be possible to use trade restrictions and sanctions for environmental ends. Pearce and Warford argue, for example, that 'trade *should* be restricted when it creates environmental degradation either by importing products that pollute the importing country or by encouraging production that may incur damages to both exporting and importing country' (1993, p. 297; emphasis added).

Supporters of the GATT/WTO rules argue that they *can* and *do* accommodate environmental protection concerns and that any amendments would undermine the integrity of free-trade principles. In this view environmentalists can (and should) use the WTO rules to pursue environmental protection. Article XX of the GATT, which provides for trade restrictions in the case of overriding public concerns, is interpreted to be amenable to environmental protection. It refers to 'measures necessary to protect human, animal or plant life or health' (article XX(b)) and 'measures relating to the conservation of exhaustible natural resources' (article XX(g)), provisions usually taken to have been included for quarantine purposes. Charnovitz argues, however, that the history of article XX shows that it 'was designed to encompass environmental measures' (1991, p. 55) and can therefore be used for such purposes. Decisions by GATT/WTO panels would seem to support this interpretation, although not when such restrictions are pursued unilaterally or as coercive measures (see Commonwealth of Australia, 1995, pp. 6–9). Test cases brought to the GATT and WTO disputes panel – the most famous are the tuna/dolphin (1991/1994) and the shrimp/turtle (1998/2001) cases (see Neumayer, 2000; and Shaw and Schwartz, 2002, for a discussion) – have revolved around the unilateral and extraterritorial imposition of domestic regulations and legislation and the problems of non-discrimination, rather than trade restrictions agreed multilaterally. The US lost both cases, although rulings in the tuna/dolphin case were not formally adopted. The WTO explains that governments have every right to protect human, animal or plant life and to use import measures to conserve exhaustible resources but that they do not have the right to apply these measures in a differentiated manner (WTO, 2003; see also Sampson, 2001). At time of writing, no case involving trade restrictions under a multilateral environmental agreement has been taken to the GATT or WTO dispute resolution process.

This balance between unilateral extraterritoriality and multilateralism has also been central to the issue of eco-labelling. While trade rules prevent unilateral discrimination against production processes, they do not preclude the use of eco-labelling in circumstances where there are internationally negotiated norms on methods of production. For example, while trade restrictions on tuna harvested in circumstances which might involve dolphin bycatch are GATT-illegal, it is acceptable to require canned tuna to be labelled to provide information on its 'dolphin-friendly' status because there are international norms on the incidental taking of dolphins. However, an Austrian attempt to enforce a sustainability labelling requirement for tropical timber products was challenged because there were no internationally accepted criteria on the determination of sustainable logging.

The trade–environment nexus has been given increasing attention by international economic institutions. In 1994, the UNCTAD (United Nations Conference on Trade and Development) established an Ad Hoc Working Group on Trade, Environment and Development. Both the OECD and the World Trade Organization (WTO) have working groups on trade and environment issues. The WTO group – the Committee on Trade and Environment (CTE) – is the heir to the GATT Group on Environmental Measures in International Trade (EMIT) which was established in 1972 after the Stockholm Conference but which did not meet until 21 January 1992. The mandate of the CTE is twofold: first, to identify the trade–environment relationship with respect to the promotion of sustainable development and, second, to recommend whether modifications to trade rules might be required to make the two areas of law mutually supportive. The CTE 'toiled for its first few years in the obscure corridors of Geneva' and has been hard put to 'reach any noteworthy conclusions' (Damian and Graz, 2001, pp. 597, 601). Certainly much of its work has focused on the first part of its mandate. Since the late 1990s, it has been attempting to pursue a more active profile, coordinating a number of high-level seminars on trade and environment and, in July 2000, convening joint sessions with UNEP and the secretariat of various MEAs. The Doha agenda (see below) will help to create a more clearly defined focus for the CTE (negotiations will take place in Special Sessions of the Committee), but it is still not clear whether the Committee will 'ever ... achieve much more than [a] discussion-based role' (Hyvarinen and Brack, 2000, p. 36). Anderson is more critical, suggesting that the CTE seems to be little more than an 'apologist for the WTO' (2002, p. 4).

A number of the MEAs discussed in earlier chapters involve various kinds of restrictions on trade which have been adopted and implemented without recourse to the GATT or WTO disputes resolution procedures. The Convention on International Trade in Endangered Species (CITES), for example, seeks to protect wildlife through the regulation of international trade (see Chapter 2). The Montreal Protocol and the Basel Convention place restrictions on trade between parties and non-parties. According to von Moltke (1991, p. 979), a ruling on the Montreal Protocol trade restrictions to the effect that the provisions were acceptable under article XX of the GATT was obtained from the GATT secretariat. Other agreements, such as the Rotterdam PIC Convention and the Stockholm POPs Convention (see Chapter 3), do not prevent trade (except in banned substances) but impose requirements on how that trade is to be managed. Trade in living modified organisms (LMOs) under the Biosafety Protocol is likely to prove more contentious in the event of a dispute between the Protocol and the WTO rules (see Chapter 2).

Sampson identifies concerns that 'uncertainty over the relationship ... is increasingly affecting MEA negotiations' and that 'the objectives of some MEAs are frustrated by WTO rules' (2001, p. 1109). Anderson, on the other hand, reflects the view that 'the adoption of many multilateral environmental treaties ... has the capacity to undermine the meaning and effectiveness of the WTO ... [and] the benefits created by the ... trade liberalisation agenda ... will be severely compromised' (2002,

p. 2). Perrez suggests, however, that 'the WTO rules will, most of the time, provide for sufficient flexibility to avoid a conflict between the WTO and MEAs' (2003, p. 19). The rule seems to be, first, that such restrictions are acceptable if there is international consensus on their inclusion in an environmental agreement (see Thompson, 1992, pp. 755–6) and, second, that the Vienna Convention on the Law of Treaties provides adequate guidance on incompatible provisions between treaties. In the event of a dispute between two countries, the provisions of the later treaty apply if both countries are parties to both treaties, otherwise the provisions of the treaty to which both are parties take precedence (see Schoenbaum, 1992, p. 719; Lallas *et al.*, 1992, p. 307).

The language adopted for the Biosafety Protocol and for the Rotterdam Convention confirms that neither of those agreements is subordinated to other international agreements (that is, the WTO agreements). Both also, however, state that this does not imply any change in the rights and obligations of any party under other international agreements. Trade and environment discussions at the WSSD continued this debate over whether WTO rules should have priority over MEA rules, or whether each should defer to the other with respect to their own areas of competence. The language adopted in the Johannesburg Plan of Implementation confirms that there is no hierarchy (that is, trade rules do not take precedence over environmental ones). However, the Doha Declaration adopted at the Fourth Ministerial Meeting of the WTO in November 2001 agreed to launch discussions on the relationship between WTO rules and the trade rules in MEAs and the issue is doubtless far from being resolved (see Shaw and Schwartz, 2002 for a useful summary of approaches to clarifying the WTO–MEA relationship). The Doha negotiations will include consideration of problems such as environmentally harmful subsidies in agriculture and fisheries and the 'effect of environmental measures on market access' (WTO, 2001, para. 32(i)). However the Declaration makes it quite clear that the trade principles of non-discrimination and an open economic system must not be compromised and that any negotiations on the relationship between WTO rules and trade obligations in MEAs will be 'limited in scope to the applicability of any such existing WTO rules as among parties to the MEA in question' (WTO, 2001, para. 31(i)). In other words, the negotiations are to address 'how WTO rules apply to WTO members who are also parties to environmental agreements' (WTO, 2002). Overlaying these debates are concerns that the WTO remains one of the least transparent and open of the global governance institutions, with its reputation in this regard described as 'not sterling' (WRI, 2003, p. 161; see also Conca, 1997), its willingness to allow NGOs to submit 'amicus briefs' to dispute panels (confirmed in the shrimp/turtle case) notwithstanding.

Market-based financial mechanisms

Financial, market-based mechanisms are expected to act as incentives for reducing environmental degradation. 'Open, competitive and rightly-framed international markets' are claimed to be the best way to achieve sustainable development (WBCSD, 2002, p. 227). Much of this analysis, grounded as it is in environmental economics (and often with a domestic focus) is beyond the scope of this text, but some brief coverage is helpful in elaborating the direction of this debate. So-called 'command-and-control' or regulatory mechanisms are posited as unwieldy and costly, spawning cumbersome bureaucratic mechanisms. David Pearce, whose work has been central to this debate, suggests that command-and-control is more expensive and less effective in the long run, especially when it comes to 'technology forcing' (1990, p. 373), that is, providing an incentive for the development of new technology. The advantages claimed for financial mechanisms, which employ the forces of the market by making use of pricing signals, are, first, that they can address issues of the externality problem (market failure) by providing a realistic valuing of environmental services and, second, that they will address pollution sources rather than 'end-of-pipe' discharges by providing incentives for conservation and technological change. Such mechanisms are also associated with corporate demands for self-regulation and voluntary codes as the 'best, most preferable and most efficient method for transforming business practices' (Karliner, 1997, p. 41).

The purpose of such financial mechanisms is twofold, although the distinction is not always clearly made. First, such mechanisms are incentives to alter behaviour, to encourage firms and individuals away from environmentally unsustainable practices and towards alternatives. Second, taxes and other mechanisms are proposed as national and international revenue-gathering exercises, the latter as a possible source of 'new and additional financial resources'. Jacobs notes of such instruments, however, that their purpose is not to determine 'the level of pollution or resource consumption. The target must be set first. The instrument is simply the method used to achieve it' (1990, p. 15). Therefore the setting of the target will involve political decisions and choices. The discussion here touches very briefly on three of the most widely canvassed financial principles and modalities – the polluter pays principle, taxes and tradable permits.

Polluter pays principle

The polluter pays principle (PPP) is argued to provide a useful means of balancing environment and trade concerns (Saunders, 1992, p. 727).

Arden-Clarke suggests that it offers 'an important adjunct and in some cases the only feasible option for internalising costs' (1992, p. 130). PPP has its genesis in OECD concerns about the allocation of the costs of pollution prevention and control measures (see Chapter 4). In 1972, that concern resulted in a formal pronouncement elaborating the principle. In effect, the principle states that the cost of such measures should be met by the polluter, without public subsidy, as a means of encouraging the internalization in the price of goods of the full costs of pollution abatement. It is, therefore, intended to 'promote efficient resource use' and to 'avoid trade and investment distortions' (Gaines, 1991, pp. 469, 470). In more general terms, the concept of polluter pays is used as a colloquial approach to liability and responsibility – that is, actors that pollute should be prepared to pay for the consequences of that pollution. In this respect, PPP has become a principle of equity as well as a principle associated with market economics. In this regard, debates over who 'pays' or who meets the financial burden of the exploitation of resources and environmental services is increasingly bound up with the concept of the ability to pay which resonates with the principles of burden-sharing explored in Chapter 6.

Taxes

Taxes are argued to be appealing because they offer an efficient way to correct for the failure of the market to value environmental services and discourage negative spillover. Green taxes are seen to have a role not only in reshaping national economies, but as new and innovative sources of global finance which could incorporate some form of redistributive justice if the tax falls most heavily on the richest or those who consume more. In this view, market mechanisms can be used for ethical ends. Martens and Paul suggest that it should be possible to reorganize existing tax systems 'on an ecological basis so that the consumption and use of resources are subject to higher taxes' (1998). One of the best known 'global tax' proposals is the Tobin tax, a tax on currency exchange transactions (although James Tobin, the author of the proposal, was as much concerned to reduce currency speculation as to generate income for social and environmental objectives). Other proposals (some of which have been noted in earlier chapters) include some form of tax on carbon emissions or the carbon content of fuels which, although difficult to administer, would both raise revenue and act as an incentive for more efficient fuel use (see Martens and Paul, 1998; UNGA, 2001b, pp. 57–8).

There is, however, a range of equity issues to be considered. Domestic taxes may well impact heavily on the poorer sections of the community. McCully argues that global taxes, such as a carbon tax, levied on all countries would be 'unfair and unworkable' (1991b, p. 245). He favours, instead, a tax on energy in the OECD countries. The imposition of any kind of global tax would also have to incorporate a 'formula for fair reductions that accounts for diverse national needs' (Jain, 1990, p. 549). Indeed Soto doubts whether a climate tax would 'encourage conservation and wise use' and wonders at what he calls the 'sanity of using consumption to pay for a move to non-consumption' (1992, p. 699). Fears are also raised that governments and institutions would become reliant on any revenue raised, which would thus act as a disincentive to further pollution abatement and ensuing revenue reduction.

Tradeable permits

Under a permit trading scheme, rights to pollute are allocated in accordance with a predetermined pollution 'target' and are then available to be traded on the open market, thus allowing the market to determine the value of a unit of pollution. The incentive structure for companies (or countries) to reduce abatement costs arises through efficiency measures or alternative technology, to the extent that it then benefits them to sell their permits or to not have to continue purchasing them. As Pearce puts it, 'basically a firm that finds it comparatively easy to abate pollution will find it profitable to sell its permits to a firm that finds it expensive to abate pollution' (1990, p. 376). Costs are internalized to the extent that the company (or country) passes them on to the consumer although this can raise equity issues not only for poorer consumers but also for companies and countries for whom both permits and abatements costs are expensive. The expectation is that through invoking market practices, emissions trading will also provide a cost-effective mechanism for managing compliance. However, such a scheme may have little impact on levels of pollution or resource use if it is based on an overall 'acceptable' level of pollution or resource use, unless a ratcheting of the overall target or the pollution-unit value of a permit is built into the permit scheme.

Until negotiations for the Kyoto Protocol (see Chapter 3), most of the focus was on the use of tradeable permits in domestic contexts. The Protocol establishes an 'artificial market ... in which the emission allowances or emission reduction units are traded [among] ... end users of emissions allowances, brokers and other actors' (Kim, 2001, p. 252). As Chapter 4 indicated, there were a range of implementation issues to be resolved, including those associated with 'hot-air' reductions, over selling and the difficult question of emissions inventories. Emissions trading under the Protocol, however, may meet neither market nor political expectations. Bohm argues, for example, that the Protocol is 'not fully cost-effective' (2002, p. 261). Nor will it necessarily meet equity concerns associated with burden-sharing between developed and developing countries. As with PPP and green taxes, equity concerns feature in debates about tradeable permits. Pan argues, for example, that 'unlimited free trading of emissions rights is likely to result in their concentration in the rich parts of the world while depriving the opportunities of the poor in the South' (2003, p. 14).

Conclusion

From a critical perspective, the sustainable development agenda reinforces the assumption that environmental and social problems in developing countries are primarily the result of insufficient capital, for which the solution is to increase Northern investment in the South; of outdated technology, for which the solution is to open up the South to Northern technologies; of a lack of expertise, for which the solution is to bring in Northern-educated managers and experts; and of faltering economic growth, for which the solution is a push for an economic recovery in the North (see Hildyard, 1993, p. 31). Thus while agreements such as the Monterrey Consensus and the Johannesburg Plan of Implementation demand that developing countries establish enabling domestic environments and mobilize domestic resources for their own sustainable development, at the same time those changes are perceived to benefit developed countries as much as they do developing ones.

Commitments on transfer of resources, either financial or technological, continue to be couched in compromise diplomatic language with a real allergy to specific timetables and targets. Serious relief of debt (as opposed to restructuring of existing debt to make it more 'sustainable') is yet to be tackled in a way that will reverse the net flow of money from recipient to donor countries or support sustainable development and environmental protection in poor countries. The principle of mutual support between trade and the environment continues, for the most part, to be driven by the trade regime rather than the environmental one, agreements like CITES, the Montreal Protocol, the Biodiversity Protocol and the Rotterdam Convention notwithstanding. Proposals for international taxes remain politically and economically contentious. One common theme in these strategic debates is cost – who pays and where will the money come from? One answer is not to emphasize *more* money, but to require a reassessment of national and global spending priorities and the redirection of existing budgets. In this context, attention is often drawn to the impact of high levels of global military spending and the lost opportunity costs and misallocation of resources involved therein. These issues are explored in the next chapter.

Chapter 9

Environmental Security

Introduction

Security is an increasingly contested concept. A reevaluation of what it means to be secure in a post-Cold War world, and how best to achieve this, has been motivated by the collapse of the familiar bipolarity of the latter half of the twentieth century and the need to understand new configurations of power and the changing nature of threats. A range of problems (or 'risk environments') bound up with the complex and confusing processes and consequences of globalization and fragmentation, are now being defined as possible sources of violence and instability, intra- and interstate conflict, transgression of state borders and threats to international peace and security. Environmental degradation is now widely accepted as one such possible threat, a relationship captured in the phrase 'environmental security'. This is a relatively new idea in both the security lexicon and in the lexicon of global environmental politics. Perhaps because of this, the meaning of the term, the processes it describes and the policy prescriptions it engenders continue to be contested.

The academic and policy debates have confirmed Brock's prediction (1991, p. 407) that the idea of environmental security could lead to either a militarization of environmental politics or a demilitarization of security thinking. The first of these can be characterized as the 'environment-*and*-security' approach in which 'the ecological crisis [is] increasingly ... defined as a threat to national security' (Finger, 1991b, p. 220). The primary referent for security is the state and the primary security concern is the potential for violence, conflict or military action as a result of and in response to environmental degradation. Thus environmental threats are added on to a traditional, geopolitical national security agenda. In this orthodox parlance, environmental security has become more of a commentary on security than on the environment and does little more than ensure that 'new issues and challenges are ... subsumed under old ... approaches' (Williams and Krause, 1997, p. xix).

The second approach emphasizes the importance of 'securing the environment', by which the integrity of the environment is both security referent and security goal and in which environmental degradation is to be taken at least as seriously as traditional military threats. In this view, the state-centric emphasis of the environmental conflict approach reinforces and legitimizes a militaristic mindset which is cast as a cause of environmental degradation and a barrier to the effective pursuit of solutions to environmental decline. Thus the concept of environmental security 'challenges established frames of mind and political conduct' (Lodgaard, cited in Brock, 1991, p. 418).

Militarizing environmental politics: the environment and security

Much attention has been paid in both the scholarly literature and the policy community to the potential for conflict to arise as a result of environmental degradation. In this view, the major concern is the relationship between environmental degradation and the 'traditional indicators of insecurity: violent conflict and the outbreak of war' (Diehl, 1998, p. 275). The environmental security project is therefore one which seeks to identify the kinds of environmental degradation and scarcities which might present threats to national security through interstate war or violence. The problem is not environmental degradation per se. Rather such degradation is a security problem *only* to the extent that it poses a challenge to either the security of the state or to international peace and security, where there is a demonstrable link with violence or conflict, or when military intervention might be required or can be justified. The questions which inform this approach are those which seek to identify how environmental degradation is likely to become a threat to security – either to internal political security, to the security of the state against incursion or threat by other states, or to international peace and security.

Resource conflict

The control of resources for strategic purposes has long been associated with the security of the state, integral to that security and important in denying a source of power to potential or actual enemy states. Thus 'the environment' has been understood as a strategic resource. Historical example exerts a powerful influence on predictions about the probability of future resource conflicts. Examples in the literature include: environmental degradation, food shortages and the rise of organized warfare in the Bronze Age (Mische, 1992); resource interests in the Peloponnesian War (Gleick, 1991); Paraguay's annexation of Bolivia's Gran Chaco wilderness in the early 1930s because of a (misplaced) belief that the region contained oil deposits (Rowlands, 1992); access to oil as an explanation for German advance into the Caucasus and for Japan's invasion of Burma and what was then the Dutch East Indies in the Second World War (Leggett, 1992); the importance of Korean tungsten, Malaysian tin and rubber, New Caledonian nickel and Indonesian oil in understanding US intervention in Korea (Lipschutz and Holdren, 1990); and minerals and fish stocks as a factor in the Falkland/Malvinas conflict between Britain and Argentina (Rowlands, 1992). Scholars have drawn on this historical evidence to argue that scarcity of resources in the future is also likely to result in conflict between states. That conflict is expected to take one of two forms – conflict over already scarce resources or military intervention to ensure access to resources which might become scarce at some time in the future including, in both cases, situations where there are competing sovereignty claims involved (the South China Sea is one such example). In one of the most widely read expositions of this position (and probably most Hobbesian in its pessimism), Robert Kaplan argued that the environment was

> the national-security issue of the early twenty-first century. The political and strategic impact of surging populations, spreading disease, deforestation and soil erosion, water depletion, air pollution, and, possibly, rising sea levels in critical, overcrowded regions like the Nile Delta and Bangladesh – developments that will prompt mass migrations and, in turn, incite group conflicts – will be the core foreign-policy challenge from which most others will ultimately emanate (1994, p. 58).

This focus on 'scarce' resources has been accompanied by a reassessment of what resources are determined to be 'strategic' and therefore important not only to national security, in traditional discourse, but also to the security of peoples and communities. The 1991 Gulf War and the 2003 war on/in Iraq have ensured that debates over war, invasion and access to oil remain part of this equation. US policy on regime change in Iraq is seen to be caught up with national (security) interest demands for reliable sources of oil as US production falls. US control of Iraqi oil would, Renner suggests, give it 'enormous leverage over the world oil market' (2003, p. 2). The conviction that oil lies at the heart of US policy in this part of the Middle East is boosted by testimony to the US Congress in 1999 by the then commander of US Central Command that the US 'must have free access to the region's resources' (cited in Paul, 2002).

Despite this sustained focus on oil and war, the new strategic resources are increasingly likely to be those which have for so long been thought of as being in plentiful supply, either because they were renewable or because they were, at least, non-exhaustible – resources such as water, arable land and the ecosystem and human services those resources supply. As earlier chapters have demonstrated, both water and land are subject to continuing degradation (loss or scarcity) through pollution, soil erosion, the depletion of aquifers, desertification and deforestation as well as from the impacts of global environmental change in the form, especially, of climate change. Water is forecast to be a major cause (perhaps even the most likely cause) of inter- and intrastate tension and possibly outright conflict in the future. Solomon suggests that this attention is hardly surprising – for the developing world, 'water availability determines the sustainability of economic development' (2000, p. 6). A concern with intrastate environmental conflict focuses on transnational water resources. One hundred and fifty-five major river systems are shared by two countries and a further 59 are shared by between three and twelve countries. The Niger, for example, runs through ten countries. The Nile and the Congo are both shared by nine countries, the Zambesi by eight and the Chad and the Volta both run through six countries. Nineteen countries receive over half their water from outside their borders (Swain, cited in Dimitrov, 2002, p. 678). In this context, cross-border conflict over shared rivers and waterways (so-called 'water wars') is thought likely (see Turton, 2000 for a useful typology of water wars).

The Middle East has attracted particular attention in this regard. Fifteen countries compete for the 'rapidly diminishing waters of the Euphrates, Jordan and Nile Rivers' (Porter and Brown, 1991, p. 100). Control over the water resources of those three rivers has been a factor in strategic posturing in the region and remains a likely source of tension. In the mid-1970s, Syria and Iraq came close to hostilities over Syria's al-Thawrah Dam on the Euphrates (see Myers, 1989, p. 29). Turkey's construction of a series of dams on the Euphrates – the Great Anatolia project – has been perceived by Iraq and Syria as a threat to their strategic interests because of its impact on their water supplies. It was also a key factor, along with the Kurdish issue, in confrontation between Turkey and Syria in 1998 (see Çarkoğlu and Eder, 2001). Israel's fears that Syria and Jordan were planning to divert the waters of the Jordan River, upon which Israel relied for almost 60 per cent of its water, was one factor in the 1967 Arab–Israeli war. By the end of the war, Israel had control of most of the water resources of the Jordan basin. When Ethiopia announced a dam construction project for the headwaters of the Blue Nile, President Anwar Sadat of Egypt warned that 'if anyone, at any moment, thinks to deprive us of our life we shall never hesitate to go to war' (cited in Gleick, 1991, pp. 19–20).

Tensions and possible conflict over water resources are not confined to the Middle East. For example, at various times, the potential for water conflict has been a possibility in the Mekong River basin (shared by Yunan Province in China, Burma, Thailand, Laos, Cambodia and Vietnam). Despite various governance structures, including the Mekong River Commission, governments remain alert to the possibility for upstream diversion of water for a range of uses (including hydro-power and irrigation) or downstream impacts of river pollution. This is particularly so because the 1995 agreement which presently regulates the use of the Mekong (and to which neither China nor Burma are signatories) does not require states to obtain the approval of their Mekong neighbours to any water diversion scheme, except during the dry season. Both Cambodia and Vietnam are heavily reliant on the waters of the Mekong for irrigation and rice production. Laos, on the other hand, wants to use the Mekong to generate electricity for domestic consumption and for export to Thailand and Vietnam. The problems are not confined to water resources. The series of dams proposed for construction on the Mekong will not only divert water resources for other purposes but, along with the impacts of deforestation, will contribute to transboundary ecological disruption including changes to the river's flood and siltation patterns, increase in salinity and, potentially, serious impacts on freshwater fishing.

Earlier chapters have described how land, particularly arable land, is under pressure from environmental degradation, including deforestation, desertification, climate change and agricultural overuse. In the 1980s the total amount of cropland in the developing world grew by only 0.25 per cent a year, a growth rate half that of the 1970s; per capita arable land dropped by almost 2 per cent a year (Homer-Dixon, 1991, p. 93). That decline was also unevenly distributed. Predictions suggested that the 1992 global per capita average of 0.28 hectares would decline to 0.17 hectares by 2025. In Asia, that figure was projected to drop as low as 0.09 hectares of arable land per person (Moss, 1993, p. 32). Whether these are conservative figures or whether they overstate the case, there seems little doubt that arable land will continue to become an increasingly scarce resource, on absolute and per capita figures, a scarcity that is likely to occur predominantly in those parts of the world which are already poor and where land is under increasing environmental pressure. Land as territory has always been a geopolitical or strategic resource for states, provided they were able to maintain control and authority over it. The extent of possible future cross-border conflict over arable land (either between local communities or between governments) is not clear. Some scholars have suggested that it was a factor in the so-called Soccer (or Football) War between El Salvador and

Honduras in 1969 (although political repression and inequities in land tenure and wealth in El Salvador were also contributory factors) (see Myers, 1989; Homer-Dixon, 1991). However the possibility that states might seek either to acquire or reclaim arable land, or that arable land inequities might be an exacerbating factor in other kinds of tensions, is not to be completely discounted.

These confident predictions about resource scarcity and environmental degradation as proximate causes of conflict or war (whether between or within states) have been subject to a range of critical examinations which expose concerns about the apparent linearity or simplicity of the 'scarcity equals conflict' approach. There are three broad themes. The first is that 'a military conflict which involves resources is not necessarily a struggle over resources' (Brock, 1991, p. 410). In this view, there is little compelling evidence that environmental scarcity has been a 'primary cause of any major sub-national or inter-state conflict' (Dupont, 1998, p. 75). The Brundtland Report observed that environmental stress is seldom the only cause of conflict within or among nations but it can be an 'important part of the web of causality', suggesting that we need to understand how 'poverty, injustice, environmental degradation and conflict interact in complex and potent ways' (WCED, 1987, p. 291). In a similar vein, Timura (2001) chastises environmental security scholars for overlooking anthropological and ethnographic research which, he argues, can offer a more nuanced explanation of conflict that apparently arises over resources. He notes, for example, that claims regarding the so-called 'Soccer War' (see above) ignore the fact that 'the conflict had as much to do with elite-propagated paranoia regarding the threat of immigrants as it did with the relative scarcity created by changes in land use practices' (2001, p. 107). The second theme is that scarcity of resources might well provide the basis for cooperation rather than conflict. The third theme is that 'greed rather than grievance [is] the motivation' as competing users 'struggle to control the rents from resource streams that [are] being exported to the global economy' (Dalby, 2003, p. 5). In other words, resource conflict is about competition for wealth rather than competition over scarcity.

Environmental inequities

The World Commission on Environment and Development suggested that 'differences in environmental endowment' could 'precipitate and exacerbate international tension and conflict', especially as poorer countries reached the limits of their environmental sustainability (1987, pp. 292–3). Homer-Dixon describes these as 'relative deprivation conflicts' (1991, p. 109). In other words, the issue is not simply one of scarcity per se, but that some are faced with greater scarcity than others (and not necessarily of their own making). A range of inequities are implicated: in the global distribution and use of resources; in the causes of environmental degradation and resource depletion; in disproportionate impacts and relative vulnerabilities; and in response capacities. At the level of conflict between states, the extent to which resentment over resource inequities will motivate governments to war is uncertain. Poor countries are unlikely to confront rich countries, which are almost always militarily better resourced, over relative deprivation. What is perhaps more likely is that relative deprivation could lead to conflict between neighbouring countries, especially in the poorer parts of the world, or to tension and violence within countries as governments and peoples attempt to adjust to the local impacts of local and global environmental stress.

In fact, this latter relationship between inequity, environmental scarcity and conflict *within* countries is equally if not more of a security issue than that associated with interstate competition for scarce resources. It has become more prominent in security debates in the context of a post-Cold War willingness on the part of the international community to define conflict and violence within countries as a threat to international peace and security and an increasingly well-established concern with human insecurities. The factors which can trigger such conflict or violence often arise in the context of inequitable access to resources and environmental services and the tensions among competing users that this can generate.

Social and political unrest

Several environmental scarcities generate tension among competing users which could, in turn, give rise to violence and unrest within countries. The first is water. Global water use doubled between 1940 and 1980 and was expected to double again in the remaining two decades of the century (Swain, 1993, p. 429). As a consequence, the world's per capita water supply is decreasing (see Chapter 2). In many parts of the world, overuse of water for agriculture, municipal and industrial use is becoming a serious challenge and the number of countries facing water stress is almost certainly increasing. Switzer (2002) examines the case of rioting and unrest in Bolivia over the privatization of water resources.

Food (in)security is another form of scarcity that is also influenced directly by economic inequities and environmental degradation (particularly desertification, soil erosion and a decline in arable land). The problem of food scarcity is exacerbated by inequitable land tenure, especially within developing countries, and also because food surpluses and scarcities are unevenly distributed. Many developing countries which used to be net food exporters are now net food importers, a problem made worse by cash mono-cropping to service not the domestic market but the global market and the imperatives of economic growth. As Chapter 2 indicated, the world's fish catch is also declining as stocks are overfished by long-distance fishing fleets and the local commercial fishing industry. Fish is an important source of protein for a large proportion of the world's population, especially in the developing world. A decline in the food resources of the oceans is a further possible source of conflict between as well as within countries as they seek to protect their access to such resources.

The social and economic consequences of this kind of environmental degradation and resource scarcity are likely factors in the disruption in what Homer-Dixon calls 'legitimised and authoritative social relations' (1991, p. 91). The consequences of environmental decline, such as increasingly limited access to food or potable water, will exacerbate the misery and despair which already exist in the poorer parts of the world. Already about one billion of the world's people do not have regular access to clean water, for example. In its 1994 *Human Development Report* (important because of its emphasis on human security) the UNDP identified 'water scarcity' as an increasing factor in 'ethnic strife and political tension' within countries (1994, p. 29). Environmental degradation, especially in rural areas in poorer countries, generates internal migration, either to other rural areas or to the cities, as people move in search of better land or work. Competition for land or for work and environmental pressures on land that is already marginal or on scarce urban infrastructure can contribute to tensions. In turn, these frustrations, tensions and resentments, the consequences of people drawing upon relatively diminished or poorly distributed resources, can result in domestic unrest. In effect, grievance becomes violence (see, for example, Goodhand, 2003).

There would seem to be plenty of examples to support these propositions. In its 1994 *Human Development Report*, the UNDP identified Afghanistan, Haiti, Angola, Iraq, Mozambique, Burma, the Sudan and Zaire as countries in which internal crises could be linked to environmental degradation and food insecurity (often compounded by inequitable internal resource distribution) (UNDP, 1994, pp. 41–3). The Commission on Global Governance nominated environmental deterioration along with population pressures as factors in the 'social breakdown and internal conflict in Somalia, Rwanda and Haiti' (Commission on Global Governance, 1995, p. 95; see also Ruff *et al.*, 1997, p. 89). In the case of Haiti, that environmental degradation includes deforestation and loss of arable land (although, curiously, analyses often make little or no reference to the former repressive regime in that country). Byers (1991, p. 70) points to Sri Lanka, Somalia and Ethiopia as countries in which pressures on the environment have exacerbated internal ethnic tensions. Extensive starvation (or food scarcity which has broadly environmental and resource causes) has been implicated in the conflict in Somalia and Liberia. The Secretary-General's 1998 report on conflict and peace in Africa also identified 'competition for scarce land and water resources' as a factor in conflict in Central Africa (UNSG, 1998a, para. 15). Indeed, the World Resources Institute reports that 'by one estimate, one quarter of the roughly 50 wars and armed conflicts active in 2001 were triggered, exacerbated or financed by legal or illegal resource exploitation' (WRI, 2003, p. 25).

The consequences of environmental degradation and loss of land are also often important factors in a range of broader political and social grievances for peoples fighting for various forms of self-determination. Environmental decline is one of a number of factors which have contributed to the struggle in Bougainville for independence from Papua New Guinea. In South Africa, environmental degradation and relative environmental deprivation, one outcome of the homelands policies which characterized the political and social violence of the apartheid regime, was one factor in the fight for freedom in that country. Homer-Dixon and his colleagues cite studies which indicate that resource scarcity, including access to land, is also an 'increasingly powerful force behind…Communist led insurgency' in the Philippines (1993, p. 20). Douglas *et al.* (2003) examine the complex relationship between oil politics, military violence and local struggle in Nigeria.

Environmental refugees

Environmental decline and internal instability result in movement of peoples. There is little disagreement that the category of displaced persons now includes environmental refugees, although this is still a rather loosely defined category and one not formally recognized in international refugee law. The numbers of environmental refugees are uncertain but those numbers do seem to be on the increase. UNEP estimates that there could be as many as 25 million environmental refugees worldwide and that this number could well double by 2010 (Töpfer, 2000). Environmental stresses have often been discounted as a cause of enforced movement of peoples. However, while refugees may be seen to be fleeing 'political upheaval and military violence', the underlying causes of the mass movements of people 'often include the deterioration of the natural resource base' (Holst, 1989, p. 125). Byers has suggested that the 'conflict-stimulating potential' 'of such massive numbers of refugees is obvious' (1991, p. 70). Forced migration (regardless of the reason) can also have environmental consequences as displaced peoples increase stresses on food sources, water and fuel such as firewood (see, for example, Switzer, 2002). As people move within countries greater environmental and social stresses can result. When those people move across (or transgress) territorial borders, environmental refugees are then defined as a threat to national security (and perhaps to international peace and security), illuminating state-based concerns about encroachment and the difficulty of protecting borders. On the other hand, it is important not to cast environmental refugees as the cause of tension rather than as the victims of environmental degradation and other forms of political marginalization and violence.

Military responses to non-military threats

The academic literature and policy pronouncements on environmental security focus on the developing world. The social and political tensions and violence which might arise from environmental decline in the Third World – distress signals from the periphery – are made cause for concern for developed countries (or their governments) because they might require intervention, contribute to international instability or undermine the stability of 'newly formed democratic regimes' (Butts, 1994, p. v). Countries suffering from environmental degradation and beset by internal conflict as a result are considered to be potentially ripe for 'authoritarian government or external subversion' (Mathews, 1989, p. 168). This then becomes an issue for developed countries, not on *humanitarian* grounds but because the '[security] interests of the North may be directly threatened' if countries develop in the direction of extremism (Homer-Dixon, 1991, p. 113).

Environmental threats are therefore identified as 'non-military' threats to national and international peace and security. This was the position formally adopted by the 1992 summit meeting of Security Council heads of state which declared that 'non-military sources of instability in the economic, social, humanitarian and ecological fields have become threats to the peace and security' (UN Security Council, 1992). The UN Secretary-General's *Agenda for Peace* identified 'ecological damage' as a new risk for stability (UNSG, 1992, p. 5). NATO's Strategic Concept observes that 'security and stability have ... environmental elements as well as the indispensable defence dimensions' (NATO, 1999, para. 25). NATO's Committee on the Challenges of Modern Society (CCMS), which was established in 1969 to give the Alliance a 'social dimension', focuses primarily on quality of life and environmental protection, including defence-related environmental problems. The UN Secretary-General's *Millennium Report* identified a 'real risk that resource depletion, especially freshwater scarcities, as well as severe forms of environmental degradation, may increase social and political tensions in unpredictable but potentially dangerous ways' (UNSG, 2000, p. 44). Just prior to WSSD in Johannesburg, US Secretary of State Colin Powell proclaimed that 'sustainable development is ... a security imperative', arguing that 'poverty, environmental degradation and despair are destroyers of people, of societies, of nations [which] ... can destabilise countries, even entire regions' (cited in Töpfer, n.d.).

But even though environmental stress is identified as a 'non-military' threat, environmental politics are militarized because the 'threat' element is defined, in the final analysis, not by the impact on human security or even economic security but by its relationship, through the potential for conflict, with the military and geopolitical security of the state. This raises, then, the question of what role is anticipated for the traditional agents of state and international security – defence forces and the Security Council – in meeting environmental security threats.

Some of the 'environmental security' literature is confined to making defence forces more ecologically conscious. Environmental security becomes operationalized as environmentally responsible defence, demonstrating an apparent willingness to 'green the military' through balancing readiness and stewardship doctrines. Military establishments are encouraged to implement environmental management strategies; to conserve resources; to protect heritage and habitat; and to develop more environmentally benign weapons acquisition and disposal strategies. The disposal issue is crucial. UNEP observes that the disposal of obsolete weapons, particularly those with explosives or dangerous chemicals, is 'both extremely expensive and environmentally risky' (UNEP, n.d.). Another theme emphasizes a precautionary role for military forces such as environmental data-gathering or disaster relief, a 'proactive' or 'protective' environmental defence role (see, for example, Finlayson, 1998, pp. 65–75). This kind of role takes military forces into the theatre of operations other than war (OOTW) and is often resisted within the military as an insidious form of 'mission creep'.

In anticipating a more traditional role for militaries in environmental security, a 'state may find it necessary to respond to serious environmental violations with ... military force to protect its own vital interests' (Murphy, 1999, p. 1199). Thus defence forces might be expected to engage in defensive or pre-emptive action in cross-border resource conflict, to gain control over scarce resources or to maintain control over resources against the threat of incursion from another state. Defence forces might be used to secure borders against environmental refugees or to maintain internal security in the event of environment-related (and often other kinds of) instabilities. States, Brock argues, 'could use military force in order to protect themselves from [the] social consequences of global environmental decay' (1991, p. 410). Military capabilities or the threat of their use could be employed to prevent activities, in or by another country, which could have a transboundary environmental impact. Finger also draws attention to the possible use of 'military force or other coercive means to force recalcitrant states or other bodies to comply with international ... agreements' (1991b, p. 223). The consequence of such analysis is that use of force is legitimized as a response to environmental decline.

Some consideration has also been given to expansion of the Security Council's mandate to maintain international peace and security to incorporate environmental security. As noted above, the Security Council has identified ecological stress as a possible threat to international peace and security. One option for expanding the Security Council mandate in this direction could involve formal amendment of the UN Charter. Indeed, Parkin suggests that 'environmental problems offer an impeccable motive for refreshing the United Nations Charter' (Parkin, 1999, p. 45). However Charter amendment is an unusual event, difficult to achieve and highly politicized. It is more likely that any role for the Security Council will arise through an interpretation of the Charter based, most likely, on analogy with the Security Council's role in humanitarian intervention (see Elliott, 2003 for a more detailed discussion). The kinds of options available to the Security Council could be accommodated under both Chapter VII of the UN Charter, on threats to and breaches of the peace, and Chapter VI on peaceful settlement of disputes. This would allow the Security Council to determine that environmental degradation is a cause of conflict (although in this case it would be the conflict itself that motivates Council action) or, much more controversially, that environmental degradation or the violence associated with it constitutes a gross abuse of human rights and therefore a threat to international peace and security.

Certainly some have suggested that military power might be garnered on behalf of the international community against environmental renegades, or as a means of enforcing international environmental law, a kind of environmental collective security. Sir Crispin Tickell, a former British diplomat, thought that 'environmental problems in one country affecting the interests of another could easily come within the purview of the Security Council with its mandate for maintaining international peace and security' (1993b, p. 23). Sir Julian Oswald (former First Sea Lord of the British Navy) also canvassed the possibility that 'poor environmental behaviour from the nations of the world' could require a 'direct active response' from military forces (1993, p. 129). However, it is most likely that any use of force mandated by the Security Council would be confined to dealing with environmental war crimes (see below). Perhaps the most important environmental role for the Security Council lies not in the authorization of military force but in its contributions to preventive diplomacy, conflict resolution and post-conflict reconstruction as they apply to environment and sustainable development vulnerabilities (see Elliott, 2003).

Demilitarizing security: securing the environment

In what has been called the 'military model' of environmental security (Finger, 1991b, p. 223), environmental degradation, resource scarcity and the impacts of differential endowment or relative deprivations are analysed in strategic terms. Environmental (in)security becomes synonymous with environmental threats to the state and to national security and with situations in which tensions over environment and resource issues increase the likelihood of armed conflict. This fits with an orthodox view of military security and is non-traditional only to the extent that the threats are non-military ones. Strategic and defence bureaucracies continue to define both the threat to national security and appropriate responses to those threats. Some have suggested that this focus on environmental threat reflects a search by strategic and defence establishments for new assignments in a post-Cold War world. Lipschutz and Holdren, for example, are trenchant in their criticism of 'strategic analysts ... busy combing the planet for new threats to be countered' by military forces (1990, p. 126).

For many this interpretation of environmental security is a problem. It is a problem because it narrows policy options by focusing on symptoms rather than causes, because it engenders inappropriate responses to the challenges of environmental degradation and because it reinforces a mindset which continues to be a direct and indirect cause of the very problems (environmental degradation and resource depletion) to which it purports to respond. In a 1982 report, well before the end of the Cold War, the UN Group of Governmental Experts on the Relationship between Disarmament and Development cautioned against moves to militarize or seek military solutions to non-military threats such as environmental degradation. Otherwise, they argued, 'there is a grave risk that the situation will deteriorate to a point of crisis where ... the use of force could be seen as a way to produce results quickly' (cited in WCED, 1987, p. 300). As the Executive Director of UNEP has put it, 'armed force is impotent in the face of ecological breakdown' (Töpfer, 2000). This conventional approach to security is therefore seen to be 'practically dysfunctional as the discursive framework for any political arrangement' (Dalby, 1997, p. 21) that could respond either to environmental degradation or to the competition and tension which might arise as a result. In short, militarizing environmental politics is argued to be inappropriate and antithetical to the real problems of environmental security.

Militarism and environmental degradation

The threat-to-state approach discourages any serious consideration of the extent to which militarization or militarism contributes to environmental degradation. As Finger argues, because environmental decline is defined as a 'threat to national security, the military is seen by many as part of the solution to the crisis rather than one of its major causes' (1991b, p. 220). Within a critical conceptualization of environmental security, the impact of war and preparation for war on the environment is at least equally as important as the potential for conflict motivated by environmental scarcity. The military and military activities contribute directly and indirectly to environmental degradation in a number of ways. One of the most obvious is through the environmental consequences of war. Arthur Westing, who has written widely on this, argues that the 'wanton disruption of the environment by armed conflict is a common occurrence in many ecogeographical regions of the world' (1989, p. 131). So-called 'scorched earth' strategies are not new. Examples within recent history would include the use of defoliants by US and other forces in Vietnam to deny cover to the Viet Cong (area denial), a strategy which destroyed 14 per cent of Vietnam's forests and severely damaged economically important mangrove swamp ecosystems (see Leggett, 1992, p. 69) as well, of course, as directly affecting the non-combatant population. Other examples include Afghanistan, Southern Sudan, Ethiopia and El Salvador (see Leggett, 1992). During the 1991 Gulf conflict, over 700 oil wells were 'damaged, destroyed and sabotaged, triggering pollution of water supplies and the seas' (Töpfer, n.d.) as well as damage to terrestrial and marine ecosystems, and environment-related health trauma in local populations. An estimated three to six million barrels of oil per day were burnt (compared with an average daily consumption of oil in all of Western Europe of 12 million barrels (Barnaby, 1991, p. 168).

As well as the deliberate destruction of the environment as a tactical manoeuvre, the conduct of war, whether between or within states, also results in 'unintended' environmental 'collateral damage'. War involves the use of 'hazardous substances, contamination of air and water resources, destruction of forests and crops' (Haque, 2002, p. 205).

Local ecosystems are damaged or destroyed by bombs (and bomb craters), by the impact of military vehicles and problems of waste management and excessive water consumption which can arise when large numbers of fighting personnel are inserted into regions where such resources are already scarce. Since the 1991 Gulf War, attention has focused also on the environmental and health consequences (for serving military personnel as well as for the people and ecosystems of target countries) of depleted uranium (DU) weapons.

War can also have a detrimental impact on wildlife and wildlife habitats (see Dudley *et al.*, 2002; UNEP, 2002a, pp. 13–14). It also has consequences for domestic agriculture – over 80 per cent of Kuwait's livestock, for example, is estimated to have died during the 1991 Gulf conflict (Pianin, 2003). The 'hardware' detritus of war also has environmental as well as humanitarian consequences. The millions of landmines scattered throughout the world as a result of conflict, for example, contribute to environmental degradation long after the war has finished. In places like Cambodia, as well as causing extensive trauma to local peoples, unmarked landmines prevent the rejuvenation of land for agriculture, thus requiring what land is available to be used intensively and often, therefore, unsustainably. The United Nations Environment Programme has established a Post Conflict Assessment Unit which, in conjunction with UN Habitat, has carried out assessments in the Balkans in 1999, in Macedonia and Albania following the conflict in Kosovo, in Afghanistan and in the occupied territory of Palestine. The Unit's report on Afghanistan found that two decades of war had degraded the country's natural resources and environmental services so badly that economic reconstruction efforts were severely compromised (UNEP, 2003a).

Environmental degradation in wartime has been subject to weak structures of accountability in international law. A number of international conventions have some partial relevance to the environmental impact of wartime, wartime-related or general military activities. This would include the environmental interpretations of the 1963 Partial Test Ban Treaty, the 1974 Threshold Test Ban Treaty, the 1976 Peaceful Nuclear Explosions Treaty, the 1980 Inhumane Weapons Convention and its protocols (which cover, among other things, the use of landmines) and the 1997 Convention on the Prohibition of the Use, Stockpiling, Production and Transfer of Anti-Personnel Mines and on their Destruction (the Ottawa Convention). Basic injunctions against environmental impact in wartime are found in the 1977 Environmental Modification Convention (ENMOD – in full the Convention on the Prohibition of Military or any other Hostile Use of Environmental Modification Techniques) but those provisions are 'ambiguous and limited' (Holst, 1989, p. 124). The Convention restricts only environmental modification techniques which have 'widespread, long-lasting or severe effects' (UNGA, 1976). Protocol I to the 1949 Geneva Convention 'explicitly requires combatants to limit environmental destruction' as part of its primary purpose to protect victims of conflict (see Diplomatic Conference, 1977). The Protocol incorporates a threshold clause similar to that of ENMOD, banning practices which cause 'widespread, long-term *and* severe damage', thus requiring all three conditions to be met before the injunction is to be invoked and assuming, of course, that warring parties are actually signatories to the Protocol.

Damage to the environment in time of war is not, however, listed under article 85 of ENMOD as a grave breach of the Protocol or the Geneva Conventions which would constitute it as a war crime. This has been rectified in the Rome Statute establishing the International Criminal Court. Article 8(2)(b)(iv) includes in its definition of war crimes 'intentionally launching an attack in the knowledge that such attack will cause ... widespread, long-term and severe damage to the natural environment which would clearly be excessive ... to the overall military advantage anticipated' (United Nations, 1998). The tests of what constitutes 'widespread', 'long-term', 'severe' and 'excessive' are interpretive but together these agreements confirm that 'destruction of the environment not justified by military necessity violates international humanitarian law' (International Committee of the Red Cross, 2000, p. 80). The importance of this was recognized in the declaration of 6 November 2002 as the first International Day for Preventing the Exploitation of the Environment in War and Armed Conflict.

However, the military's war on the environment goes beyond wartime. Globally, the military has been and remains a major polluter of the environment and a disproportionate user of resources. Barnett suggests that 'worldwide military activity may be responsible for more greenhouse gas emissions than all of the United Kingdom' (2003, p. 13). At the end of the Cold War, the Pentagon identified over 15,000 toxic waste sites at over 1,600 military bases in the United States alone. The German government listed 4,000 sites potentially contaminated by military waste (Anon., 1993c). A 1991 study by the organization Medical Association for Prevention of War (MAPW) cited reports which estimated that up to 10 per cent of the former East Germany may have been contaminated by the Soviet military (MAPW, 1991, p. 5). The costs of cleaning up the environmental legacy of the Cold War are extensive. The Pentagon estimated that something between $US11 and $US15 billion (Pirages, 1991, p. 132; Schneider, 1991) would be needed to deal with military-related toxic waste sites in the United States. The costs of permanent and environmentally safe disposal of Cold War nuclear by-products – 'an estimated 257 tons of weapons-grade plutonium and at least 1,300 tons of Highly Enriched Uranium' (Renner, 1994, p. 141) – was thought likely to cost much more than it cost to make the plutonium in the first place (see Taylor, 1989, p. 158).

The military is also a disproportionate user of world energy and mineral resources using, for example, about 25 per cent of all jet fuel (Renner, cited in Finger, 1991b, p. 221). Militaries and defence bureaucracies also often have an important role in decision-making on resource use. Harbinson (1992) describes how the military-dominated State Law and Order Restoration Council (SLORC) (as it was then) which continues to rule Burma as the State Peace and Development Council (SPDC) has sold oil and mineral exploration rights and logging concessions to pay for its campaign against the democracy movement and the Karen tribal resistance movement. The cost and impact of the struggle against SLORC has also placed pressure on the Karen to abandon their traditional slash-and-burn agriculture in order to survive as well as to fund their struggle (see Harbinson, 1992). The Khmer Rouge military regime in Cambodia was estimated to have made up to $240 million a year from the exploitation of Cambodia's forests (Töpfer, n.d.). For many years, the US military was the largest single holder of agricultural land in the Philippines (land which was often left idle; see MAPW, 1991). An analysis of the impact of militarism on the environment points also to the closed nature of military activity and the extent to which such impact is often subject to little or no scrutiny, often in the name of national security. In the build-up to the 1991 Gulf War, the Pentagon was exempted from having to conduct Environmental Impact Assessments on its projects (Finger, 1991b, p. 222). Boulding (1991, p. 80) describes the practice of militaries in constructing 'sacrifice areas' for the conduct of military exercises or weapons-testing, practices that are damaging to both the environment and people. French testing at Mururoa Atoll, US testing in the Marshall Islands, or the British use of Maralinga in Australia for its atomic tests would all fall into this category.

The contribution of militaries and military activity to environmental degradation is measured also in lost opportunity costs and a misallocation of resources. Global military spending totals approximately $US800 billion, with military spending in some countries close to 50 per cent of GNP. The global level of military spending declined in the 1990s, driven as much by economic necessity as any commitment to disarmament or the peace dividend. The Stockholm International Peace Research Institute (SIPRI) reports, however, that military spending increased by 6 per cent in real terms in 2002 with current levels of world military expenditure 14 per cent higher than in 1998 although still

16 per cent below its Cold War peak level in 1988 (SIPRI, 2003). Tolba, El-Kholy *et al.* (1992, p. 592) remind us that UNEP's expenditure in the decade 1982–92, a sum of $US450 million, was the equivalent of less than five hours of global military spending for the same period of time. Funds absorbed by the military are therefore denied to other areas of spending, including environmental repair, a view summed up in President Eisenhower's oft-quoted aphorism, 'Every gun that is made, every warship launched, every rocket fired represents, in the final analysis, a theft from those who hunger and are not fed, who are cold and are not clothed' (cited in Renner, 1989, p. 137). The Brundtland Commission expressed its concern about this misallocation of resources when it noted that 'arms competition and armed conflict create major obstacles to sustainable development' (WCED, 1987, p. 294). Former UN Secretary-General Boutros Boutros-Ghali also took up this theme, observing in his *Agenda for Development* that 'preparation for war absorbs inordinate resources ... which diminish the prospects for development' (UNSG, 1994, para. 17).

Opportunity costs are calculated not just in terms of direct military spending. In the last years of the Cold War, up to 40 per cent of the world's scientific and technological capabilities was directed towards military-related activities (Lipschutz and Holdren, 1990, p. 130). Even where spin-offs are available, reports have suggested they could have been achieved more efficiently and effectively with direct civilian investment (see Renner, 1989, pp. 139–41). Seymour Melman, among others, has challenged the idea that 'military goods and services are a source of wealth' (1988, p. 55), a proposition that has been supported by a number of studies which, using neo-classical economic growth models, show that 'military spending is a drain on the economy' (see Ward and Davis, 1992).

Flawed discourse?

As noted above, the security discourse which informs militarism and the environmental threat literature is argued to be both inappropriate and antithetical to the pursuit of environmental security. Military action is an ineffective response to resource scarcity and there is little evidence to support the proposition that 'trying to defend resources access militarily pays off' (Lipschutz and Holdren, 1990, p. 122). It is suggested that, for developed countries at least, non-renewable resources are unlikely to reach a point of actual rather than strategic scarcity, such that national security is considered to be at stake, because technological and financial capacity, along with public concerns about the increasing profligate use of resources, should ensure that substitutes are developed long before a state of scarcity is reached. However, this does require us to consider what defines scarcity in a resource context. Scarcity is often determined by politics rather than by the 'physical limitations of natural resources' (Brock, 1991, p. 410). There are, therefore, dangers that defining scarcity in strategic terms runs the risk of transforming 'every single resource into a potentially strategic one' (Finger, 1991a, p. 5). If what is considered strategic is linked to the pursuit of national security, then any resource defined as strategic or scarce becomes a potential source of conflict.

Traditional security discourse is also based on the assumption that threats to national security and identity come from 'others', usually other states or groups of states. Secure states, through the protection of borders, make (in theory) for a secure world and for secure citizens. Security against other states is to be pursued through military-related strategies, either unilaterally, through the deterrent acquisition of military capability or through alliance strategies and confidence-building. Yet, as explored in Chapter 4, environmental degradation does not always fit comfortably with this geopolitical, state-centric analysis. Environmental degradation does not respect state borders and states cannot rely on unilateral action to attain and maintain the security of their own environment. Traditional security responses which focus on military capability cannot ensure the security of the state and its people against environmental degradation. In the face of ecological insecurities, states and peoples cannot be secure unless the ecosystem is secure. Environmental degradation as a threat to state security arises not just through the potential for war or other forms of violence and unrest. Climate change, for example, presents 'the most serious security problem' for low-lying island states which may simply cease to exist – or at least become inhospitable to their people – as a result of sea-level rises (Barnett, 2003, p. 7). Neither is it helpful to identify an enemy 'other', whose intent is the violation of territorial integrity and state sovereignty. The 'enemy', the source of the threat, is not the environment but the everyday activities of humans and corporations, the former primarily in pursuit of quality of life and the latter in pursuit of profit. Töpfer argues that 'it is relentless ecological degradation, rather than any external enemy, which poses the greatest threat to international and national security today' (2000). State-centric and national security interpretations of environmental security have also restricted who can contribute to the 'security' discourse. Defining and providing security is determined to be the responsibility of state actors, nationally and internationally. When this is joined with 'environmental' threats, it can preclude ideas and concepts which do not have states as the key structures. Thus traditional security discourse is not only inappropriate as a basis for environmental security but it may also stand in the way of creative and successful solutions to environmental insecurity.

The traditional security discourse also engenders a focus on environmental conflict as a symptom and pays less attention to the underlying causes of environmental degradation that have been explored in earlier chapters in this book. Yet it is failure to take action on environmental degradation that is 'likely to lead to escalating insecurity and instabilities in which the forces of traditional security will be heavily engaged' (Oswald, 1993, p. 113). Rather than a focus on conflict as an outcome of resource and environmental scarcity, attention should be given to *preventing* resource scarcity. Rather than anticipating the extent to which internal tensions and conflict as a result of environmental degradation may spill over into neighbouring countries and pose a threat to international peace and security, greater attention should be given to mitigating the causes of that environmental degradation. As noted earlier, a focus on the adversarial model of security can also overlook the extent to which environmental scarcities might be amenable to cooperation rather than conflict. Dimitrov (2002) and Sadoff and Grey (2002) suggest, for example, that there are plenty of examples in international water law to demonstrate that shared water resources can provide the basis for conflict resolution and the development of cooperative management schemes (see also Turton, 2000, who argues that water wars are unlikely).

The expansion of the national security discourse to include economic security concerns provides some space for incorporating environmental challenges but, for those working within a critical perspective, it remains limited and problematic. These issues have, in effect, been canvassed in Chapters 7 and 8 and are therefore revisited only briefly here. The 'economic security' agenda was a recognition that the survival of the state over the longer term depends as much (and perhaps more) on economic capability as on military capacity. However, the pursuit of economic security, through growth strategies, can itself result in environmental degradation. Thus, for both military and economic securities, we have the environmental equivalent of the classic security dilemma. As states seek either territorial or economic security through unilateral initiatives and often unrestricted development and consumption, the less secure they become through the pressures of environmental decline.

The antidote has been sought in conceptualizations of global security which revive the value of common security and emphasize the importance of human security. In its 1994 *Human Development Report*, the United Nations Development Programme argued that the concept of security had 'for too long ... been shaped by the potential for conflict between states ... equated with ... threats to a country's borders' (UNDP, 1994, p. 3). In articulating a persuasive view of human security as universal, interdependent and people-centred, the UNDP emphasized 'human life and dignity' rather than weapons or territory (1994, p. 22) as the key features of global security and argued that early prevention rather than later intervention was the best strategy for pursuing such security. Human security is also *more* than security defined at the level of the individual. It is conceptually and practically interwoven with global security, 'as important to global peace as arms control and disarmament' (Axworthy, 1997, p. 184). It also invites a reassessment of the probability of particular kinds of insecurities. The Commission on Global Governance reported, for example, that 'threats to the earth's life support systems [*inter alia*] ... challenge the security of people far more than the threat of external aggression' (1995, p. 79). A human security approach provides a broader window on the relationship between environmental decline and insecurity. It accommodates situations, such as ecological disasters, where there is no violent conflict or social unrest but in which the lives of people and the stability of the ecosystem are clearly under threat.

There is some resistance to use of the term 'environmental security' from within both the traditional security community and the environmental community, albeit for quite different reasons. In the former case, security scholars are concerned at what they consider to be a weakening of 'real' security with the addition of what they often define as welfare concerns. Gleick, for example, argues that it is not a 'redefinition of international or national security' that is required but a 'better understanding of the nature of certain threats' (1991, p. 17). Scholars such as Brock and Deudney, on the other hand, caution against claiming the term security for the environmental discourse because in their view, it sends us off in the wrong direction and because it locks environmental concerns into an inappropriate, state-centric framework (see Brock, 1991, p. 418; Deudney, 1990). Thus Deudney argues that the 'environmental crisis is not a threat to national security, but it does challenge the utility of thinking in "national" terms' (1990, p. 468). Brock asks whether 'it make[s] sense at all to talk about environmental matters in terms of aggression and security' (1991, p. 408). Deudney is concerned that 'efforts to harness the emotive power of nationalism', which he sees as a logical outcome of the use of a security discourse, 'may prove counterproductive' (1990, p. 461). For others, however, the concept provides a 'powerful analytical tool ... and a powerful rhetorical tool, allowing [environmentalists] to argue in favour of the environment as a question of survival' (Switzer, 2002, p. 1).

Revisiting environmental security

The achievement of environmental security requires two things. First, because traditional security discourse is inappropriate for environmental security issues, non-traditional approaches to environmental security must be adopted, approaches which do not seek to identify the enemy 'other', and which do not seek to identify security only in terms of states, conflict, and military and territorial security. However, establishing a separate discourse for environmental insecurity is insufficient if the assumptions and practices of the traditional security agenda, which are antithetical to the pursuit of environmental security, are left unchallenged. Therefore achieving environmental security requires a demilitarizing of security, the second of Brock's propositions outlined at the beginning of this chapter. Security has to be demilitarized by reducing global military expenditure, by taking the planning and implementation of global security away from strategists who cannot accept or are unwilling to accept this broader vision, and by encouraging new ways of thinking about what it means to be secure. The UNDP (1994, pp. 22–5) urges that environmental security should be part of a comprehensive approach to security, one that moves away from a narrow military and defensive meaning of security to one which is integrative and focuses on human security. The Brundtland Report urges turning away from the 'destructive logic of an "arms culture"', a process which should include reductions in both military spending and arms trading, and acting 'in concert to remove the growing environmental sources of conflict' (WCED, 1987, p. 304). Soroos (in what may be an unintended appropriation of the language of traditional security) calls for an 'assault on business-as-usual practices' (1994a, p. 320). It is worthwhile also heeding Prins's words. He argues that environmental security is 'not something in the here and now. It is a *goal*' (Prins, 1993, p. xiv; emphasis added). What we have, he reminds us, is environmental insecurity!

In this view, environmental security stands for security of the environment, valuable in its own right and as a crucial component of human security. Buzan argues that 'environmental security concerns the maintenance of the local and planetary biosphere as the essential support system on which all other human enterprises depend' (1991, p. 433). Thus, as a report by UNEP and the Peace Research Institute in Oslo (PRIO) has argued, 'in the context of comprehensive international security, the significance of environmental security extends far beyond the environmental sector itself' (PRIO, 1989, p. 13). It also extends far beyond what has usually been defined and claimed as the security sector in international politics.

Chapter 10

The Global Politics of the Environment

There has clearly been no lack of attention to the global environment in the years since the Rio Conference. Thousands of committed people have worked hard to keep environmental issues on the agenda. Negotiation and debate on environment-related issues continue apace. Within the UN system and outside it, there are any number of committees, working groups, expert panels, subsidiary bodies, workshops, commissions and other fora, convened by governments, intergovernmental organizations and NGOs, which have focused and continue to focus on a wide range of transboundary and global environmental issues. Much has also been made in those years of the imperative for a global partnership (as Agenda 21 has it) in support of our common future (as the World Commission on Environment and Development described it).

Yet there are serious grounds for arguing that while we have seen considerable activity, we have yet to see the decisive action that the world's seven most industrialized countries (the G7) thought imperative when, in 1989, they stated that 'decisive action' on global environmental issues was urgently needed. Indeed they have themselves not heeded their own injunction. As Richard Falk reminds us, the 'geopolitical leadership of the world is not meeting the environmental challenge in a responsible fashion' (1995, p. 32). There is little evidence that the much-vaunted New World Order is becoming a green world order. UNEP's first *Global Environment Outlook (GEO)* suggested that 'from a global perspective, the environment has continued to degrade ... [and] progress towards a sustainable future is just too slow' (UNEP, 1997a). In its second *GEO*, UNEP again argued that 'the global system of environmental management is moving ... much too slowly' (1999a, p. xxiii). The third in this series, published in 2002 just before WSSD, was hardly any more comforting, arguing that 'sustainable development remains largely theoretical for the majority of the world's population' (2002a, p. xx). For many there has been 'precious little global sharing' (Agarwal and Narain, 1991, p. 1) and we continue to suffer from 'green planet blues' (Conca *et al.*, 1995).

223

Two broadly based responses to environmental degradation and unsustainable development have come to characterize the global politics of the environment. The divergence between those ideas which have been described in this book as reformist and those which have been identified as critical or transformative is manifest in approaches to description and analysis (how can we describe and understand the politics of this process?), to prescription (what policies will best meet the goals of reversing environmental decline?) and to our epistemological and normative framework (what unquestioned assumptions do we bring to the study and practice of the global politics of the environment and what kinds of norms and values are most appropriate for the goals we set ourselves?). This chapter turns now to draw those themes together.

Problem-solving and critique

In the view of many, the ecological confidence which was proclaimed after UNCED has yet to be justified and, if the experiences of UNGASS and WSSD are any indication, may well be misplaced. Caroline Thomas's view that 'at the most fundamental level, the *causes* of environmental degradation have not been addressed and ... efforts to tackle the crisis are bound to fail' (1993, p. 1; emphasis added) has not lost its relevance. Many scholars claim that what is therefore required to tackle this environmental crisis is a 'rethinking of fundamental concepts and assumptions' (Williams, 1996, p. 43). However, others whose views have also been explored here have cautioned against unrealistic expectations of decision-making processes that, while not perfect and perhaps slower than would be ideal, still provide the best hope for progress in international environmental governance, the development of international environmental law and better practice in the pursuit of sustainable development. In other words, this is a position which fears that the demands for radical change would be, to coin a phrase, akin to throwing babies out with the bathwater.

An important distinction which helps make sense of the different views and strategies which have been explored in this book is that which Robert Cox makes between problem-solving and critical approaches. For Cox, problem-solving

> takes the world as it finds it, with the prevailing social and power relationships and the institutions into which they are organized, as the given framework for action. The general aim of problem-solving is to make these relationships and institutions work smoothly (1986, p. 208).

This characterizes the reformist tradition, one which not only accepts but reinforces and helps to maintain the dominant social paradigm. At the risk of simplifying the views which have been explored in earlier chapters, reformist approaches share a general understanding that the environmental crisis and the search for solutions are as much managerial or technical problems as they are political ones. They can be resolved through making the existing political and economic order, which is not itself at fault, work more effectively and efficiently. For those who adopt this view, a system of international governance based primarily on sovereign states (of the kind explored in Chapter 4) is a reality and it is, therefore, simply unhelpful or unrealistic either to advocate or expect extensive change. Rather, the environmental problematic – and the energies of those involved in environmental decision-making – should focus on finding ways of strengthening institutional competence, particularly through the United Nations which, in this view, offers the best hope for progress. This problem-solving approach also views the principles and institutions of the liberal international economic order as fundamental to any attempts to mitigate and reverse global environmental degradation. Thus an open and supportive trading system can only contribute to the overall goal of sustainable development, and economic growth, albeit pursued in a sustainable manner, remains a basic condition for managing the environmental crisis. Nevertheless, these views are not, as various chapters in this book have demonstrated, simply business-as-usual strategies. If sustainable development is to be achieved, environmental concerns must be factored into the very centre of economic decision-making; environmental governance must be democratized; the poverty, misery and despair faced by such a large proportion of the world's people must be addressed and overcome.

At a rhetorical level, there is little disagreement with these propositions among policy-makers and commentators. However, as explored in this book, there is frequently a chasm (some would suggest one of insurmountable proportion) between statements of principle and subsequent commitments to act on such principles. For those who continue to advocate reform of the contemporary system of governance and political economy, the problem lies not in the strategies themselves but in the fact that those strategies have not yet been effectively operationalized because of the intervention of political and economic interests.

This is hardly an explanation to satisfy those who adopt a critical approach. As Cox elaborates it, such an approach

> stands apart from the prevailing order ... [it] does not take institutions and social and power relations for granted but calls them into question by concerning itself with their origins ... [it appraises] the

very framework for action which problem-solving accepts as its parameters (1986, p. 208).

Critical approaches, Cox argues, are 'directed to the social and political complex as a whole rather than to the separate parts' (1986, p. 208). Environmental issues are explored, therefore, not in isolation but as a manifestation of and intimately connected in their causes with a range of historical and contemporary social and political relationships. Rather than reinforcing the dominant social paradigm, these are the views which 'challenge established frames of mind and political conduct' (Lodgaard, cited in Brock, 1991, p. 418).

In calling the prevailing order into question, critical approaches extend the environmental problematic from one which focuses primarily on institutions and cooperation, the effective functioning of the market and processes of transfer and exchange to one which explores the environmental crisis in the context of questions about equity and justice, the importance of 'social forces above and below the state' (Thomas, 1993, p. 4) and the negative synergies between militarism and environmental degradation. In this view, the neo-liberal problematic of the reformist or problem-solving position provides a partial and incomplete picture of the global politics of the environment. At worst, the commitment to neo-liberalism is discursively complicit in sustaining particular hegemonic ideologies and practices (see Elliott, 2002b). Economic and political interests are not simply intervening factors in an otherwise value-free and effective process as the problem-solvers would have it. Rather they are inextricably bound up with the ways in which environmental problems are articulated and understood, with the causes of the environmental crisis and with the dysfunctions of the contemporary political and economic world order. Prevailing power relationships, which reflect and constitute the contemporary world order, are perceived as an ecological 'double assault' – as a cause of the environmental crisis and a barrier to its resolution. Thus strategies which continue to emphasize primarily state-centric governance (even if mediated through 'collective sovereignty' and democratization), or the more effective implementation of the liberal international economic order, are considered to be ineffective in the final analysis because they do not embody the kinds of fundamental normative change which, in a critical view, are necessary for a sound ecological future.

The different analytical traditions which are the basis for the reformist and critical approaches give rise to some quite different perspectives on just what constitutes the global politics of the environment. In reformist or problem-solving terms, politics is understood primarily as a process of arbitration between competing interests and the resolution of conflicts among actors with different preferences. Global environmental governance is characterized as a 'revamped liberal multilateralism' (Law, 1997, p. 171). Thus the global politics of the environment can be studied by identifying the actors and their interests, and by describing and analysing negotiations on environmental degradation as a collective action problem. As Sheldon Kamieniecki suggests in the introduction to his edited collection, 'global environmental issues can best be understood by studying environmental movements, ecological parties, international organisations and regimes, international law and the problems and policies of specific nations in different regions of the world' (1993, p. 1).

From a critical perspective, with its emphasis on underlying power structures, the problem-solving approach is flawed because of its 'exclusion of normative debate from social and political life' (Smith, 1996, p. 25). In this view, politics also arises (and is implicated in) the disenfranchisement of the powerless and the means by which particular environmental (and other) ideologies are reproduced. The global environment is presented as something more than an issue area. Rather it is an 'expression of privilege and power' (Wapner, 1997, p. 216), 'part of a larger process of systemic transformation' that is 'grounded in [and] related to the economic, social and political structures of the current world order' (Conca and Lipschutz, 1993, pp. 3, 5). Global environmental governance is therefore neither normatively neutral nor materially benign. Rather it is seen to accommodate and legitimize the rehabilitation of the state, the centralization of neo-liberal values in institutions such as the World Bank and the World Trade Organization, individualistic conceptions of justice and the 'efficiency-focused rationalisation discourse' (Hobson, 2002, p. 95).

Critical perspectives are grounded also in an increasingly widely held perception that it has become 'impossible to comprehend the causes of environmental concern' and the problems of environmental change within contemporary disciplinary orthodoxies (see Vogler, 1996, p. 13). In other words, our theoretical frameworks are inadequate for thinking about the environmental crisis and, therefore, for offering strategies and solutions. Benton and Redclift suggest that 'serious attempts to come to terms with issues posed by our environmental crisis expose to critical examination some very basic "settled" assumptions of the "mainstream" traditions of the social sciences' (Benton and Redclift, 1994, p. 2). Benton makes a similar point about what he calls the 'technological environmental ideology' (1994, p. 37). Such an ideology is, he argues, flawed for two reasons: first, because it cannot 'contemplate qualitatively different lines of sociocultural and economic change' and, second, because it tends to 'undertheorise the social, legal and political processes of environmental regulation' (Benton, 1994, p. 37). One finds, therefore, demands for a serious investigation of the ways in which theories 'might need to be broadened, recast or transformed in order to understand global environmental problems and the ways in which these can, or should be, tackled' (Hurrell, 1995, p. 136).

A critical global politics of the environment is now well-established in the discipline of International Relations whose key ideas have informed the questions explored in this book. It draws on a range of theoretical interventions to contemplate more normatively driven and politically nuanced ways of understanding environmental change. A detailed investigation of those theories, and what is termed 'green theory' in particular, is beyond the scope and purpose of this chapter (see Elliott, 2002b). It is, however, at least worth identifying many of the shared purposes in those theoretical debates which span disciplines and which have been touched upon in other chapters of this book. These common themes include concerns about the relationship between humans and non-human species, important debates about the values and normative imperatives which should inform policy-making, about social goals, about the ideologies of industrialism and anthropocentrism and about democratization, decentralization and appropriate forms of political practice.

As earlier chapters in this book have demonstrated, competing reformist and critical analytical traditions diverge also in their understanding not just of the causes of global environmental degradation but also of the kinds of strategies that are likely to be most effective in mitigating and reversing the environmental crisis. These issues of political practice and appropriate strategies illuminate differences over the question of agency. At the risk of simplifying the intellectual debates over agency (which are themselves beyond the scope of this discussion), the reformist or problem-solving approaches explored in earlier chapters tend to look to the collective actions of individuals as the basis for solutions to the environmental crisis on the grounds that it is human action (whether individual, collective or corporate) that is at the root of the environmental crisis. For critical scholars, this is rather too simple and rather too easy. Saurin argues, for example, that environmental change is not so much just the outcome of human agency, whether deliberative or otherwise, but the 'cumulative or systematic consequences of a set of structured practices and processes' (1996, p. 85), which for Saurin at least are further embedded in capitalism. Therefore, in this view, simply changing human behaviour is inadequate as a solution to the environmental crisis if those 'structured practices and processes' remain. It becomes, to borrow a much-used phrase, a necessary but not sufficient condition for overcoming environmental insecurity.

At a more fundamental level, this question of effective strategies is related to the degree of confidence or otherwise in the 'basic assumptions of modern western society' (Sessions, cited in Paehlke, 1994, p. 350) and the 'capacity of western institutions to redress or reverse the environmental crisis' (Fischer and Black, 1995a, p. xiii). Those assumptions are based on a commitment to the market and industrialism, international institutions based on the state, decision-making informed by democratic pluralism, and a belief in the importance of objective science and technology, a position Rees describes as 'techno-optimism' (2002, p. 17). For those of a reformist persuasion, while a modern western society characterized by governance based on democratic pluralism and a liberal economic order might have some previously unforeseen side effects which need to be managed and overcome, it still holds out the best promise for progress for humanity and for managing the environmental crisis. For others, the consequences for the environment of these practices and assumptions of the contemporary world order 'have been devastating' (Doran, 1995, p. 194).

Interrogating the contemporary world order

Debates over the defining features of the contemporary world order focus on the structures and values associated with neo-liberalism, globalization and modernity and the practices they inscribe on the axes of world politics – states and markets, the global and the local (see Elliott, 2002c). One of the major characteristics of the post-Cold War and post-Rio era has been the continued globalization of a neo-liberal international economic order and the spread (some would claim the triumph) of capitalism, engendering the 'hegemony of neo-liberal economic assumptions' (Paterson, 1995, p. 216). As Chapters 7 and 8 have indicated, for many whose positions can be characterized as reformist or problem-solving, this is to be welcomed. In this view, free(r) trade along with the free movement of capital, supported by limited interference in the market, provide the basis for increased economic welfare, greater equity and, as a welcome consequence, the potential for greater environmental protection. Environmental values and costs will be internalized and major economic players will be encouraged, through competition and market-based mechanisms, to act in a more environmentally sustainable and sound manner. The problem of sustainability is here located 'within the context of a global economy of mutually interdependent actors' which renders nature as a commodity and assumes that a properly functioning market will determine the most 'efficient use of resources' (Williams, 1996, p. 53). This is a position which understands 'the economy as an independent, self-regulating and self-sustaining system whose productivity and growth are not seriously constrained by the environment' (Rees, 2002, p. 17). Therefore there is no questioning of the assumption that economic growth per se is a good thing nor, indeed, that sustainable growth can be pursued within the contemporary international economic order.

In contrast to this general optimism, critical positions raise 'doubts about the compatibility of an increasingly globalized world economy with any notion of global ecological rationality ... [giving] rise to an emerging radical ecological critique of the world economy' (Hurrell, 1995, p. 143). This is a tradition which, as explored in Chapters 7 and 8, challenges the 'expansionist vision' (Rees, 2002, p.16) reflected in the 'predominantly market-liberal assumptions that characterize Northern policies and attitudes' (Hurrell, 1995, p. 144). From a critical position, the deep integration of the global economy, rather than providing the basis for global economic growth and increased welfare, 'has enabled the majority of the population in the North to greatly expand its capacity for consuming the resources of the Southern hemisphere' (Redclift and Sage, 1998, p. 507). This is so *precisely* because of the continuing emphasis on resource-intensive growth and trade, the maintenance of debt and global inequities, and the powerful and central role played by global corporate and business interests. The very institutions which are advantaged by a globalized world economy – multinational corporations and the multinational development banks – are those which continue to pose 'major environmental threats' (see Shiva, 1993, p. 149). In the most orthodox forms of neo-liberal economics, environmental concerns are treated as consumer preferences and the individual as an 'active citizen, mobilised by responsibility and duty (Hobson, 2002, p. 101) is discounted. Problems of ecology become cast as 'problem[s] of technology transfer and finance' (Shiva, 1993, p. 153). Prevailing inequities in resources are identified primarily as a statement of geography rather than a 'consequence of centuries of colonialism as well as [of] contemporary forms of international economic domination' (Soroos, 1986, p. 356). The consequence is that the practices and consequences of globalization are depoliticized.

Neo-liberal approaches to the functioning of the global economy have sought to respond to the practical challenges associated with the negative consequences of globalization in a way that rejects the 'crude reductionism of orthodox neo-classical analysis' (Sandbrook, 2000, p. 1071). What is sometimes known as the 'post-Washington consensus' (see Stiglitz, 1998; Fine, 2001) or, in domestic contexts, the 'third way' (see Arestis and Sawyer, 2001) is hospitable to a more active role for the state in providing social safety nets and overcoming the problems of market failure, including those associated with environmental degradation and sustainable development. This 'pragmatic neoliberalism' adopts 'human well-being rather than mere growth as its goal' (Sandbrook, 2000, p. 1071). It seeks to reinsert concerns with good governance, social rights and freedoms, and sustainability into the structures of both domestic and global economies and into economic policy. From a critical perspective, however, this still presents serious intellectual and policy flaws. Fine perceives in the post-Washington consensus the colonization of the social sciences by economics in a way that treats 'non-economic or non-market relations as if they were economic' without 'once mentioning the economic and political power and structures' embodied in financial or economic systems (2001, p. 7). Sandbrook argues that this more human-centred approach still 'purveys a false promise to the poor and socially excluded' (2000, p. 1071).

Knowledge, science and risk

Reformist traditions tend also to be characterized by a growing confidence in scientific knowledge as an essential basis for action, one which accepts, explicitly or implicitly, that 'increased scientific understanding of environmental problems will ... facilitate international cooperation' (Hurrell, 1995, p. 134). Critical scholars, while recognizing the imperatives for agreement, cooperation and the growth of knowledge, are cautious about an unbridled commitment to and belief in technology and science as the solution to the environmental crisis. This wariness arises, first, from concern about the impact of science and technology which has, Sachs argues, 'successfully transform[ed] nature on a vast scale, but so far, with unpleasant as well as unpredictable consequences' (1993b, p. 20). It arises also because of a perception that the 'ascendant ideology of global environmental management' which characterizes this position is not value-free but reproduces the 'values and interests of existing international institutions and their most powerful members' (Doran, 1995, p. 193).

Critical scholars are concerned that this reformist faith in science and technology as the basis for environmental progress has also closed any 'serious consideration of alternatives' (Torgerson, 1995, p. 16). In particular, it marginalizes and disenfranchises 'diverse and competent communities of knowledge which embrace numerous ways of understanding, perceiving, experiencing and defining reality, including relations between people and people and their environment' (Doran, 1995, p. 201). Attempts to incorporate indigenous knowledge and indigenous communities, or declarations that women have a vital role to play in environmental management, are viewed therefore with some concern, perceived not as democratization but as examples of the mining of competing knowledge systems as and when necessary and appropriate in order to shore up the central reformist paradigm.

The role that technology and science have in enhancing our understanding of the often severe environmental consequences of the technological and scientific 'progress' which characterizes globalization and modernization exposes the ecological paradox of a globalized modernity. This paradox and the challenges of the ecological crisis have informed the literature on risk society and ecological modernization, both of which seek to rehabilitate globalization and modernity through contemplating a more complex and reflexive phase of contemporary society. The concept of risk society, associated most closely with the work of German sociologist Ulrich Beck, defines the ecological crisis in part as a product of the institutional practices associated with the technological advances of industrial modernity. As Marshall summarizes it, 'the risk society becomes gripped by the hazards and potential threats unleashed by the exponentially growing productive forces in the modernisation process' (1999, p. 264). In turn, the risks associated with modern society impel the transformation of that society. The 'political and economic processes of globalisation' are argued to 'contain within them the promise of global governance shaped by ethical globalisation' (Lacy, 2002, p. 43). Nevertheless, knowledge has an ambiguous role in this transformation, where 'more and better knowledge often means more uncertainty' (Beck, cited in Lacy, 2002, p. 45).

Ecological modernization is similarly 'concerned with the transformation of societies', in this case 'via the integration of environmental concerns into production and consumption practices' (Murphy, 2001, p. 1). In fact, ecological modernization has been explicitly linked to the 'third way' rehabilitation of neo-liberal globalization discussed above (see Curran, 2001). One of the central themes of ecological modernization theory is that the pressures that ecological interests and ideas impose on economic and industrial practices are being mediated through science and technology to transform modern society in a way that can strengthen rather than undermine environmental reform (see Vogel, 2002/03). In other words, science and technology provide mechanisms by which society confronts the consequences of environmental decline. Economic development and globalization are presented not as sources of environmental decline but as opportunities and mechanisms for improving environmental protection. Ecological modernization also has a more specifically emancipatory and reflexive form which departs from a techno-industrial focus to emphasize the importance of negotiated public dialogue, a position shared by risk society. Despite this emphasis on democratization and the public sphere, risk society and ecological modernization theories have attracted criticism similar to that directed to 'third way' and the post-Washington consensus – that they reinforce the problem-solving dimensions of a reformist agenda, that their generalizability is limited, that they fail to deal adequately with equity issues, that they abstract agency (particularly that of the nation-state) from global structures, and that they provide an environmental façade for industrialism and elite (especially western) values (see Marshall, 1999; Curran, 2001; Toke, 2001).

Global environmental governance

Differences over the capacity of the practices and values of the contemporary world to address the causes of environmental degradation also engender, at minimum, some ambivalence about the value of existing international state-centric institutions. The crisis of state legitimacy and capacity has been explored in Chapter 4. In a globalized world, the state is under siege territorially from environmental degradation and institutionally from the forces of globalization, especially the globalized world economy. As Linklater argues, 'globalisation has seriously reduced [states'] scope for independent action' (1995, p. 250). The state is also under challenge because it is increasingly unable to fulfil the social contract to provide citizens with security: its normative appeal is, as Hurrell (1994, p. 147) notes, diminishing. Thus we have a process of deterritorialization: the territorial integrity of the state is increasingly precarious and vulnerable to a range of challenges, including environmental ones, and the normative appeal of the state as the primary referent for identity is weakened. Political processes are increasingly detached from national spaces (Scholte, cited in Paterson *et al.*, 2003, p. 7). Yet if international environmental agreements are to be implemented and if environmental commitments are to be put into practice, then the paradox is that a strong state may be required. Thus French argues that 'sustainable development ... relies on the organisational ability of the state to manage change and to promote a particular vision of public policy' (2002, p. 137). The paradox of the contemporary state is that it is ' too large to deal with the local problems of modern life and too small to deal with the global problems of modernity' (Saurin, 1996, p. 92).

Despite concerns about the adequacy and capacity of the state (and the state system), a general reformist optimism claims that the increase in multilateral environmental agreements and international institutions and the development of a web of environmental norms, including sustainable development, are evidence that governance based on the state as the major legitimate site of policy-making, while not perfect, is working reasonably well. This problem-solving emphasis on efficiency and effectiveness also engenders, as Chapter 5 suggested, a commitment to pluralism and the participation of a range of stakeholders. There can be little doubt that this is a precondition for addressing environmental concerns. Yet a reformist emphasis on democratic efficiency remains more attuned to elite dynamics and, as Marc Williams notes, has 'tended to have little to say about non-elite social movements' (1996, p. 51). Advocating participation as a strategy in the problem-solving tradition reveals little about the power relationships which determine the extent or nature of that participation. Its assumptions about democratic outcomes are open to question.

From a critical perspective the pluralism of reformist approaches and the commitment to international institutions based on cooperative sovereignty establish and reinforce political processes which represent the privileged interests of the few rather than the democratic interests of the many. International institutions and the processes of environmental governance are not, in this view, democratized despite the participation (some would suggest the incorporation or cooption) of NGOs. Rather environmental governance continues, from this critical perspective, to 'represent a coalition of the rich and powerful political regimes, their corporations and their military establishments' (Aigbokhan, 1993, p. 32). As earlier chapters have suggested, one of the consequences of the commitment to state-centric institutions, regardless of demands for reform, has been to move the debate about solutions to the environmental crisis, and the implementation of those solutions, out of the hands of those who are most directly affected (see Stoett, 2002). What exists, according to Shiva, is not a 'democratic distillation of all local and national concerns worldwide but the imposition of a narrow group of interests from a handful of nations on a world scale' (1993, p. 154), a condition Sachs calls the 'hegemony of globalism' (1993b, p. 17) and which Fischer and Black argue 'inherently privilege[s] the view of elite industrialists' (1995a, p. xvi).

A reformist or problem-solving emphasis on this particular form of global governance also ensures that environmental concerns which do not meet the privileged criteria of the global are excluded from the arena of responsibility of the world community of states, thereby narrowing rather than expanding the global environmental agenda. Yet, to paraphrase Conca and Lipschutz (1993, p. 3), there are multiple meanings of the global. Local concerns may be global in that they occur in many parts of the world (that is, global issues may be a cluster of local issues) but they have not been defined as *international* because they have been excluded from the definition of transboundary or multilateral collective action problems. As Lipschutz and Conca point out, 'phenomena such as soil erosion and land degradation that are depicted as "local" – and thus relegated to a lesser sense of urgency – are ... linked by economic, political and social institutions of much broader, and often global, extent' (1993b, p. 331). Some environmental problems, Sachs suggests, also become more global than others in terms of whose interests dominate: did Senegalese peasants, he asks, 'ever pretend to have a say in Europe's energy consumption, or did the people of Amazonia ever rush to North America to protect the forests in Canada and the North-West Pacific' (1993a, p. xvii). The 'global', then, is not simply a geographic term appropriated to describe increasing environmental interdependence, as it is most often used in the reformist tradition. Rather it is a political term and one which, according to scholars such as Shiva (1993, p. 154), provides the North with a new political space in which to control the South, thus creating the moral base for green imperialism.

Future conditional?

For some, the twenty-first century is a turning point and we must now be certain that we make the right choice. For others, the problem is no longer one of deciding which way to turn: rather we have lost our direction, 'wandering between the modern world of the past half-millennium and a different world if civilisation and perhaps humanity is to survive' (Caldwell, 1990, p. xiii). The problems are, at one level, clear. This book has identified the difficulties of securing effective environmental protection in a decentralized world of sovereign states, while also pointing out problems with increasing centralization of environmental governance. It has drawn attention to the gap between statements of principle and rhetoric, on the one hand, and political and financial commitments on the other. It has illuminated the ways in which global environmental degradation is embedded in the global political economy and explored the imperatives for reform (at minimum) and, perhaps, a radical reorienting of the international economic order. It has suggested, as have many before, that the hopes ignited at Rio remain largely unfulfilled.

There is no shortage of general prescriptions for an environmentally secure future. There are calls for a 'new global order for environmental care' (Shiva, 1993, p. 155) and a new planetary paradigm (Caldwell, 1990). Lester Brown, from the WorldWatch Institute, has argued that we need nothing short of an environmental revolution to rival the agricultural and industrial revolutions in scope as 'one of the greatest economic and social transformations of human history' (1992, p. 174). William Rees urges us to 'rise above history in an unprecedented cooperative effort to engineer the global-scale "paradigm shift" necessary for collective survival' (2002, p. 44). Yet, as suggested throughout this book, there is a considerable divergence between the kinds of strategies advocated by those who look to a better and more effective functioning of the contemporary world order to provide solutions to the environmental crisis and those who argue that the contemporary world order is not only inappropriate for reversing ecological decline but is, in the long run, antithetical to that purpose. Can we address, halt and reverse global environmental degradation and its social and economic impacts, as Torgerson asks, through better 'policy planning or management' or does it require a 'process of basic social change' (1995, p. 3)?

Critical approaches call, implicitly and sometimes explicitly, for a 'fundamentally different approach' (Thomas, 1993, p. 2) to political and economic practice. If the critical position that the causes of the environmental crisis are to be found in the structures of the contemporary world order is right, then 'unless these structures are overturned, sustainable development will remain an aspiration rather than a practical goal' (Williams, 1996, p. 55). Paterson argues that what is required is a challenge to 'prevailing power relationships, between states, within states, within capitalist economies and within patriarchal forms of power' (1995, p. 212). What is common to these alternative paths is an emphasis on humane governance, globalization from below (rather than a globalization characterized by further centralization of power and authority) and a reclaiming of the local and of different ways of knowing and understanding. A major theme of this critical tradition has been the 'empowerment of both individuals and communities, combined with a strong emphasis on decentralised forms of political organisation' (Hurrell, 1994, p. 158). There is a fundamental concern with equity and social justice, and for ecological values to inform decision-making, issues which have been explored in earlier chapters in this book. Falk refers to this as 'normative democracy' which highlights 'ethical and legal norms ... reconnecting politics with moral purpose and values' (1998, p. 106). As a minimum requirement, the imperatives of a truly participatory democracy and the empowerment of those who are presently disempowered cannot be gainsaid on either environmental or human rights grounds. In this sense, rather than simply questions of strategy and efficiency, the debate about solutions to the problems of global environmental change becomes one of 'informed ethics and morality' (Caldwell, 1990, p. xiii).

This would involve a stronger recognition of ecological responsibility, environmental stewardship, an emphasis on welfare and human rather than state security, equity and respect for the diversity of cultures and traditions. Rees argues that 'sustainability with social justice can be achieved only through an unprecedented level of international cooperation rooted in a sense of compassion for other peoples and other species'

(2002, p. 15). The values and institutions of governance need to recognize ecological interdependence as the force which shapes political and economic interdependence. Rather than the biosphere at the service of the economy, 'the economic sphere must now find its place within the biosphere' (Damian and Graz, 2001, p. 602). Demands for radical transformation are accompanied by hopes for a 'return to small-scale technologies, decentralised bioregions and participatory democracy' (Fischer and Black, 1995a, p. xiv). Shiva argues that the reversal of ecological decline will only be achieved with a strengthening of local rights, including the right to information and prior consent along with recognition of the rights of non-human nature (1993, pp. 155–6). A new global order for environmental care would see local communities equipped with rights and obligations, rather than the current trend which is to move rights further upwards to centralized agencies (such as the World Bank or the World Trade Organization) in which local concerns are rarely heard. In this view, the global must accede to the local, and must be informed by the right to information and the right of prior consent.

Yet the paradox of the state explored in Chapter 4 and revisited earlier in this chapter is matched, as Chapter 5 hinted, by the paradox of civil society. Chartier and Deléage point out that NGOs are 'at one and the same time, in continuity with and in rupture from dominant social structures' (1998, p. 36). While some, such as Breyman, argue that 'ecology movements, despite their imperfections, inspire hope for the future' (1993, p. 124), others are cautious about this confidence in civil society and a concomitant decentralization of governance. Ford, for example, questions whether the inclusion of global civil society 'actually acts as a distraction from questions of democracy' within the institutions of global governance (1999, p. 69; see also Raustiala, 1997, p. 720).

The prospects for even a reformed, green world order are not looking good on present performance as earlier chapters have suggested. If enthusiasm over the prospects for reform is muted then the prospects for a transformed world order must be even more constrained. It seems clear that 'environmental security requires a willingness to make ... fundamental changes' (Falk, 1995, p. 169). There is, however, much to make us cautious about the likelihood of any fundamental change in the short term. It is unclear quite how such transformations could be achieved in a world characterized by continued high levels of military spending, parlous levels of development assistance, continued inequities between rich and poor, centralization of decision-making and, paradoxically, the crisis of the capacity of the state in the absence, at this stage, of widely accepted decentralized sites of decision-making and implementation.

The agenda of global environmental politics is likely to continue much as it did in the decade between Rio and Johannesburg. On the one hand the emphasis on sectoral issues will ensure continued debate and discussion on particular environmental problems, the status of scientific knowledge, the kinds of targets that should be established and how best to ensure implementation of those agreements. If past experience is a guide, however, progress on sectoral issues may not keep pace with the environmental problems themselves. This is in large part because of a lack of political will in addressing fundamental cross-sectoral concerns – issues of funding and technology transfer, trade, debt, poverty and inequities in wealth, the nature of international environmental institutions and the role of actors such as multinational corporations and non-governmental organizations. Many of those issues were on the agenda at Stockholm in 1972. They were addressed by the World Commission on Environment and Development in 1987 and were on the agenda again in Rio in 1992, UNGASS in 1997 and Johannesburg in 2002. At the Stockholm Conference, one observer suggested that debates amounted to little more than 'fighting a fire with a thermometer' (in Rowland, 1973, p. 33). It is doubtful whether we can claim to have moved in any significant way to dealing with the fire in the years since, despite the many activities described in this book.

At the conclusion of the United Nations Conference on Environment and Development in 1992, the then United Nations Secretary-General Boutros Boutros-Ghali reminded, indeed cautioned, his audience that 'one day we will have to do better' (cited in Brenton, 1994, p. 231). Yet a decade later, in a lecture delivered at the London School of Economics and Political Science in February 2002, the incumbent UN Secretary-General Kofi Annan expressed his fears that the concept of sustainability at the centre of sustainable development and environmental protection had 'become a pious invocation rather than the urgent call to concrete action that it should be' (Annan, 2002, p. 7). We would do well to heed their words.

Further Reading

The growing interest in global environmental issues among political scientists and international relations scholars has been reflected in a developing corpus of literature. Many of those works are cited in various chapters of this book and are listed in the bibliography. This guide to further reading is therefore brief, suggesting only some *starting* points for those who want to delve more deeply into some of the issues which have been covered in this book. For the most part, it excludes the immense number of journal articles available to readers except where those works are considered seminal to the debates or where they fill a gap in the book-length literature. A number of issue-specific texts are mentioned throughout this section and in individual chapters of this book. For more recent overviews see, *inter alia*, Schreurs and Economy (1997), Vig and Axelrod (1999), French (2000), Porter *et al.* (2000), Vogler (2000), Chasek (2000b), DeSombre (2002) and Lipschutz (2003). Thomas (1992) and Brenton (1994) are still useful for historical surveys.

Keeping up to date on environmental issues is time-consuming, which is why the Internet has become such a boon to researchers. The websites of the secretariat for the various environmental conventions are always a useful starting point. One of the best journals for information, although less so for analysis, is *Environmental Policy and Law*. The annual *Yearbook of International Cooperation on Environment and Development* is a good reference resource. The journal *Environment* provides a useful balance of commentary and analysis, as do *Global Environmental Change: Human and Policy Dimensions*, the *Review of European Community and International Environmental Law* (*RECIEL*) and *International Environmental Agreements*. Among the best analytical journals are *Global Environmental Politics*, *Environmental Politics* and the *Journal of Environment and Development*. For a more self-consciously critical perspective on environmental issues, *The Ecologist* is worth exploring.

1 From Stockholm to Rio to Johannesburg

Little has been written on the politics of the Stockholm Conference. Rowland (1973) provides a readable and what was then a contemporary commentary. See also Brenton (1994, pp. 35–50) for a brief analysis. UNCED, on the other hand, generated a flurry of publishing activity. Halpern (1992), Johnson (1993) and Grubb *et al.* (1993) are worth consulting on the detail and, in some respects, the analysis of the Conference. Chatterjee and Finger (1994) offer a more critical approach to UNCED and its achievements (or lack thereof). Campiglio *et al.* (1994) cover UNCED and the post-Rio agenda. Osborn and

Bigg provide an overview of UNGASS and its outcomes. See Brack *et al.* (2001) for a good overview of the background to the Johannesburg World Summit on Sustainable Development.

2   The Global Politics of Conservation: Species, Resources and Habitat

One of the difficulties with literature on the global environmental agenda is the time lag between the events and the publication of academic commentaries. The *Global Environment Outlook* publications produced by the United Nations Environment Programme provide a detailed overview of the environmental challenges facing decision-makers that are explored in Chapter 2 and in Chapter 3. The various commentaries produced by the International Institute for Sustainable Development (particularly the journal *Earth Negotiations Bulletin*) provide detailed day-by-day accounts of individual meetings and negotiations. McConnell (1996) provides a negotiating history of the Biodiversity Convention from the perspective of someone closely involved with those negotiations. See Le Prestre (2002) also for an exploration of how global biodiversity has been 'governed'. Cosbey and Burgiel (2000) provide a helpful overview of the Biosafety Protocol and see Bail *et al.* (2002) for an investigation of the trade implications of the Protocol. See also the special issue of *International Affairs* (vol. 76, no. 2, 2000) on biodiversity. On endangered species, CITES and the trade in wildlife see Hutton and Dickson (2000), Reeve (2002) and Stoett (2002). Humphreys (1996b) is helpful for an overview of the early debates on international cooperation on forests. See also Humphreys (1999), Tarasofsky (2000) and Rosendal (2001) for more recent coverage. The negotiations for the Desertification Convention are covered in Corell (1999).

3   The Global Politics of Pollution

The historical analysis of the negotiations for many of the conventions covered in this chapter remain useful. Krueger (1999b) and O'Neill (2000) provide a good overview of the key issues related to the Basel Convention and the trade in hazardous wastes. See Hough (2000) and Van den Bilcke (2002) for introductory overviews, respectively, of the Rotterdam Convention on hazardous chemicals and pesticides and the Stockholm Convention on persistent organic pollutants. On global atmospheric issues, Benedick (1991) is of interest on the ozone negotiations, given his 'insider' status as head of the US delegation. Litfin (1994) and Rowlands (1995a) both tackle the ozone issue in the context of broader theoretical questions related to global politics concerns and Paterson (1996) does likewise on climate change. One of the most interesting texts on the early negotiations is Mintzer and Leonard (1994a) which views the climate negotiations from a range of participant perspectives. See also Fermann (1997). Grubb *et al.* (1999) provide a guide to the Kyoto Protocol and Victor (2001) examines the politics of the Protocol in some detail. Dunn (2002) provides an environmentalist perspective of climate policy between the Rio and Johannesburg summits and Faure *et al.* (2003) examine the institutions associated with the governance of climate change.

4   Global Environmental Governance: The State and Institutional Design

The whole issue of environmental governance is so broad that almost all books on global environmental issues, and a goodly number of articles as well, touch on this at some stage. Many of the books referred to in the introduction to this section are relevant here. The problem of the inadequate state is well-covered in Hurrell (1994). See also French (2000). For a helpful exploration of the sovereignty issue, see Litfin (1998). The exploration in Haas *et al.* (1993) of what effective environmental institutions might look like remains relevant even if the issue coverage is now a little dated. Victor *et al.* (1998) and Weiss and Jacobson (2000) examine the challenges associated with the implementation of and compliance with international environmental agreements. The critical perspective on debates about global governance and international institutions, including the UN, is explored in the various chapters in Sachs (1993c) and in Chatterjee and Finger (1994). For a more detailed but immensely readable study of environmental governance in the United Nations, Imber (1994) provides a good starting point. Elliott (2001) provides a concise summary of the more recent debates. Sjöberg (1999) and Streck (2001) are helpful on the Global Environment Facility. See Charnovitz (2002) for a discussion of the issues surrounding a world environment organization. Hyvarinen and Brack (2000) summarize and analyse key issues regarding institutions for environmental governance.

5   Global Environmental Governance: Democratization and Local Voices

Starkey and Welford (2001) provide a good collection of readings on business and sustainable development, which is relevant also to Chapters 7 and 8. For a critical perspective on the corporate world in environmental politics, see Beder (1997) and Karliner (1997). There is now an extensive body of work which documents and analyses the role of non-governmental organizations. Wapner (1996) and Princen and Finger (1994) still count as seminal pieces. See also Keck and Sikkink (1998) for an exploration of NGOs in the context of theory and practice. Various sources in Chapter 5 refer to specific case studies of NGO influence on environmental governance. The issue of gender and environmental degradation has most often been dealt with in the broader context of the impact of development on women, particularly in the developing world. Bretherton (2003) provides a useful overview and analysis of the key themes of a gender perspective on global environmental governance. See Kurian (2000) for an investigation of gender issues in the environmental policies of the World Bank. The politics of the relationship between indigenous peoples and environmental degradation is explored in Clad (1998), Aguilar (2001) and Fourmile (2001).

6   Normative Challenges: Justice, Obligations and Rights

The challenges of justice and ethics in international politics, including those relating to the environment, are often explored in more general texts on international ethics and principled world politics. For a good introduction focusing specifically on the ethical challenges of displacement associated with environmental degradation, see Wapner (1997). Shue (1981) and (1995) are important. Gleeson and Low (2001) and Low (1999) – indeed many of the works by these two authors – also explore these challenges in more detail. O'Riordan *et al.* (2001) cover a range of views on the precautionary principle. Freestone and Hey (1996) cover the development of the polluter pays principle. Weiss (1988) remains a seminal work on intergenerational equity and Thompson (2001) is also insightful on the ethical dimensions of this issue. Aaron Sachs (1996), Bosselman (2001) and Wagner *et al.* (2003) all provide useful examinations of the issue of human rights and the environmental. See Ganguli (1998) and Khor (2002) for analysis of some of the important intellectual property rights issues which are relevant to environmental protection and sustainable development. Corpuz-Tauli (1999) and Prakash (2000) provide different views on how IPRs relate to indigenous rights.

7   The International Political Economy of the Environment

Most books on the global politics of the environment examine, at some stage, the international political economy (IPE) of the environment. The Brundtland Report (WCED, 1987) remains a key work on sustainable development. See de la Court (1990) for a specific critique of the report. Glasby (2002) examines the contemporary relevance of the concept. Pearce *et al.* (1994) examine sustainable development in a Third World context. Daly and Cobb (1994) is also useful. Rajamani (2003) provides a brief but useful introduction from a critical perspective to the 'anatomy of dissonance' which characterizes the relationship between developed and developing countries; see also Redclift and Sage (1998) and the chapters in Sachs (1993c). Miller (1995) provides a more conventional interpretation. On the principle of common but differentiated responsibilities, see Matsui (2002) and Segger *et al.* (2003).

8   Strategies for Sustainable Development

Much of the literature related to the strategies discussed in this chapter is to be found in journal articles and book chapters rather than in full-length works. Two issues have become prominent – trade and the environment, and the use of market-based mechanisms such as emissions trading in the climate change regime. The debates on trade and the environment can be traced over time through Esty (1994), Fijalkowski and Cameron (1998), Ulph (2001) and Gaines (2002). Rich (1994), Wade (1997) and Zoe Young (2002) analyse the environmental role of the World Bank, sometimes from a highly critical perspective. The chapters in Kerr (2000) examine the issue of emissions trading. IIED (2002) explores the challenges of financing for sustainable development and the chapters in Keohane and Levy (1996) remain useful for discussions of environmental aid.

9   Environmental Security

As the chapter suggests, there is an extensive journal-based literature which addresses the potential for conflict over particular resources and debates over the usefulness of the term 'environmental security'. Two edited collections which remain useful and which cover reformist and critical positions on the environmental security issue are Käkönen (1992 and 1994). Two excellent critical examinations are Dalby (2002) and Barnett (2001). See also Lowi and Shaw (2000). Westing (1988) examines the relationship between the conduct of war and environmental degradation. The chapters in Austin and Bruch (2000) also explore various aspects of the environmental consequences of war. See Page and Redclift (2002) for an investigation which draws specifically on the human security literature. For more on protection of the environment during wartime, see Vöneky (2000), Henckaerts (2000) and Elliott (2003). Solomon and Turton (2000) provide a theoretical and empirically nuanced exploration of the likelihood of water wars; see also Barnett (2000).

10   The Global Politics of the Environment

There is a growing literature which locates the environmental agenda within particular disciplinary debates. Doran (1995) and Vogler and Imber (1996) – the latter an edited collection – are particularly useful on International Relations and the environment. Another edited collection – Lipschutz and Conca (1993a) – focuses on the state and social power in global environmental politics. Paterson (2000) provides a critical interrogation and Laferrière and Stoett (1999) explore the relationship between International Relations theory and ecological thought. Benton and Redclift (1994) cover social theory more generally. These issues are also examined in Fischer and Black (1995b) and, particularly, Torgerson (1995) in that collection. See Falk (2001) and Bernstein (2001) on neo-liberalism and the environment. Mol (2001) and Murphy (2001) explore ecological modernization.

Bibliography

Abate, Dejen and Shahid Akhtar (1994) 'Information and knowledge inputs: combatting desertification in Africa and transboundary air pollution in Europe', *Environmental Policy and Law*, vol. 24, no. 2/3, June, pp. 71–84.

Adler, Jonathan H. (2000) 'More sorry than safe: assessing the precautionary principle and the proposed international biosafety protocol', *Texas International Law Journal*, vol. 35, pp. 173–205.

AEFJN (Africa–Europe Faith and Justice Network) (2002) *Making Intellectual Property Rights Work for Developing Countries*, Update, September (Brussels: AEFJN).

Agarwal, Anil and Sunita Narain (1991) *Global Warming in an Unequal World: A Case of Environmental Colonialism* (New Delhi: Centre for Science and Environment).

Aguilar, Grethel (2001) 'Access to genetic resources and protection of traditional knowledge in the territories of indigenous peoples', *Environmental Science and Policy*, vol. 4, nos 4–5, pp. 241–56.

Aigbokhan, Ben E. (1993) 'Peaceful, people-centred and ecologically sensitive development', in Jeremy Brecher, John Brown Childs and Jill Cutler (eds), *Global Visions: Beyond the New World Order* (Boston, Mass.: South End Press).

American Association for the Advancement of Science (2002) *Integrating Human Rights and the Environment within the United Nations*, Submission to the Joint OHCHR–UNEP Seminar on Human Rights and the Environment, January 16 (http://shr.aaas.org/hrenv/docs/wssd12_2001.htm; accessed 8 July 2003).

Anderson, Troy (2002) 'The Cartegena Protocol on Biosafety to the Convention on Biological Diversity: trade liberalisation, the WTO and the environment', *Asia Pacific Journal of Environmental Law*, vol. 7, no. 1, pp. 1–38.

Andresen, Steinar and Shardul Agrawala (2002) 'Leaders, pushers and laggards in the making of the climate regime', *Global Environmental Change*, vol. 12, no. 1, pp. 41–51.

Annan, Kofi (2002) 'From Doha to Johannesburg by way of Monterrey: how to achieve, and sustain, development in the 21st century', lecture at the London School of Economics and Political Science, 25 February.

Anon. (1991) 'International environmental law', *Harvard Law Review*, vol. 104, no. 7, May, pp. 1484–639.

Anon. (1993a) 'Basel Convention: more action?', *Environmental Policy and Law*, vol. 23, no. 1, February, pp. 12–14.

Anon. (1993b) 'UNEP: 17th Governing Council', *Environmental Policy and Law*, vol. 23, no. 3/4, June/August, pp. 118–42.

Anon. (1993c) 'Germany faces expensive world war military waste cleanup', *The Canberra Times*, 29 July, p. 9.

Anon. (1994a) 'Small Island Developing States: Prepcom meets', *Environmental Policy and Law*, vol. 24, no. 1, February, pp. 5–8.

Anon. (1994b) 'Desertification convention finalised', *Environmental Policy and Law*, vol. 24, no. 5, September, pp. 229–30.

Anon. (1994c) 'Biodiversity convention ratified', *Environmental Policy and Law*, vol. 24, no. 5, September, p. 265.

Anon. (1995a) 'Ozone Protocol: sixth meeting of the Parties', *Environmental Policy and Law*, vol. 25, no. 1/2, February/April, pp. 21–3.

Anon. (1995b) 'Commission on Sustainable Development: third session', *Environmental Policy and Law*, vol. 25, no. 4/5, August/September, pp. 163–77.

Anon. (1995c) 'UN/GA: fourth Fisheries conference', *Environmental Policy and Law*, vol. 25, no. 415, August/September, pp. 178–80.

Anuradha, R. V. (2001) 'IPRs: implications for biodiversity and local and indigenous communities', *RECIEL*, vol. 10, no. 1, pp. 27–36.

Archibugi, Daniele (2001) 'The politics of cosmopolitical democracy', in Brendan Gleeson and Nicholas Low (eds), *Governing for the Environment: Global Problems, Ethics and Democracy* (Basingstoke: Palgrave Macmillan).

Arden-Clarke, Charles (1992) 'South–North terms of trade: environmental protection and sustainable development', *International Environmental Affairs*, vol. 4, no. 2, Spring, pp. 122–38.

Arestis, Philip and Malcolm Sawyer (2001) 'The economic analysis underlying the "Third Way"', *New Political Economy*, vol. 6, no. 2, pp. 255–78.

Argawal, Bina (2001) 'Participatory exclusions, community forestry, and gender: an analysis for South Asia and a conceptual framework', *World Development*, vol. 29, no. 12, pp. 1623–48.

ASEAN Secretariat (2002) *ASEAN Report to the World Summit on Sustainable Development* (Jakarta: ASEAN Secretariat).

Asian and Pacific NGO Working Group (1993) 'Draft plan of action: women, environment and development', Asian and Pacific Symposium of non-governmental organizations of women in development, Philippines, November 1993 (convened by the UN Economic and Social Commission for Asia and the Pacific (ESCAP) and the National Commission on the Role of Filipino Women (NCRFW)).

Asian and Pacific Women's Resource Collection Network (1992) *Environment* (Kuala Lumpur: Asian and Pacific Development Centre).

Asian Development Bank (2002) *Southeast Asia Regional Report for the World Summit on Sustainable Development* (Manila: Asian Development Bank).

Austin, Jay and Carl Bruch (eds) (2000) *The Environmental Consequences of War: Legal, Economic and Scientific Perspectives* (Cambridge: Cambridge University Press).

Axworthy, Lloyd (1997) 'Canada and human security: the need for leadership', *International Journal*, vol. 52, no. 2, pp. 183–96.

Babiker, Mustafa H., Henry D. Jacoby, John M. Reilly and David M. Reiner (2002) 'The evolution of a climate regime: Kyoto to Marrakech and beyond', *Environmental Science and Policy*, vol. 5, no. 3, pp. 195–206.

Bail, Christoph, Robert Falkner and Helen Marquard (2002) *The Cartegena Protocol on Biosafety: Reconciling Trade and Biotechnology with Environment and Development* (London: Royal Institute of International Affairs).

Baldwin, Elizabeth B. (1997) 'Reclaiming our future: international efforts to eliminate the threat of persistent organic pollutants', *Hastings International and Comparative Law Review*, vol. 20, no. 4, Summer, pp. 855–99.

Barbier, Edward B. (1995) 'Elephant ivory and tropical timber: the role of trade interventions in sustainable management', *Journal of Environment and Development*, vol. 4, no. 2, Summer, pp. 1–32.

Barkenbus, Jack (2001) 'APEC and the environment: civil society in an age of globalization', *AsiaPacific Issues*, no. 51 (Hawaii: East–West Center).

Barnaby, Frank (1991) 'The environmental impact of the Gulf War', *The Ecologist*, vol. 21, no. 4, July/August, pp. 166–72.

Barnes, J. (1984) 'Non-governmental organisations: increasing the global perspective', *Marine Policy*, vol. 8, no. 2, April, pp. 171–81.

Barnett, Jon (2000) 'Destabilizing the environment-conflict thesis', *Review of International Studies*, vol. 26, no. 2, pp. 271–88.

—— (2001) *The Meaning of Environmental Security: Environmental Politics and Policy in the New Security Era* (London: Zed Books).

—— (2003) 'Security and climate change', *Global Environmental Change*, vol. 13, no. 1, pp. 7–17.

Beder, Sharon (1997) *Global Spin: The Corporate Assault on Environmentalism* (Melbourne: Scribe Publications).

—— (2001) 'Neoliberal think tanks and free market environmentalism', *Environmental Politics*, vol. 10, no. 2, pp. 128–33.

Begg, K. G. (2002) 'Implementing the Kyoto protocol on climate change: environmental integrity, sinks and mechanisms', *Global Environmental Change*, vol. 12, no. 4, pp. 331–6.

Benedick, Richard (1991) *Ozone Diplomacy: New Directions in Safeguarding the Planet* (Cambridge, Mass.: Harvard University Press).

Bengwayan, Michael A. (2000) 'Deaths and illnesses from pollution in Asia increasing', *Earth Times*, 11 March (http://www.earthtimes.org/mar/environmentdeathsandillnessmar11_01.htm).

Benton, Ted (1994) 'Biology and social theory', in Michael Redclift and Ted Benton (eds), *Social Theory and the Environment* (New York: Routledge).

Benton, Ted and Michael Redclift (1994) 'Introduction', in Michael Redclift and Ted Benton (eds), *Social Theory and the Environment* (New York: Routledge).

Bergesen, Helge Ole and Georg Parmann (eds) (1996) *Green Globe Yearbook* (Oxford: Oxford University Press).

Berlin, Kenneth and Jeffrey M. Lang (1993) 'Trade and the environment', *The Washington Quarterly*, vol. 16, no. 4, Autumn, pp. 35–51.

Bernstein, Steven (2000) 'Ideas, social structure and the compromise of liberal environmentalism', *European Journal of International Relations*, vol. 6, no. 4, pp. 464–512.

Bernstein, Steven F. (2001) *The Compromise of Liberal Environmentalism* (New York: Columbia University Press).

Betsill, Michelle M. and Roger A. Pielke Jr (1998) 'Blurring the boundaries: domestic and international ozone politics and lessons for climate change', *International Environmental Affairs*, vol. 10, no. 3, pp. 147–72.

Bhat, Mahadev G. (1996) 'Trade-related intellectual property rights to biological resources: scoioeconomic implications for developing countries', *Ecological Economics*, vol. 19, no. 3, pp. 205–17.

Biermann, Frank (2002) 'Strengthening green global governance in a disparate world society: would a World Environment Organisation benefit the South?', *International Environmental Agreements*, vol. 2, no. 4, pp. 297–315.

Birnie, Patricia (1992) 'International environmental law: its adequacy for present and future needs', in Andrew Hurrell and Benedict Kingsbury (eds), *The International Politics of the Environment* (Oxford: Clarendon Press).

Blumenfeld, Jared (1994) 'Institutions: the United Nations Commission on Sustainable Development', *Environment*, vol. 36, no. 10, pp. 2–5, 33.

Bodansky, Daniel (1994) 'Prologue to the Climate Change Convention', in Irving M. Mintzer and J. Amber Leonard (eds), *Negotiating Climate Change: The Inside Story of the Rio Convention* (Cambridge: Cambridge University Press).

—— (2002) *US Climate Policy after Kyoto: Elements for Success*, Policy Brief No. 15 (Washington, DC: Carnegie Endowment for International Peace).

Boehmer-Christiansen, Sonja (2002) 'The geo-politics of sustainable development: bureaucracies and politicians in search of the holy grail', *Geoforum*, vol. 33, no. 3, pp. 351–65.

Bohm, Peter (2002) 'Improving cost-effectiveness and facilitating participation of developing countries in international emissions trading', *International Environmental Agreements*, vol. 2, no. 3, pp. 261–75.

Bolin, Bert (1998) 'The Kyoto negotiations on climate change: a science perspective', *Science*, vol. 279, no. 5349, pp. 330–1.

Bosselmann, Klaus (2001) 'Human rights and the environment: redefining fundamental principles', in Brendan Gleeson and Nicholas Low (eds), *Governing for the Environment: Global Problems, Ethics and Democracy* (Basingstoke: Palgrave Macmillan).

Boulding, Elise (1991) 'States, boundaries and environmental security in global and regional conflicts', *Interdisciplinary Peace Research*, vol. 3, no. 2, October/November, pp. 78–93.

Bowman, Michael (1991) 'Global warming and the international protection of wildlife', in Robin Churchill and David Freestone (eds), *International Law and Global Climate Change* (London: Graham & Trotman).

Boyd, Emily and Emma Lisa Schipper (2002) 'The Marrakech Accord – at the crossroad to ratification: seventh conference of parties to the United Nations Framework Convention on Climate Change', *Journal of Environment and Development*, vol. 11, no. 2, June, pp. 184–90.

Boyle, Alan E. (1994) 'The Convention on Biological Diversity', in Luigi Campiglio *et al.* (eds), *The Environment after Rio: International Law and Economics* (London: Graham & Trotman).

Brack, Duncan, Fanny Calder and Müge Dolun (2001) *From Rio to Johannesburg: The Earth Summit and Rio+10*, Briefing Paper No. 19

(London: Royal Institute of International Affairs, Energy and Environment Programme).

Brack, Duncan, Kevin Gray and Gavin Hayman (2002) *Controlling the International Trade in Illegally Logged Timber and Wood Products* (London: Royal Institute of International Affairs).

Bradbury, Roger (1997) 'Sustainable development as a subversive issue', *Nature and Resources*, vol. 34, no. 4, pp. 7–11.

Bragdon, Susan H. (1992) 'National sovereignty and global environmental responsibility: can the tension be reconciled for the conservation of biological diversity?', *Harvard International Law Journal*, vol. 33, no. 2, Spring, pp. 381–92.

Braidotti, Rosi, Ewa Charkiewicz, Sabine Häusler and Saskia Wieringa (1994) *Women, the Environment and Sustainable Development: Towards a Theoretical Synthesis* (London: Zed Books).

Brenton, Tony (1994) *The Greening of Machiavelli: The Evolution of International Environmental Politics* (London: Royal Institute of International Affairs/Earthscan).

Bretherton, Charlotte (2003) 'Movements, networks, hierarchies: a gender perspective on global environmental governance', *Global Environmental Politics*, vol. 3, no. 2, pp. 103–19.

Breyman, Steve (1993) 'Knowledge as power: ecology movements and global environmental problems', in Ronnie D. Lipschutz and Ken Conca (eds), *The State and Social Power in Global Environmental Politics* (New York: Columbia University Press).

Brock, Lothar (1991) 'Peace through parks: the environment on the peace research agenda', *Journal of Peace Research*, vol. 28, no. 4, November, pp. 407–23.

Brown, Lester R. (1992) 'Launching the environmental revolution', in Lester R. Brown, Holly Brough, Alan Durning, Christopher Flavin, Hilary French, Jodi Jacobson, Nicholas Lensson, Marcia Lowe, Sandra Postel, Michael Renner, John Ryan, Linda Starke and John Young (eds), *State of the World 1992* (London: Earthscan).

Browne, Anthony (2000) 'Mass slaughter threat to whales: Norway and Japan accused of buying Third World support to bring back industrial-scale hunting', *Observer* (UK), 9 April (via csdgen@undp.org, 11 April 2000).

Bruno, Kenny (2002) *Greenwash+10: The UN's Global Compact, Corporate Accountability and the Johannesburg Earth Summit* (San Francisco: CorpWatch).

Bruno, Kenny and Joshua Karliner (2002) 'The UN's Global Compact, corporate accountability and the Johannesburg Summit', *Development*, vol. 45, no. 3, pp. 33–8.

Burger, Julian (1990) *The Gaia Atlas of First Peoples* (London: Robertson McCarta).

Burgiel, Stanley W. (2002) 'The Cartegena Protocol on Biosafety: taking the steps from negotiation to implementation', *RECIEL*, vol. 11, no. 1, pp. 53–61.

Burke, Tom (1982) 'Friends of the Earth and the conservation of resources', in Peter Willetts (ed.), *Pressure Groups in the Global System: The Transnational*

Relations of Issue-oriented Non-governmental Organisations (London: Frances Pinter).

—— (1997) 'A swing in the climate of change', *New Statesman*, 19 December, p. 16.

Butts, Kent Hughes (ed.) (1994) *Environmental Security: A DOD Partnership for Peace*, Strategic Studies Institute Special Report, US Army War College.

Buzan, Barry (1991) 'New patterns of global security in the twenty-first century', *International Affairs*, vol. 67, no. 3, pp. 431–51.

Byers, Bruce (1991) 'Ecoregions, state sovereignty and conflict', *Bulletin of Peace Proposals*, vol. 22, no. 1 pp. 65–76.

Caldwell, Lynton Keith (1990) *Between Two Worlds: Science, the Environmental Movement and Policy Choice* (Cambridge: Cambridge University Press).

—— (1991) 'International responses to environmental issues', *International Studies Notes*, vol. 16, no. 1, Winter, pp. 3–7.

Campiglio, Luigi, Laura Pineschi, Domenico Siniscalo and Tullio Treves (eds) (1994) *The Environment after Rio: International Law and Economics* (London: Graham & Trotman).

Carbone, Maurizio (2002) 'A world environment organisation: issues in global governance', *The Courier ACP-EU*, July–August, pp. 38–9.

Çarkoğlu, Ali and Mine Eder (2001) 'Domestic concerns and the water conflict over the Euphrates–Tigris river basin', *Middle Eastern Studies*, vol. 37, no. 1, pp. 41–71.

Caron, David D. (1991) 'Protection of the stratospheric ozone layer and the structure of international environmental lawmaking', *Hastings International and Comparative Law Review*, vol. 14, no. 4, Summer, pp. 755–79.

Chadwick, Michael J. (1994) 'Foreword', in Irving M. Mintzer and J. Amber Leonard (eds), *Negotiating Climate Change: The Inside Story of the Rio Convention* (Cambridge: Cambridge University Press).

Charnovitz, Steve (1991) 'Exploring the environmental exceptions in GATT article XX', *Journal of World Trade*, vol. 25, no. 5, October, pp. 37–55.

—— (2002) *A World Environment Organization* (Tokyo: United Nations University Institute of Advanced Studies).

Chartier, Denis and Jean-Paul Deléage (1998) 'The international environmental NGOs: from revolutionary alternative to the pragmatism of reform', *Environmental Politics*, vol. 7, no. 3, Autumn, pp. 26–41.

Chasek, Pamela S. (2000a) 'The UN Commission on Sustainable Development: the first five years', in Pamela S. Chasek (ed.), *The Global Environment in the Twenty-first Century: Prospects for International Cooperation* (Tokyo: United Nations University Press).

—— (ed.) (2000b) *The Global Environment in the Twenty-first Century: Prospects for International Cooperation* (Tokyo: United Nations University Press).

Chatterjee, Pratap and Matthias Finger (1994) *The Earth Brokers* (London: Routledge).

CITES Secretariat (2002) 'Illegal ivory trade driven by unregulated domestic markets', Press Release, 4 October.

Clad, James C. (1998) 'Conservation and indigenous peoples: a study of convergent interests', in John H. Bodley (ed.), *Tribal Peoples and Development Issues: A Global Overview* (Mountain View, Calif.: Mayfield Publishing).

Clapp, Jennifer (1994) 'The toxic waste trade with less-industrialised countries: economic linkages and political alliances', *Third World Quarterly*, vol. 15, no. 3, September, pp. 505–18.

Clapp, Roger Alex and Carolyn Crook (2002) 'Drowning in the magic well: Shaman Pharmaceuticals and the elusive value of traditional knowledge', *Journal of Environment and Development*, vol. 11, no. 1, March, pp. 79–102.

Claussen, Eileen (2001) 'Beyond Bonn: forging a global agreement', *Asia Perspectives*, vol. 4, no. 1, pp. 1–5.

COICA (Coordinating Body of Indigenous Organizations of the Amazon Basin) (n.d.) '[A letter] To the Community of Concerned Environmentalists', [reproduced in] Ken Conca, Michael Alberty and Geoffrey D. Dabelko (eds) (1995) *Green Planet Blues: Environmental Politics from Stockholm to Rio* (Boulder, Colo: Westview Press).

Colchester, Marcus (1988) 'The global threat to tribal peoples: strategies for survival', in Asia–Pacific Peoples' Environmental Network (ed.), *Global Development and Environment Crisis: Has Humankind a Future?* (Penang: Sahabat Alam Malaysia).

—— (1990) 'The International Tropical Timber Organisation: kill or cure for the rainforests?', *The Ecologist*, vol. 20, no. 5, September/October, pp. 166–73.

—— (1994) 'The new sultans: Asian loggers move in on Guyana's forests', *The Ecologist*, vol. 24, no. 2, March/April, pp. 45–52.

Commission on Global Governance (1995) *Our Global Neighbourhood* (Oxford: Oxford University Press).

Commonwealth of Australia, Department of Foreign Affairs and Trade (1995) *The Relationship Between the Provisions of the Multilateral Trading System and Trade Measures Pursuant to Multilateral Environmental Agreements: a discussion paper*, prepared by the GATT Projects Section, Multilateral Trade Organizations Branch, Trade Negotiations and Organizations Division, 3 February 1995.

Conca, Ken (1997) 'The WTO and the undermining of global environmental governance', *Review of International Political Economy*, vol. 7, no. 3, pp. 484–94.

Conca, Ken and Ronnie D. Lipschutz (1993) 'A tale of two forests', in Ronnie D. Lipschutz and Ken Conca (eds), *The State and Social Power in Global Environmental Politics* (New York: Columbia University Press).

Conca, Ken, Michael Alberty and Geoffrey D. Dabelko (eds) (1995) *Green Planet Blues: Environmental Politics from Stockholm to Rio* (Boulder, Colo: Westview Press).

Cooper, H. David (2002) 'The international treaty on plant genetic resources for food and agriculture', *RECIEL*, vol. 11, no. 1, pp. 1–16.

Corell, Elisabeth (1999) 'Non-state actor influence in the negotiations of the Convention to Combat Desertification', *International Negotiation*, vol. 4, no. 1, pp. 197–223.

Corell, Elisabeth and Michelle Betsill (2001) 'A comparative look at NGO influence in international environmental negotiations: desertification and climate change', *Global Environmental Politics*, vol. 1, no. 4, pp. 86–107.

Corpuz-Tauli, Victoria (1999) *Indigenous Peoples and Intellectual Property Rights*, Briefing Paper No. 5 (Baguio City, The Philippines: Tebtebba Foundation).

Corral, Thais (2002) 'The Women's Action Agenda for a Healthy and Peaceful Planet', *Development*, vol. 45, no. 3, pp. 28–32.

Corry, Stephen (1993) 'The rainforest harvest: who reaps the benefits?', *The Ecologist*, vol. 23, no. 4, July/August, pp. 148–53.

Cosbey, Aaron and Stas Burgiel (2000) *The Cartagena Protocol on Biosafety: An Analysis of Results* (Winnipeg: International Institute for Sustainable Development).

Cox, Robert W. (1986) 'Social forces, states and world orders: beyond International Relations theory', in Robert O. Keohane (ed.), *NeoRealism and its Critics* (New York: Columbia University Press).

Curran, Giorel (2001) 'The Third Way and ecological modernization', *Contemporary Politics*, vol. 7, no. 1, pp. 41–55.

Dalby, Simon (1997) 'Contesting an essential concept: reading the dilemmas in contemporary security discourse', in Keith Krause and Michael C. Williams (eds), *Critical Security Studies* (Minneapolis: University of Minnesota Press).

—— (2002) *Environmental Security* (Minneapolis: University of Minnesota Press).

—— (2003) 'Resources and conflict: contesting constructions of environmental security', paper prepared for presentation to a conference on 'Resources: Conceptions and Contestations', Kathmandu, January (available at http://www.carleton.ca/~sdalby/DalbyKathmandu.pdf; accessed 30 July 2003).

Daly, Herman E. (2002) 'Reconciling the economics of social equity and environmental sustainability', *Population and Environment*, vol. 24, no. 1, pp. 47–53.

Daly, Herman E. and John B. Cobb Jr (1994) *For the Common Good: Redirecting the Economy toward Community, the Environment and a Sustainable Future*, 2nd edn (Boston, Mass.: Beacon Press).

Damian, Michel and Jean-Christophe Graz (2001) 'The World Trade Organization, the environment and the ecological critique', *International Social Science Journal*, vol. 53, no. 170, pp. 597–610.

Davis, Shelton H. (ed.) (1993) *Indigenous Views of Land and the Environment*, World Bank Discussion Paper No. 188 (Washington, DC: The World Bank).

Davison, Aidan and Ian Barns (1992) 'The Earth Summit and the ethics of sustainable development', *Current Affairs Bulletin*, vol. 69, no. 1. June, pp. 4–12.

de la Court, Thijs (1990) *Beyond Brundtland: Green Development in the 1990s* (London: Zed Books).

Den Elzen, Michel G. J and André P. G. de Moor (2002) 'Evaluating the Bonn-Marrakesh agreement', *Climate Policy*, vol. 2, no. 1, pp. 111–17.

DeSombre, Elizabeth R. (2002) *The Global Environment and World Politics* (London/New York: Continuum).

Deudney, Daniel (1990) 'The case against linking environmental degradation and national security', *Millennium*, vol. 19. no. 3, Winter, pp. 461–76.

Diehl, Paul F. (1998) 'Environmental conflict: an introduction', *Journal of Peace Research*, vol. 35, no. 3, pp. 275–7.

Dimitrov, Radoslav S. (2002) 'Water, conflict and security: a conceptual mine-field', *Society and Natural Resources*, vol. 15, no. 8, pp. 677–91.

Diplomatic Conference (1977) *Protocol Additional to the Geneva Conventions of 12 August 1949, and relating to the Protection of Victims of International Armed Conflicts (Protocol 1)*, adopted on 8 June 1977 by the Diplomatic Conference on the Reaffirmation and Development of International Humanitarian Law applicable in Armed Conflicts.

Doran, Peter (1995) 'Earth, power, knowledge: towards a critical environmental politics', in John MacMillan and Andrew Linklater (eds), *Boundaries in Question: New Directions in International Relations* (London: Pinter Publishers).

—— (1996) 'The UN Commission on Sustainable Development, 1995', *Environmental Politics*, vol. 5, no. 1, Spring, pp. 100–7.

Douglas, Oronto, Von Kemedi, Ike Okonta and Michael Watts (2003) *Alienation and Militancy in the Niger Delta: A Response to CSIS on Petroleum, Politics and Democracy in Nigeria*, FPIF Special Report (Silver City, N. Mex. and Washington, DC: Foreign Policy in Focus) (http://www. foreignpolicy-infocus.org/papers/nigeria2003_body.html; accessed 29 July 2003).

Downie, David L. and Marc A. Levy (2000) 'The UN Environment Programme at a turning point: options for change', in Pamela S. Chasek (ed.), *The Global Environment in the Twenty-first Century: Prospects for International Cooperation* (Tokyo: United Nations University Press).

Dubner, Barry Hart (1999) 'Recent developments in the international law of the sea', *International Lawyer*, vol. 33, no. 2, pp. 627–36.

Dudley, Joseph P., Joshua R. Ginsberg, Andrew J. Plumptre, John A. Hart and Liliana C. Campos (2002) 'Effects of war and civil strife on wildlife and wildlife habitats', *Conservation Biology*, vol. 16, no. 2, pp. 319–29.

Dunn, Seth (1998) 'Can the North and South get in step?', *World Watch*, November/December, pp. 19–27.

—— (2002) *Reading the Weathervane: Climate Policy from Rio to Johannesburg* (Washington, DC: Worldwatch Institute).

Dupont, Alan (1998) *The Environment and Security in Pacific Asia*, Adelphi Paper 319 (London: Oxford University Press/International Institute for Strategic Studies).

Dutfield, Graham (2000) 'The public and private domains: intellectual property rights in traditional knowledge', *Science Communication*, vol. 21, no. 3, pp. 274–95.

Dyer, Hugh (2001) 'Environmental security and international relations: the case for enclosure', *Review of International Studies*, vol. 27, no. 3, pp. 441–50.

Easterly, William (2002) 'How did Heavily Indebted Poor Countries become heavily indebted? Reviewing two decades of debt relief', *World Development*, vol. 30, no. 10, pp. 1677–96.

Eckersley, Robyn (1992) *Environmentalism and Political Theory: Towards an Ecocentric Approach* (London: UCL Press).

Egenhofer, Christian and Jan Cornillie (2001) *Reinventing the Climate Negotiations: An Analysis of COP6*, CEDS Policy Brief No. 1 (Brussels: CEPS).

El-Ashry, Mohamed T. (1993) 'Development assistance institutions and sustainable development', *The Washington Quarterly*, vol. 16, no. 2, Spring, pp. 83–95.

Elliott, Lorraine M. (1994) *International Environmental Politics: Protecting the Antarctic* (London: Macmillan – now Palgrave Macmillan).

—— (2001) *Global Environmental Governance: A Report Card for the United Nations*, Manchester Papers in Politics, No. 1/01 (Manchester: Department of Government, University of Manchester).

—— (2002a) 'Australia in world environmental affairs', in John Ravenhill and James Cotton (eds), *The National Interest in a Global Era: Australia in World Affairs 1996–2000* (Melbourne: Oxford University Press).

—— (2002b) 'The global politics of the environment', in Stephanie Lawson (ed.), *The New Agenda for International Relations* (Cambridge: Polity Press).

—— (2002c) 'Global environmental governance', in Rorden Wilkinson and Steve Hughes (eds), *Global Governance: Critical Perspectives* (London: Routledge).

—— (2002d) *Global environmental (in)equity and the cosmopolitan project*, CSGR Working Paper No. 95/02, (Coventry: Centre for the Study of Globalisation and Regionalisation, University of Warwick).

—— (2003) 'Imaginative adaptations: a possible environmental role for the UN Security Council', *Contemporary Security Policy*, vol. 24, no. 2, pp. 47–68.

Esty, Daniel C. (1994) *Greening the GATT: Trade, Environment and the Future* (Washington, DC: Institute for International Economics).

—— (2001) 'A term's limit', *Foreign Policy*, Issue 126, September/October, pp. 74–5.

European Commission (2002) *Sustainable Production and Consumption* (Brussels: European Commission).

European Environment Agency (1999) *Environment in the European Union at the Turn of the Century* (Copenhagen: European Environment Agency).

Evans, Senator Gareth (1994) *Reintegrating the United Nations*, Statement to the 49th General Assembly of the United Nations, 3 October.

Fabig, Heike and Richard Boele (1999) 'The changing nature of NGO activity in a globalising world: pushing the corporate responsibility agenda', *IDS Bulletin*, vol. 30, no. 3, pp. 58–67.

Fairclough, A. J. (1991) 'Global environmental and natural resource problems – their economic, political and security implications', *The Washington Quarterly*, vol. 14, no. 1, Winter, pp. 81–98.

Falk, Richard (1995) *On Humane Governance: Toward a New Global Politics* (Cambridge: Polity Press).

—— (1998) 'Global civil society: perspectives, initiatives, movements', *Oxford Development Studies*, vol. 26, no. 1, pp. 99–110.

—— (2001) 'Humane governance and the environment: overcoming neo-liberalism', in Brendan Gleeson and Nicholas Low (eds), *Governing for the*

Environment: Global Problems, Ethics and Democracy (Basingstoke: Palgrave Macmillan).

Falkner, Robert (2003) 'Private environmental governance and International Relations: exploring the links', *Global Environmental Politics*, vol. 3, no. 2, pp. 72–87.

Faure, Michael, Joyeeta Gupta and Andries Nentjes (eds) (2003) *Climate Change and the Kyoto Protocol: The Role of Institutions and Instruments to Control Global Change* (Cheltenham: Edward Elgar).

Favre, David (1993) 'Debate within the CITES community: what direction for the future?', *Natural Resources Journal*, vol. 33, no. 4, Fall, pp. 875–918.

—— (2001) 'Elephants, ivory and international law', *RECIEL*, vol. 10, no. 3, pp. 277–86.

Fearnside, Philip M. (2003) 'Conservation policy in Brazilian Amazonia: understanding the dilemmas', *World Development*, vol. 31, no. 5 , pp. 757–79.

Fermann, Gunnar (ed.) (1997) *International Politics of Climate Change: Key Issues and Critical Actors* (Oslo: Scandinavian University Press).

Fijalkowski, Agata and James Cameron (eds) (1998) *Trade and the Environment: Bridging the Gap* (London: Cameron May).

Fine, Ben (2001) 'Neither the Washington nor the Post-Washington consensus: an introduction' (http://www.globalpolicy.org/socecon/bwi-wto/wbank/2001/esrc.pdf; accessed 15 August 2003).

Finger, Matthias (1991a) *Unintended Consequences of the Cold War: Global Environmental Degradation and the Military*, Occasional Paper No. 10 (Syracuse, NY: Program on the Analysis and Resolution of Conflict, Maxwell School of Citizenship and Public Affairs, Syracuse University).

—— (1991b) 'The military, the nation-state and the environment', *The Ecologist*, vol. 21, no. 5, September/October, pp. 220–5.

—— (1993) 'Politics of the UNCED process', in Wolfgang Sachs (ed.), *Global Ecology: A New Arena of Political Conflict* (London: Zed Books).

Finlayson, Ian (1998) 'Environmental security and the Australian Defence Force', in Alan Dupont (ed.), *The Environment and Security: What are the Linkages?*, Canberra Papers on Strategy and Defence No. 125 (Canberra: Strategic and Defence Studies Centre, Australian National University).

Fischer, Frank and Michael Black (1995a) 'Introduction', in Frank Fischer and Michael Black (eds), *Greening Environmental Policy: The Politics of a Sustainable Future* (New York: St Martin's Press).

Fischer, Frank and Michael Black (eds) (1995b) *Greening Environmental Policy: The Politics of a Sustainable Future* (New York: St Martin's Press).

Flanders, Lowell (1997) 'The United Nations Department for Policy Coordination and Sustainable Development (DPCSD)', *Global Environmental Change*, vol. 7, no. 4, pp. 391–4.

Ford, Lucy H. (1999) 'Social movements and the globalisation of environmental governance', *IDS Bulletin*, vol. 30, no. 3, pp. 68–74.

—— (2003) 'Challenging global environmental governance: social movement agency and global civil society', *Global Environmental Politics*, vol. 3, no. 2, pp. 120–34.

Fourmile, Henrietta (1998) 'Using prior informed consent procedures under the Convention on Biological Diversity to protect indigenous traditional ecological knowledge and natural resource rights', *Indigenous Law Bulletin*, vol. 4, no. 16, pp. 14–17.

—— (2001) 'Indigenous peoples, the conservation of traditional ecological knowledge, and global governance', in Brendan Gleeson and Nicholas Low (eds), *Governing for the Environment: Global Problems, Ethics and Democracy* (Basingstoke: Palgrave Macmillan).

Freestone, David and Ellen Hey (eds) (1996) *The Precautionary Principle and International Law: The Challenge of Implementation* (The Hague: Kluwer Law International).

French, Duncan A. (2002) 'The role of the state and international organisations in reconciling sustainable development and globalisation', *International Environmental Agreements*, vol. 2, no. 2, pp. 135–50.

French, Hilary F. (1995) *Partnership for the Planet: An Environmental Agenda for the United Nations*, Worldwatch Paper No. 107 (Washington, DC: Worldwatch Institute).

—— (2000) *Vanishing Borders: Protecting the Planet in the Age of Globalization* (New York: W. W. Norton & Co).

Gaines, Sanford E. (1991) 'Taking responsibility for transboundary environmental effects', *Hastings International and Comparative Law Review*, vol. 14, no. 4, Summer, pp. 781–809.

—— (2002) 'International trade, environmental protection and development as a sustainable development triangle', *RECIEL*, vol. 11, no. 3, pp. 259–74.

Ganguli, Prabuddha (1998) 'Intellectual property rights in transition', *World Patent Information*, vol. 20, pp. 171–80.

Gehring, Thomas and Sebastian Oberthür (1993) 'The Copenhagen meeting', *Environmental Policy and Law*, vol. 23, no. 1, February, pp. 6–13.

Gerlach, Luther P. (1991) 'Global thinking, local acting: movements to save the planet', *Evaluation Review*, vol. 15, no. 1, February, pp. 120–48.

Giorgetta, Sueli (2002) 'The right to a healthy environment, human rights and sustainable development', *International Environmental Agreements*, vol. 2, no. 2, pp. 173–94.

Glasby, Geoffrey P. (2002) 'Sustainable development: the need for a new paradigm', *Environment, Development and Sustainability*, vol. 4, no. 4, pp. 333–45.

Gleick, Peter H. (1991) 'Environment and security: the clear connections', *Bulletin of Atomic Scientists*, April, pp. 17–21.

Gleeson, Brendan and Nicholas Low (eds) (2001) *Governing for the Environment: Global Problems, Ethics and Democracy* (Basingstoke: Palgrave Macmillan).

Global Commons Institute (2003) *Contraction and Convergence: A Global Solution to a Global Problem* (http:// http://www.gci.org.uk/; accessed 13 July 2003).

GMEF (Global Ministerial Environmental Forum) (2000) Malmö Ministerial Declaration (UNEP: Nairobi).

Godwin, Diana L. (1993) 'The Basel Convention on Transboundary Movements of Hazardous Wastes: an opportunity for industrialized nations to clean up their acts?', *Denver Journal of International Law and Policy*, vol. 22, no. 1, Fall, pp. 193–208.

Goodhand, Jonathan (2003) 'Enduring disorder and persistent poverty: a review of the linkages between war and chronic poverty', *World Development*, vol. 31, no. 3, pp. 629–46.

Gray, Andrew (1990) 'Indigenous peoples and the marketing of the rainforest', *The Ecologist*, vol. 20. no. 6, November/December, pp. 223–27.

Gray, Kevin R. (2002) 'Foreign direct investment and environmental impacts – is the debate over?', *RECIEL*, vol. 11, no. 3, pp. 306–13.

Gray, Mark Allan (1990) 'The United Nations Environment Programme: an assessment', *Environmental Law*, vol. 20, no. 2, pp. 291–319.

Griffith, Mark D. (1995) 'Reflections on the implementation of the Programme of Action on the Sustainable Development of Small Island Developing States (SIDS)', *Ocean and Coastal Management*, vol. 29, nos 1–3, pp. 139–63.

Grubb, Michael (1990) 'The greenhouse effect: negotiating targets', *International Affairs*, vol. 66, no. 1, January, pp. 67–89.

—— (1998) 'International emissions trading under the Kyoto Protocol: core issues in implementation', *RECIEL*, vol. 7, no. 2, pp. 140–6.

Grubb, Michael, Matthias Koch, Abby Munson, Francis Sullivan and Koy Thompson (1993) *The Earth Summit Agreements: A Guide and Assessment* (London: The Royal Institute of International Affairs/Earthscan).

Grubb, Michael, Christiaan Vrolijk and Duncan Brack (1999) *The Kyoto Protocol: A Guide and Assessment* (London: The Royal Institute of International Affairs/Earthscan).

Gudynas, Eduardo (1993) 'The fallacy of Ecomessianism: observations from Latin America', in Wolfgang Sachs (ed.), *Global Ecology: A New Arena of Political Conflict* (London: Zed Books).

Gupta, Joyeeta (2002) 'Global sustainable development governance: institutional challenges from a theoretical perspective', *International Environmental Agreements*, vol. 2, no. 4, pp. 361–88.

Guruswamy, Lakshman D. (1999) 'The Convention on Biological Diversity: exposing the flawed foundations', *Environmental Conservation*, vol. 26, no. 2, pp. 79–82.

Haas, Peter M. (1990) 'Obtaining international environmental protection through epistemic consensus', *Millennium*, vol. 19, no. 3, Winter, pp. 347–63.

Haas, Peter M., Robert O. Keohane and Marc A. Levy (eds) (1993) *Institutions for the Earth: Sources of Effective Environmental Protection* (Cambridge, Mass.: The MIT Press).

Haas, P., Marc A. Levy and Edward A. Parson (1992) 'Appraising the Earth Summit: how should we judge UNCED's success?', *Environment*, vol. 34, no. 8, pp. 6–11, 26–33.

Haites, Erik and Farhana Yamin (2000) 'The clean development mechanism: proposals for its operation and governance', *Global Environmental Change*, vol. 10, no. 1, pp. 27–45.

Halpern, Shanna (1992) *The United Nations Conference on Environment and Development: Process and Documentation* (Providence, RI: Academic Council on the United Nations System) (http://www.ciesin.org/docs/008-585/unced-home.html).

Hamilton, Kirk and John A. Dixon (2003) 'Measuring the wealth of nations', *Environmental Monitoring and Assessment*, vol. 86, nos 1–2 , pp. 75–89.

Hamilton, Kirsty (1998) *The Oil Industry and Climate Change* (Amsterdam: Greenpeace International).

Hanisch, Ted (1992) 'The Rio Climate Convention: real solutions or political rhetoric?', *Security Dialogue*, vol. 23, no. 4, December, pp. 63–73.

Haque, M. Shamsul (2002) 'Environmental security in East Asia: a critical view', *The Journal of Strategic Studies*, vol. 24, no. 4, pp. 203–34.

Harbinson, Rod (1992) 'Burma's forests fall victims to war', *The Ecologist*, vol. 22, no. 2, March/April, pp. 72–3.

Hardin, Garrett (1968) 'The tragedy of the commons', *Science*, vol. 162, no. 3859, 13 December, pp. 1243–8.

—— (1974) 'Living on a lifeboat', *BioScience*, vol. 24, no. 10, October, pp. 561–8.

Hawkins, Ann (1993) 'Contested ground: international environmentalism and global climate change', in Ronnie D. Lipschutz and Ken Conca (eds), *The State and Social Power in Global Environmental Politics* (New York: Columbia University Press).

Hecht, Alan D. (1999) 'The triad of sustainable development: promoting sustainable development in developing countries', *Journal of Environment and Development*, vol. 8, no. 2, pp. 111–32.

Held, David (1997) 'Democracy and global order', in James Bohman and Matthias Lutz-Bachmann (eds), *Perpetual Peace: Essays on Kant's Cosmopolitan Ideal* (Cambridge, Mass.: The MIT Press).

—— (1998) 'Democracy and globalisation', in Daniele Archibugi, David Held and Martin Köhler (eds), *Re-imagining Political Community: Studies in Cosmopolitan Democracy* (Cambridge: Polity Press).

Henckaerts, Jean-Marie (2000) 'Toward better protection for the environment in armed conflict: recent developments in international humanitarian law', *RECIEL*, vol. 9, no. 1, pp. 13–19.

Hendrickx, Frederic, Veit Koesler and Christian Prip (1993) 'Convention on Biological Diversity – access to genetic resources: a legal analysis', *Environmental Policy and Law*, vol. 23, no. 6, December, pp. 250–8.

Herkenrath, Peter (2002) 'The implementation of the Convention on Biological Diversity – a non-government perspective ten years on', *RECIEL*, vol. 11, no. 1, pp. 29–37.

Hildyard, Nicholas (1993) 'Foxes in charge of the chickens', in Wolfgang Sachs (ed.), *Global Ecology: A New Arena of Political Conflict* (London: Zed Books).

Hobson, Kersty (2002) 'Competing discourses of sustainable consumption: does the "rationalisation of lifestyles" make sense?', *Environmental Politics*, vol. 11, no. 2, pp. 95–120.

Holmberg, Johan (1992) 'Judgement on Rio', *People and the Planet*, vol. 1, no. 3, p. 4.

Holst, Johan Jørgen (1989) 'Security and the environment: a preliminary exploration', *Bulletin of Peace Proposals*, vol. 20, no. 2, June, pp. 123–8.

Homer-Dixon, Thomas F. (1991) 'On the threshold: environmental changes as causes of acute conflict', *International Security*, vol. 16, no. 2, Fall, pp. 76–116.

Homer-Dixon, Thomas F., Jeffrey H. Boutwell and George W. Rathjens (1993) 'Environmental change and violent conflict', *Scientific American*, vol. 268, no. 2, February, pp. 38–45.

Hontelez, John (1988) 'Friends of the Earth International: an international movement to fight for environment and a better future for humankind', in Asia–Pacific Peoples' Environmental Network (ed.), *Global Development and Environment Crisis* (Penang: Sahabat Alam Malaysia).

Hough, Peter (2000) 'Institutions for controlling the global trade in hazardous chemicals: the 1998 Rotterdam Convention', *Global Environmental Change*, vol. 10, no. 2, pp. 161–4.

Houghton, J. T., G. J. Jenkins and J. J. Ephraims (eds) (1990) *Climate Change: The IPCC Scientific Assessment*, Final Report of Working Group I, IPCC (Cambridge: Cambridge University Press).

Howard, Kathleen (1990) 'The Basel Convention: control of transboundary movement of hazardous wastes and their disposal', *Hastings International and Comparative Law Review*, vol. 14, no. 1, Fall, pp. 223–46.

Hughes, Steve and Rorden Wilkinson (2001) 'The Global Compact: promoting corporate responsibility?', *Environmental Politics*, vol. 10, no. 1, pp. 155–9.

Hulme, Mike and Mick Kelly (1993) 'Exploring the links between desertification and climate change', *Environment*, vol. 35, no. 6, July/August, pp. 4–11, 39–45.

Humphreys, David (1996a) 'The global politics of forest conservation since the UNCED, *Environmental Politics*, vol. 5, no. 2, Summer, pp. 231–56.

—— (1996b) *Forest politics: The Evolution of International Cooperation* (London: Earthscan).

—— (1998) 'The report of the Intergovernmental Panel on Forests', *Environmental Politics*, vol. 7, no. 1, Spring, pp. 214–21.

—— (1999) 'The evolving forests regime', *Global Environmental Change*, vol. 9, no. 3, pp. 251–4.

Hurrell, Andrew (1994) 'A crisis of ecological viability? Global environmental change and the nation state', *Political Studies*, vol. XLII, pp. 146–65.

—— (1995) 'International political theory and the global environment' in Ken Booth and Steve Smith (eds), *International Relations Theory Today* (Cambridge: Polity Press).

Hurrell, Andrew and Benedict Kingsbury (eds) (1992a) *The International Politics of the Environment* (Oxford: Clarendon Press).

—— (1992b) 'Introduction', in Andrew Hurrell and Benedict Kingsbury (eds), *The International Politics of the Environment* (Oxford: Clarendon Press).

Hutton, Jon and Barnabas Dickson (eds) (2000) *Endangered Species, Threatened Convention: The Past, Present and Future of CITES* (London: Earthscan).

Hyvarinen, Joy and Duncan Brack (2000) *Global Environmental Institutions: Analysis and Options for Change* (London: Royal Institute of International Affairs).

IIED (International Institute for Environment and Development) (ed.) (2002) *Financing for Sustainable Development* (London: IIED).

IISD (International Institute for Sustainable Development) (1993) 'Desertification and the UN system', *Earth Negotiations Bulletin*, ENB:04:01 (Winnipeg: International Institute for Sustainable Development) (http://www.iisd.ca/linkages/vol04/0401018e.html).

—— (1996a) *The Montreal Process* (Winnipeg: International Institute for Sustainable Development) (http://www.iisd.ca/linkages/forestry/mont.html).

—— (1996b) *The Helsinki Process* (Winnipeg: International Institute for Sustainable Development) (http://www.iisd.ca/linkages/forestry/hel.html).

—— (1996c) 'Summary of the ninth session of the INC for the Convention to Combat Desertification: 3–13 September 1996', *Earth Negotiations Bulletin*, ENB:04:95 (Winnipeg: International Institute for Sustainable Development) (http://www.iisd.ca/linkages/vol04/0495001e.html).

—— (1996d) 'A brief analysis of INCD-9', *Earth Negotiations Bulletin*, ENB:04:95 (Winnipeg: International Institute for Sustainable Development) (http://www.iisd.ca/linkages/vol04/0495020e.html).

—— (2003a) 'A daily report of the 3rd World Water Forum', *Forum Bulletin*, vol. 82, no. 8, 25 March.

—— (2003b) 'WSSD: challenges and opportunities', *Earth Negotiations Bulletin*, vol. 22, no. 51, pp. 17–18.

—— (2003c) 'WSSD: accomplishments behind the negotiations', *Earth Negotiations Bulletin*, vol. 22, no. 51, p. 17.

Imber, Mark (1994) *Environment, Security and UN Reform* (London: Macmillan – now Palgrave Macmillan).

—— (1999) 'The impasse in UN reform', *Global Environmental Change*, vol. 9, no. 4, pp. 329–32.

Indigenous Peoples and Local Communities Caucus on Climate Change (2001) 'Statement to the Seventh Session of the Conference of the Parties, UNFCCC, Marrakech', in *Indigenous Peoples and the WSSD*, Briefing Paper No. 8 (Baguio City, The Philippines: Tebtebba Foundation).

International Chamber of Commerce (n.d.) *The Business Charter for Sustainable Development* (http://www.iccwbo.org/home/environment/charter.asp; accessed 23 July 2003).

International Committee of the Red Cross (2000) 'ICRC Guidelines for military manuals and instructions on the protection of the environment in times of armed conflict', *RECIEL*, vol. 9, no. 1, 2000, pp. 80–2.

International Indigenous Forum on Biodiversity (2001) 'Statement at the Ad Hoc Open-Ended Working Group on Access and Benefit Sharing, Convention on Biological Diversity, 22–26 October 2001, Bonn, Germany', in *Indigenous Peoples and the WSSD*, Briefing Paper No. 8 (Baguio City, The Philippines: Tebtebba Foundation).

International Peoples' Tribunal (1997) 'Statement on human rights and the environment: sustainable development in the context of globalisation', [reproduced in] *Alternatives*, vol. 23, no. 1, Jan.–March, 1998, pp. 109–47.

International Union for the Conservation of Nature (2002) 'The 2002 IUCN Red List of Threatened Species', News Release, 8 October (http://www.iucn.org/themes/ssc/redlist2002/rl_news.htm; accessed 12 July 2003).

International Water Management Institute (2001) 'Growing water scarcity threatens global good and environmental security', Press Release, 13 August (http://www.iwmi.org).

IPCC (Intergovernmental Panel on Climate Change) (1990) *Impacts Assessment of Climate Change: The Policy-makers' Summary of the Report of Working Group II* (Canberra: Australian Government Publishing Service).

—— (1995) IPCC *Second Assessment: Synthesis of Scientific Technical Information Relevant to Interpreting Article 2 of the UN Framework Convention on Climate Change 1995* (Geneva: UNEP) (http://www.unep.ch/ipcc/syntrep.html).

—— (2001) *Summary for Policymakers: Working Group I* (Geneva: IPCC).

Jacobs, Michael (1990) *Sustainable Development: Greening the Economy* (London: The Fabian Society).

Jacobson, Jodi (1992) *Gender Bias: Roadblock to Sustainable Development*, WorldWatch Paper No. 110 (Washington, DC: WorldWatch Institute).

Jain, Peeyush (1990) 'Proposal: a pollution added tax to slow ozone depletion and global warming', *Stanford Journal of International Law*, vol. 26, no. 2, Spring, pp. 549–72.

Jasanoff, Sheila (1997) 'NGOs and the environment: from knowledge to action', *Third World Quarterly*, vol. 18, no. 3, pp. 579–94.

Johnson, Craig and Timothy Forsyth (2002) 'In the eyes of the state: negotiating a "rights-based approach" to forest conservation in Thailand', *World Development*, vol. 30, no. 9, pp. 1591–1605.

Johnson, Stanley P. (1993) *The Earth Summit: The United Nations Conference on Environment and Development (UNCED)* (London: Graham & Trotman).

Johnston, Sam (1997) 'The Convention on Biological Diversity: the next phase', *RECIEL*, vol. 6, no. 3, pp. 219–30.

Joint Declaration (1997), *Joint Declaration for a Global Initiative on Sustainable Development*, issued by the Department of Foreign Affairs, Pretoria, 23 June (http://www.polity.org.za/html/govdocs/pr/1997/pr0623c. html?rebookmark=1, accessed 15 August 2003).

Jones, Tom (2002) 'Policy coherence, global environmental governance and poverty reduction', *International Environmental Agreements*, vol. 2, no. 4, pp. 389–401.

Jordan, Andrew and Heather Voisey (1998) 'The "Rio process": the politics and substantive outcomes of "Earth Summit II"', *Global Environmental Change*, vol. 8, no. 1, pp. 93–7.

Juma, Calestous (2000) 'The perils of centralizing global environmental governance', *Environment*, vol. 42, no. 9, pp. 44–6.

Kaiser, Jocelyn (2002) 'World summit adopts voluntary action plan', *Science*, vol. 297, 13 September, p. 1785.

Käkönen, Jyrki (ed.) (1992) *Perspectives on Environmental Conflict and International Relations* (London: Pinter Publishers).

—— (ed.) (1994) *Green Security or Militarized Environment* (Aldershot: Dartmouth Publishing).

Kaldor, Mary (2000) ' "Civilising" globalisation? The implications of the "Battle in Seattle" ', *Millennium*, vol. 29, no. 1, pp. 105–12.

Kamieniecki, Sheldon (1993) 'Emerging forces in global environmental politics', in Sheldon Kamieniecki (ed.), *Environmental Politics in the International Arena: Movements, Parties, Organizations and Policy* (Albany, NY: State University of New York Press).

Kaplan, Robert (1994) 'The coming anarchy', *The Atlantic Monthly*, vol. 273, no. 2, pp. 44–76.

Karliner, Joshua (1997) *The Corporate Planet: Ecology and Politics in the Age of Globalization* (San Francisco: Sierra Club Books).

Karno, Valerie (1991) 'Protection of endangered gorillas and chimpanzees in international trade: can CITES help?', *Hastings International and Comparative Law Review*, vol. 14, no. 4, pp. 989–1015.

Kassas, M. (2002) 'Biodiversity: gaps in knowledge', *The Environmentalist*, vol. 22, no. 1, pp. 43–9.

Keck, Margaret E. and Kathryn Sikkink (1998) *Activists Beyond Borders: Advocacy Networks in International Politics* (Ithaca, NY: Cornell University Press).

Kennedy Cuomo, Kerry (1993) 'Human rights and the environment: common ground', *Yale Journal of International Law*, vol. 18, no. 1, Winter, pp. 227–33.

Keohane, Robert O. and Marc A. Levy (eds) (1996) *Institutions for Environmental Aid* (Cambridge, Mass.: The MIT Press).

Kerr, Suzi (ed.) (2000) *Global Emissions Trading: Key Issues for Industrialised Countries* (Cheltenham: Edward Elgar).

Khor, Kok Peng (Martin) (2002) *Intellectual Property, Biodiversity and Sustainable Development: The TRIPS Agreement and the Issues to be Resolved* (London: Zed Books).

Khor, Martin (1994) 'The Commission on Sustainable Development: paper tiger or agency to save the earth?', in Helge Ole Bergesen and Georg Parmann (eds), *Green Globe Yearbook 1994* (Oxford: Oxford University Press).

Khosla, Ashok (2002) 'Expectations of the World Summit on Sustainable Development', *Development*, vol. 45, no. 3, pp. 6–11.

Kildow, Judith T. (1992) 'The Earth Summit: we need more than a message', *Environmental Science and Technology*, vol. 26, no. 6, pp. 1077–8.

Kim, Joy Aeree (2001) 'Institutions in conflict? The climate change flexibility mechanisms and the multinational trading system', *Global Environmental Change*, vol. 11, no. 3, pp. 251–5.

Kimball, Lee A. (1997) 'International linkages between the Convention on Biological Diversity and other international conventions', *RECIEL*, vol. 6, no. 3, pp. 239–48.

Koenig, Dieter (1995) 'Sustainable development: linking global environmental change to technology cooperation', in O. P. Dwivedi and Dhirendra K. Vajpeyi (eds), *Environmental Politics in the Third World: A Comparative Analysis* (Westport, Conn.: Greenwood Press).

Korten, David C. (1997) 'The responsibility of business to the whole', reproduced in Richard Starkey and Richard Welford (eds) (2001) *Business and Sustainable Development* (London: Earthscan).

Krueger, Jonathan (1999a) 'Prior Informed Consent and the Basel Convention: the hazards of what isn't known', *Journal of Environment and Development*, vol. 7, no. 2, June, pp. 115–37.

—— (1999b) *International Trade and the Basel Convention* (London: Royal Institute of International Affairs/Earthscan).

Kummer, Katharina (1998) 'The Basel Convention: ten years on', *Review of European Community and International Environmental Law*, vol. 7, no. 3, pp. 227–36.

Kurian, Priya A. (2000) *Engendering the Environment? Gender in the World Bank's Environmental Policies* (Aldershot: Ashgate).

Lacy, Mark J. (2002) 'Deconstructing risk society', *Environmental Politics*, vol. 11, no. 4, pp. 42–62.

Laferrière, Eric and Peter J. Stoett (1999) *International Relations Theory and Ecological Thought* (London: Routledge).

Lallas, Peter L., Daniel C. Esty and Daniel J. van Hoogstraten (1992) 'Environmental protection and international trade: towards mutually supportive rules and policies', *Harvard Environmental Law Review*, vol. 16, no. 2, pp. 271–342.

Lanchbery, John (1998) 'Expectations for the climate talks in Buenos Aires', *Environment*, vol. 40, no. 8, pp. 16–21, 42–5.

Lang, Winfried (1991) 'The international waste regime', in Winfried Lang, Hanspeter Neuhold and Karl Zemanek (eds), *Environmental Protection and International Law* (London: Graham & Trotman).

Laurance, William F. (1999) 'Reflections on the tropical deforestation crisis', *Biological Conservation*, vol. 91, no. 2/3, pp. 109–17.

Law, David (1997) 'Global environmental issues and the World Bank', in Stephen Gill (ed.), *Globalization, Democratization and Multilateralism* (London/Tokyo: Macmillan/United Nations University Press).

Leclair, Mark S. (2003) 'Fighting back: the growth of alternative trade', *Development*, vol. 46, no. 1, pp. 66–73.

Leggett, Jeremy (1992) 'The environmental impact of war: a scientific analysis and Greenpeace's reaction', in Glen Plant (ed.), *Environmental Protection and the Law of War* (London: Belhaven Press).

Leggett, Jeremy and Paul Hohnen (1992) 'The Climate Convention: a perspective from the environmental lobby', *Security Dialogue*, vol. 23, no. 4, December, pp. 75–81.

Le Prestre, Philippe G. (2002) *Governing Global Biodiversity: The Evolution and Implementation of the Convention on Biological Diversity* (Aldershot: Ashgate).

Leubuscher, Susan (1996) 'Ozone depletion: seventh meeting of the Parties to the Montreal Protocol', *RECIEL*, vol. 5, no. 2, pp. 186–7.

Levy, David L. and Daniel Egan (2003) 'A neo-Gramscian approach to corporate political strategy: conflict and accommodation in the climate change negotiations', *Journal of Management Studies*, vol. 40, no. 4, pp. 803–29.

Levy, Marc A. (1993) 'European acid rain: the power of tote-board diplomacy', in Peter M. Haas. Robert O. Keohane and Marc A. Levy (eds), *Institutions for the Earth: Sources of Effective International Environmental Protection* (Cambridge, Mass.: The MIT Press).

Levy, Marc A., Peter M. Haas and Robert O. Keohane (1992) 'Institutions for the Earth: promoting international environmental protection', *Environment*, vol. 34, no. 4, pp. 12–17, 29–36.

Lewis, Tammy L. (2003) 'Environmental aid: driven by recipient need or donor interests?', *Social Science Quarterly*, vol. 84, no. 1, pp. 144–61.

Lidskog, Rolf and Göran Sundqvist (2002) 'The role of science in environmental regimes: the case of LRTAP', *European Journal of International Relations*, vol. 8, no. 1, pp. 77–101.

Linklater, Andrew (1995) 'Neo-realism in theory and practice' in Ken Booth and Steve Smith (eds), *International Relations Theory Today* (Cambridge: Polity Press).

—— (1998) 'Cosmopolitan citizenship', *Citizenship Studies*, vol. 2, no. 1, pp. 23–41.

—— (2002) 'The problem of harm in world politics: implications for the sociology of states-systems', *International Affairs*, vol. 78, no. 2, pp. 319–38.

Liotta, P. H. (2002) 'Boomerang effect: the convergence of national and human security', *Security Dialogue*, vol. 33, no. 4, pp. 473–88.

Lipschutz, Ronnie D. (1991) 'One world or many? Global sustainable economic development in the 21st century', *Bulletin of Peace Proposals*, vol. 22, no. 2, pp. 189–98.

—— (1993) 'Learn of the green world: global environmental change, global civil society and social learning', paper presented at the Annual Conference of the International Studies Association, 23–27 March.

—— (2003) *Global Environmental Politics: Power, Perspectives and Practice* (Washington, DC: Congressional Quarterly Press).

Lipschutz, Ronnie D. and Ken Conca (eds) (1993a) *The State and Social Power in Global Environmental Politics* (New York: Columbia University Press).

—— (1993b) 'The implications of global ecological interdependence', in Ronnie D. Lipschutz and Ken Conca (eds), *The State and Social Power in Global Environmental Politics* (New York: Columbia University Press).

Lipschutz, Ronnie D. and John P. Holdren (1990) 'Crossing borders: resource flows, the global environment and international security', *Bulletin of Peace Proposals*, vol. 21, no. 2, pp. 121–33.

Lisowski, Michael (2002) 'The emperor's new clothes: redressing the Kyoto Protocol', *Climate Policy*, vol. 2, no. 2–3, pp. 161–77.

Litfin, Karen (1993) 'Ecoregimes: playing tug of war with the nation-state', in Ronnie D. Lipschutz and Ken Conca (eds), *The State and Social Power in Global Environmental Politics* (New York: Columbia University Press).

—— (1994) *Ozone Discourses: Science and Politics in Global Environmental Cooperation* (New York: Columbia University Press).

—— (1997) 'Sovereignty in world ecopolitics', *Mershon International Studies Review*, vol. 41, no. 2, pp. 167–204.

—— (ed.) (1998) *The Greening of Sovereignty in World Politics* (Cambridge, Mass.: The MIT Press).

—— (1999) 'Constructing environmental security and ecological interdependence', *Global Governance*, vol. 5, no. 3, pp. 359–77.

Lodefalk, Magnus and John Whalley (2002) 'Reviewing proposals for a world environment organisation', *The World Economy*, vol. 25, no. 5, pp. 601–17.

Low, Nicholas (ed.) (1999) *Global Ethics and Environment* (London: Routledge).

Low, Nicholas and Brendan Gleeson (1999) 'Global governance for environmental justice', *Pacifica Review*, vol. 11, no. 2, June, pp. 177–93.

Lowi, Miriam R. and Brian R. Shaw (eds) (2000) *Environment and Security: Discourses and Practices* (Basingstoke: Palgrave Macmillan).

Lu, Flora E. (2001) 'The common property regime of the Huaorani Indians of Ecuador: implications and challenges to conservation', *Human Ecology*, vol. 29, no. 4, pp. 425–47.

McConnell, Fiona (1996) *The Biodiversity Convention: A Negotiating History* (London: Kluwer Law International).

McCormick, John (1989) *The Global Environment Movement* (London: Belhaven Press).

McCully, Patrick (1991a) 'Discord in the greenhouse: how WRI is attempting to shift the blame for global warming', *The Ecologist*, vol. 21, no. 4, July/August, pp. 157–65.

—— (1991b) 'The case against climate aid', *The Ecologist*, vol. 21, no. 6, November/December, pp. 244–51.

McGinn, Anne Platt (2000) 'POPs culture', *World Watch*, vol. 13, no. 2, March/April, pp. 26–36.

McGraw, Désirée M. (2002) 'The CBD – key characteristics and implications for implementation', *RECIEL*, vol. 11, no. 1, pp. 17–28.

MacKenzie, James (2000) Oil as a finite resource: when is global production likely to peak? (Washington, DC: World Resources Institute) (http://www.wri.org/wri/climate/jm_oil_000.html; accessed 19 August 2003).

McNeely, Jeffrey A., Martha Rojas and Caroline Martinet (1995) 'The Convention on Biological Diversity: promise and frustration', *Journal of Environment and Development*, vol. 4, no. 2, Summer, pp. 33–53.

MacNeill, Jim, Pieter Winsemius and Taizo Yakushiji (1991) *Beyond Interdependence: The Meshing of the World's Economy and the Earth's Ecology* (New York: Oxford University Press).

Maddox, John (1972) *The Doomsday Syndrome* (London: Macmillan – now Palgrave Macmillan).

Mahony, Rhona (1992) 'Debt-for-Nature Swaps: who really benefits?', *The Ecologist*, vol. 22, no. 3, May/June, pp. 97–103.

MAPW (Medical Association for Prevention of War) (1991) *Environmental Effects of Warfare* (Canberra: MAPW).

Marshall, Brent K. (1999) 'Globalisation, environmental degradation and Ulrich Beck's Risk Society', *Environmental Values*, vol. 8, no. 2, pp. 253–75.

Martens, Jens (2002) 'Sustainable development and the effectiveness of ODA', in International Institute for Environment and Development (ed.), *Financing for sustainable development* (London: IIED).

Martens, Jens and James A. Paul (1998) *The Coffers Are Not Empty: Financing for Sustainable Development and the Role of the United Nations*

(New York: Global Policy Forum) (http://www.globalpolicy.org/socecon/global/paul.htm; accessed 16 June 2003).

Mathews, Jessica Tuchman (1989) 'Redefining security', *Foreign Affairs*, vol. 68, no. 2, pp. 162–77.

Matsui, Yoshiro (2002) 'Some aspects of the principle of common but differentiated responsibilities', *International Environmental Agreements*, vol. 2, no. 2, pp. 151–71.

Matthew, Richard A. and Ted Gaulin (2001) 'Conflict or cooperation? The social and political impacts of resource scarcity on small island states', *Global Environmental Politics*, vol. 1, no. 2, pp. 48–70.

Meadows, Donella, Debbus, I. Meadows, Jorgen Randers and William W. Behrens III (1972) *The Limits to Growth* (London: Earth Island Ltd).

Melman, Seymour (1988) 'Law for economic conversion: necessity and characteristics', *ENDPapers*, no. 18, Summer/Autumn, pp. 54–60.

Meyer, Anja (2001) 'International environmental law and human rights: towards the explicit recognition of traditional knowledge', *RECIEL*, vol. 10, no. 1, pp. 37–46.

Michaelowa, Katharina (2003) 'The political economy of the enhanced HIPC-initiative', *Public Choice*, vol. 114, no. 3–4, pp. 461–76.

Miller, Kenton R. (1983) 'The Earth's living terrestrial resources: managing their conservation', in David A. Kay and Harold K. Jacobson (eds), *Environmental Protection: The International Dimension* (Totowa, NJ: Allenheld, Osmun).

Miller, Marian A. L. (1995) *The Third World in Global Environmental Politics* (Boulder, Colo: Lynne Reinner).

Mintzer, Irving M. and J. Amber Leonard (eds) (1994a) *Negotiating Climate Change: The Inside Story of the Rio Convention* (Cambridge: Cambridge University Press).

—— (1994b) 'Visions of a changing world', in Irving M. Mintzer and J. Amber Leonard (eds), *Negotiating Climate Change: The Inside Story of the Rio Convention* (Cambridge: Cambridge University Press).

Mische, Patricia M. (1989) 'Ecological security and the need to reconceptualise sovereignty', *Alternatives*, no. XIV, pp. 389–427.

—— (1992) 'Security through defending the environment: citizens say yes!', in Elise Boulding (ed.), *New Agendas for Peace Research* (Boulder, Colo: Lynne Rienner).

Mitchell, Ronald (1993) 'International oil pollution of the oceans', in Peter M. Haas, Robert O. Keohane and Marc A. Levy (eds), *Institutions for the Earth: Sources of Effective Environmental Protection* (Cambridge, Mass.: The MIT Press).

Mol, Arthur P. J. (2001) *Globalization and environmental reform: the ecological modernization of the global economy* (Cambridge, Mass.: The MIT Press).

Molina, Mario J. and F. S. Rowland (1974) 'Stratospheric sink for chlorofluoromethanes: chlorine atom-catalysed destruction of ozone', *Nature*, vol. 249, no. 5460, 28 June, pp. 810–12.

Momsen, Janet Henshall (1991) *Women and Development in the Third World* (London: Routledge).

Moody-O'Grady, Kristin (1995) 'Nuclear waste in the oceans: has the Cold War taught us anything?', *Natural Resources Journal*, vol. 35, no. 3, Summer, pp. 695–709.

Moomaw, William, Kilparti Ramakrishna, Kevin Gallagher and Tobin Freid (1999) 'The Kyoto Protocol: a blueprint for sustainable development', *Journal of Environment and Development*, vol. 8, no. 1, March, pp. 82–90.

Morrisette, Peter M. (1989) 'The evolution of policy responses to stratospheric ozone depletion', *Natural Resources Journal*, vol. 29, no. 3, Summer, pp. 793–820.

Moss, Richard H. (1993) 'Resource scarcity and environmental security', *SIPRI Yearbook 1994* (Oxford: Oxford University Press).

Muchie, Mammo (2000) 'Old wine in new bottles: a critical exploration of the UN's conceptions and mechanisms for the transfer of environmentally sound technology to industry', *Technology in Society*, vol. 22, no. 2, pp. 201–20.

Mucklow, Fiona (2000) 'The integration of environmental principles into the World Bank', *RECIEL*, vol. 9, no. 2, pp. 100–11.

Müller-Kraenner, Sascha (2002) 'On the road to Johannesburg', *Development*, vol. 45, no. 3, pp. 18–23.

Muradian, Roldan and Joan Martinez-Alier (2001) 'Trade and the environment: from a "Southern" perspective', *Ecological Economics*, vol. 36, no. 2, pp. 281–97.

Murphy, Joseph (2001) *Ecological Modernisation: The Environment and the Transformation of Society*, Research Paper No. 20 (Oxford: Oxford Centre for the Environment, Ethics and Society).

Murphy, Michael K. (1999) 'Achieving economic security with swords as ploughshares: the modern use of force to combat environmental degradation', *Virginia Journal of International Law*, vol. 39, no. 4, pp. 1181–1219.

Murphy, Sean D. (1994) 'Prospective liability regimes for the transboundary movement of hazardous wastes', *American Journal of International Law*, vol. 88, no. 1, January, pp. 24–75.

Murray, Martyn (1993) 'The value of biodiversity', in Gwyn Prins (ed.), *Threats Without Enemies* (London: Earthscan).

Myers, Norman (1989) 'Environment and security', *Foreign Affairs*, no. 74, Spring, pp. 23–41.

—— (1992) 'The anatomy of environmental action: the case of tropical deforestation', in Andrew Hurrell and Benedict Kingsbury (eds), *The International Politics of the Environment* (Oxford: Clarendon Press).

Najam, Adil (1999) 'World Business Council for Sustainable Development: the greening of business or a greenwash?', in Helge Ole Bergesen, Georg Parmann and Øystein B. Thommessen (eds), *Yearbook of International Cooperation on Environment and Development* 1999/2000 (London: Earthscan).

Nanda, Ved P. (1991) 'International environmental protection and developing countries' interests: the role of international law', *Texas International Law Journal*, vol. 26, no. 3, Summer, pp. 497–519.

Native Peoples of Sarawak (1991) 'Statement by representatives to the 11th meeting of the ITTO', *ECO*, Issue no. 1, Article 4 (http://bioc09.uthscsa.edu/natnet/archive/nl/9202/ 0163.html).

NATO (North Atlantic Treaty Organisation) (1999) *The Alliance's Strategic Concept*, Approved by the Heads of State and Government participating in the meeting of the North Atlantic Council in Washington, DC on 23rd and 24th April 1999, Press Release NAC-S(99)65, 24 April 1999.

Neumayer, Eric (2000) 'Trade and the environment: a critical assessment and some suggestions for reconciliation', *Journal of Environment and Development*, vol. 9, no. 2, pp. 138–59.

Newell, Peter (2002) 'A world environment organisation: the wrong solution to the wrong problem', *The World Economy*, vol. 25, no. 5, pp. 659–71.

—— (2003) 'Globalisation and the governance of biotechnology', *Global Environmental Politics*, vol. 3, no. 2, pp. 56–71.

Newell, Peter and Ruth Mackenzie (2000) 'The 2000 Cartegena Protocol on biosafety: legal and political dimensions', *Global Environmental Change*, vol. 10, no. 4, pp. 313–17.

NOAA (National Oceanic and Atmospheric Administration) (2000) 'Tropical waters in Northern Hemisphere heating at an accelerated rate', Press Release, 28 July (via Climate Change Impacts Network, ccin@dar.csiro.au, 4 August 2000).

Ntambirweki, John (1991) 'The developing countries in the evolution of an international environmental law', *Hastings International and Comparative Law Review*, vol. 14, no. 4, Summer, pp. 905–28.

Oberthür, Sebastian (1996) 'UNFCCC: the second Conference of the Parties', *Environmental Policy and Law*, vol. 26, no. 5, October, pp. 195–201.

Oberthür, Sebastian and Hermann Ott (1995) 'UN Convention on Climate Change: the First Conference of the Parties', *Environmental Policy and Law*, vol. 24, no. 4/5, August/September, pp. 144–56.

Obiora, Amede (1999) 'Symbolic episodes in the quest for environmental justice', *Human Rights Quarterly*, vol. 21, no. 2, pp. 464–512.

OECD (Organisation for Economic Co-operation and Development) (2003) *Policy Brief: The OECD Guidelines for Multinational Enterprises* (Paris: OECD).

Oilwatch (2002) *Oil Companies: The New Partners of the United Nations – a Critique of the Type II Partnership Initiatives in the WSSD*, Position Paper No. 3 (Quito, Ecuador: Oilwatch International Secretariat).

O'Neill, Kate (1998) 'Out of the backyard: the problems of hazardous waste management at a global level', *Journal of Environment and Development*, vol. 7, no. 2, June, pp. 138–63.

—— (2000) *Waste Trading Among Rich Nations: Building a New Theory of Environmental Regulation* (Cambridge, Mass.: The MIT Press).

Ong, David M. (1998) 'The Convention on International Trade in Endangered Species (CITES, 1973): implications of recent developments in international and EC environmental law', *Journal of Environmental Law*, vol. 10, no. 2, pp. 291–314.

Opschoor, Johannes B. (1989) 'North–South trade, resource degradation and economic security', *Bulletin of Peace Proposals*, vol. 20, no. 2, June, pp. 135–42.

Opschoor, J. (Hans) B. (2003) 'Conference report: The World Summit on Sustainable Development (WSSD), Johannesburg (24 August–4 September 2002)' *African Affairs*, vol. 102, no. 406, pp. 145–6.

O'Riordan, Tim, James Cameron and Andrew Jordan (eds) (2001) *Reinterpreting the Precautionary Principle* (London: Cameron May).

Osborn, Derek and Tom Bigg (1998) *Earth Summit II: Outcomes and Analysis* (London: Earthscan).

Osman, Sabihah (2000) 'Globalisation and democratisation: the response of the indigenous peoples of Sarawak', *Third World Quarterly*, vol. 21, no. 6, pp. 977–88.

Oswald, Julian (1993) 'Defence and environmental security', in Gwyn Prins (ed.), *Threats Without Enemies* (London: Earthscan).

Ott, Hermann E. (1998) 'The Kyoto Protocol: unfinished business', *Environment*, vol. 40, no. 6, pp. 17–20, 41–5.

—— (2001) 'The Bonn agreement to the Kyoto Protocol: paving the way for ratification', *International Environmental Agreements*, vol. 1, no. 4, pp. 469–76.

Paehlke, Robert (1994) 'Environmental values and public policy', in Norman J. Vig and Michael K. Kraft (eds), *Environmental Policy in the 1990s: Toward a New Agenda*, 2nd edn (Washington, DC: CQ Press).

Page, Edward (1999) 'Intergenerational justice and climate change', *Political Studies*, vol. XLVII, no. 1, pp. 53–66.

Page, Edward and Michael Redclift (eds) (2002) *Human Security and the Environment* (Cheltenham: Edward Elgar).

Pallemaerts, Marc (2003) 'International law and sustainable development: any progress in Johannesburg?', *RECIEL*, vol. 12, no. 1, pp. 1–11.

Palmer, Geoffrey (1992) 'New ways to make international environmental law', *American Journal of International Law*, vol. 86, no. 2, April, pp. 259–83.

Pan, Jiahua (2003) 'Emission rights and their transferability: equity concerns over climate change mitigation', *International Environmental Agreements*, vol. 3, no. 1, pp. 1–16.

Parkin, Sara (1999) 'Environment and security: issues and agenda', *Disarmament Forum*, no. 1, pp. 41–8.

Parson, Edward A. (1993) 'Protecting the ozone layer', in Peter M. Haas, Robert O. Keohane and Marc A. Levy (eds), *Institutions for the Earth: Sources of Effective Environmental Protection* (Cambridge, Mass.: The MIT Press).

Parson, Edward A., Peter M. Haas and Marc A. Levy (1992) 'A summary of major documents signed at the Earth Summit and the Global Forum', *Environment*, vol. 34, no. 8, pp. 12–15, 34–6.

Paterson, Matthew (1995) 'Radicalising regimes? ecology and the critique of IR theory', in John MacMillan and Andrew Linklater (eds), *Boundaries in Question: New Directions in International Relations* (London: Pinter Publishers).

—— (1996) *Global Warming and Global Politics* (New York: Routledge).

—— (2000) *Understanding Global Environmental Politics: Domination, Accumulation, Resistance* (New York: St Martin's Press).

Paterson, Matthew and Michael Grubb (1992) 'The international politics of climate change', *International Affairs*, vol. 68, no. 2, pp. 293–310.

Paterson, Matthew, David Humphreys and Lloyd Pettiford (2003) 'Conceptualising global environmental governance: from interstate regimes to counter-hegemonic strategies', *Global Environmental Politics*, vol. 3, no. 2, pp. 1–10.

Patterson, Alan (1990) 'Debt-for-Nature Swaps and the need for alternatives', *Environment*, vol. 32, no. 10, December, pp. 5–13, 31–2.

Paul, James A. (2002) 'Iraq: the struggle for oil', December (New York: Global Policy Forum) (http://www.globalpolicy.org/security/oil/2002/08jim.htm; accessed 29 July 2003).

Peace Research Institute Oslo (1989) *Environmental Security: A Report Contributing to the Concept of Comprehensive International security* (Oslo: Peace Research Institute, Oslo/United Nations Environment Programme).

Peake, Stephen (2002) 'The Jo'burg summit: what did it really mean for renewables?', *Refocus*, November/December, pp. 46–9.

Pearce, David (1990) 'Economics and the global environmental challenge', *Millennium*, vol. 19, no. 3, Winter, pp. 365–87.

Pearce, David W. and Jeremy J. Warford (1993) *World Without End: Economics, Environment and Sustainable Development* (New York: Oxford University Press).

Pearce, David, Edward Barbier and Anil Markandya (1994) *Sustainable Development: Economics and Environment in the Third World* (London: Earthscan).

Peet, John (1992) *Energy and the Ecological Economics of Sustainability* (Washington, DC: Island Press).

Pegg, Scott (2003) *Poverty Reduction or Poverty Exacerbation? World Bank Group Support for Extractive Industries in Africa* (New York: Environmental Defense).

Perreault, Thomas (2003) 'Changing places: transnational networks, ethnic politics and community development in the Ecuadorian Amazon', *Political Geography*, vol. 22, no. 1, pp. 61–88.

Perrez, Franz Xaver (2003) 'The World Summit on Sustainable Development: environment, precaution and trade – a potential for success and/or failure', *RECIEL*, vol. 12, no. 1, pp. 12–22.

Pettifor, Ann and Andrew Simms (2002) 'Debt and sustainable development: a new paradigm', in International Institute for Environment and Development (ed.), *Financing for Sustainable Development* (London: IIED).

Pianin, Eric (2003) 'Impending war threatens Gulf: environment damage could eclipse 1990–1991 Gulf War', *The Washington Post*, 19 March (http:www.washingtonpost.com/wp-dyn/articles/A54640-2003Mar19.html; accessed 28 July 2003).

Pirages, Dennis Clark (1991) 'The greening of peace research', *Journal of Peace Research*, vol. 28, no. 2, May, pp. 129–33.

Pollock, Mark A. and Gregory C. Shaffer (2000) 'Biotechnology: the next transatlantic trade war', *The Washington Quarterly*, vol. 23, no. 4, pp. 41–54.

Porras, Ileana M. (1993) 'The Rio Declaration: a new basis for international cooperation', in Philippe Sands (ed.), *Greening International Law* (London: Earthscan).

Porter, Gareth and Janet Welsh Brown (1991) *Global Environmental Politics* (Boulder, Colo: Westview Press).

Porter, Gareth, Janet Welsh Brown and Pamela S. Chasek (2000) *Global environmental politics*, 3rd edn (Boulder, Colo: Westview Press).

Posey, Darrell A. (1996) 'Protecting indigenous peoples' rights to biodiversity', *Environment*, vol. 38, no. 8, pp. 7–9, 37–45.

—— (2002) 'Commodification of the sacred through intellectual property rights', *Journal of Ethnopharmacology*, vol. 83, no. 1, pp. 3–12.

Posey, Darrell A. and Graham Dutfield (1996) *Beyond Intellectual Property: Toward Traditional Resource Rights for Indigenous Peoples and Local Communities* (Ottawa: International Development Research Centre).

Postel, Sandra and Christopher Flavin (1991) 'Reshaping the global economy', in Lester R. Brown *et al.* (eds), *State of the World 1991* (New York: W. W. Norton & Co.).

Postiglione, Amedeo (2001) 'An international court of the environment', in Brendan Gleeson and Nicholas Low (eds), *Governing for the Environment: Global Problems, Ethics and Democracy* (Basingstoke: Palgrave Macmillan).

Prakash, Siddhartha (2000) *Indigenous Knowledge and Intellectual Property rights*, IK Notes No. 19 (Washington, DC: World Bank).

Princen, Thomas and Matthias Finger (1994) 'Introduction', in Thomas Princen and Matthias Finger (eds), *Environmental NGOs in World Politics: Linking the Global and the Local* (London: Routledge).

Prins, Gwyn (1990) 'Politics and the environment', *International Affairs*, vol. 66, no. 4, pp. 711–30.

—— (1993) 'Putting environmental security in context', in Gwyn Prins (ed.), *Threats Without Enemies* (London: Earthscan).

Puckett, Jim (1994) 'Disposing of the waste trade: closing the recycling loophole', *The Ecologist*, vol. 24, no. 2, March/April, pp. 53–8.

Pulvenis, Jean-François (1994) 'The Framework Convention on Climate Change', in Luigi Campiglio *et al.* (eds), *The Environment after Rio: International Law and Economics* (London: Graham & Trotman).

Rajamani, Lavanya (2003) 'From Stockholm to Johannesburg: the anatomy of dissonance in the international environmental dialogue', *RECIEL*, vol. 12, no. 1, pp. 23–32.

Ramakrishna, Kilaparti (1990) 'North–South issues, common heritage of mankind and global climate', *Millennium*, vol. 19, no. 3, Winter, pp. 429–45.

Raustiala, Kal (1997) 'States, NGOs and international environmental institutions', *International Studies Quarterly*, vol. 41, no. 4, pp. 719–40.

Raustiala, Kal and David G. Victor (1996) 'Biodiversity since Rio: the future of the Convention on Biological Diversity', *Environment*, vol. 38, no. 4, May, pp. 17–20, 37–45.

Reader, Melvyn (1993) 'The International Whaling Commission (IWC)', *Environmental Politics*, vol. 2, no. 1, Spring, pp. 81–5.

Redclift, Michael (1984) *Development and the Environmental Crisis* (London: Methuen).

—— (1987) *Sustainable Development: Exploring the Contradictions* (London: Methuen).

Redclift, Michael and Ted Benton (1994) (eds), *Social theory and the environment* (New York: Routledge).

Redclift, Michael and Colin Sage (1998) 'Global environmental change and global inequality: North/South perspectives', *International Sociology*, vol. 13, no. 4, December, pp. 499–516.

Redgwell, Catherine (1992) 'Has the Earth been saved? A legal evaluation of the 1992 United Nations Conference on Environment and Development', *Environmental Politics*, vol. 1, no. 4, Winter, pp. 262–7.

Rees, William E. (1990) 'The ecology of sustainable development', *The Ecologist*, vol. 20, no. 1, January/February, pp. 18–23.

—— (2002) 'An ecological economics perspective on sustainability and prospects for ending poverty', *Population and Environment*, vol. 24, no. 1, pp. 15–46.

Reeve, Rosalind (2002) *Policing International Trade in Endangered Species: The CITES Treaty and Compliance* (London: Earthscan).

Reid, Walter V. (1992) 'Conserving life's diversity: can the extinction crisis be stopped?', *Environmental Science and Technology*, vol. 26, no. 6, June, pp. 1090–5.

—— (1997) 'Strategies for conserving biodiversity', *Environment*, vol. 39, no. 7, pp. 16–20, 39–43.

Reinstein, R. A. (1993) 'Climate negotiations', *The Washington Quarterly*, vol. 16, no. 1, Winter, pp. 78–95.

Renner, Michael (1989) 'Enhancing global security', in Lester R. Brown *et al.* (eds), *State of the World 1989* (New York: W. W. Norton & Co.).

—— (1994) 'Cleaning up after the arms race', in Lester R. Brown, Alan Thein Durning, Christopher Flavin, Hilary F. French, Nicholas Lenssen, Marcia D. Lowe, Ann Misch, Sandra Postel, Michael Renner, Linda Starke, Peter Weber and John E. Young (eds), *State of the World 1994* (New York: W. W. Norton & Co.).

—— (2003) *Post-Saddam Iraq: Linchpin of a New Oil Order*, Policy Report, Foreign Policy in Focus, January.

Renner, Rebecca (1998) 'International POPs treaty faces implementation hurdles', *Environmental News*, vol. 32, no. 17, 1 September, pp. 394A–395A.

Repetto, Robert (1992) 'Earth in the balance sheet: incorporating natural resources in national income accounts', *Environment*, vol. 34, no. 7, September, pp. 13–20, 43–5.

Reuters News Service (2000) 'World Bank admits to failure of forest policy', 28 January (http://www.planetark.org/avantgo/dailynewsstory.cfm?newsid= 5566; accessed 25 July 2003).

Rich, Bruce (1994) *Mortgaging the Earth: The World Bank, Environmental Impoverishment and the Crisis of Development* (London: Earthscan).

Richardson, Benjamin J. (2001) 'Indigenous peoples, international law and sustainability', *RECIEL*, vol. 10, no. 1, pp. 1–12.

Richardson, Elliot L. (1992) 'Climate change: problems of law-making', in Andrew Hurrell and Benedict Kingsbury (eds), *The International Politics of the Environment* (Oxford: Clarendon Press).

Ringius, Lasse (1997) 'Environmental NGOs and regime change: the case of ocean dumping and radioactive waste', *European Journal of International Relations*, vol. 3, no. 1, pp. 61–104.

Rodenburg, Eric and Dirk Bryant (1994) 'Water: conditions and trends', in World Resources Institute, *World Resources 1994–95* (New York: Oxford University Press).

Rogers, Adam (1997) 'Earth Summit+5 talks run into impasse at 11th hour', WETV/Webcast (http://www.SustainableDevelopment.net/empire/?SubSystemID=2&ComponentID=332).

Rosenau, James (1993) 'Environmental challenges in a turbulent world', in Ronnie D. Lipschutz and Ken Conca (eds), *The State and Social Power in Global Environmental Politics* (New York: Columbia University Press).

Rosencranz, Armin and Christopher L. Eldridge (1992) 'Hazardous waste: Basel after Rio', *Environmental Policy and Law*, vol. 22, no. 5/6, November/December, pp. 318–22.

Rosendal, G. Kristin (2001) 'Overlapping international regimes: the case of the Intergovernmental Forum on Forests between climate change and biodiversity', *International Environmental Agreements*, vol. 1, no. 4, pp. 447–68.

Rowland, Wade (1973) *The Plot to Save the World: The Life and Times of the Stockholm Conference on the Human Environment* (Toronto: Clarke Irwin & Co.).

Rowlands, Ian (1991) 'The security challenges of global environmental change', *The Washington Quarterly*, vol. 14, no. 1, Winter, pp. 99–114.

—— (1992) 'The international politics of environment and development: the post-UNCED agenda', *Millennium*, vol. 21, no. 2, Summer, pp. 209–24.

—— (1995a) *The Politics of Global Atmospheric Change* (Manchester: Manchester University Press).

—— (1995b) 'The climate change negotiations: Berlin and beyond', *Journal of Environment and Development*, vol. 4, no. 2, Summer, pp. 145–63.

—— (1997) 'International fairness and justice in addressing global climate change', *Environmental Politics*, vol. 6, no. 3, Autumn, pp. 1–30.

Ruff, Nathan, Robert Chamberlain and Alexandra Cousteau (1997) *Report on Applying Military and Security Assets to Environmental Problems*, Environmental Change and Security Project Report No. 3 (Washington, DC: Woodrow Wilson International Center for Scholars).

Rummel-Bulska, Iwona (1998) 'Compliance with and enforcement of the Basel Convention on the Control of Transboundary Movement of Hazardous Wastes and their Disposal', in *Proceedings of the Fifth International Conference on Environmental Compliance and Enforcement* (Washington, DC: International Network for Environmental Compliance and Enforcement).

Runyan, Curtis and Magnar Norderhaug (2002) *The path to Johannesburg* (Washington DC: Worldwatch Institute).

Sachs, Aaron (1996) 'Upholding rights and environmental justice', in Lester R. Brown, Janet N. Abramovitz, Chris Bright, Christopher Flavin, Gary

Gardner, Hal Kane, Anne E. Platt, Sandra Postel, David Malin Roodman, Aaron Sachs and Linda Starke (eds), *State of the World 1996* (New York: W. W. Norton & Co.).

Sachs, Wolfgang (1993a) 'Introduction', in Wolfgang Sachs (ed.), *Global Ecology: A New Arena of Political Conflict* (London: Zed Books).

—— (1993b) 'Global ecology and the shadow of "development"', in Wolfgang Sachs (ed.), *Global Ecology: A New Arena of Political Conflict* (London: Zed Books).

—— (ed.) (1993c) *Global Ecology: A New Arena of Political Conflict* (London: Zed Books).

—— (2002) 'Fairness in a fragile world: the Johannesburg agenda', *Development*, vol. 45, no. 3, pp. 12–17.

Sadoff, Claudia W. and David Grey (2002) 'Beyond the river: the benefits of cooperation on international rivers', *Water Policy*, vol. 4, no. 5, pp. 389–403.

Salt, Julian E. (1998) 'Kyoto and the insurance industry: an insider's perspective', *Environmental Politics*, vol. 7, no. 2, pp. 160–65.

Sampson, Gary P. (2001) 'Effective multilateral environmental agreements and why the WTO needs them', *World Economy*, vol. 24, no. 9, pp. 1109–34.

Samson, Colin, James Wilson and Jonathan Mazower (1999) *Canada's Tibet: The Killing of the Innu* (London: Survival International).

Sand, Peter H. (1993) 'International environmental law after Rio', *European Journal of International Law*, vol. 4, no. 3, pp. 377–89.

Sandbrook, Richard (1999) 'New hopes for the United Nations Environment Programme (UNEP)?', *Global Environmental Change*, vol. 9, no. 2, pp. 171–4.

—— (2000) 'Globalisation and the limits of neoliberal development doctrine', *Third World Quarterly*, vol. 21, no. 6, pp. 1071–80.

Sanders, Jerry W. (1990) 'Global ecology and world economy: collision course or sustainable future', *Bulletin of Peace Proposals*, vol. 24, no. 1, December, pp. 395–401.

Sands, Philippe J. (1989) 'The environment, community and international law', *Harvard International Law Journal*, vol. 30, no. 2, Spring, pp. 393–420.

—— (1992) 'The United Nations Convention on Climate Change', *Review of European Community and International Environmental Law*, vol. 1, no. 3, pp. 270–7.

—— (1993) 'Enforcing environmental security: the challenges of compliance with international obligations', *Journal of International Affairs*, vol. 46, no. 2, Winter, pp. 367–90.

Saunders, J. Owen (1992) 'Trade and environment: the fine line between environmental protection and environmental protectionism', *International Journal*, vol. XLVII, Autumn, pp. 722–50.

Saurin, Julian (1996) 'International relations, social ecology and the globalisation of environmental change', in John Vogler and Mark F. Imber (eds), *The Environment and International Relations* (London: Routledge).

Schmidheiny, Stephan (1992) *Changing Course: a global business perspective on environment and development* (Cambridge, Mass.: The MIT Press).

Schmidt, Eleonore (1998) 'The Forest Stewardship Council: using the market to promote responsible forestry', in Øystein B. Thommessen, Helge Ole

Bergesen and Georg Parmann (eds), *Yearbook of International Cooperation on Environment and Development 1998/99* (London: Earthscan).

Schneider, Keith (1991) 'US escalates war on waste', *Financial Review* (Australia), 20 September, p. 30.

Schoenbaum, Thomas J. (1992) 'Free international trade and protection of the environment: irreconcilable conflict?', *American Journal of International Law*, vol. 86, no. 4, October, pp. 700–27.

Schreurs, Miranda A. and Elizabeth Economy (eds) (1997) *The Internationalisation of Environmental Protection* (Cambridge: Cambridge University Press).

Schrijver, Nico (1989) 'International organisation for environmental security', *Bulletin of Peace Proposals*, vol. 20, no. 2, pp. 115–22.

Schwarzer, Gudrun (1993) 'The international long-range air pollution regime', *Aussenpolitik*, vol. 44, no. 1, pp. 13–22.

Sears, Robin R., Lilian M. Dávalos and Gonçalo Ferraz (2001) 'Missing the forest for the profits: the role of multinational corporations in the international forest regime', *Journal of Environment and Development*, vol. 10, no. 4, pp. 345–64.

Segger, Marie-Claire Cordonier, Ashfaq Khalfan, Markus Gehring and Michelle Toering (2003) 'Prospects for principles of international sustainable development law after the WSSD: common but differentiated responsibilities, precaution and participation', *RECIEL*, vol. 12, no. 1, pp. 54–68.

Selin, Henrik and Noelle Eckley (2003) 'Science, politics and persistent organic pollutants: the role of scientific assessments in international environmental cooperation', *International Environmental Agreements*, vol. 3, no. 1, pp. 17–42.

Shackley, Simon (1997) 'The Intergovernmental Panel on Climate Change: consensual knowledge and global politics', *Global Environmental Change*, vol. 7, no. 1, pp. 77–9.

Sharma, Sohan and Surinder Kumar (2002) 'Debt relief – indentured servitude for the Third World', *Race and Class*, vol. 43, no. 4, pp. 45–56.

Shaw, Sabrina and Risa Schwartz (2002) 'Trade and environment in the WTO: state of play', *Journal of World Trade*, vol. 36, no. 1, pp. 129–54.

Shea, Cynthia Pollock (1989) 'Protecting the ozone layer', in Lester Brown *et al.* (eds), *State of the World 1989* (New York: W. W. Norton & Co.).

Shelton, Dinah (1991) 'Human rights, environmental rights and the right to environment', *Stanford Journal of International Law*, vol. 28, no. 1, Fall, pp. 103–38.

Shiva, Vandana (1989) *Staying Alive: Women, Ecology and Development* (London: Zed Books).

—— (1990) 'Biodiversity, biotechnology and profit: the need for a people's plan to protect biodiversity', *The Ecologist*, vol. 20, no. 2, March/April, pp. 44–7.

—— (1993) 'The greening of the global reach', in Wolfgang Sachs (ed.), *Global Ecology: A New Arena of Political Conflict* (London: Zed Books).

—— (2000) 'Ecological balance in an era of globalisation', in Paul Wapner and Lester Edwin J. Ruiz (eds), *Principled World Politics: The Challenge of Normative International Relations* (Boulder, Colo: Rowman & Littlefield).

Shrybman, Steven (1990) 'International trade and the environment: an environmental assessment of the General Agreement on Tariffs and Trade', *The Ecologist*, vol. 20, no. 1, January/February, pp. 30–4.

Shue, Henry (1981) 'Exporting hazards', *Ethics*, vol. 91, no. 4, pp. 579–606.

—— (1992) 'The unavoidability of justice', in Andrew Hurrell and Benedict Kingsbury (eds), *The International Politics of the Environment* (Oxford: Clarendon Press).

——(1993) 'Subsistence emissions and luxury emissions', *Law and Policy*, vol. 15, no. 1, January, pp. 39–59.

——(1995) 'Ethics, the environment and the changing international order', *International Affairs*, vol. 71, no. 3, pp. 453–61.

Shutkin, William Andrew (1991) 'International human rights and the Earth: the protection of indigenous peoples and the environment', *Virginia Journal of International Law*, vol. 31, no. 3, Spring, pp. 479–511.

Simms, Andrew (1993) 'If not then, when? Non-governmental organisations and the Earth Summit process', *Environmental Politics*, vol. 2, no. 1, pp. 94–100.

Simon, Julian and Herman Kahn (eds) (1984) *The Resourceful Earth: Response to Global 2000* (Oxford: Basil Blackwell).

Simonis, Udo E. (2001) 'NIEO revisited: a new international environmental order in the making', *The Environmentalist*, vol. 21, no. 2, pp. 103–7.

——(2002) 'Advancing the debate on a world environment organisation', *The Environmentalist*, vol. 22, no. 1, pp. 29–42.

Simpson, Tony and Vanessa Jackson (1997) 'Human rights and the environment', *Environmental and Planning Law Journal*, vol. 14, no. 4, pp. 268–81.

SIPRI (Stockholm International Peace Research Institute) (2003) *SIPRI Yearbook 2003: Armaments, Disarmament and International Security* (Oxford: Oxford University Press, 2003), summary of Chapter 10 (http://editors.sipri.org/pubs/yb03/ch10.html; accessed 28 July 2003).

Sitarz, Daniel (ed.) (1994) *Agenda 21: The Earth Summit Strategy to Save Our Planet* (Boulder, Colo: Earthpress).

Sjöberg, Helen (1999) *Restructuring the Global Environment Facility*, Working Paper 13 (Washington, DC: Global Environment Facility Secretariat).

Smith, Richard (1996) 'Sustainability and the rationalisation of the environment', *Environmental Politics*, vol. 5, no. 1, Spring, pp. 25–47.

Solomon, Hussein (2000) 'Introduction', in Hussein Solomon and Anthony Turton (eds), *Water Wars: Enduring Myth or Impending Reality*, Africa Dialogue Monograph Series No. 2 (Durban: African Centre for the Constructive Resolution of Disputes (ACCORD)/Green Cross International).

Solomon, Hussein and Anthony Turton (eds) (2000) *Water Wars: Enduring Myth or Impending Reality*, Africa Dialogue Monograph Series No. 2 (Durban: African Centre for the Constructive Resolution of Disputes (ACCORD)/Green Cross International).

Soroos, Marvin S. (1986) *Beyond Sovereignty: The Challenge of Global Policy* (Columbia, SC: University of South Carolina Press).

——(1991) 'Introduction', *International Studies Notes*, vol. 16, no. 1, Winter, pp. 1–2.

——(1994a) 'Global change, environmental security and the Prisoner's Dilemma', *Journal of Peace Research*, vol. 31, no. 3, August, pp. 317–32.

Soroos, Marvin S. (1994b) 'From Stockholm to Rio: the evolution of environmental governance', in Norman J. Vig and Michael E. Kraft (eds), *Environmental Policy in the 1990s*, 2nd edn (Washington, DC: CQ Press).

—— (1997) *The endangered atmosphere: preserving a global commons* (Columbia, SC: University of South Carolina Press).

——(1998) 'Preserving the atmosphere as a global commons', *Environment*, vol. 40, no. 2, March, pp. 7–13, 32–4.

Soto, Alvaro (1992) 'The global environment: a Southern perspective', *International Journal*, vol. XLVII, Autumn, pp. 679–705.

Stairs, Kevin and Peter Taylor (1992) 'Non-governmental organisations and the legal protection of the oceans: a case study', in Andrew Hurrell and Benedict Kingsbury (eds), *The International Politics of the Environment* (Oxford: Clarendon Press).

Starke, Linda (1990) *Signs of Hope: Working Towards Our Common Future* (Oxford: Oxford University Press).

Starkey, Richard and Richard Welford (eds) (2001) *Business and Sustainable Development* (London: Earthscan).

Steiner, Melanie (2001) 'After a decade of global forest negotiations, where are we now?', *RECIEL*, vol. 10, no. 1, pp. 98–105.

——(2003) 'NGO reflections on the World Summit: Rio + 10 or Rio − 10?', *RECIEL*, vol. 12, no. 1, pp. 33–8.

Stiglitz, Joseph (1998) 'More instruments and broader goals: moving toward the post-Washington consensus', The 1998 WIDER [World Institute for Development Economics Research] Annual Lecture, Helsinki, Finland.

Stoett, Peter (2002) 'The international regulation of trade in wildlife: institutional and normative considerations', *International Environmental Agreements*, vol. 2, no. 2, pp. 195–210.

Stokke, Olav Schram (1998) 'Beyond dumping? The effectiveness of the London Convention', in Øystein B. Thommessen, Helge Ole Bergesen and Georg Parmann (eds), *Yearbook of International Cooperation on Environment and Development 1998/99* (London: Earthscan).

Streck, Charlotte (2001) 'The Global Environment Facility: a role model for international governance', *Global Environmental Politics*, vol. 1, no. 2, pp. 71–94.

Strong, Maurice (1972a) Opening statement by Secretary-General of the United Nations Conference on the Human Environment, Stockholm, Sweden, 5 June (Association for Progressive Communications: gopher://infoserver.ciesin.org/00/human/domains/political-policy/intl/confs/conf72/SGs_Open_72).

——(1972b) Statement by Secretary-General of the United Nations Conference on the Human Environment to Closing Plenary Meeting, Stockholm, Sweden, 16 June (Association for Progressive Communications: gopher://infoserver.ciesin.org/00/human/domains/political-policy/intl/confs/conf72/SGs_Close_ 72).

——(1973) 'Introduction' to Wade Rowland, *The Plot to Save the World: The Life and Times of the Stockholm Conference On the Human Environment* (Toronto: Clarke, Irwin & Co.).

——(1990) 'Foreword', in Julian Burger, *The Gaia Atlas of First Peoples* (London: Robertson McCarta).

——(1991) 'ECO '92: critical challenges and global solutions', *Journal of International Affairs*, vol. 44, no. 2, Winter, pp. 287–300.

Susskind, Lawrence E. (1994) *Environmental Diplomacy: Negotiating More Effective Global Agreements* (New York: Oxford University Press).

Susskind, Lawrence E. and Connie Ozawa (1992) 'Negotiating more effective international environmental agreements', in Andrew Hurrell and Benedict Kingsbury (eds), *The International Politics of the Environment* (Oxford: Clarendon Press).

Swain, Ashok (1993) 'Conflicts over water: the Ganges water dispute', *Security Dialogue*, vol. 24, no. 4, December, pp. 429–39.

Swanson, Timothy M. (1992) 'The evolving trade mechanisms in CITES', *Review of European Community and International Environmental Law*, vol. 1, no. 1, pp. 57–63.

Switzer, Jason (2002) *Environmental Insecurity: Moving from Crisis to Sustainability*, IISD Commentary (Winnipeg: International Institute for Sustainable Development).

Szekely, Alberto (1994) 'The legal protection of the world's forests after Rio '92', in Luigi Campiglio *et al.* (eds), *The Environment after Rio: International Law and Economics* (London: Graham & Trotman).

Tarasofsky, Richard (2000) 'UN Intergovernmental Forum on Forests ends – UN Forum on Forests to begin', *Environmental Policy and Law*, vol. 30, no. 1–2, pp. 32–3.

Taylor, Theodore (1989) 'Roles of technological innovation in the arms race', in J. Rotblat and V. I. Goldanski (eds), *Global Problems and Common Security: Annals of Pugwash 1988* (Berlin: Springer-Verlag).

Tegart, W. J. McG., G. W. Sheldon and D. C. Griffiths (1990) *Climate Change: The IPCC Impacts Assessment*, Final Report of Working Group II, Intergovernmental Panel on Climate Change (Canberra: Australian Government Publishing Service).

Thacher, Peter S. (1991) 'Multilateral cooperation and global change', *Journal of International Affairs*, vol. 44, no. 2, Winter, pp. 433–55.

Thomas, Caroline (1992) *The Environment in International Relations* (London: Royal Institute of International Affairs).

——(1993) 'Beyond UNCED: an introduction', *Environmental Politics*, vol. 2, no. 3, Winter, pp. 1–27.

——(1999) 'Where is the Third World now?', *Review of International Studies*, vol. 25, no. 5, pp. 225–43.

Thomas, Urs P. (2000) 'Improving integration between the WTO and the UN system', *Bridges between Trade and Sustainable Development*, vol. 4, no. 8, pp. 13–14.

Thompson, Dixon (1992) 'Trade, resources and the international environment', *International Journal*, vol. XLVII, Autumn, pp. 751–75.

Thompson, Janna (2001) 'Planetary citizenship: definition and defence of an ideal', in Brendan Gleeson and Nicholas Low (eds), *Governing for the Environment: Global Problems, Ethics and Democracy* (Basingstoke: Palgrave Macmillan).

Thomson, Koy (1992) 'Lowering sights on the road to Rio', *IIED Perspectives*, no. 8, Spring, pp. 3–5.

Tickell, Crispin (1993a) 'The world after the Summit meeting at Rio', *Washington Quarterly*, vol. 16, no. 2, Spring, pp. 75–82.

——(1993b) 'The inevitability of environmental security', in Gwyn Prins (ed.), *Threats Without Enemies* (London: Earthscan).

Tickell, Oliver and Nicholas Hildyard (1992) 'Green dollars, green menace', *The Ecologist*, vol. 22, no. 3, May/June, pp. 82–3.

Timura, Christopher T. (2001) ' "Environmental conflict" and the social life of environmental security discourse', *Anthropological Quarterly*, vol. 74, no. 3, pp. 104–13.

Tinker, Catherine J. (1993) 'NGOs and environmental policy: who represents global civil society?', paper presented to the Annual Meeting of the International Studies Association, Acapulco, Mexico.

Toke, Dave (2001) 'Ecological modernisation: a reformist review', *New Political Economy*, vol. 6, no. 2, pp. 279–91.

Tolba, Mostafa K., Osama A. El-Kholy E. El-Hinnawi, M. W. Holdgate, D. F. McMichael and R. E. Munn (1992) *The World Environment: 1972–1992: Two Decades of Challenge* (London: Chapman & Hall).

Tolbert, David (1991) 'Global climate change and the role of international non-governmental organisations', in Robin Churchill and David Freestone (eds), *International Law and Global Climate Change* (London: Graham & Trotman).

Töpfer, Klaus (n.d.) 'In defence of the environment: putting poverty to the sword', Editorial, http://www.unep.org/Documents; accessed 29 July 2003.

——(1998) 'United Nations Task Force on Environment and Human Settlements', *Linkages Journal*, vol. 3, no. 3 (www.iisd.ca/linkages/journal/toepfer.html).

——(2000) 'Environmental security, stable social order and culture', 21 February, http://www.unep.org/documents; accessed 29 July 2003.

Torgerson, Douglas (1995) 'The uncertain quest for sustainability: public discourse and the politics of environmentalism', in Frank Fischer and Michael Black (eds), *Greening Environmental Policy: The Politics of a Sustainable Future* (New York: St Martin's Press).

TRAFFIC (2002) 'Illegal ivory trade driven by unregulated domestic markets', Press Release, 4 October.

Turton, Anthony (2000) 'Water wars in Southern Africa: challenging conventional wisdom', in Hussein Solomon and Anthony Turton (eds), *Water Wars: Enduring Myth or Impending Reality*, Africa Dialogue Monograph Series No. 2 (Durban: African Centre for the Constructive Resolution of Disputes (ACCORD)/Green Cross International).

Ulph, Alistair (ed.) (2001) *Environmental Policy, International Agreements and International Trade* (Oxford: Oxford University Press).

UNCED (United Nations Conference on Environment and Development) (1992a) *Report of the UN Conference on Environment and Development: Annex I, Rio Declaration on Environment and Development*, A/CONF. 151/26 (vol. I), 12 August.

——(1992b) *Report of the UN Conference on Environment and Development: Annex II, Agenda 21*, A/CONF.151/26 (vol. I–III), 12 August.

——(1992c) *Non-legally Binding Authoritative Statement of Principles for a Global Consensus on the Management, Conservation and Sustainable Development of All Types of Forests*, A/CONF.151/26 (vol. III), 14 August.

UN-DESA (United Nations Department of Economic and Social Affairs) (1999) *Executive Committee on Economic and Social Affairs* (http://www.un.org/esa/coordination/ecesa/ecesa.htm; accessed 9 August 1999).

——(2002) 'Sustainable development summit concludes in Johannesburg: UN Secretary-General Kofi Annan says it's just the beginning', Johannesburg Summit 2002, (http://www.johannesburgsummit.org/html/whats_new/feature_story39.htm; accessed 5 September 2002).

UNDP (United Nations Development Programme) (1994) *Human Development Report 1994* (New York: Oxford University Press).

——(1995) *Human Development Report 1995* (New York: Oxford University Press).

——(1996) *Human Development Report 1996* (New York: Oxford University Press).

——(1998) *Human Development Report 1998: Consumption for Human Development* (New York: Oxford University Press).

——(1999) *Human Development Report 1999: Globalisation with a Human Face* (New York: Oxford University Press).

——(2003) *Human Development Report 2003: Millennium Development Goals: A Compact Among Nations to End Human Poverty* (New York: Oxford University Press).

UNDPI (United Nations Department of Public Information) (1997) 'Earth Summit review ends with few commitments', Round-up Press Release, DPI/1916/SD, July (http://www.un.org/ecosocdev/geninfo/sustdev/es5final.htm; accessed 4 March 1998).

UNEP (United Nations Environment Programme) (1992) *Convention on Biological Diversity* (Nairobi: UNEP/CBD Secretariat).

——(1994a) 'Experts to meet in Nairobi to finalise agreement for Africa Wildlife Task Force', Press Release HE/853, 27 May (Nairobi: UNEP) (gopher://gopher.undp.org:70/00/uncurr/ press_releases/HE/94_05/853).

——(1994b) 'Resolutions on interim arrangements and on urgent action for Africa', INCD, Fifth Session, Paris, 6–17 June, Agenda item 2 (available at http://www.unep.ch/incd/resol-e.html).

——(1994c) 'Bahamas to host first convention of parties to Biodiversity Convention', Press Release HE/858, 22 June (Nairobi: UNEP) (gopher://gopher.undp.org:70/00/uncurr/ press_releases/HE/94_06/858).

——(1994d) *United Nations Convention to Combat Desertification in Countries Experiencing Serious Drought and/or Desertification, Especially in Africa* (Nairobi: UNEP/CCD Interim Secretariat).

——(1995a) *Fact Sheet 3 – The Consequences of Desertification* (Geneva: Interim Secretariat of the Convention to Combat Desertification/Information Unit for Conventions of UNEP) (available at http://www.unep.ch/incd/fs3.html).

——(1995b) *The United Nations Convention to Combat Desertification: An Explanatory Leaflet* (Geneva: Interim Secretariat of the Convention to

Combat Desertification/Information Unit for Conventions of UNEP) (available at http://www.unep.ch/incd/leaflet.html).

UNEP (1997a) *Global Environment Outlook: Executive Summary* (Nairobi: UNEP) (http://www.unep.org/unep/eia/geo1/exsum/ex2.htm; accessed 10 March 1998).

—— (1997b) *Nairobi Declaration on the Role and Mandate of UNEP* (Nairobi: UNEP).

—— (1999a) *Global Environment Outlook 2000* (London: Earthscan).

—— (1999b) 'Stable, adequate and predictable funding for the United Nations Environment Programme', Decision 20/33, 20th Governing Council Session, 4 February.

—— (2001a) 'Impacts of climate change to cost the world over $300 billion a year', UNEP News Release 2001/11, 3 February (Nairobi: UNEP).

—— (2001b) 'Global warming: Africa hit hardest', UNEP News Release 01/27, 22 February (Nairobi: UNEP).

—— (2001c) 'Tiger enforcement task force to target criminal networks', UNEP News Release 01/45, 2 April (Nairobi: UNEP).

—— (2001d) 'Netherlands gives big backing to UNEP in run up to World Summit on Sustainable Development', UNEP News Release 2001/114, 28 November.

—— (2001e) *Illegal Trade in Ozone Depleting Substances: Is There a Hole in the Montreal Protocol?, OzonAction Newsletter,* Special Supplement, no. 6 (Paris: UNEP Division of Technology, Industry and Economics).

—— (2002a) *Global Environment Outlook 3* (London: Earthscan).

—— (2002b) 'Hazardous wastes experts seek to strengthen Basel Convention', Press Release, 14 January (UNEP: Geneva).

—— (2002c) 'Global survey shows slow progress on UN sustainable consumption guidelines', UNEP News Release 2002/43, 3 June.

—— (2002d) 'The state of Africa's environment chronicled in ground-breaking report: hard facts, tough choices', UNEP News Release 2002/50, 4 July.

—— (2002e) Report of the sixth meeting of the Conference of the Parties to the Convention on Biological Diversity UNEP/CBD/COP/6/20, 27 May.

—— (2003a) 'UNEP report chronicles environmental damage of the Afghan conflict', UNEP News Release, 29 January.

—— (2003b) 'How does petroleum become a pollutant in the coastal and marine environment?', Global Marine Oil Pollution Information Gateway (http://oils.gpa.unep.org/facts/sources.htm; accessed 21 August 2003).

—— (n.d.) 'Weapons as waste', UN System-Wide Earthwatch (http://earthwatch.unep.net/hazardousw/weapons.php; accessed 29 July 2003).

UNEP and United Nations Centre for Human Settlements (1999) *The Kosovo conflict: consequences for the environment and human settlements,* (Geneva: UNEP/UNCHS).

UNFCCC (United Nations Framework Convention on Climate Change) (2003) 'Rich countries see higher greenhouse gas emissions: upward trend set to continue', Press Release, 3 June.

UNGA (United Nations General Assembly) (1976) *Convention on the Prohibition of Military or any Other Hostile Use of Environmental Modification Techniques,* A/RES/31/72, 10 December.

——(1982) *World Charter for Nature*, A/RES/37/7, 28 October.

——(1983) 'Process of preparation of the Environmental Perspective to the year 2000 and beyond', A/RES/38/161, 19 December (gopher://gopher.undp.org:70/00/undocs/gad/RES/38/161).

——(1988) 'Protection of global climate for present and future generations of mankind', A/RES/43/53, 70th Plenary Meeting, 6 December.

——(1989a) 'Protection of global climate for present and future generations of mankind', A/RES/44/207, 85th Plenary Meeting, 22 December.

——(1989b) 'International cooperation in the monitoring, assessment and anticipation of environmental threats and in assistance in cases of environmental emergency', A/RES/44/224, 85th Plenary Meeting, 22 December.

——(1989c) 'United Nations Conference on Environment and Development', Resolution 44/228, 85th Plenary Meeting, 22 December.

——(1990) 'Protection of global climate for present and future generations of mankind', A/RES/45/212, 71st Plenary Meeting, 21 December.

——(1994) *Report of the Global Conference on the Sustainable Development of Small Island Developing States*, A/CONF.167/9, October.

—— (1997), *Environment and sustainable development: Special Session for the purpose of an overall review and appraisal of the implementation of Agenda 21 – Outcome of the nineteenth special session of the General Assembly: report of the Secretary-General*, A/52/280, 14 August.

——(1999), *Report of the Secretary-General on environment and human settlements*, A/RES/53/242, 10 August.

——(2000), *Ten-year review of progress achieved in the implementation of the outcome of the United Nations Conference on Environment and Development*, A/RES/55/199, 20 December.

——(2001a) 'Ten year review of progress achieved in the implementation of the outcome of the United Nations Conference on Environment and Development', A/RES/55/1999, 5 February.

——(2001b) *Report of the High-level Panel on Financing for Development* (the Zedillo Report), A/55/1000, 26 June.

UNHCHR (United Nations High Commissioner for Human Rights) (2003) *Human Rights and the Environment as Part of Sustainable Development*, Commission on Human Rights Resolution 2003/71, 25 April.

UNICEF/UNFPA (1991) *Women and Children First*, Report of the symposium on the impact of poverty and environmental degradation on women and children, Geneva, 27–30 May.

UNIFEM (1993) *Agenda 21: An Easy Reference to the Specific Recommendations on Women* (New York: UNIFEM) (also available at http://iisd1.iisd.ca/women/unifema.htm).

United Nations (1998) *Text of the Rome Statute on the International Criminal Court*, circulated as document A/CONF.183/9 of 17 July 1998 (and corrected by subsequent procès-verbaux).

——(1999) *Report of the Ad Hoc Committee of the Whole of the Twenty-second Special Session of the General Assembly*, A/S-22/9/Rev.1.

——(2002a) *Final Outcome of the International Conference on Financing for Development: The Monterrey Consensus*, A/CONF.198/3, 1 March.

United Nations (2002b) *Report of the World Summit on Sustainable Development*, A/CONF.199/20 (New York: United Nations).

United Nations Division for Sustainable Development (2003) *Small Island Developing States* (http://www.un.org/esa/sustdev/sids/sids.htm; accessed 22 May 2003).

United Nations Economic and Social Council (1994) *Human Rights and the Environment: Final Report of the Special Rapporteur*, E/CN.4/Sub.2/1994/9, 6 July.

United Nations Economic Commission for Europe (1998) The *Convention on Access to Information, Public Participation in Decision-making and Access to Justice in Environmental Matters*, Doc. ECE/CEP/43, June.

United Nations INC/FCCC (1991) 'Climate change negotiations set to shift from drafting to political "give and take" ', Press Release ENV/DEV/21, 19 December.

—— (1992) *United Nations Framework Convention on Climate Change* (Bonn: Climate Change Secretariat) (http://www.un/ccc.def.fccc/conv-toc.html).

United Nations Security Council (1992) *Statement by the President*, A/47/253, 31 January.

United Nations Task Force on Environment and Human Settlements (1999) *Report*, annexed to *Report of the Secretary General on Environment and Human Settlements*, General Assembly, A/53/463.

UNSG (United Nations Secretary-General) (1992) *An Agenda for Peace*, Report of the Secretary General pursuant to the Statement adopted by the Summit Meeting of the Security Council on 31 January 1992, 47th Session, Security Council S/24111; General Assembly A/47/277, 17 June.

—— (1994) *Development and International Economic Co-operation: An Agenda for Development*, Report of the Secretary General, 48th session, A/48/935, 6 May.

—— (1997a) *Global Change and Sustainable Development: Critical Trends*, Report of the Secretary General, Commission on Sustainable Development, Fifth Session 1997 (http://www.un.org/dpcsd/dsd/trends.htm; accessed 5 March 1998).

—— (1997b) *Environment and development: Special Session for the purpose of an overall review and appraisal of the implementation of Agenda 21, Outcome of the nineteenth special session of the General Assembly*, Report of the Secretary General, A/52/280, 14 August.

—— (1997c) *Renewing the United Nations: A Programme for Reform*, A/51/950 (New York: United Nations Secretariat).

—— (1997d) *Overall Progress Achieved since the United Nations Conference on Environment and Development, Addendum: International Legal Instruments and Mechanisms*, E/CN.17/1997/2/Add.2, 21 January.

—— (1998a) *Report on the Causes of Conflict and the Promotion of Durable Peace and Sustainable Development in Africa*, 13 April, S/1998/318.

—— (1998b) *Promotion and Protection of Human Rights: Science and Environment*, Report submitted to the Commission on Human Rights in accordance with Commission decision 1997/102, 22 December, E/CN.4/1999/89.

——(2000) *The Millennium Report – We the Peoples: The Role of the United Nations in the 21st Century*, A/54/2000 (New York: UN Secretariat).

——(2001) *Implementing Agenda 21: Report of the Secretary-General*, 19 December, E/CN.17/2002/PC.2/7.

USIS (United States Information Service) (1992) 'US proposes survey of Earth's biodiversity', *Backgrounder* (Canberra: USIS), 16 June.

Van den Bilcke, Christian (2002) 'The Stockholm Convention on Persistent Organic Pollutants', *RECIEL*, vol. 11, no. 3, pp. 328–42.

van Trotsenburg, Axel and Alan MacArthur (1999) *The HIPC Initiative: Delivering Debt Relief to Poor Countries* (Washington, DC: The World Bank).

Vellinga, Pier, Richard Howarth and Joyeeta Gupta (2002) 'Improving global environmental governance', *International Environmental Agreements*, vol. 2, no. 4, pp. 293–6.

Victor, David (2001) *The Collapse of the Kyoto Protocol and the Struggle to Slow Global Warming* (Princeton, NJ: Princeton University Press).

Victor, David, Kal Raustiala and Eugene B. Skolnikoff (eds) (1998) *The Implementation and Effectiveness of International Environmental Commitments* (Cambridge, Mass.: The MIT Press).

Vig, Norman J and Regina S. Axelrod (1999) *The Global Environment: Institutions, Law and Policy* (London: Earthscan).

Vigneron, Giselle (1998) 'Compliance and international environmental agreements: a case study of the 1995 United Nations Straddling Fish Stocks Agreement', *The Georgetown International Environmental Law Review*, vol. 10, no. 2, pp. 581–623.

Vogel, David (2002/03) 'Review of *Globalisation and Environmental Reform: The Ecological Modernisation of the Global Economy*', *Political Science Quarterly*, vol. 117, no. 4, pp. 691–3.

Vogler, John (1996) 'The environment in International Relations: legacies and contentions', in John Vogler and Mark F. Imber (eds), *The Environment and International Relations* (London: Routledge).

——(2000) *The Global Commons: Environmental and Technological Governance*, 2nd edn (Chichester: John Wiley).

Vogler, John and Mark F. Imber (eds) (1996) *The Environment and International Relations* (London: Routledge).

Vöneky, Silja (2000) 'A new shield for the environment: peacetime treaties as legal restraints of wartime damage', *RECIEL*, vol. 9, no. 1, pp. 20–32.

von Moltke, Konrad (1991) 'Debt-for-Nature: the second generation', *Hastings International and Comparative Law Review*, vol. 14, no. 4, Summer, pp. 973–87.

——(2001) 'The organisation of the impossible', *Global Environmental Politics*, vol. 1, no. 1, pp. 23–8.

——(2002) 'Governments and international civil society in sustainable development: a framework', *International Environmental Agreements*, vol. 2, no. 4, pp. 341–59.

von Moltke, Konrad and Paul J. DeLong (1990) 'Negotiating in the global arena: debt-for-nature swaps', *Resolve*, no. 22, pp. 1–10.

Wackernagel, Mathis, Chad Monfreda and Diana Deumling (2002) *Ecological footprint of nations: November 2002 update*, (Oakland, Calif.: Redefining Progress).

Wade, Robert (1997) 'Greening the Bank: the struggle over the environment, 1970–1995', in Devesh Kapur, John P. Lewis and Richard Webb (eds), *The World Bank: Its First Half Century, Vol. 2: Perspectives* (Washington, DC: The Brookings Institution).

Wagner, J. Martin, Marcello Mollo, Alyssa Johl, Jocelyn Garovoy, Neil Popovic and Yves Lador (2003) *Human Rights and the Environment* (Oakland, Calif.: Earthjustice).

Wapner, Paul (1996) *Environmental Activism and World Civic Politics* (Albany, NY: State University of New York Press).

—— (1997) 'Environmental ethics and global governance: engaging the international liberal tradition', *Global Governance*, vol. 3, no. 2, May–August, pp. 213–31.

—— (1998) 'Reorienting state sovereignty: rights and responsibilities in the environmental age', in Karen T. Litfin (ed.), *The greening of sovereignty in world politics* (Cambridge, Mass.: The MIT Press).

—— (2003) 'World Summit on Sustainable Development: toward a post-Jo'burg environmentalism', *Global Environmental Politics*, vol. 3, no. 1, pp. 1–10.

Ward, Michael D. and David R. Davis (1992) 'Sizing up the peace dividend: economic growth and military spending in the United States, 1948–1996', *American Political Science Review*, vol. 86, no. 3, September, pp. 748–55.

Watson, Robert T. (1999) 'New strategies, strengthened partnerships', *Environment Matters Annual Review*, June, pp. 4–7.

WBCSD (World Business Council for Sustainable Development) (2002) 'The business case for sustainable development: making a difference towards the Earth Summit 2002 and beyond', *Corporate Environmental Strategy*, vol. 9, no. 3, pp. 226–35.

WCED (World Commission on Environment and Development) (1987) *Our Common Future* (Oxford: Oxford University Press).

Weber, Peter (1994) 'Safeguarding oceans', in Lester R. Brown, Alan Thein Durning, Christopher Flavin, Hilary F. French, Nicholas Lensson, Marcia D. Lowe, Ann Misch, Sandra Postel, Michael Renner, Linda Starke, Peter Weber and John E. Young (eds), *State of the World 1994* (New York: W. W. Norton & Co.).

WEDO (Women's Environment and Development Organization) (1992) *Official Report: World Women's Congress for a Healthy Planet, 8–12 November 1991, Miami, Florida* (New York: WEDO).

—— (1998) *Women Transform the Mainstream* (New York: WEDO).

Weiss, Edith Brown (1988) *In Fairness to Future Generations: International Law, Common Patrimony and Intergenerational Equity* (Dobbs Ferry, NY: Transnational Publishers).

—— (1992) 'Environment and trade as partners in sustainable development: a commentary', *American Journal of International Law*, vol. 86, no. 4, October, pp. 728–35.

Weiss, Edith Brown and Harold K. Jacobson (eds) (2000) *Engaging countries: Strengthening Compliance with International Environmental Accords* (Cambridge, Mass.: The MIT Press).

Werksman, Jacob D. (1993) 'Greening Bretton Woods', in Philippe Sands (ed.), *Greening International Law* (London: Earthscan).

—— (ed.) (1996) *Greening International Institutions* (London: Earthscan).

—— (1998) 'The clean development mechanism: unwrapping the "Kyoto surprise" ', *RECIEL*, vol. 7, no. 2, pp. 147–58.

Westing, Arthur H. (ed.) (1988) Cultural Norms, War and the Environment (Oxford: Oxford University Press).

—— (1989) 'The environmental component of comprehensive security', *Bulletin of Peace Proposals*, vol. 20, no. 2, pp. 129–34.

Wettestad, Jørgen (1995) 'Science, politics and institutional design: some initial notes on the long-range transboundary air pollution regime', *Journal of Environment and Development*, vol. 4, no. 2, Summer, pp. 165–83.

Wiggins, Armstrong (1993) 'Indian rights and the environment', *Yale Journal of International Law*, vol. 18, no. 1, pp. 345–54.

Wilder, Martijn (1995) 'Quota systems in international wildlife and fisheries regimes', *Journal of Environment and Development*, vol. 4, no. 2, Summer, pp. 55–104.

Williams, Marc (1996) 'International political economy and global environmental change', in John Vogler and Mark F. Imber (eds), *The Environment and International Relations* (London: Routledge).

Williams, Maurice (1992) 'Guidelines to strengthening the institutional response to major environmental issues', *Development*, no. 2, pp. 22–7.

Williams, Michael C. and Keith Krause (1997) 'Preface: toward critical security studies', in Keith Krause and Michael Williams (eds), *Critical Security Studies* (Minneapolis: University of Minnesota Press).

Wood, William B., George J. Demko and Phyllis Mofson (1989) 'Ecopolitics in the global greenhouse', *Environment*, vol. 31, no. 7, September, pp. 12–17, 32–4.

Woodliffe, John (1991) 'Tropical forests', in Robin Churchill and David Freestone (eds), *International Law and Global Climate Change* (London: Graham & Trotman).

World Bank (2001a) *Making Sustainable Commitments: An Environment Strategy for the World Bank* (Washington, DC: The World Bank).

—— (2001b) *Comprehensive Development Framework: Meeting the Promise? Early Experience and Emerging Issues* (Washington, DC: CDF Secretariat).

—— (2002) *Financing for Sustainable Development* (Washington, DC: The World Bank, prepared with the International Monetary Fund and the United Nations Environment Programme).

—— (2003) *World Development Report 2003* (New York: Oxford University Press).

World Energy Council (2001) *Living In One World* (London: World Energy Council) (http://www.worldenergy.org/wec-geis/publications/reports/liow/stresses/land.asp; accessed 19 August 2003).

Worldwatch Institute (2000) 'Earth Day 2000: a 30-year report card', *World Watch*, vol. 13, no. 2, March/April, pp. 10–11.

World Water Council (2003) Summary Forum Statement of the 3rd World Water Forum, (http://www.world.water-forum3.com/en/statement.html; accessed 12 July 2003).

WRI (World Resources Institute) (2003) *World Resources 2002–2004* (Washington, DC: World Resources Institute).

WRM (World Rainforest Movement) (1990) *Rainforest Destruction: Causes, Effects and False Solutions* (Penang: WRM).

WTO (World Trade Organisation) (2001) *Ministerial Declaration*, adopted at the Ministerial Conference, Doha, 9–14 November, WT/MIN(01)/DEC/1, 20 November.

——(2002) Doha explained: trade and environment (http://www.wto.org/english/tratop_e/dda_e/dohaexplained_e.htm; accessed 24 July 2003).

——(2003) 'Environmental disputes in GATT/WTO' (http://www.wto.org/english/tratop_e/envir_e/edis00_e.thm; accessed 25 July 2003).

WWF (World Wide Fund for Nature) (2003) Endangered species: African elephant (http://www.panda.org/about_wwf/what_we_do/species/what_we_do/flagship_species/elephants/african_elephant/population.cfm; accessed 12 July 2003).

Yamin, Farhana (n.d.) *The United Nations Framework Convention on Climate Change: The Need for a Protocol on Energy Efficiency and New and Renewable Sources of Energy* (London: Foundation for International Environmental Law and Development).

Yap, Nonita (1989–90) 'NGOs and sustainable development', *International Journal*, vol. XLV, no. 1, Winter, pp. 75–105.

Young, Oran R. (ed.) (1997) *Global governance: drawing insights from the environmental experience* (Cambridge, Mass.: The MIT Press).

——(ed.) (1999) *The effectiveness of international environmental regimes: causal connections and behavioral mechanisms* (Cambridge, Mass.: The MIT Press).

——(2002) 'Evaluating the success of international environmental regimes: where are we now?', *Global Environmental Change*, vol. 12, no. 1, pp. 73–7.

Young, Zoe (2002) *A New Green Order? The World Bank and the Politics of the Global Environment Facility* (London: Pluto Press).

Yu, Douglas (1994) 'Free trade is green: protectionism is not', *Conservation Biology*, vol. 8, no. 4, December, pp. 989–96.

Index

287